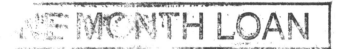

The Chef's Compendium of
Professional Recipes by Fuller,
John

THE CHEF'S COMPENDIUM
OF PROFESSIONAL RECIPES

Other books by
John Fuller

Kitchen Planning & Management (with D. Kirk)
Essential Table Service
Modern Restaurant Service
Advanced Food Service
Guéridon & Lamp Cookery
A Hotel and Catering Career (with D. Gee)
The Waiter (with A. J. Currie)
Professional Kitchen Management
The Menu, Food and Profit (with Keith Waller)
Hotelkeeping and Catering as a Career
The Caterer's Potato Manual
The Professional Chef's Manual of Kitchen Management
   (in USA: with J.B. Knight and C.A. Salter)

as editor

The Complete Book of Pub Catering
Pellaprat's L'Art Culinaire Moderne
Meat Dishes in the International Cuisine
Catering and Hotelkeeping
Catering Management in the Technological Age
Productivity and Profit in Catering (with J. Steel)

THE CHEF'S COMPENDIUM
OF PROFESSIONAL RECIPES

John Fuller

and

Edward Renold

THIRD EDITION

ELSEVIER
BUTTERWORTH
HEINEMANN

AMSTERDAM BOSTON HEIDELBERG LONDON NEW YORK OXFORD
PARIS SAN DIEGO SAN FRANCISCO SINGAPORE SYDNEY TOKYO

Elsevier Butterworth-Heinemann
Linacre House, Jordan Hill, Oxford OX2 8DP
200 Wheeler Road, Burlington,

First published 1963
Reprinted 1996, 1968, 1971
Second edition 1972
Reprinted 1973, 1975, 1978, 1979, 1982, 1984, 1985, 1986, 1987, 1988
Third edition 1992
Reprinted 1993, 1997 (twice), 1 2000, 2001, 2003, 2004

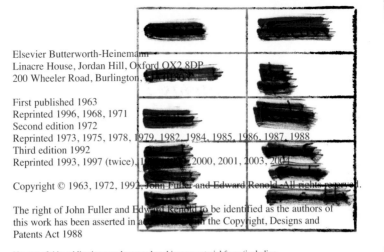

Permissions may be sought directly from Elsevier's Science and Technology Rights
Department in Oxford, UK: phone: (+44) (0) 1865 843830; fax: (+44) (0) 1865 853333;
e-mail: permissions@elsevier.co.uk. You may also complete your request on-line
via the Elsevier homepage (http://www.elsevier.com), by selecting 'Customer
Support' and then 'Obtaining Permissions'.

British Library Cataloguing in Publication Data
Fuller, John
    Chef's Compendium of Professional
    Recipes. – 3Rev.ed
    I. Title II. Renold, Edward
    641.5

Library of Congress Cataloguing in Publication Data
Fuller, John, 1916–
    The chef's compendium of professional recipes/John Fuller
    and Edward Renold. – 3rd ed
    Includes bibliographical references and index.
    1. Quantity cookery. I. Renold, Edward. II. Title
    TX820.F84   1992
    641.5'7–dc20   92–6037
                                                    CIP

ISBN 0 7506 0490 5

For more information on all Butterworth-Heinemann publications
please visit our website at www.bh.com

Composition by Genesis Typesetting, Laser Quay, Rochester, Kent
Printed and bound in Great Britain by MPG Books Ltd, Bodmin, Cornwall

Contents

Preface

The *Compendium* aims to provide a range of recipes useful throughout catering. It is so titled because a selection was made and any temptation to include every possible recipe resisted. The examples chosen should enable users to prepare a wide repertoire.

In addition to covering restaurant cookery, the recipes are also deemed suitable for employee catering at the work-place and in institutions such as hospitals (NHS and private), schools, colleges and in travel catering (motorways, aircraft, rail and at sea). Indeed the present level of general catering makes recipes widely interchangeable.

Though designed for working chefs, the *Compendium* has been prepared to meet the requirements of those taking BTEC National Diplomas, Higher National Diplomas, BA Hospitality Management Degrees and, in particular, City & Guilds of London Institute's examination 706 series, NCVQ levels 1, 2 and 3.

It is assumed that *Compendium* readers will have a knowledge of cookery, but most recipes have been reduced to steps sufficiently simple to be followed by beginners as well as chefs. Recipe instructions are concise but generally include each step in each recipe. Elementary points are reiterated in some cases to ensure that every stage may be followed and excessive cross-reference avoided.

Because the *Compendium* concentrates on providing recipes, principles have been incorporated in them rather than by coverage in separate sections. To help link the text and interpret recipes, occasional short observations on general culinary processes have been included; but this is not a book of cookery theory.

It covers professional cookery in the conventional professional (generally French) style in the belief that understanding underlying first-class cookery principles is helped through this tradition. Nevertheless reforms and simplifications are incorporated where these have become accepted.

Some recipes from previous editions have been dropped because they have become less popular or are less frequently demanded through public concern, eg some offal, such as heads. This edition takes into account trends towards healthy and safe eating and suggests alternatives to certain ingredients to meet this demand. Also reflecting change in demand, further vegetable and vegetarian recipes have been added. (See *How to use the Compendium*, p. x.) However, Chapter 8, 'Pastry and Sweets', has been extended to include recipes that have consolidated their popularity since this book first appeared. This accords with the idea that unsatisfactory nutrition lies less in poor foods (refined sugar being often so identified) than in poor eating patterns, and that a healthier diet can also be interesting and feature many favourite foods.

It is hoped that these changes will make this revised edition of the *Compendium* as useful to a new generation of chefs and students as the former versions, which have been continuously in print for some 30 years.

Acknowledgements

Despite the additional recipes and revisions introduced to make this collection more useful in today's kitchens, the work of my greatly missed friend and co-author, the late Edward Renold, remains an important element in the *Compendium*. His awards from the French government of Chevalier de Mérite Agricole and the Palmes Académiques underline not only his services to French cuisine but the esteem in which he and his culinary skill were held by his fellow chefs and teachers. His work endures in this new edition.

Thanks for assistance in the original edition are gratefully accorded to Charles Jarvie, Gordon Sinclair and Ian T, Marshall (all at that time lecturers at the Scottish Hotel School). I am indebted to Daniel Stevenson, MHCIMA, Cert.Ed., Head of the Department of Catering, Tourism & Hotel Operations, and John Bodley, Senior Lecturer in Bakery and Pâtisserie, both of Bournemouth and Poole College of Further Education, for suggestions (especially regarding Chapter 8, 'Pastry and Sweets') and for the guidance of my former colleague at Oxford Polytechnic, Dr David Atkinson, BA, PhD, in regard to French dish names and terms. Many usages (for example contracting names such as Moules marinière rather than Moules à la marinière, Sauce au raifort to Sauce raifort or Tournedos chasseur (rather than Tournedos à la (sauce) chasseur) are still commonplace even in modern, authoritative French language culinary works. Dr Atkinson is, of course, in no way responsible for any such instances which might linger here. Acknowledgement and gratitude are especially due to Professor David Foskett, BEd(Hons), Cert.Ed., MHCIMA, Director of Hospitality, Education and Training, Polytechnic of West London, for his help as Consultant Editor, for his amendments and for his provision of additional recipes.

J.F.

How to use the Compendium

For some 30 years the *Compendium* has been used as an *aide-mémoire* by chefs and as a guide by students in their cuisine practicals (as a 'kitchen lab' manual). Because of this latter use: **recipes are for four covers.** Since its first appearance in 1963, however, changes in practice have prompted adaptations in this book. Readers are advised to note the following in order to gain maximum benefit from it.

Metric and Imperial measures
All recipes are in metric measures (with Imperial equivalent following in brackets). However, a conversion guide is also included on p. xii.

Oven temperatures
As the oven temperature guide on p. xiii relates to general descriptions such as 'cool', 'hot', etc., and to degrees Celsius and Fahrenheit or gas 'marks', these are not all incorporated in each recipe. However, accuracy is important, especially in baking and pâtisserie work. A competent chef is distinguished by his ability to gauge times and temperatures in relation to varying sizes of meat joints, pies and so on and the age and quality of vegetables; so that even the most precise recipes can never entirely replace the skills in timing and temperature derived from day-to-day experience.

Frozen and other processed foods
Processed food development brought (and continues to bring) change into kitchens, but chefs with a sound grasp of good professional cookery are able to adapt recipes of the best tradition to manufacturers' reconstitution or defrosting instructions. Indeed, because freezing (and other forms of processing) encourage the reappearance over a longer season of some vegetables, it is even more necessary for chefs to be versatile in applying sauces, garnishes and varied dressings to vegetables and other commodities.

Healthy eating
As the preface indicates, this book is not one of theory; nor is it a guide to nutrition. Recipes may need to serve a range of markets. Many operations may still cater to those dining out for pleasure who on some occasions will be self-indulgent rather than mindful of health precepts. Such diners may be resistant to substitutes. Attitudes constantly change. Some people still believe (despite objection to their over-use) that butter, cream and eggs are not yet doomed to eternal banishment from kitchens.

However, there is now widespread agreement that to avoid obesity, heart disease and other health problems, changes in eating habits are desirable, and that this should be reflected in recipes. Much traditional fine cooking is unacceptably over-rich and heavily dependent on butter, cream, sugar and starch thickenings.

In assessing the nutritional content and hence healthiness of recipes it is now generally accepted that:

- Energy (calorie) intake should suffice to maintain optimum body weight and to fuel adequate exercise.
- Total fat should not exceed 80–85 g/day.
- Saturated fat should not exceed 20–23 g/day.
- Sugar should not exceed 50 g/day.
- Dietary fibre should be increased to 30 g/day.
- Salt should not exceed 5 g/day.

Modifying recipes
Many recipes have been altered (or substitute ingredients suggested) but not every recipe has been modified, for it is eating patterns that are often at fault rather than individual foods or even recipes. Chefs can aim to effect changes in traditional recipes to help achieve nutritional balance in every meal.

The following notes are added as further guidance for those seeking to modify their cooking to meet present perceptions of healthy eating.

Thickenings
Present reaction against roux and other starch thickenings may not be permanent, for the amount of flour used (and actually consumed per customer) in some roux-thickened sauces and other dishes can often be small. Techniques such as the oven-browning of flour-dredged items again does not inevitably cause the ingestion of much starch per head. Dishes long popular have suffered perhaps at the hands of inept practitioners rather than in lack of innate appeal.

Nevertheless alternatives have been highlighted in this edition. Many sauces that were formerly thickened with flour starch are now given body by reductions of good quality stock. Such light thickening comes from the reduction being of a gelatinous nature. The reduction is sometimes finished with a little butter, margarine, fromage frais, egg yolk, natural yogurt or similar ingredient. Vegetable purées are also used as replacement or partial substitute for starch thickening in suitable dishes, especially soups and some sauces. Even finely chopped (brunoise) or shredded (julienne) vegetables may also be used in a flavoured fumet or jus to add body to a sauce. Carrot, celery, celeriac and concassé tomato are often used in this way.

Substitutions
Some other ingredients may be replaced as follows:

Instead of	*Choose*
Whole milk	Skimmed or semi-skimmed milk
Butter or hard margarine	Polyunsaturated margarine
Lard, hard vegetable fat	Pure vegetable oils, eg sunflower oil, rape seed, olive oil

Full-fat cheese	Lower fat cheeses, eg low-fat Cheddar has half the fat
Fatty meats	Lean meat (smaller portion), chicken or fish
Cream	Plain yogurt, quark, fromage frais

Adjusting seasoning
When using substitutes, eg natural unseasoned low fat yogurt in place of seasoned mayonnaise, always adjust the seasoning and in some cases add extra flavourings as required – say finely chopped fresh herbs, lemon juice, vinegar, etc.

Kitchen French
In professional British (or American) kitchens French (as well as English equivalent) terms for commodities, utensils and preparations are still used. Chefs are as likely to speak of 'demi-glace' as of 'half-glaze', or of 'lié' as frequently as 'thickening'; and to refer to 'maître d'hôtel butter' (a mixture of French and English) as often as 'parsley butter'. Recipes in the *Compendium* reflect such normal working usage by including terms either in their French or English versions; and it has seemed appropriate to write recipes in a way chefs are, or tend to become, used to.

A French title of a dish is followed by its English version; but some French terms (in headings or in the text) lack adequate translation. These include older words, such as mirepoix, and as *The Times* (8 March 1991) observed, 'for some new dairy products such as fromage frais, fromage battu, fromage blanc or petit suisse the English have not even found names'.

Safe eating
Finally this recipe collection is not a manual of hygiene, but, in cooking, chefs must be mindful of today's food hazards, especially those associated with new processes, e.g. battery and intensive farming. Dishes such as calves' heads (and other offal dishes) have lost popularity or have been outlawed because of new awareness of risks. It is perhaps too early to be sure whether the eclipse of such foods will be permanent, but for now the *Compendium* makes appropriate suggestions about, for example, the use of pasteurized eggs and egg yolk in recipes.

METRIC CONVERSION APPROXIMATE EQUIVALENTS

Mass or weight
¼ oz = 7 g
½ oz = 15 g
1 oz = 30 g
16 oz = 480 g (500 g in large-scale recipes)
2 lb = 1 kg
10 lb = 5 kg

Capacity or Volume
1 pint = 500 ml
1 quart = 1000 ml = 1 litre

Spoon measures
British Standard 1348 measures available as a complete set:

1.25 ml = ¼ teaspoon
2.50 ml = ½ teaspoon
5.00 ml = 1 teaspoon
10.00 ml = 1 dessertspoon
15.00 ml = 1 tablespoon
20.00 ml = 4 teaspoons

Length
⅛ inch = 0.3 cm
¼ inch = 0.5 cm
½ inch = 1.0 cm
1 inch = 2.0 cm

OVEN TEMPERATURES

	Gas Mark	*Degrees Celsius*	*Degrees Fahrenheit*
Very cool	¼	115	240
	½	120	250
Cool	1	135	275
	2	150	300
Warm	2	150	300
	3	160	325
Moderate	3	160	325
	4	175	350
Moderately hot	5	190	375
	6	200	400
Hot	7	215	425
	8	230	450
Very hot	9	245	475

1 Culinary Basics, Stocks, and Sauces

DURING the past quarter of a century many changes have taken place in professional kitchens. Not only those catering for industry, hospitals, and schools, but even hotel and restaurant kitchens once organized along traditional *partie* (or sectional) lines, have been affected. Some changes simplify basic culinary preparations, owing to such factors as cost and public demand. To make economical use of craft skills in kitchens is as important as economizing in ingredients, energy or other cost elements. Public demand favours simpler, shorter meals (but meals well prepared and presented), and is more health-conscious. Thus many recipies once popular may need modification to reduce richness – by eliminating or using less fat, especially animal fat, including butter); and cutting down on sugar and conserve nutrients by correct cooking.

Changes in kitchen practices are not, however, always accurately reflected in professional cookery manuals. Many chefs pay lip-service to classic recipes that are seldom carried out in full in the kitchens of today.

Yet first-class work still requires properly prepared stocks and similar culinary basics, though, nowadays, stocks may not always contain the high proportion of poultry and butcher's meat formerly considered essential. Modern methods, in certain operations, make use of pre-processed bases for stocks, soups and sauces. Nevertheless, kitchens of the finest grade, even those run on modest lines, must still use basic preparations produced by their own staff. Therefore, a sound knowledge of culinary foundations is essential for all who intend to practise good cooking.

Mis-en-place. Despite the changes, traditional kitchen methods, whether for table d'hôte or à la carte service, still include the idea of mise-en-place; that is, the preparation of culinary items in advance. By this means dishes can be assembled at service time with the minimum fuss and bother, the maximum efficiency, and attractively presented.

Fonds de cuisine. The basic elements of the chef's mise-en-place are described as 'fonds de cuisine' of which a literal translation might be 'foundations of the kitchen or of cookery'. The following recipes for fonds de cuisine are based on traditional principles, though reconciled with present-day practice and possibilities, in the belief that building good cookery on sound foundations is still of the utmost importance.

(Basic preparations for fish and fish sauces are dealt with in Chapter 5; larder preparations and those for cold cookery appear in Chapter 2.)

BASIC FLAVOURINGS FOR STOCKS, SAUCES, AND SOUPS

In his work the chef uses many seasonings; these various aromatics, spices, and herbs are specified in all the recipes, but there are a few basic, composed flavourings used so frequently in savoury liquors that it is convenient to list them here.

1 Bouquet garni

1 *sprig thyme*	15 *g (½ oz) parsley*	2 *pieces green leek*
1 *bay-leaf*	*stalk*	1 *piece celery*

1 Bunch together the thyme, bay-leaf, celery and parsley stalk.
2 Wrap the green of leek round the bundle and tie with fine string.

Used for stocks, soups, sauces and entrées.

2 Mirepoix

240 *g (½ lb) carrots*	240 *g (½ lb) celery*	120 *g (¼ lb)* onions
1 *bay-leaf*	1 *sprig thyme*	60 *ml vegetable oil*

1 Cut all vegetables into medium dice.
2 Fry the vegetables and herbs in the oil to a light golden colour.

Used in soups, sauces, stews, and for braising.

3 Matignon (for large joints)

240 *g (½ lb) carrots*	240 *g (½ lb) celery*	3 *large onions*
1 *bay-leaf*	1 *sprig thyme*	6 *crushed peppercorns*

1 Cut the vegetables in large thick slices.
2 Place under large joints.

Used in roasting, poêlé, and the subsequent flavouring of jus or sauce.

4 Mirepoix à la Bordelaise

240 *g (½ lb) carrots*	1 *sprig thyme*	30 *g (1 oz)* butter
30 *g (1 oz) raw, lean ham*	240 *g (½ lb) white celery*	240 *g (½ lb)* onions
		1 *bay-leaf*

1 Dice the vegetables as brunoise.
2 Stew the raw ham and butter.
3 Add the vegetables and herbs and continue to sweat until soft.

Used for chicken, game, etc., and for the subsequent flavouring of jus (gravy) or sauce.

5 Oignon clouté (or piqué) – Studded onion

1 *large onion*
4 *cloves*
1 *blade bay-leaf*

Stud the peeled onion with the spices, impaling the bay-leaf to the onion with cloves.

Used generally, e.g. for infusing in milk or other liquors for sauces, particularly white sauces.

STOCKS

General Directions. As the function of stock is to add to the flavour and to give 'body' (that is, a gelatinous consistency) to the soups and sauces for which it is used, it will be obvious that a stock-pot should not be considered a dumping ground for any old kitchen scraps and left-overs. Moreover, as stocks are prepared in advance for later use they invariably have to be stored in the kitchen. Measures have to be taken, therefore, to prevent the souring or 'turning' of stock during storage. With these two factors in mind the following general points in stock-making should be remembered:

(i)   Choose sound ingredients ensuring that they are fresh and cleaned.
(ii)   Ensure that stock-pots and utensils are scrupulously clean.
(iii)   Break bones into small sizes to aid in extracting the maximum flavour, calcium, and gelatine.
(iv)   Use cold water (normally about twice as much water as the bulk of solid ingredients) and bring slowly to the boil for maximum extraction.
(v)   Carefully skim all scum and fat as they rise to the surface, particularly before the stock actually boils.
(vi)   Simmer gently, continuing to skim as required.
(vii)   Do not allow vegetables to remain in stock longer than is needed for extracting flavour otherwise these merely re-absorb flavour from the liquor.
(viii) Observe storage precautions to prevent sourness by careful skimming and straining, and by leaving the stock-pot raised on its storage surface to allow air to circulate.
(ix)   Store stock in a refrigerator at 3°C and bring to the boil daily, and after any storage period.

Note. Various types of commercial bouillons can be used as an aid to stock-making.

6 Fonds blanc – White stock [to yield 10 litres (10 quarts)]

10 *kg (20 lb) beef*	500 *g (1 lb) celery*	4 *onions cloutés*
bones	500 *g (1 lb) leeks*	14 *litre (14 qt) cold*
1 *kg (2 lb) whole*	1 *bouquet garni*	*water*
carrots		

1 Chop or saw the bones small; clean and prepare the vegetables.
2 Place bones in large saucepan or stock-pot with the water.
3 Bring to the boil slowly; remove scum as it rises.
4 Add the vegetables and bouquet garni.

5 Simmer for at least 4 hours, skimming frequently. (Simmering throughout the day, i.e. up to 8 hours, is customary. But excessive cooking fulfils no useful purpose.)
6 Remove all fat; strain and reserve for use.

Used for soups, sauces, and white stews.

7 Fonds brun ordinaire – Ordinary brown stock [to yield 10 litres (10 quarts)]

10 *kg* (20 *lb*) *beef* *bones*	12 *litre* (12 *qt*) *water*	60 *ml vegetable oil*
500 *g* (1 *lb*) pork rind (*optional*)	1 *bouquet garni*	1 *kg* (2 *lb*) *onions*
	1 *kg* (2 *lb*) *carrots*	

1 Chop the bones small.
2 Cut the vegetables into large dice.
3 Place bones, oil, and vegetables in the oven and cook until golden brown.
4 Add bones and vegetables to the water.
5 Bring to the boil, skim, add bouquet garni and simmer for 8 hours.
6 Strain and reserve for use.

This ordinary brown stock is the one most commonly used in trade practice when a brown stock is required.

8 Estouffade – Brown stock [to yield 10 litres (10 quarts)]

5 *kg* (10 *lb*) *shin of beef* (*bone and meat*)	750 *g* (1½ *lb*) diced pork rind (*optional*)	1 *kg* (2 *lb*) *onions*
5 *kg* (10 *lb*) shin of veal (*bone and meat*) *or* veal bones	1 *kg* (2 *lb*) *carrots*	12 *litre* (12 *qt*) *water*

1 Bone the meat and break bones finely.
2 Brown the bones in the oven with stock fat.
3 Place in large stock-pot with roughly sliced pork-rind, onions, carrots, bouquet garni; add the cold water.
4 Bring to the boil and skim; cover with lid and simmer for 8 hours.
5 Remove all fat; strain and allow to cool.
6 Place the meat in a saucepan with a little stock fat and brown over a brisk heat.
7 When brown, drain off the fat and add 1 litre (2 pints) of the stock; simmer under cover until the stock has nearly reduced, taking care to turn the meat during this process.
8 Pour on the remainder of the stock; bring to the boil and simmer with the lid off till the meat is cooked.
9 Remove fat; strain and reserve for use.

Used for braisings (including vegetables) and the preparation of basic sauces and gravies.

9 Fonds de veau – Veal stock [to yield 10 litres (10 quarts)]

10 *kg* (20 *lb*) *shin of*	750 *g* (1½ *lb*) *carrots*	360 *g* (¾ *lb*) *celery*
veal (*bone and meat*)	4 *onions cloutés*	14 *litre* (14 *qt*) *cold*
or veal bones	360 *g* (¾ *lb*) *leeks*	*water*
4 *raw chicken carcases*	1 *bouquet garni*	

1 Bone the shin of veal and break the bones into small pieces.
2 Place the bones in the water; bring to the boil; skim and simmer for 4 hours, skimming frequently.
3 Strain the stock in a clean saucepan; add the meat, whole vegetables, and bouquet garni and simmer for 4 hours.
4 Skim off all fat; strain and use as required.

Used for chicken poêlé, blanquettes, fricassées, etc.

10 Fonds de veau brun – Brown veal stock [to yield 10 litres (10 quarts)]

Ingredients: as for White Veal Stock; Method: as for Estouffade.

Used for jus lié (thickened gravy), and braisings (including vegetables).

11 Fonds de volaille – Chicken stock [to yield 10 litres (10 quarts)]

1 *old fowl* [2.5 *kg*	1 *kg* (2 *lb*) *whole*	360 *g* (¾ *lb*) *leeks*
(5–6 *lb approx*.)]	*carrots*	1 *bouquet garni*
5 *kg* (10 *lb*) *veal bones*	4 *onions cloutés*	14 *litre* (14 *qt*) *cold*
	360 *g* (¾ *lb*) *celery*	*water*

1 Break the bones into small lengths [approximately 4 cm (2 inches)].
2 Cover with cold water and simmer for 4 hours.
3 Strain the stock into a clean saucepan; add the fowl, vegetables, and bouquet garni and simmer for 4 hours.
4 Skim off all fat; strain through muslin and reserve for use.

Used for clear soups, veloutés, cream soups, aspic and chaud-froid sauces.

12 Fonds de gibier – Game stock [to yield 10 litres (10 quarts)]

NB. For economy, 15 kg (30 lb) game bones may be substituted for the venison, hare trimmings and pheasant below.

4.5 *kg* (9 *lb*) *neck or*	240 *g* (½ *lb*) *diced*	240 *g* (½ *lb*) *celery*
breast of venison	*carrots*	(*diced*)
1.5 *kg* (3 *lb*) *hare*	480 *g* (1 *lb*)	1 *bouquet garni*
trimmings	*mushrooms* (*diced*)	2 *onions cloutés**
4 *old pheasants*	240 *g* (½ *lb*) *leeks*	12 *litre* (12 *qt*) *cold*
	(*diced*)	*water*

1 Chop the venison, hare, and pheasant into small pieces.
2 Brown these same pieces with the carrots in the oven to a golden colour.

* Brown onions in the oven before sticking in cloves.

3 Place all in a large saucepan, cover with water, bring to the boil and remove the scum.
4 Add the mushrooms, celery, leeks, bouquet garni, and onions cloutés.
5 Simmer under cover for 4 hours.
6 Skim the stock and pass through muslin and allow to cool.

Used for game sauces, aspic, soups.

Essences. An Essence is stock reduced to half its quantity.

12a White vegetarian stock

120g (4 oz) onion	120g (4 oz) celery	1½ litre (3 pt) water
120 g (4 oz) carrots	120g (4 oz) leeks	

1 Roughly chop vegetables.
2 Place into pan with other ingredients, add water, bring to boil.
3 Allow to simmer for approx. 1 hour, skim. Strain and use.

For use in vegetarian soups and sauces.

12b Brown vegetarian stock

120 g (4 oz) onion	60 ml (⅛ pt) sunflower	6 peppercorns
120 g (4 oz) carrots	(or other vegetable	1½ litre (3 pt) water
120 g (4 oz) celery	oil)	7 g (¼ oz) yeast
120 g (4 oz) leeks	60g (2 oz) mushroom	extract
	trimmings	

1 Roughly chop the vegetables.
2 Fry the onions, carrots, celery and leeks in the sunflower oil until golden brown.
3 Drain the vegetables, place into a suitable saucepan.
4 Add all the other ingredients except the yeast extract.
5 Cover with the water, bring to the boil.
6 Add the yeast extract, simmer gently for approx. 1 hour.
7 Skim if necessary, strain and use.

For use in vegetarian soups and sauces.

12c Fonds de legumes – vegetable stock [to yield 10 litres (10 quarts)]

750 g (1½ lb) leeks	360g (¾ lb) cauliflower	750 g (1½ lb)
360 g (¾ lb) celery (or	(See Note 2 below)	tomato or 200 ml
celeriac)	125 g (¼ lb) mushroom	(½ pt) tomato
750 g (1½ lb) carrots	stalks and	purée
360 g (¾ lb) cabbage	trimmings.	10 litre (10 qt) water
(See Note 2 below)	Bouquet garni	750 g (1½ lb) onions
360 g (¾ lb) kohlrabi	360 g (¾ lb) scrubbed,	
(See Note 2 below)	unpeeled potatoes	

Seasoning for broth usage: salt, pepper, nutmeg, chopped parsley and/or other herbs

1 Wash and clean vegetables.
2 Peel celeriac, onion, scrub or scrape carrots.
3 Chop the onion.
4 Cut the vegetables into large dice.
5 In the stock-pot, fry the chopped onion until beginning to colour.
6 Add the leeks, carrots and celery (or celeriac) and continue to fry gently for a few minutes.
7 Add remaining ingredients with a little salt.
8 Simmer for 1 hour, skimming to remove scum as it rises.

Notes on vegetable stock
1 Recipe 12c accords with the precepts of Dr M.O. Bircher-Benner (Swiss pioneer of muesli and healthy eating) for service both as broth and as foundation for soups and sauces.
2 Substitutions and additions may be made to vegetable stock (according to intended use) but caution should be exercised in using leaf vegetables, especially cabbage, kohlrabi and cauliflower.
3 *Vegetable liquor.* Vegetarian cookery also uses liquor remaining when such vegetables as mushrooms, celery, potatoes, leeks, onions, carrots and other roots and leaf items have been cooked.

GLACES – GLAZES

Glazes are used in good-class cookery mainly for enriching sauces, though in some instances a thread of glaze added at a dish's finishing point may also have the effect of enhancing its appearance. Glazes are prepared by reducing stock until a thick and barely flowing liquid is achieved. Proprietary extracts of beef, poultry or yeast (e.g. Marmite) are on the market and have been substituted for glazes made by the chef in his own kitchens. However, it will become apparent that these substitutes have their limitations if fine, individual work in the classic tradition is sought.

Yield of Glazes from Stock

Glaze	Stock and Quantity Required		Yield	
13 Glace de viande – meat glaze	8 l. (8 qt) meat stock	250 ml	(½ pint)
14 Glace de volaille – chicken glaze	9 l. (9 qt) chicken stock	375 ml	(¾ pint)
15 Glace de gibier – game glaze	8 l. (8 qt) game stock	250 ml	(½ pint)
16 Glace de veau – veal glaze	9 l. (9 qt) veal stock	375 ml	(¾ pint)

1 Boil the stock in a thick pan.
2 Reduce on moderate fire for 3½ to 4 hours.
3 Reduce to given amount; when ready, the glaze should be sticky to the touch.
4 Pour in jars when hot.
5 Store for use as required.

16a Glace de légume – Vegetable glaze

Glace de legúme or vegetable glaze has not featured in the professional culinary tradition. Commerically produced yeast extracts (e.g. Marmite), owe something of their flavour and consistency to the reduction of vegetable liquor. Yeast/vegetable extracts may be used in substitution for meat glaze in vegetarian cookery.

GRAVIES

17 Jus – Gravy

The importance of accompanying simpler dishes, such as roasts, with good gravy is frequently underestimated. In modest establishments too great a reliance is often placed on packaged aids rather than on correct methods that capture the true flavour of the main item which the gravy accompanies. When roasting small joints or birds, it is important to place them on a bed of roots and aromates embodying the principle of the mirepoix and matignon (see Recipes 3 and 4), for this enriches the residue after cooking and improves the gravy.

Jus lié – *Thickened gravy*
See Recipe 30.

18 Jus rôti – Roast gravy
   500 *ml* (1 *pt*) *brown stock*

1 After cooking the joint, poultry or game, pour away surplus fat, retaining the residue.
2 Add a pinch of salt and pour in sufficient brown stock for the number of persons.
3 Strain through muslin.
4 Remove all fat.

Note. Never add flour to jus rôti to thicken.

THICKENINGS AND BINDING AGENTS

Most sauces are given body and consistency by combining their flavoursome liquor with a thickening agent. Similarly, thickening agents can be used to give body to soups. They may, therefore, be regarded as basic or fundamental kitchen preparations.

19 Beurre manié – Manipulated butter [to thicken 1 litre (1 quart)]

   120 *g* (4 *oz*) *butter or unsaturated*   90 *g* (3 *oz*) *sifted flour*
   margarine

1 Mix the butter and sieved flour together with palette knife to a smooth paste.
2 Add to the liquor to be thickened, just prior to service.
3 Avoid boiling after addition of beurre manié as the sauce would acquire a disagreeable taste.

Used for quick liaison, i.e. matelotes, vegetables and fish sauces.

20 Fécule thickening – Potato-starch thickening [to thicken 1 litre (1 quart)]

45 g (1½ oz) fécule   *125 ml (¼ pt) cold water*

1 Dilute fécule in water to a smooth paste.
2 Strain into boiling-liquid and simmer.

Used to thicken sauces and gravy (jus lié).

21 Liaison à l'œuf et à la crème – Egg and cream liaison [to thicken 1 litre (1 quart)]

250 ml (½ pt) fresh cream (or   *3 egg yolks*
fromage frais or heat-stable,
non-dairy creamer)

1 Beat egg yolks with cream.
2 Add to boiling liquid but do not allow to boil after the addition.
3 Mix well and draw to side of fire.

Note. Liaison may also be effected with egg yolks alone. Soups may similarly be enriched with butter and cream: 30 g (1 oz) butter, 125 ml (¼ pt) cream to 1 litre (1 quart) soup.

Used for chicken and fish sauces, entrées, and soups, etc.

22 Liaison au sang – Blood thickening [to thicken 1 litre (1 quart)]

500 ml (1 pt) blood   *125 ml (¼ pt) water*

1 This liaison is added at the last minute.
2 Mix blood with water with a whisk.
3 Add to the sauce and draw to the side of the stove-top away from the intense heat.

Used for thickening game soups and dishes such as jugged hare.

ROUX

Although equal quantities of fat and flour are given in roux recipies following, reducing the proportion of flour [to 100 g (3½ oz) in these recipes] results, in the author's experience, in a smoother sauce.

23 Roux blanc – White roux [to thicken 1 litre (1 quart) of white sauce)]

120 g (4 oz) flour   *120 g (4 oz) butter, sunflower oil or*
                               margarine

1 Melt the butter in a thick saucepan.
2 Sift and add the flour; mix well with wooden spoon.
3 The cooking must be limited to a few minutes, sufficient only to do away with the taste of the flour.
4 Cook on low heat.

Used for white sauces, Béchamel and derivatives.

24 Roux blond – Blond roux [to thicken 1 litre (1 quart of velouté sauce)]

120g (4 oz) flour   120 g (4 oz) butter or margarine

1 Melt the butter in a thick saucepan.
2 Sift the flour and add to the butter and mix well with wooden spoon.
3 Cook on low heat.
4 Cooking must cease as soon as the colour of the roux begins to change.

Used for veloutés.

25 Roux brun – Brown roux [to thicken 1 litre (1 quart)]

150 g (4 oz) flour   120g (4 oz) dripping or unsaturated
                                      vegetable oil

1 Melt the fat, add the flour using a thick saucepan.
2 Place in moderate oven or on side of stove.
3 Stir often with wooden spoon until a light brown colour and a scent
   resembling hazelnut exudes.

Note. Use more flour than fat when making a brown roux, because the flour
dextrinizes, thus losing some of its thickening property. If the roux is cooked
too quickly the flour burns. In addition to this fault imparting a burnt taste it
also makes it difficult to obtain the right consistency.

Used for Espagnole and other brown sauces.

SAUCES

The importance of sauces in good cookery hardly needs emphasis. The true
value of most important dishes depends upon the contribution made by the
sauce. Some sauces may be regarded as a vehicle for capturing the basic
flavour of the food they are to enhance. While certain sauces may act as a
foil, others may complement a food.

Common and obvious examples of the way in which a sauce completes a
dish is where a rich, fatty food such as pork or goose is off-set by a sharper or
more piquant sauce; or contrarywise, where a completely fatless food, like
white fish, is enriched by the presence of an emollient sauce in which butter
or oil has been emulsified. It is natural, therefore, that the basic sauces
should be regarded as fonds de cuisine – foundations of cookery.

Sauces are so implicit in good professional cookery that excellent, simple
sauces have been adapted by a variety of means including changes of flavours
and colour to meet the needs of different dishes and foods. The principal
sauces from which variants are derived have come to be regarded as basic or
mother sauces. To master the making of principal 'mother' sauces, that also
have their own uses in many dishes, is vital to the development of a full,
cookery repertory. The main kinds of basic sauces are:

(i)   Roux-thickened white sauce such as Béchamel and velouté.
(ii)   Roux-thickened brown sauce such as Espagnole and demi-glace.
(iii) Warm egg and butter-emulsion sauce, basic Hollandaise.

(iv) Cold egg and oil-emulsion sauce, basic Mayonnaise. (See 'Cold Preparations' Chapter 2.)

(v) The 'hard' sauce or flavoured cold butter, such as Maître d'Hôtel.

Note. There are, of course, sauces such as vinaigrette and sweet sauces which are not made from the foregoing basics; just as jus liés, thickened gravies, are similarly fundamental to good cookery but not derivative from the foregoing. Some of the miscellaneous savoury sauces are used sufficiently frequently by themselves, or in combination with other sauces, for them to be listed below as secondary or non-derivative sauces. The principal basic sauces in common use are:

BASIC SAUCES FROM STOCKS

Note: Substitutions and omissions
In the following recipes sunflower oil or margarine (or other unsaturated vegetable oils) may be substituted for butter in health-conscious catering. Enriching with butter (monter au beurre) in finishing sauces may also be omitted for the same reason.

VELOUTÉS

Veloutés classified here as derived from stocks are also regarded as constituting a basic white sauce, though Béchamel and Butter Sauce have wider use in forming true white sauces.

26 Velouté de veau – Veal velouté [to yield 1 litre (1 quart)]

1.5 *litre* (1½ *qt*) *veal* *stock* (*Recipe* 9) 1 *bouquet garni* 12 *ground peppercorns*	120g (4oz) *sifted flour* 120g (4 oz) *butter or* *margarine*	15 g (½ oz) *mushroom* *trimmings*

1 Bring the veal stock to the boil.
2 Make a blond roux (Recipe 24).
3 Allow roux to cool slightly and mix in stock slowly using a wooden spoon.
4 Continue to boil, skimming carefully.
5 Add peppercorns, mushroom trimmings and bouquet garni.
6 Simmer over low heat until reduced to 1 litre (1 quart), strain and reserve for use.

27 Velouté de volaille – Chicken velouté [to yield 1 litre (1 quart)]

Ingredients and method as for Velouté de veau, substituting white chicken stock (Recipe 11).

BROWN SAUCES

28 Espagnole – Basic brown sauce [to yield 1 litre (1 quart)]

120g (4 oz) sunflower oil or dripping	*120 g (4 oz) diced onions*	*125 ml (¼ pt) tomato purée*
120g (4 oz) flour	*2.5 litre (2½ qt) estouffade*	*15 g (½ oz) mushroom peelings*
30 g (1 oz) diced fat bacon (optional)	*480 g (1 lb) fresh tomatoes or*	
120 g (4 oz) diced carrots		

1 Make a brown roux (Recipe 25).
2 Allow to cool and add the boiling estouffade, slowly mixing to smoothness with a wooden spoon.
3 Bring slowly to the boil. Add tomato.
4 Remove all scum by careful skimming.
5 Fry the bacon to extract the fat. Add the vegetables and cook to a golden-brown colour.
6 Add the vegetables to the sauce and simmer 4 hours, skimming frequently.
7 Strain through fine chinois and reserve for use.

29 Demi-glace – Half-glaze (or refined basic brown sauce) [to yield 1 litre (1 quart)]

1 litre (1 qt) estouffade (Recipe 8)	*25 ml (1 fluid oz) truffle essence*
1 litre (1 qt) espagnole (Recipe 28)	

1 Mix together both liquids and essence.
2 Reduce by boiling to l litre (1 quart).
3 Strain and season.

SECONDARY OR NON-DERIVATIVE SAUCES

Many sauces today are based on reductions of well-made stock. They are not flour-thickened but have their own gelatinous body (or light thickening), resulting from reduction. They may sometimes be finished with a little butter (monté au beurre) or with egg yolk, cream, fromage frais, yogurt or similar ingredients.

30 Jus lié – Thickened gravy [to thicken 1 litre (1 quart)]

1.5 litre (1½ qt) brown veal stock (Recipe 10)	*15 g (½ oz) diced bacon rind*	*45 g (1½ oz) fécule or arrowroot*
120 g (4 oz) meat trimmings	*1 bouquet garni*	*12 crushed peppercorns*
60 g (2 oz) diced onions	*240 g (½ lb) fresh mashed tomatoes or*	*30 g (1 oz) mushroom peelings*
60 g (2 oz) diced carrots	*125 ml (¼ pt) tomato purée*	*salt*

1 Fry off the bacon rind to extract the fat.
2 Continuing to fry, add the diced meat and allow to brown.
3 Add the vegetables and colour slightly.
4 Strain off surplus fat.
5 Add the meat and vegetables to the stock. Bring to the boil and skim.
6 Add the bouquet garni, tomato, peppercorns and mushroom peelings.
7 Simmer 45 minutes, skimming frequently.
8 Dilute fécule with water and add to the liquid; re-boil, skim, season and strain through fine chinois.

31 Sauce à la bigarade [to yield 1 litre (1 quart)]

Juice of 3 oranges	*zest of 1 orange*	*1 litre (2 pts)*
Juice of ½ lemon	*zest of 1 lemon*	*thickened*
		braising stock*

1 Strain the braising-liquor and remove all fat.
2 Add the orange and lemon-juice and reduce to 1 litre (2 pints).
3 Strain through a muslin cloth.
4 Cut the zest of orange and lemon into fine julienne and blanch for 2 minutes.
5 Season the sauce and add the julienne of lemon and orange.

32 Sauce kari – Curry sauce [to yield 1 litre (1 quart)]

60 g (2 oz) sunflower margarine or sunflower oil (or butter)	*15 g (½ oz) chopped, fresh ginger*	*65 ml (⅛ pt) warm, fresh cream (or natural yogurt, fromage frais or*
60 g (2 oz) sifted flour	*90 g (3 oz) finely chopped onions*	*heat-stable non-dairy creamer)*
15 g (½ oz) curry powder	*125 ml (¼ pt) cold milk*	*¼ clove garlic*
65 ml (⅛ pt) tomato purée	*7 g (¼ oz) desiccated coconut*	*1 bouquet garni*
15 g (½ oz) chopped chutney		*salt and pepper*
1 finely chopped apple		*pinch cayenne*
		1 litre (1 qt) brown stock (Recipe 8)

1 Sweat the onions in butter.
2 Add the curry powder continuing to sweat.
3 Blend in the flour and cook for a few minutes at the side of the stove (or over low heat).
4 Mix in thoroughly the tomato purée.
5 Add the stock; mix smoothly; allow to boil and skim.
6 Add the crushed garlic, bouquet garni, chopped apple, ginger and chutney.

---

* This sauce is used to accompany braised and poêléd ducklings and the braising-stock, being thickened, constitutes a sauce.

7 Simmer 1 hour skimming frequently; then remove bouquet garni.
8 Soak the coconut in the cold milk for ½ hour and squeeze the resulting liquid out. (Some add the coconut direct.)
9 Add this coconut (or liquor) to the sauce and simmer for a further few moments; season and finish off with cream.
10 The sauce need not be strained.

Note. This is not intended to represent a true Indian curry but typifies the curry-flavoured sauce used not only alone but to flavour other sauces in professional Western cookery.

33 Sauce provençale I

60 g (2 oz) finely-chopped shallots	15 g (½ oz) fines herbes	120 g (¼ lb) butter
1 clove crushed garlic	100 ml (⅕ pt) olive oil	725 g (1½ lb) tomato concassé
	125 ml (¼ pt) white wine	

1 Sweat of the shallots and garlic in the oil.
2 Add the wine and make a reduction.
3 Add the tomato concassé and fines herbes.
4 Cook for approximately 10 minutes on the side of the stove.
5 Blend in the butter and season; do not strain.

33a Sauce provençale II

60 g (2 oz) finely-chopped shallots	480 g (1 lb) tomato concassé	120 g (¼ lb) butter
1 clove crushed garlic	250 ml (½ pt) tomato sauce	15 g (½ oz) fines herbes
125 ml (¼ pt) white wine		15 g (½ oz) meat glaze (Recipe 13)

1 Sweat off the shallots in 30 g (1 oz) butter.
2 Make a reduction of the wine.
3 Add the tomato concassé and garlic and stew for a few minutes.
4 Add the tomato sauce and fines herbes and simmer for 10 minutes.
5 Add the meat glaze.
6 Blend in the butter and adjust seasoning; do not strain.

34 Sauce à la tomate – Tomato sauce

60 g (2 oz) diced fat pork (optional)	240 g (½ lb) tomato purée or	7 g (¼ oz) sugar
15 g (½ oz) butter (or sunflower oil or margarine)	1 kg (2 lb) raw mashed tomatoes	1 sprig thyme
60 g (2 oz) flour	1.25 litre (2½ pt) fonds blanc (Recipe 6)	1 clove crushed garlic
1½ diced onions		salt and pepper
45 g (1½ oz) diced carrots		1 bay-leaf

Notes
1 When using fresh tomato in lieu of purée, reduce quantity of fonds blanc (white stock) to 750 ml (1½ pt).
2 A gatric, which is a light caramel reduction of 30 g (1 oz) sugar with 70 ml (⅛ pt) vinegar, may be added at step 4, with the tomatoes.
1 Fry the diced pork in butter.
2 Add the vegetables and sweat on.
3 Add the flour, thus making a blond roux.
4 Add the tomatoes and mix well.
5 Blend in the stock; boil and skim.
6 Add the garlic, herbes and seasoning.
7 Cook under cover in a moderate oven for 1½ hours.
8 Pass through chinois; butter the surface to avoid the formation of a skin.

34a Coulis de tomates – Tomato coulis (to be served hot)

> 500 g (1 lb) fresh tomatoes,
> skinned, de-seeded and diced
> 60 g (2 oz) finely chopped onion

> 60 g (2 oz) butter (or sunflower oil
> or margarine)
> 125 ml (¼ pt) white wine
> Seasoning

1 Sweat the finely chopped onion in the butter (or alternative) without colouring.
2 Add the tomatoes. Season and simmer for 5 minutes.
3 Moisten with white wine, bring to boil and reduce by one third.
4 Liquidize, pass through a fine strainer, correct seasoning and consistency.
5 Use as required.

DERIVATIVE BROWN SAUCES

In the following group of sauces, demi-glace plays an important role, although in some instances sauces are 'doubly derivative', e.g. sauce Charcutière, which is an elaboration of sauce Robert.

35 Sauce bordelaise

> 60 g (2 oz) finely-
> chopped shallots
> 250 ml (½ pt) red wine
> 6 crushed peppercorns
> 1 bay-leaf

> 1 sprig of thyme
> 30 g (1 oz) meat glaze
> (Recipe 13)
> 30 g (1 oz) diced
> marrow

> 750 ml (1½ pt)
> demi-glace
> (Recipe 29) (or
> jus lié or well-
> reduced meat
> stock)
> 90 g (3 oz) butter
> (or sunflower
> margarine or oil)

1 Sweat off the shallots and peppercorns in 30 g (1 oz) butter.
2 Add the thyme and bay-leaf and make a reduction of the wine.
3 Add the demi-glace and simmer to 500 ml (1 pint).
4 Strain the sauce and add the diced marrow which has been soaked in a little warm stock.
5 Add butter, meat glaze, and season.

Sauce bourguignonne

500*ml* (1 *pt*) demi-glace (*Recipe* 29) (*or jus lié or reduced stock*)	120*g* (4 *oz*) butter (or *sunflower margarine or oil*)
12 *crushed peppercorns*	250 *ml* (½ *pt*) red wine
1 *bay-leaf*	30 *g* (1 *oz*) finely-chopped shallots
	1 *sprig thyme*

1 Sweat off the shallots and peppercorns in 30 g (1 oz) butter.
2 Add bay-leaf and thyme, pour on red wine and make a reduction.
3 Moisten with demi-glace and reduce to 375 ml (¾ pt).
4 Strain the sauce; blend in the remainder of butter and season.

Note. See also Sauce bourguignonne for fish in Chapter 5, Recipe 381.

37 Sauce charcutière

500 *ml* (1 *pt*) sauce Robert (*Recipe* 49)	30 *g* (1 *oz*) julienne of gherkins

Toss the julienne of gherkins in a little butter and add to the sauce Robert as a garnish; do not strain.

38 Sauce chasseur

250 *ml* (½ *pt*) demi-glace (*Recipe* 29) (*or jus lié or reduced stock*)	240 *g* (½ *lb*) tomato concass	1 *small liqueur-glass brandy*
125 *ml* (¼ *pt*) tomato sauce (*Recipe* 34)	8 *medium mushrooms*	250 *ml* (½ *pt*) white wine
15 *g* (½ *oz*) meat glaze (*Recipe* 13)	15 *g* (½ *oz*) diced onions	90 *g* (3 *oz*) butter (*or sunflower margarine or oil*)
	15 *g* (½ *oz*) fines herbes	

1 Sweat the onions in 30 g (1 oz) butter (or margarine or oil).
2 Peel and slice mushrooms and add to onions and cook for a few minutes.
3 Make a reduction of the wine and brandy.
4 Add the tomato concassé, moisten with demi-glace and tomato sauce and simmer for 10 minutes.
5 Add the meat glaze and fines herbes.
6 Thicken with butter (optional) – season but do not strain.

39 Sauce Chateaubriand

60 *g* (2 *oz*) finely-chopped shallots	180 *g* (6 *oz*) parsley butter (*or parsley margarine*) (*Recipe* 89)	500 *ml* (1 *pt*) demi-glace (*Recipe* 29) (*or jus lié or reduced stock*)
60 *g* (2 *oz*) mushroom peelings	15 *g* (½ *oz*) chopped tarragon	250 *ml* (½ *pt*) white wine
1 *sprig thyme*		
2 *bay leaves*		

1 Sweat off shallots in 30 g (1 oz) butter.
2 Add the bay-leaves, thyme and make a reduction of the wine.

3 Moisten with demi-glace and reduce by one-third.
4 Strain, blend with the parsley butter.
5 Season and garnish with the chopped tarragon.
6 Add the mushroom peelings while making the reduction of demi-glace.

40 Sauce diable – Devilled sauce

60 g (2 oz) finely-chopped shallots	*165 ml (⅓ pt) white wine*	*1 sprig thyme seasoning*
12 crushed peppercorns	*165 ml (⅓ pt) wine vinegar*	*pinch cayenne pepper*
90 g (3 oz) butter (or sunflower margarine or oil)	*375 ml (¾ pt) half-glaze (Recipe 29) (or jus lié or reduced stock)*	*1 bay-leaf*

1 Sweat off shallots and peppercorns in 30 g (1 oz) butter.
2 Add the thyme and bay-leaf.
3 Make a reduction of the wine and vinegar.
4 Add the demi-glace and simmer to 250 ml (½ pint).
5 Strain and season – blend in the butter (optional).

41 Sauce Grand-Veneur

30 g (1 oz) meat glaze (Recipe 13)	*500 ml (1 pt) game stock (Recipe 12)*	*125 ml (¼ pt) fresh cream*
500 ml (1 pt) sauce poivrade (Recipe 47)	*3 × 20 ml spoon [4 tablespoons] red-currant jelly*	*120 g (¼ lb) butter*

1 Reduce sauce poivrade and game stock to 500 ml (1 pint).
2 Dissolve red-currant jelly and meat glaze in the sauce.
3 Finish with the cream and butter.

Note. The quantities of cream and butter may be reduced or even omitted, or fromage frais substituted for cream.

42 Sauce italienne

240 g (½ lb) dry duxelles (Recipe 101)	*¼ clove crushed garlic*
60 g (2 oz) diced lean cooked ham	*90 g (3 oz) butter (or sunflower margarine or oil)*
30 g (1 oz) finely-chopped shallots	*375 ml (¾ pt) half-glaze (Recipe 29) (or jus lié or reduced stock)*
125 ml (¼ pt) tomato sauce (Recipe 34) (or fresh tomato coulis)	*7 g (¼ oz) fines herbes*

1 Sweat the shallots in 30 g (1 oz) butter.
2 Add the garlic and finely chopped ham.
3 Add the duxelle and cook for a few minutes.
4 Moisten with the two sauces.
5 Simmer for 10 minutes; skim; add the fines herbes and blend in the butter.
6 Season but do not strain.

43 Sauce lyonnaise

120 g (4 oz) thinly sliced onions 90 g (3 oz) butter (or sunflower margarine or oil)	125 ml (¼ pt) white wine 125 ml (¼ pt) wine vinegar	750 ml (1½ pt) demi-glace (Recipe 29) (or jus lié or reduced stock)

1 Stew the onions gently in 60 g (2 oz) butter to a light colour.
2 Make a reduction of the wine and vinegar.
3 Moisten with the demi-glace and simmer to 500 ml (1 pint).
4 Skim and season; thicken with 30 g (1 oz) butter; do not strain.

44 Sauce madère – Madeira sauce

750 ml (1½ pt) demi-glace (Recipe 29) (or jus lié or reduced stock)
100 ml (⅕ pt) Madeira wine

60 g (2 oz) butter (or sunflower margarine or oil)
seasoning

1 Reduce the demi-glace to 500 ml (1 pint).
2 Add the Madeira wine.
3 Season, blend in the butter (optional) and strain.

45 Sauce Périgueux

500 ml (1 pt) sauce madère (Recipe 44)

90 g (3 oz) chopped truffles
85 ml (⅙ pt) truffle essence

Add the truffles and truffle essence to 500 ml (1 pint) of prepared sauce madère.

46 Sauce piquante

250 ml (½ pt) sauce diable (Recipe 40)
60 g (2 oz) chopped gherkins

30 g (1 oz) chopped capers
15 g (½ oz) fines herbes

Add the chopped gherkins, capers and fines herbes to the basic sauce diable.

47 Sauce poivrade

480 g (1 lb) fine mirepoix (Recipe 4) 120 g (4 oz) butter (or sunflower margarine or oil) 125 ml (¼ pt) vinegar	18 crushed peppercorns 750 ml (1½ pt) demi-glace (Recipe 29) (or jus lié or reduced stock) ½ clove crushed garlic	250 ml (½ pt) red wine 2 bay-leaves 1 sprig thyme 30 g (1 oz) meat glaze (Recipe 13)

1 Fry off mirepoix in butter.
2 Make a reduction of the wine and vinegar with the bay-leaves and thyme.
3 Add the demi-glace and reduce to 500 ml (1 pint).
4 Add the peppercorns and simmer for 5 minutes.

5 Strain the sauce and skim.
6 Season and thicken with butter (optional).

48 Sauce Reform

500 ml (1 pt) demi-glace (Recipe 29)	250 ml (½ pt) sauce poivrade (Recipe 47)	3 × 20 ml (spoon [4 tablespoons] red-currant jelly
4 chopped shallots	240 g (½ lb) butter (or sunflower margarine or oil)	
250 ml (½ pt) red wine		

1 Sweat shallots in 30 g (1 oz) butter (or margarine or oil).
2 Make a reduction of the red wine.
3 Moisten with the 2 sauces and reduce to 500 ml (1 pint).
4 Add the red-currant jelly and dissolve well.
5 Season; thicken with butter (monter au beurre) (optional).
6 Strain.

Used with côtelette d'agneau (lamb cutlet Reform) incorporating the following garnish: *Julienne of ham, tongue, gherkin, cooked egg-white, beetroot, truffles.*

49 Sauce Robert

60 g (2 oz) finely-chopped onions	750 ml (1½ pt) half-glaze (Recipe 29)	30 g (1 oz) meat glaze (Recipe 13)
165 ml (⅓ pt) white wine	5 ml spoon [1 teaspoon] English mustard	60 g (2 oz) butter (or sunflower margarine or oil)

1 Fry the onions gently in butter but do not colour.
2 Make a reduction of the white wine.
3 Add the demi-glace and reduce to 500 ml (1 pint).
4 Finish off with diluted mustard and meat glaze.
5 Blend in the butter (optional) and season; do not strain.

50 Sauce salmis

750 ml (1½ pt) demi-glace (Recipe 29) (or jus lié or reduced stock)	65 ml (⅛ pt) truffle essence	240 g (½ lb) game bones
150 g (5 oz) fine mirepoix (Recipe 4)	125 ml (¼ pt) sherry 125 ml (¼ pt) mushroom essence	120 g (4 oz) butter

1 Fry off the game bones and mirepoix in butter to golden colour.
2 Add the mushrooms, truffle essence, and demi-glace.
3 Reduce to 500 ml (1 pint).
4 Add the sherry and adjust the seasoning.
5 Pass through a fine chinois.

Use with venison and other game.

BASIC WHITE SAUCE

In addition to the veloutés, the following white sauces may be considered basic or mother sauces for savoury purposes and they are used to provide variants.

51 Béchamel sauce – Basic white savoury sauce [to yield 1 litre (1 quart)]

120 g (4 oz) butter (or sunflower margarine or oil)	1 litre (1 qt) milk (or skimmed or semi-skimmed milk)	1 onion clouté 1 bouquet garni salt and pepper
120 g (4 oz) sifted flour		

1 Make an infusion by boiling the milk with the onion clouté.
2 Make a white roux (Recipe 23) with the butter and flour and allow to cool.
3 Remove the onion from the infused milk.
4 Add the milk slowly to the roux mixing with a wooden spoon to a smooth sauce.
5 Add the bouquet garni.
6 Bring to boil slowly in moderate heat.
7 Simmer 20 minutes; season, strain and cover top with greased paper.

52 Sauce au beurre – Butter sauce [to yield 1 litre (1 quart)]

60 g (2 oz) melted butter	7 g (¼ oz) salt	125 ml (¼ pt) cream (or fromage frais,
60 g (2 oz) sifted flour	6 egg yolks	plain yogurt or
1 litre (1 qt) boiling water	juice of ½ lemon 150 g (5 oz) butter	heat-stable non-dairy creamer)

1 Melt butter and stir in flour in a thick pan over low heat and without allowing to cook.
2 Add the boiling water with salt added and whisk to make a smooth sauce but do not boil.
3 Immediately add the egg yolks mixed with the cream and then follow with the lemon-juice and mix thoroughly.
4 Finish off the sauce by adding walnut-size pieces of butter, blending well.

DERIVATIVE WHITE SAUCES (FROM BÉCHAMEL AND VELOUTÉ)

53 Sauce Albuféra (or Sauce ivoire) [to yield 1 litre (1 quart)]

1 litre (1 qt) sauce suprême (Recipe 61)	45 g (1½ oz) meat glaze (Recipe 13)

Add the warm meat glaze to sauce suprême and strain.

54 Sauce allemande [to yield 1 litre (1 quart)]

750 *ml* (1½ *pt*) *white veal stock* (*Recipe* 9)	1 *bay-leaf*	250 *ml* (½ *pt*) *fresh cream*
750 *ml* (1½ *pt*) *veal velouté* (*Recipe* 26)	*juice of* ½ *lemon*	*salt and cayenne pepper*
	5 *egg yolks*	24 *crushed peppercorns*
	60 *g* (2 *oz*) *mushroom peelings*	

1 Mix stock with velouté and add peppercorns, bay-leaf and mushroom peelings.
2 Reduce liquid to 1 litre (1 quart).
3 Season with salt, cayenne pepper and lemon juice.
4 Draw to side of stove.
5 Beat egg yolks with cream and add to sauce.
6 Strain and cover with buttered paper.
7 Do not allow to boil after adding egg yolks and cream.

55 Sauce aurore [to yield 1 litre (1 quart)]

750 *ml* (1½ *pt*) *chicken velouté* (*Recipe* 27)	125 *ml* (¼ *pt*) *fresh cream* (*or fromage frais or non-dairy creamer*)	250 *ml* (½ *pt*) *basic tomato sauce* (*Recipe* 34) (*or tomato coulis, Recipe* 34a)
180 *g* (6 *oz*) *butter*	*salt and pepper*	

1 Mix chicken velouté and basic tomato sauce together.
2 Simmer for a few minutes; add cream.
3 Season and pass through tammy-cloth.
4 Blend in the butter (optional).

56 Sauce Bonnefoy [to yield 1 litre (1 quart)]

60 *g* (2 *oz*) *finely-chopped shallots*	250 *ml* (½ *pt*) *chicken velouté*
250 *ml* (½ *pt*) *white wine*	(*Recipe* 27)
150 *g* (5 *oz*) *butter* (*or sunflower margarine or oil*)	5 *ml spoon* (1 *teaspoon*) *chopped tarragon*

1 Sweat off the shallots in 30 g (1 oz) butter.
2 Add the white wine and reduce to half.
3 Moisten the reduction with the chicken velouté and reduce to 125 ml (¼ pint).
4 Rub through a tammy-cloth.
5 Blend in the butter slowly (optional), garnish with chopped tarragon and season.

Serve separately with grilled fish or grilled white meat.

57 Sauce hongroise [to yield 1 litre (1 quart)]

90 g (3 oz) finely-chopped onions
250 ml (½ pt) white wine
1 litre (1 qt) well-reduced chicken
   velouté (Recipe 27)
120 g (4 oz) butter (or sunflower
   margarine or oil)

15 g (½ oz) paprika
1 small bouquet garni
250 ml (½ pt) cream (or fromage
   frais or natural yogurt or quark
   or non-dairy creamer)

1 Take 30 g (1 oz) of the butter and gently cook the onions without colouring.
2 Add the paprika to the onions and cook for a few minutes.
3 Add the white wine and the bouquet garni and reduce the wine to one-third of its volume.
4 Add the velouté and simmer for approximately 10 minutes.
5 Add the cream; blend in the butter.
6 Strain and season.

Note. When required for fish, substitute fish veoluté for chicken.

57a Sauce ivoire

See Recipe 53.

58 Sauce Mornay [to yield 1 litre (1 quart)]

1 litre (1 qt) Béchamel
   (Recipe 51)
60 g (2 oz) grated
   gruyère (or low-fat
   cheddar) cheese

65 ml (⅛ pt) fresh
   cream (or non-dairy
   creamer)
2 egg yolks

60 g (2 oz) grated
   parmesan
salt and pepper
pinch cayenne

1 Stir the cheese into the Béchamel with a whisk until the cheese is melted and thoroughly blended.
2 Effect a liaison with the egg yolks and cream and add this at the last minute to the sauce.

The above sauce is used for vegetables and for general purposes. If required for fish, a little fish glaze should be added.

59 Sauce poulette [to yield 1 litre (1 quart)]

1 litre (1 pt) sauce allemande
   (Recipe 54)
120 g (4 oz) butter
strained juice of ½ lemon

5 ml spoon [1 teaspoon] chopped
   parsley
25 ml (1 fluid oz) mushroom liquor

Blend the butter, parsley, lemon juice and mushroom liquor into the sauce allemande.

60 Sauce Soubise

1 kg (2 lb) onions	125 ml (¼ pt) cream	5 ml spoon [1
250 ml (½ pt) thick	(or fromage frais,	teaspoon] caster
Béchamel (Recipe	yogurt, quark or	sugar
51)	non-dairy creamer)	salt and pepper
	120 g (4 oz) butter (or	
	sunflower	
	margarine)	

1 Chop the onions finely.
2 Blanch for 3 minutes and drain well.
3 Stew the onions in the butter but do not allow them to colour.
4 Add the Béchamel; mix well; season and add the sugar.
5 Cook gently for ½ hour; rub first through a fine sieve and then through a tammy-cloth.
6 Finish off by adding cream.

61 Sauce suprême

1.5 litre (1½ qt)	500 ml (½ pt) fonds de	120 g (4 oz) butter
chicken velouté	volaille (Recipe 11)	(or sunflower
(Recipe 27)	125 ml (¼ pt)	margarine)
250 ml (½ pt) fresh	mushroom stock	
cream (or fromage		
frais or non-dairy		
creamer)		

1 Reduce the chicken stock to ⅓ of its volume.
2 Add the velouté and mushroom stock. Reduce the total liquid to 1 litre (1 quart).
3 Blend in the cream and butter.
4 Season and pass through tammy-cloth.

ENGLISH-STYLE WHITE SAUCE DERIVATIVES

62 Caper sauce

500 ml (1 pt) velouté	60 g (2 oz) butter (or	seasoning
(as Recipe 26 but	sunflower	30 g (1 oz) capers
using mutton stock)	margarine)	(whole)
	125 ml (¼ pt) cream	
	(or fromage frais or	
	non-dairy creamer)	

1 Add the whole capers to the velouté.
2 Blend in the butter and cream; season.

Note. When making caper sauce for fish use 500 ml (1 pint) of Béchamel in place of mutton velouté.

63 Cream sauce

500 *ml* (1 *pt*) *Béchamel (Recipe*   60 *g* (2 *oz*) *butter (or sunflower*
51)   *margarine)*
125 *ml* (¼ *pt*) *fresh cream*   *seasoning*

1 Add the cream to the Béchamel and reduce to 500 ml (1 pint).
2 Add the butter, season and strain.

64 Egg sauce

500 *ml* (1 *pt*) *Béchamel*   60 *g* (2 *oz*) *butter (or*   125 *ml* (¼ *pt*) *cream*
(*Recipe* 51)   *sunflower*   (*or fromage frais*
                                 margarine)   *or non-dairy*
                                 3 *hard-boiled eggs*   *creamer)*
                                                                  seasoning

1 Chop the hard-boiled eggs small.
2 Add the eggs to the Béchamel.
3 Blend in the cream and butter.
4 Season.

65 Mustard sauce I – English style

500 *ml* (1 *pt*) *Béchamel*   30 *g* (1 *oz*) *butter* (or   15 *ml spoon*
(*Recipe* 51)   *sunflower*   [1 *tablespoon*]
25 *ml* [1 *fluid oz*] *water*   *margarine)*   *mustard*
                                 salt and pepper

1 Dilute mustard in 25 ml (1 fluid oz) water.
2 Place in sauté-pan and reduce by half.
3 Add the Béchamel and mix well.
4 Strain, blend in butter and season; heat but do not boil.
5 Keep in bain-marie; butter the top to avoid skin formation.

66 Mustard sauce II – Classic style

Proceed as Method I above but substitute 500 ml (1 pint) of butter sauce
(Recipe 52) for the pint of Béchamel.

67 White onion sauce

500 *ml* (1 *pt*) *Béchamel*   30 *g* (1 *oz*) *butter (or*   250 *ml* (½ *pt*) *water*
(*Recipe* 51)   *sunflower*   *salt and pepper*
120 *g* (4 *oz*) *diced*   *margarine)*   *little grated nutmeg*
onions   125 *ml* (¼ *pt*) *cream*
                                 (*or fromage frais,*
                                 yogurt or non-dairy
                                 creamer)

1 Simmer the onions with the water and butter until soft.
2 Add the cooked onions and liquid to 500 ml (1 pint) of stiff Béchamel.

3 Warm the cream and add to the sauce.
4 Season.
5 Serve without straining.

68 Parsley sauce I

> 500 *ml* (1 *pt*) *cream sauce* (*Recipe*   *30 g* (1 *oz*) *butter* (*or sunflower*
>   63)   *margarine*)
> 15 *g* (½ *oz*) *blanched chopped*   *seasoning*
>   *parsley*

1 Blanch and chop the parsley.
2 Blend the cream and butter into the cream sauce and season.
3 Add the blanched chopped parsley.

Note. Blanching the parsley ensures that the sauce has a nice colour.

69 Sauce persil – Parsley sauce II

> 500 *ml* (1 *pt*) *butter sauce*   15 *g* (½ *oz*) *blanched chopped*
>   (*Recipe* 52)   *parsley*

Mix all ingredients; do not boil.

Note. Further white sauce derivatives are included in Chapter 5.

HOLLANDAISE SAUCE

In the preparation of warm dishes, Hollandaise is the mother of the classic egg-and-butter emulsion sauces; just as in cold cookery, Mayonnaise (see Chapter 2) is the parent egg-and-oil emulsion sauce. Hollandaise and some of its derivatives are extensively used with fish dishes such as Poached Turbot Sauce Hollandaise, and they are also widely used with vegetables and garnishes.

70 Sauce hollandaise

> 480 *g* (1 *lb*) *melted*   *50 ml* (2 *fluid oz*) *water*   *pinch cayenne*
>   *butter* (*or sunflower*   *12 crushed*   *pinch salt and*
>   *margarine*)   *peppercorns*   *pepper*
> 6 *egg yolks*   *juice of* ½ *lemon*
> 25 *ml* (1 *fluid oz*)
>   *vinegar*

1 Reduce vinegar and peppercorns in a sauteuse.
2 Allow to cool and add cold water.
3 Whisk in the egg and cook to ribbon stage, whisking all the time in the bain-marie.
4 Add the melted butter in a thin stream, whisking all the time.
5 Add the lemon juice and season.
6 Strain through muslin; keep warm.

Notes. Hollandaise curdles when an emulsion is not achieved. This may result if the butter (or its substitute) is added too quickly, or excessive heat causes the eggs to harden, shrink and separate from the liquid. (Even when the sauce is finished, do not over-heat or it will curdle.) If the sauce curdles, place a teaspoon of boiling water or a fresh egg yolk in a basin and gradually whisk in the curdled sauce.

To stabilize the sauce during the service period, add 60 ml thick Béchamel or velouté before straining. Hollandaise sauce (and its derivatives), however, should be freshly made for each service and never allowed to stand in a warm condition for long.

DERIVATIVES OF SAUCE HOLLANDAISE

71 Sauce béarnaise

300 g (10 oz) melted butter (or sunflower margarine)	15 g (½ oz) finely-chopped shallots	15 g (½ oz) chopped tarragon
5 egg yolks	60 ml [4 tablespoons] vinegar	juice of ½ lemon
12 crushed peppercorns	15 ml spoon [1 tablespoon] water	7 g (¼ oz) chopped chervil
cayenne pepper	30 g (1 oz) tarragon stalks	salt

1 Make a reduction of the vinegar, peppercorns, shallots and tarragon stalks.
2 Cool pan, add water and egg yolks.
3 Cook to ribbon stage in the bain-marie, whisking all the time.
4 Add the melted butter slowly, whisking to form an emulsion.
5 Season with lemon juice, salt and cayenne.
6 Strain through muslin.
7 Garnish with the chopped tarragon and chervil.

72 Sauce Choron

Basic béarnaise (Recipe 71) plus one-third pint fresh tomato purée. *

Mix warm tomato purée well with béarnaise.

72a Sauce divine

To sauce hollandaise (Recipe 70) add a reduction of sherry (1 sherry glassful reduced to half). Fold in 125 ml (¼ pint) whipped cream before serving.

73 Sauce Foyot (or Sauce valoise)

Basic béarnaise (Recipe 71) plus 3 × 15 ml spoon [3 tabelspoons] of warm meat glaze (Recipe 13).

* *To make fresh tomato purée.* Blanch tomatoes, remove all seeds, toss in butter and rub through fine sieve.

Blend the meat glaze with Béarnaise and put a thread of meat glaze on top before serving.

74 Sauce maltaise

> *Basic hollandaise*   *juice of 2 small blood*
> *(Recipe 70)*   *oranges*
>   *grated zest of ½ orange*

Add the strained orange juice and grated zest to basic hollandaise.

75 Sauce mousseline

> *Basic hollandaise (Recipe 70) plus* 125 ml (¼ *pint) stiffly whipped fresh cream.*

Fold cream gently into hollandaise sauce.

76 Sauce noisette

> *Basic hollandaise (Rceipe 70) plus* 60 g (2 oz) *beurre noisette (Recipe 82).*

Blend in the warm noisette butter with hollandaise just before serving.

77 Sauce Valoise

> (As Sauce Foyot, Recipe 73 above.)

Substitutions for butter. If sunflower (or similar margarine) is used in place of butter in warm butter sauces, warm butters and compound butters, their names will have to change (to avoid the term butter) to conform with the Trades Description Act.

VEGETARIAN SAUCES

Several of the sauces among the foregoing (such as Béchamel, Mornay and others) are suitable for vegetarian use. Others may be adapted for vegetarian use by substituting vegetable stock (Recipe 12c) for non-vegetarian stock (Recipes 6–12, as, for example, in Sauce Kari, Tomato sauce and others). The following small additional selection may also suggest further possibilities.

78 Sauce d'asperges – Asparagus sauce

> 360 g (12 oz) *cooked (or drained*   60 ml (⅛ pt) *double cream (or*
>   *canned) asparagus*   *fromage frais, natural yogurt or*
> 250 ml (½ pt) *vegetable stock*   *smetana)*
>   *(Recipe* 12c)   *seasoning*
> 125 ml (¼ pt) *white wine*

1 Liquidize the asparagus, stock and wine until smooth.
2 Bring to the boil

3 Strain through a fine strainer, season, reheat, finish with cream (or alternative).
4 Correct seasoning and consistency.

Use to accompany fried vegetable cutlets and similar vegetarian dishes.

78a Green peppercorn and paprika sauce

240 g (8 oz) plum tomatoes
(canned)
30 g (1 oz) crushed green
peppercorns
15 g (½ oz) paprika

juice of ½ lemon
250 ml (½ pt) double cream (or
vegetable creamer, natural yogurt
or fromage frais)

1 Purée the plum tomatoes, place in a pan with the peppercorns and bring to the boil. Simmer for 5 minutes.
2 Add paprika, simmer for a further 5 minutes.
3 Finish with cream (or substitute), bring back to the boil.
4 Add lemon juice, pass through a fine strainer, cool and serve chilled.

79 Groundnut and sesame sauce

120 g (4 oz) raisins
120 g (4 oz) peanut butter
2 tbsp. tahini (sesame seed paste)
2 tbsp. sesame seed oil
seasoning

2 tbsp. red wine vinegar
4 tbsp. concentrated apple juice
pinch ground cinnamon
375 ml (¾ pt) water

1 Place the raisins in a saucepan of cold water. Bring to the boil, refresh and drain.
2 Liquidize all ingredients together until smooth.
3 Correct seasoning and consistency. Pass through a coarse strainer and use as required.

79a Herb sauce

375 ml (¾ pt) marinade (wine
vinegar and oil with mixed
herbs and bay-leaf used to
marinade vegetarian kebabs)
125 ml (¼ pt) vegetable stock
(Recipe 12c)
15 g (½ oz) yeast extract
60 g (2 oz) tomato purée

60 g (2 oz) finely chopped onions
1 crushed and chopped clove of
garlic
15 g (½ oz) sunflower margarine
(or oil)
15 g (½ oz) arrowroot
seasoning

1 In a saucepan bring the marinade, vegetable stock, yeast extract and tomato purée to the boil.
2 Separately sweat the onion and garlic in the margarine for 2–3 minutes without colouring.
3 Add the marinade and stock and bring to boil.
4 Mix the arrowroot in a little cold water and stir into the liquid.
5 Bring back to boil, stirring continuously and simmer for 2 minutes.
6 Correct consistency. Season, strain and use as above.

WARM BUTTERS

Butter is widely used as an emollient and as a flavoursome accompaniment with many vegetable, fish, meat, and poultry dishes in good cookery. Therefore, in effect, prepared butters may be classified as sauces.

80 Beurre fondu – Melted butter

120 g (¼ lb) best butter   few drops lemon juice

1 Melt butter slowly, add lemon juice.
2 Strain off the whey.

81 Beurre noir – Black butter

120 g (4 oz) butter   juice of ½ lemon
15 g (½ oz) chopped parsley   15 ml spoon [1 tablespoon] vinegar

1 Brown the butter in a frying-pan.
2 Add the vinegar, lemon juice and parsley.

82 Beurre noisette

120 g (4 oz) butter   juice of ½ lemon

Brown butter in a frying-pan and add lemon juice.

83 Beurre meunière

Same as noisette plus a little chopped parsley.

Note. Optionally, it is sometimes the custom when using beurre meunière to surround the article with a thread of jus lié before pouring the beurre meunière on top. This constitutes a type of meunière sauce.

84 Clarified butter

Though clarified butter is used more as a cooking medium than as an accompaniment, its function may conveniently be noted here. This form of butter is cooked slowly until all the whey in the butter has evaporated, and the pure butter fat is separated from any milk solids. Clarified butter is used for making omelettes and for fine types of griddle-frying.

84a Beurre blanc – White butter

62 ml (⅛ pt) white wine vinegar   120 g (4 oz) unsalted butter
62 ml (⅛ pt) Muscadet (or other   seasoning
   dry white wine)   squeeze of lemon juice (optional)
30 g (1 oz) finely chopped shallot

1 Place the wine, vinegar and shallot in suitable saucepan. Bring to the boil.
2 Reduce to a syrup-like consistency.
3 Add the butter in small pieces. Whisk until the mixture becomes creamy.
4 Remove from heat. Season, add the lemon juice (if desired).
5 Serve lukewarm, ie at 60°C (140°F).

Notes
1 Originally used for pike (brochet) from the Loire, beurre blanc now has more extensive usage as an accompaniment to other fish and vegetables (such as asparagus, artichoke and warm vegetable mousses).
2 Techniques vary. Some chefs allow the reduction to cool before adding the butter, and then reheat gently. Others do not allow the butter to melt completely. Some include a little crème fraîche when adding butter to the bubbling reduced liquor to aid thickening.
3 In recent extended use of beurre blanc, some incorporate cream or additional flavourings, e.g. thyme or bay-leaf. Proportions may be varied (wine to wine vinegar and even substitution of water for some wines).
4 In a maigre version butter can be reduced from 120 g (¼ lb) to 30 g (1 oz) with half tablespoon crème fraîche and 100 g (3¼ oz) fromage blanc. Once the reduction has been achieved, the cold butter is added to the boiling reduction. As thickening takes place with the butter's melting, the cream is added. This mix is allowed to cool away from the heat. Then the fromage blanc is beaten in and the seasoning adjusted.

84b Beurre rouge

As for Beurre blanc, but substitute red wine and red wine vinegar for the white. Some chefs add a little meat glaze (Recipe 13) to the reduction before blending in the butter.

BEURRE COMPOSÉ

Composed butters or 'Hard sauces'. Butter blended with other flavouring agents is widely used, particularly to accompany grilled meats and fish. In most cases the butter, when completed with its additives, is rolled in greaseproof or butter paper or aluminium foil into a cylindrical shape and chilled. Roundels are sliced off as required. These slices are normally served in a sauce-boat containing iced water. (For butters with fish flavourings, see the section on fish sauces in Chapter 5.)

85 Beurre Bercy I

30 g (1 oz) finely-chopped shallots	125 ml (¼ pt) white wine
30 g (1 oz) meat glaze (Recipe 13)	5 ml spoon [1 teaspoon] chopped
240 g (½ lb) butter	parsley
30 g (1 oz) diced marrow	juice of ¼ lemon

1 Cream the butter and soften marrow in a little warm stock.
2 Reduce the shallots in the white wine, allow pan to cool.
3 Blend in the butter, marrow, meat glaze, parsley, and lemon juice.
4 Strain marrow before adding.

Note. This butter should not be melted and is used for grilled meats.

86 Beurre Bercy II

120 g (4 oz) butter	15 g (½ oz) chopped	30 g (1 oz) chopped
5 ml spoon [1	parsley	shallots
teaspoon] meat glaze	¼ clove chopped garlic	pinch cayenne
(optional)		juice of ½ lemon

1 Blanch and refresh shallots.
2 Work the shallots, garlic, cayenne, parsley, meat glaze, and butter together.
3 Roll in greaseproof paper or aluminium foil and keep until required.

Used for grills of meat, escargots (snails).

87 Beurre diable – Devilled butter

120 g (4 oz) butter	2.5 ml ([½ teaspoon]	juice of ½ lemon
2.5 ml spoon [½	curry powder	pinch cayenne
teaspoon] paprika		
pepper		

1 Mix all ingredients well.
2 Roll in greaseproof paper or aluminium foil and keep until required.

88 Beurre a l'echalote – Shallot butter

120 g (4 oz) finely chopped	juice of ½ lemon
shallots	pinch of cayenne pepper
120 g (4 oz) butter	

1 Blanch and refresh shallots.
2 Work shallots into butter with lemon juice and cayenne pepper.
3 Roll in greaseproof paper or aluminium foil and keep until required.

89 Beurre maître d'hôtel – Parsley butter

120 g (4 oz) butter	15 g (½ oz) chopped parsley
juice of ½ lemon	pinch of cayenne pepper

1 Work the lemon juice, parsley, and cayenne into the butter.
2 Roll in greaseproof paper or aluminium foil and keep until required.

90 Beurre Madras

120 g (4 oz) butter	juice of ½ lemon
60 g (2 oz) chopped chutney	pinch of cayenne pepper

1 Pound the chutney and butter.
2 Add lemon juice, cayenne, and salt.
3 Roll in greased paper or aluminium foil and keep in refrigerator till required.

91 **Beurre de moutarde** – Mustard butter

120 g (4 oz) butter   juice of ½ lemon
5 ml spoon [1 teaspoon] mustard   pinch cayenne

1 Work mustard, pepper and lemon juice into the butter.
2 Roll in greaseproof paper or aluminium foil and leave until required.

92 **Beurre Montpellier**

30 g (1 oz) parsley	7 g (¼ oz) capers	4 hard-boiled eggs
60 g (2 oz) cooked	15 g (½ oz) tarragon	cayenne pepper
spinach	and chervil	120 g (4 oz) butter
2 boned anchovies	15 g (½ oz) chives	2 gherkins

1 Blanch and refresh parsley, spinach, tarragon, chives, chervil.
2 Drain well.
3 Pound the anchovies and the herbs in the mortar.
4 Add the butter, eggs, chopped gherkins, capers.
5 Pound the whole mixture to a smooth paste.
6 Rub through a medium sieve.
7 Roll in greaseproof paper (or aluminium foil), keep until required.

93 **Beurre au paprika**

120 g (4 oz) butter   5 ml spoon [1   juice of ½ lemon
                           teaspoon] paprika

1 Work the lemon juice and paprika well into butter.
2 Roll in greaseproof paper and keep in refrigerator until required.

94 **Beurre de raifort** – Horse-radish butter

120 g (4 oz) butter   juice of ½ lemon
15 g (½ oz) horse-radish   pinch salt and cayenne pepper

1 Chop the horse-radish finely.
2 Work the butter, horse-radish, lemon juice, salt and cayenne together.
3 Roll in greaseproof paper and keep until required.

UNCLASSIFIED ENGLISH SAUCES

Although one or two of the non-classified sauces might appear in the following chapter, 'Cold Preparations', it was thought more convenient to group them together in this section. Many are known by their French designations, but they constitute a miscellaneous collection of sauces belonging to the British tradition of cookery.

95 Apple sauce – Sauce aux pommes

750 g (1½ lb) apples   30 g (1 oz) sugar   juice of ¼ lemon
30 g (1 oz) butter (or
    sunflower
    margarine)   125 ml (¼ pt) water

1 Peel and core apples and cut.
2 Add the water.
3 Cook quickly under cover till soft.
4 Pass through a medium sieve.
5 Add the butter, lemon juice and mix well.

The sauce may be served hot or cold as appropriate with hot or cold roast pork, duck, goose.

96 Bread sauce

500 ml (1 pt) milk   60 g (2 oz) butter (or   salt and pepper
90 g (3 oz)   sunflower
    breadcrumbs   margarine)
1 onion clouté

1 Boil milk with onion clouté.
2 Remove the onion and stir in the crumbs; mix well for the sauce must be of a smooth texture.
3 Simmer for a few minutes at the side of the stove.
4 Blend in the butter and season.
5 Keep warm in the bain-marie.
6 Cover with butter paper.

Served warm with roast poultry or feathered game (though butter-fried breadcrumbs are a preferred alternative with game).

97 Cranberry sauce – Sauce aux airelles

480 g (1 lb) cranberries   250 ml (½ pt) water
45 g (1½ oz) caster sugar   pinch salt

1 Wash cranberries.
2 Add the sugar, water, and salt to cranberries.
3 Cook quickly under cover.
4 Pass through a sieve.

The sauce may be served hot or cold. Usually accompanies turkey or game.

98 Cumberland Sauce

2.5 ml [½ teaspoon] English   65 ml (⅛ pt) orange juice
    mustard   juice of ½ lemon
240 g (½ lb) half-melted red-   zest of ½ orange cut in julienne
    currant jelly   15 g (½ oz) finely-chopped shallots
65 ml (⅛ pt) port wine

1 Place in a china bowl the half-melted red-currant jelly.
2 Add the English mustard and whisk in the port wine and the orange juice.
3 Blanch and refresh the shallots and add to the emulsion.
4 Complete the sauce with the julienne of the zest of orange.

Serve cold with cold meat (particularly venison), cold chicken or duck.

99 Horse-radish sauce – Sauce au raifort

1 *stick horse-radish*	125 *ml* (¼ *pt*) *lightly*	1 *ml* [¼ *teaspoon*]
25 *ml* (1 *fluid oz*)	*whipped cream* (*or*	*diluted mustard*
vinegar	*fromage frais or*	125 *ml* (¼ *pt*) *milk*
120 *g* (4 *oz*) *fine white*	*whipped non-dairy*	*salt and pepper*
breadcrumbs	*creamer*)	

1 Scrub and peel carefully the horse-radish.
2 Grate finely into china bowl.
3 Pour on the vinegar and mix in the mustard.
4 Soak the breadcrumbs in 125 ml (one gill) of milk.
5 Allow this mixture to stand for 1 hour.
6 Squeeze the milk from the crumbs and mix into the marinated horse-radish.
7 Fold in the cream and season.

Serve cold in sauce-boat with roast beef (hot or cold).

100 Mint sauce – Sauce à la menthe

For 1 litre (1 quart)

1 *litre* (1 *qt*) *malt vinegar*	30 *g* (1 *oz*) *caster sugar*
120 *g* (4 *oz*) *chopped mint*	*juice of* ½ *lemon*

1 Pick leaves from stalks and wash well and chop finely with the sugar.
2 Add the sugar and mint to vinegar and allow to stand for 1 hour.
3 Add the lemon juice and mix well.

Serve cold with hot or cold roast lamb.

Note. If using dried mint use 45 g (1½ oz. and bring to boil in the vinegar and allow to get cold before using.

DUXELLE

Duxelle has a wide culinary use, particularly as a base for stuffing vegetables, and in completing the garnish for meat entrées, fish, and vegetable dishes. A culinary basic, Duxelle is normally part of the kitchen mise-en-place.

101 Duxelle

1 *large finely chopped onion*	30 *g* (1 *oz*) *chopped parsley*
480 *g* (1 *lb*) *freshly chopped*	*nutmeg, pinch salt, pepper*
mushroom débris (*stalk and*	30 *g* (1 *oz*) *butter* (*or sunflower*
peel)	*margarine*) 12 *ml* (½ *fluid oz*) *oil*

1 Fry the onions in butter and oil without colouring.
2 Squeeze mushrooms in kitchen cloth to remove moisture.
3 Add mushrooms to onions and continue to cook until dry.
4 Add seasoning and chopped parsley.
5 Retain in china bowl covered with buttered paper until required.

102 Duxelle for stuffing vegetables

1 Mix Duxelle with 120 g (¼ lb) white breadcrumbs, moisten with tomatéd demi-glace and white wine.
2 Flavour with crushed, chopped garlic and simmer until reduced to consistency desired.

SALPICONS

A simple *salpicon* is a single item as chicken, diced and combined with sauce. Salpicons may be compounded of a variety of ingredients but always diced and always blended with a sauce. Mainly composed of cooked meat, poultry, and quenelles, they are commonly used to fill vol-au-vent, boucheés, croustades, etc. Combined with sauces given in previous recipes, salpicons may be considered one of the basic preparations for many different dishes. Examples of salpicon for fish are included in Chapter 5.

103 Financière

quenelles of veal	*mushrooms*	*stoned olives*
(*Recipe* 199)	*sweetbread*	*diced ham* (*lean*)
diced tongue		*may be added*

Sweat ingredients in butter and cohere with demi-glace (Recipe 29).

104 Godard

chicken quenelles	*mushrooms*	*lamb's sweetbreads*
(*Recipe* 199)	*diced truffle*	

Sweat ingredients in butter and cohere with sauce madère (Recipe 44).

105 Régence

truffles	*quenelles of veal*	*diced white part of*
	(*Recipe* 199)	*boiled fowl*

Sweat ingredients in butter and cohere with sauce suprême (Recipe 61). Garnish with sliced truffles.

106 Reine

| *diced, cooked chicken* | *truffles* | *sweetbreads* |
| *mushrooms* | | |

Sweat ingredients in butter, cohere with sauce suprême (Recipe 61).

107 Royale

| *diced foie-gras* | *chicken* | *sweetbreads* |
| *mushrooms* | | |

Sweat ingredients in butter, cohere with sauce crème (Recipe 63).

108 St-Hubert

| *truffles* | *mushrooms* | *dice of cooked game* |

Sweat ingredients in butter and cohere with sauce salmis (Recipe 50).

109 Toulousaine

| *chicken quenelles* | *mushrooms* | *slices of truffle* |
| *(Recipe* 199) | *sweetbreads* | |

Sweat ingredients in butter, cohere with sauce suprême (Recipe 61); garnish with slices of truffle.

Note. Pre-prepared vol-au-vents, etc. may be used with any of these fillings.

2 Cold Preparations

THE term cold area is often used nowadays to describe the larder (garde-manger, in French). In the past the larder (or cold area) was more than a food-storing section. It was where meat, fish, poultry and game were prepared and portioned for other sections (or parties), as well as undertaking its own cold cookery, buffet dishes, salad and hors d'œuvre making. In recent times economic (especially labour costs) and technological change (factory production) have resulted in greater reliance on the purchase of prepared food; but whatever their origin, basic preparations and sauces remain important in cold cookery.

COLD SAUCES AND LARDER BASICS

MAYONNAISE

While mayonnaise and its derivative sauces have a widespread application in cold cookery, the use of them with hot fried and grilled fish is, of course, a major one.

To reduce the risk of salmonella food poisoning, it is advisable to use pasteurized egg yolk instead of fresh in all mayonnaise type sauces.

110 Sauce mayonnaise [to yield 1 litre (1 quart)]

6 *egg yolks*	2.5 *ml spoon*	5 *ml (spoon*
5 *ml spoon*	[½ *teaspoon*] *salt*	[1 *teaspoon*]
[1 *teaspoon*] *English*	1 *litre* (1 *qt*) *salad oil*	*ground pepper*
mustard	*juice of* ½ *lemon*	
65 *ml* (⅛ *pt*) *vinegar*		

1 Place egg yolks in basin.
2 Add half the vinegar with the salt, pepper and mustard.
3 Whisk briskly.
4 Whisking all the time add the oil in a thin stream.
5 Add the lemon juice.

Note. If the sauce becomes too thick add up to 2 × 15 ml spoon [2 tablespoons] boiling water and a little vinegar. A well-made sauce should keep its shape when heaped on a spoon.

DERIVATIVES OF SAUCE MAYONNAISE

111 Cambridge sauce [to yield 1 litre (1 quart)]

6 *hard-boiled eggs*
30 *g* (1 *oz*) *anchovy fillets*
7 *g* (¼ *oz*) *chopped parsley*
pinch cayenne pepper
15 *g* (½ *oz*) *capers*

15 *g* (½ *oz*) *blanched and refreshed
chervil, tarragon, chives*
1 *litre* (1 *qt*) *mayonnaise*
(*Recipe* 110)

1 Pass the hard-boiled eggs through a medium sieve.
2 Pound in a mortar to a smooth paste the following: sieved eggs, anchovies, chives, chervil and tarragon.
3 Pass the resulting purée through a fine sieve.
4 Add the mixture to 1 litre (1 qt) basic mayonnaise.
5 Mix well and season – garnish with chopped parsley.

112 Gloucester sauce [to yield 1 litre (1 quart)]

1 *litre* (1 *qt*) *basic
mayonnaise*
(*Recipe* 110)

250 *ml* (½ *pt*) *sour
cream* (*or natural
yogurt*)

15 *g* (½ *oz*) *chopped
fennel*

Add to the basic mayonnaise the sour cream and chopped fennel.

Use with cold meats, particularly pork and duck.

113 Sauce rémoulade [to yield 1 litre (1 quart)]

1 *litre* (1 *qt*) *basic
mayonnaise*
(*Recipe* 110)
15 *ml spoon* [1
tablespoon] *anchovy
essence*

30 *g* (1 *oz*) *chopped
capers*
30 *g* (1 *oz*) *chopped
gherkins*

10 *ml spoon*
[2 *teaspoons*]
French
(*preferably Dijon
fort*) *mustard*

Add anchovy-essence, capers, gherkins, French mustard to basic mayonnaise.

Use with cold eggs, fried fish, grilled meats.

114 Sauce tartare [to yield 1 litre (1 quart)]

30 *g* (1 *oz*) *finely-
chopped shallots*
30 *g* (1 *oz*) *chopped
gherkins*
60 *g* (2 *oz*) *chopped
capers*

1 *litre* (1 *qt*) *basic
mayonnaise*
(*Recipe* 110)
15 *g* (½ *oz*) *chopped
chives*

15 *g* (½ *oz*) *tarragon*
15 *g* (½ *oz*) *chopped
parsley*
15 *g* (½ *oz*) *chopped
chervil*

Add the finely-chopped gherkins, capers, tarragon, parsley, chervil and chives to 1 litre (1 qt) basic mayonnaise.

Used particularly with fried and grilled fish.

115 Sauce tyrolienne [to yield 1 litre (1 quart)]

1 *litre (1 qt) basic mayonnaise (Recipe* 110)	240 *g (½ lb) tomato concassé*	1 *bay-leaf*
30 *g (1 oz) finely-chopped shallots*	12 *ml (½ fluid oz) salad oil*	½ *clove, chopped garlic*
		15 *g (½ oz) chopped fines herbes*

1 Sweat the shallots and garlic in oil.
2 Add the tomato concassé and bay-leaf.
3 Sweat the above under cover till a purée is made.
4 Pass through a fine sieve.
5 Allow to cool, add to basic mayonnaise and finish with the fines herbes.

Use with fried fish and with cold meats.

116 Sauce verte

1 *litre (1 qt) basic mayonnaise (Recipe* 110)	90 *g (3 oz) blanched leaves of spinach, watercress, tarragon, chervil and chives*

1 Squeeze the blanched and refreshed leaves free of all water.
2 Purée in a food processor and, if necessary, pass through a fine sieve.
3 Mix this purée with basic mayonnaise.

Use particularly with cold fish, fried and grilled fish.

117 Sauce Vincent

500 *ml (1 pt) sauce verte (Recipe* 116)	500 *ml (1 pt) sauce tartare (Recipe* 114)

Mix both sauces together.

Use particularly with cold and fried fish.

Salad dressings. The basic blend of oil and vinegar (sauce vinaigrette) and its possible permutations are used, of course, not only to dress lettuce and leaf salads, potato and other vegetable salads, but shredded meats, fish, and similar dishes for hors-d'œuvre and other dishes for cold service.

117a Sauce au Roquefort – Roquefort sauce

60 *g (2 oz) Roquefort cheese*	62 *ml (⅛ pt) white wine vinegar*
62 *ml (⅛ pt) whipping cream*	½ *teaspoon Dijon mustard*
pinch cayenne pepper, salt	

Place all ingredients into a food processor or a liquidizer, and blend to a smooth sauce. Pass through a suitable strainer, if necessary.

OIL AND VINEGAR DRESSINGS

118 Sauce vinaigrette [to yield 1 litre (1 quart)]

750 *ml* (1½ *pt*) *salad oil*   10 *ml spoon* [2 *teaspoons*] *French*
250 *ml* (½ *pt*) *wine vinegar*   *mustard*
½ *teaspoon salt*   1.25 *ml* (spoon [¼ *teaspoon*]
                                     ground pepper

1 Place mustard, salt, pepper and vinegar in a bowl.
2 When the salt has dissolved add the salad oil, gradually whisking till it forms an emulsion.

Note. This is basic vinaigrette. To it many chefs may add a garnish of one or all of the following: chopped capers, parsley, chervil, tarragon, shallot.

119 Sauce ailloli – Garlic dressing [to yield 1 litre (1 quart)]

4 *small cloves*   4 *pasteurized egg yolks*   1.25 *ml* (*spoon*
crushed garlic   750 *ml* (1½ *pt*) *oil*   [¼ *teaspoon*]
12 *ml* (½ *fluid oz*)   25 *ml* (1 *fluid oz*) *wine*   *ground pepper*
water   *vinegar*   2.5 *ml spoon*
                                                 [½ *teaspoon*] *salt*

1 Chop and crush the garlic finely.
2 Add the egg-yolks, salt, pepper and work the mixture well.
3 Gradually add the oil in a thin stream.
4 Finally add a few drops of water 10 ml spoon (½ fluid oz) to prevent curdling.
5 Pass sauce through fine muslin.

Note. Garlic-based *aillade* varies slightly according to French region. In Provençe, for example, there is sauce aillade: virtually a garlic vinaigrette (sometimes garnished with shallot and chives); and pain à l'aillade: slices of toast well-rubbed with garlic and sprinkled with olive oil (similar to chapon). Elsewhere preparations named aillade may be simply aioli (as above) or aioli blended, for example, in Toulouse style with blanched and pounded nuts.

120 Sauce ravigote [to yield 1 litre (1 quart)]

1 *litre* (1 *qt*) *basic vinaigrette*   30 *g* (1 *oz*) *chopped capers*
(*Recipe* 118)   30 *g* (1 *oz*) *chopped tarragon*,
30 *g* (1 *oz*) *finely-chopped shallots*   *chervil, chives, parsley*

1 Blanch and refresh chopped shallots and dry on cloth.
2 Blend shallots, herbs and chopped capers with vinaigrette.

Use for calf's head and other meat salads.

121 Thousand Island dressing [to yield 1 litre (1 quart)]

1 *litre (1 qt) basic dressing*
(Recipe 118)
4 chopped hard-boiled eggs
15 *g (½ oz) cooked lobster coral*
(optional)

125 *ml (¼ pt) tomato ketchup*
15 *g (½ oz) chopped parsley*
15 *g (½ oz) chopped tarragon*
30 *g (1 oz) finely-chopped shallots*

1 Dry the lobster coral and chop finely.
2 Blanch and refresh the shallots.
3 Add the coral, chopped eggs, parsley, tarragon and tomato ketchup to the basic vinaigrette.
4 Mix well. (This may also be used as a sea-food cocktail sauce.)

This sauce can also be made using 750 ml of basic mayonnaise instead of dressing.

121a Roquefort dressing

120 *g (4 oz) Roquefort cheese*
240 *ml (½ pt) sunflower (or olive)*
oil

2 *tbsp. white wine vinegar*
large teaspoon Dijon mustard
pinch cayenne pepper and salt

1 Place all ingredients into a food processor or liquidizer and blend until smooth.
2 Adjust the seasoning.

Note. Other blue cheese dressings may be made, e.g. blending 120 g (4 oz) Danish blue with 500 ml (1 pt) thinned mayonnaise (with cream, say) and appropriately seasoned.

121b Coulis de tomates – Fresh tomato sauce (raw)

500 *g (1 lb) tomatoes, skinned and*
pips removed
½ *tbsp. wine vinegar*
3 *tbsp. oil*

salt and pepper mill
1 *tbsp. chopped parsley and*
tarragon

1 Squeeze the tomatoes to remove excess juice and liquidize the flesh.
2 Place in a bowl and gradually whisk in the vinegar and oil.
3 Season and mix in the herbs.

ASPICS

Aspic is widely used in cold cookery as a glaze to inhibit moisture loss and enhance appearance. Its clear, solid consistency allows it to be cut into decorative shapes or chopped. It is used as a garnish, for lining moulds, or for incorporation into pâtés and pies to fill up crevices with its rich gelatinous material. The common faults to avoid in making aspic and when using the following recipes are:

(i)   Forgetting the preliminary soaking of gelatine in water.
(ii) Boiling too fast.
(iii) Not ladling gently when passing the aspic through muslin.

General guidance. For every litre (quart) of good, gelatinous stock of veal, chicken or fish, use 60 to 120 g [2 to 4 oz (according to warmth of weather)] of good gelatine (leaf gelatine for preference) and 1 raw egg-white. *Strong or heavy aspic.* For 'heavy' aspic, i.e. for pressed brisket, the proportion of gelatine is further increased.

Caution

Aspic jelly is an ideal medium for growing micro-organisms, so ensure that you understand the dangers and take safety precautions. In bare summary these include:

1 Always use fresh aspic (bring to boil, simmer a minimum of 10 minutes and cool quickly) and use sparingly.
2 Avoid using warm aspic (especially avoid exposure at room temperature for long periods).
3 For further use, rapidly rechill, store in refrigerator (and, again, follow step 1 above).
4 Use aspic-glazed dishes quickly (for consumption within 8 hours maximum); discard after 24 hours.
5 For aspic goods use refrigerated display units when possible.

122 Stock for aspic jelly [to yield 10 litres (10 quarts)]

5 kg (10 lb) chopped veal knuckle-bone	2 large onions	45 g (1½ oz) salt
	1 leek	12 litre (12 qt) water
2 kg (4 lb) shin of beef minced	1 stick celery	1 bouquet garni
	2 calf's feet	4 large carrots

1 Blanch and bone the calf's feet.
2 Oven-brown the veal knuckle-bone lightly to uniform colour.
3 Draw fat from bones and place in a large pan with the minced shin of beef.
4 Mix well with water; add the calf's feet, bring slowly to the boil; add the salt.
5 When boiling remove the scum and place in the vegetables.
6 Simmer for 4 to 5 hours, taking care to remove vegetables when they are cooked.
7 Remove fat often from the surface.
8 When cooked, pass through muslin-cloth and cool.
9 To make aspic from this base, add gelatine in accordance with the notes in *General guidance* above.

Note. Flavouring of aspic jelly may be appropriately varied by using chicken and game stocks.

123 Fish aspic [to yield 10 litres (10 quarts)]

1 *kg (30 oz) gelatine leaf*	1 *bouquet garni*	500 *g (1 lb) diced carrots*
10 *litre (10 qt) fish stock (Recipe 374)*	4 *sprigs tarragon*	500 *g (1 lb) diced onions*
1 *bottle white wine*	22 *crushed peppercorns*	10 *egg whites*
	½ *bottle sherry*	

1 Allow fish stock to become very cold and remove all scum.
2 Beat the egg whites to a froth and add the cold stock. Add the white wine.
3 Soak the leaf-gelatine until soft in cold water; when soft, squeeze out all the water.
4 Add the vegetables, gelatine, peppercorns, to the stock and bring quickly to the boil, stirring all the time.
5 When boiling, add the bouquet garni and tarragon leaves and simmer slowly until the clarification is complete (approximately 1 hour).
6 Add the sherry and strain carefully through muslin.
7 Remove all fat and season.
8 Use a kitchen paper to remove any surplus fat that may be on the surface.

MARINADE

A marinade is a liquor which flavours and helps to make tender the flesh of meat or fish. Marinading could be described as a mild form of pickling. It is used more often for meat than fish and has special value in dealing with game such as hare.

124 Marinade cuite – Cooked marinade [to yield 2 litres (2 quarts)]

1.5 *litre (3 pt) red wine*	1 *sliced onion*	2 *sprigs marjoram*
250 *ml (½ pt) malt vinegar*	1 *sliced carrot*	1 *sprig thyme*
125 *ml (¼ pt) brandy*	*juice of ½ lemon*	½ *clove crushed garlic*
125 *ml (¼ pt) olive oil*	60 *g (2 oz) green celery*	30 *g (1 oz) parsley stalks*
3 *cloves*	12 *crushed peppercorns*	2 *bay-leaves*
2.5 *ml spoon* [½ *teaspoon*] *salt*	2 *blades mace*	

1 Boil the vinegar and wine.
2 Pour over the other ingredients.
3 Allow to cool.
4 Season the meat with salt before marinading.
5 Turn over the items daily in marinade.

Used for game, meat, venison.

125 Marinade instantanée – Instant marinade [to yield 1 litre (1 quart)]

1 *litre* 1 *qt) oil*	60 *g* (2 *oz) finely*	2.5 *ml spoon*
240 *g* (½ *lb) thinly*	*minced shallots*	[½ *teaspoon*] *salt*
sliced onion	*juice of* 1 *lemon*	1.25 *ml spoon*
5 *ml spoon*	15 *g* (½ *oz) chopped*	[¼ *teaspoon*]
[1 *teaspoon*]	*chives*	*ground pepper*
powdered thyme	15 *g* (½ *oz) chopped*	2 *bay-leaves*
	parsley	

1 Mix all ingredients.
2 Allow to stand 2 hours before use.

Used with fish before frying, e.g. Filet de Sole Orly and à la juive.

126 Marinade for braised beef [to yield 1 litre (1 quart)]

500 *ml* (1 *pt) red wine*	½ *clove, crushed garlic*	1 *sprig thyme*
125 *ml* (¼ *pt) brandy*	30 *g* (1 *oz) parsley*	1.25 *ml spoon*
120 *g* (¼ *lb) diced*	*stalks*	[¼ *teaspoon*] *salt*
celery	120 *g* (¼ *lb) sliced*	125 *ml* (¼ *pt) olive*
12 *crushed*	*carrots*	*oil*
peppercorns	2 *bay-leaves*	
120 *g* (¼ *lb) diced*		
onions		

1 Mix all ingredients together in a large china bowl.
2 Allow to stand for 1 hour before use.
3 Keep in very cold place.

Use for large pieces of braising-beef (salt-seasoned before marinading). Turn in the marinade each day.

127 Marinade for soused herring [to yield 1 litre (1 quart)]

750 *ml* (1½ *pt) malt*	15 *g* (½ *oz) chopped*	5 *ml spoon*
vinegar	*parsley*	[1 *teaspoon*] *salt*
250 *ml* (½ *pt) water*	2 *cloves*	1.25 *ml spoon*
60 *g* (2 *oz) carrots*	1 *bay-leaf*	[¼ *teaspoon*]
(*paysanne cut*)	*pinch sugar*	*pepper*
60 *g* (2 *oz) thin onion*	*pinch allspice*	6 *black peppercorns*
rings		2 *slices lemon*
6 *chillies*		

1 Mix all ingredients.
2 Bring to boil.
3 Pour in china bowl and allow to cool; do not strain.

128 Marinade for Bismarck herring [to yield 1 litre (1 quart)]

750 *ml* (1½ *pt*) *white* *vinegar* 250 *ml* (½ *pt*) *dry white* *wine* 60 *g* (2 *oz*) *thinly-sliced* *onion*	1.25 *ml spoon* [¼ *teaspoon*] *salt* 8 *chillies* *pinch allspice* 2 *bay-leaves*	2 *black peppercorns* 8 *white peppercorns* *juice of* ½ *lemon* 2 *cloves*

Mix all the ingredients, allow to cool, then strain.

Used to pickle raw herring.

129 Marinade à la grecque – Marinade Greek style [to yield 1 litre (1 quart)]

1 *litre* (1 *qt*) *water* *juice of* 4 *lemons* 10 *ml spoon* [2 *teaspoons*] salt	1 *sprig thyme* 2 *bay-leaves* 12 *crushed* *peppercorns*	125 *ml* (¼ *pt*) *oil* ¼ *root of fennel* 4 *celery sticks*

1 Boil the lemon juice and water with the ingredients until they are cooked before adding the oil.
2 Cook in the resultant 'cuisson' whatever you wish to cook in the style 'à la grecque', i.e. cauliflower, onions, artichoke, marrow, etc.

130 Marinade à la portugaise [to yield 1 litre (1 quart)]

Add to the above recipe:

15 *ml spoon* [1 *tablespoon*] *tomato* *purée*	1 *clove crushed garlic* 480 *g* [1 *lb* (*net*)] *tomato concassé*

131 Spiced vinegar [to yield 1 litre (1 quart)]

7 *g* (¼ *oz*) *allspice* 7 *g* (¼ *oz*) *cloves* 7 *g* (¼ *oz*) *root-ginger*	7 *g* (¼ *oz*) *mace* 7 *g* (¼ *oz*) *black* *peppercorn*	7 *g* (¼ *oz*) *cinnamon bark* 1.5 *litre* (1½ *qt*) *vinegar*

1 Bruise all ingredients by crushing with a rolling-pin.
2 Tie in a muslin-bag.
3 Boil the vinegar; infuse the crushed ingredients in the vinegar just off the boil; allow to cool.

Used for pickling red cabbage, cauliflower, onions, etc.

BRINE

General points in brine-making. Brine joints such as silverside of beef for 4 to 5 days. (Ox-tongues because of tough skin may take about three weeks unless injection method is used):

(i)   Wash and dry meat before putting it into brine.
(ii) After removing the meat from the brine, run cold-tap water over it.
(iii) Keep in very cold place.
(iv) Wash the tub scrupulously after use.

132 Sweet brine [to yield 9 litres (2 gallons)]

9 *litre (2 gallons) water*	360 *g (¾ lb) brown sugar*
3 *kg (6 lb) bay-salt*	45 *g (1½ oz) saltpetre*

1 Place all ingredients in a pan and boil for 20 minutes.
2 Allow to get cold and pour into porcelain or other suitable container; keep covered.

Use for salt beef, pork, tongues, ham.

133 Dry pickle [sufficient for 7 kg (14 lb of meat)]

750 *g (1½ lb) salt*	120 *g (¼ lb) brown sugar*
30 *g (1 oz) saltpetre*	120 *g (¼ lb) allspice*

1 Rub meat in sugar and let it stand for 2 hours.
2 Rub on a little saltpetre, allspice and salt a little at a time.
3 Turn and knead the meat well.
4 Let it lie for about 10 weeks in a very cold place, turning daily.

Note. Dry pickling certainly does not involve the use of culinary liquor but is included here as it is often used as an alternative to pickling in brine; particularly for belly of pork, bath chaps, silverside of beef.

CHAUD-FROID SAUCES

The chaud-froid sauces (literally, hot-cold sauces) are those which, though cooked and thus, initially hot, are intended specifically for cold use as buffet items and similar purposes. See Recipe 745, for example.

Points to note in making and using chaud-froid sauces. When cooling, stir often to avoid lumps for the sauce must be a smooth texture while coating. Chaud-froid can also be reheated slowly in the bain-marie; re-strain before using.

134 Chaud-froid blanc – White chaud-froid [to yield 1.5 litres (3 pints)]

1 *litre (1 qt) chicken velouté* (*Recipe* 27)	250 *ml (½ pt) chicken stock* (*Recipe* 11)
250 *ml (½ pt) fresh cream (or fromage frais, yogurt or non-dairy creamer)*	500 *ml (1 pt) chicken aspic-jelly* (*Recipe* 123 *made with chicken stock*)
	seasoning

1 Mix the velouté with chicken stock and reduce on quick fire.
2 While the sauce is reducing, add the aspic, 125 ml (¼ pt) at a time; yield after total reduction should be 1.25 (2½ pints).
3 Season, blend in the cream and strain through muslin.

Note. To make a quick type add 45 g (1½ oz) leaf gelatine softened in water to 1 litre (1 quart) of sauce allemande (Recipe 54). Be sure to allow the gelatine to melt thoroughly and to strain it through a muslin.

135 Chaud-froid à l'aurore – Pink, tomaté chaud-froid [to yield 1 litre (1 quart)]

1 *litre* (1 *qt*) *white chaud-froid*   125 *ml* (¼ *pt*) *fine tomato-pulp*
(*Recipe* 134)

Add 125 ml (¼ pt) of fine tomato-pulp to basic chaud-froid while hot and strain through muslin.

This pink chaud-froid is used in dishes such as Poularde Rose de Mai.

Chaud-froid brun – Brown chaud-froid [to yield 1 litre (1 quart)]

1.25 *litre* (2½ *pt*) *demi-glace*   *seasoning*
(*Recipe* 29) (*or jus lié or*   100 *ml* (⅕ *pt*) *truffle essence*
reduced stock)   (*optional*)
1 *glass* (70 *ml or* ⅛ *pt*) *Madeira*   500 *ml* (1 *pt*) *aspic jelly*
wine

1 Add the truffle-essence to demi-glace and reduce on quick fire.
2 While the sauce is reducing add the aspic jelly, 125 ml (¼ pt) at a time.
3 Add the Madeira wine and season.
[Yield of total reduction should be 1 litre (1 quart).]

The use of this type of aspic jelly is determined by the article to be coated, i.e. for game, use game aspic-jelly.

137 Chaud-froid blanc de poisson – White fish chaud-froid [to yield 1 litre (1 quart)]

Same recipe and method as white chaud-froid but using fish velouté (Recipe 377) instead of chicken velouté.

138 Chaud-froid au vin rouge (for fish) – Red wine chaud-froid (fish) [to yield 1 litre (1 quart)]

Same method as chaud-froid brun, using 1.25 litre (2½ pints) Genevoise Sauce (Recipe 385), and 500 ml (1 pint) of fish aspic (Recipe 123) instead of demi-glace and ordinary aspic.

HORS-D'ŒUVRE

Hors-d'œuvre are meant to stimulate the appetite. Therefore, their presentation is as important as taste: items must be dainty, petite, and fresh with eye-appealing colour contrasts. But simplicity should be the watchword;

do not over-elaborate. Left-overs may be used, but hors-d'œuvre should not depend entirely on these elements, and certainly they must never look like left-overs. Merely pouring oil and vinegar on to vegetables will not make an hors-d'œuvre.

An hors-d'œuvre may be a single item (or a single item with simple accompaniments) or a variety of items. Examples of single hors-d'œuvre are: caviar, oysters, lobster, smoked ham, foie gras, pâtés and terrines, smoked salmon, trout, and smoked poultry; potted or cocktail shrimps, or other sea-food cocktails; fruits such as melon, avocado pear, grapefruit, and fruit cocktails; cold asparagus or artichoke with vinaigrette. Even fruit and tomato juices may be served as an appetizer course.

Recipes for mixed and plain hors-d'œuvre are practically inexhaustible. It would, indeed, be easier to compile a list of food that should not be used. Discretion, commonsense, imagination, and good taste should determine the selection.

A few of the standard hors-d'œuvre expected in a selection include: salads (particularly potato, tomato, cucumber, Russian); vegetables (especially cauliflower, onions, mushrooms) and fish cooked à la grecque, i.e. in the à la grecque marinade (Recipe 129); other fish like soused, pickled, and smoked herrings, anchovies and sardines; egg mayonnaise, salami, celery, cheese, and olives.

Grapefruit or oysters are normally served as single appetizers, but many of the dishes in this section may also be featured as part of a selection of hors-d'œuvre varié. Although most hors-d'œuvre are served cold, there are also hot appetizers; one or two of these are included in this chapter.

FRUITS AND FRUIT JUICES

AVOCAT – AVOCADO PEAR

Avocado pear has widespread use as an appetizer.

Simple presentations. Halve the fruit lengthwise, remove the centre stone, carefully scoop out the soft flesh and cut into small dice, then blend with a dressing and replace the flesh in the half-shell of skin. Another alternative presentation is, after halving and removing the stone, to remove the flesh from the skin, then slice (without completely severing) to enable fanning of the slices on a plate. Garnish with either a simple composed salad or cottage cheese or citrus fruit with a raspberry vinaigrette. Diced avocado may, be combined with other ingredients (as in the examples which follow) and also used in mixed salads.

139 Avocat épicure

2 *avocado pears*	30 *g* (1 *oz*) *gherkins*	62 *ml* (⅛ *pt*)
4 *pickled walnut halves*	*paprika*	*mayonnaise*
15 *g* (½ *oz*) *walnuts*		(*Recipe* 110) (*or*
		fromage frais,
		yogurt or quark)

1 Halve the pears, remove stone and flesh, taking care not to break the skin.
2 Dice the pear flesh and combine with diced gherkins, walnuts, and mayonnaise; season with paprika.
3 Garnish the top with half a pickled walnut.
4 Present on a bed of crisp lettuce-hearts.

140 Avocat Singapour

2 *avocado pears*	7.5 *ml* [½ *tablespoon*]	*lemon juice*
60 *g* (2 *oz*) *flaked,*	*whipped cream**	*cayenne pepper*
white crab meat	7 *g* (⅛ *oz*) *freshly*	
62 *ml* (⅛ *pt*)	*grated root ginger*	
*mayonnaise**		
(*Recipe* 110)		

1 Cut the pears in half, lengthwise, and remove the stone.
2 Dice the flesh and sprinkle with a few drops of vinegar.
3 Mix the crab meat, mayonnaise, cream, ginger and lemon juice together and replace in the half-pear shells.
4 Serve on crushed ice with quarters of lettuce and slices of lemon.

**Note.* Some, or all of the mayonnaise and cream may be replaced by fromage frais, yogurt or quark.

MELON

141 Cantaloup or Honeydew melon

1 Cut into sections and remove seeds.
2 Serve on crushed ice.
3 Decorate with orange slivers and/or cherries impaled on cocktail sticks, and also frills for melon-end points.
4 Ground ginger and caster sugar served separately.

142 Melon de Charente au porto – Charentais melon with port wine

1 Cut small piece from top in form of lid.
2 Remove seeds – macerate with port wine.
3 Replace lid and serve on crushed ice.

PAMPLEMOUSSE – GRAPEFRUIT

Grapefruit may be served plainly in halves with the segments loosened to facilitate eating. Grapefruit juice may be served chilled in goblets (or double vessels with ice liner) as an appetizer.

143 Demi-pamplemousse frappé au kirsch – Chilled half grapefruit, kirsch-flavoured

1 Prepare grapefruit in halves.
2 Add a little kirsch and a 5 ml spoon [teaspoon] of caster sugar to each half.
3 Serve on crushed ice; garnish with cocktail cherries.

144 Grapefruit cocktail

> 4 *grapefruit*   125 *ml* (¼ *pt*) *stock*   30 *ml* (1 *tbsp.*)
> 4 *cherries*   *syrup* (*Recipe* 992)   *kirsch*
>   4 *goblets*

1 Rim goblets with sugar as follows: (a) colour the sugar or leave plain as desired; (b) dip the rim of glass into egg-white and then in sugar.
2 Skin and fillet grapefruit.
3 Place the fillets in the stock syrup with the kirsch.
4 Serve very cold in goblets. Garnish with cocktail cherries.

145 Cocktail Florida

Combine equal parts of orange fillets with grapefruit to make this variant cocktail.

146 Pamplemousse mexicaine – grapefruit Mexicaine (hot)

> 2 *grapefruit*   15 *g* (½ *oz*) *caster sugar*
> ½ glass sherry   1 *pimento*

1 Prepare grapefruit in halves.
2 Add 7.5 ml spoon [½ tablespoon] of brown sugar and 7.5 ml spoon [½ tablespoon] sherry. All to stand 1 hour.
3 Sprinkle some caster sugar on top of each, brown under the grill.
4 Garnish with pimento. Serve hot.

147 Fresh tomato juice

> 12 *blanched tomatoes*   1 *piece bruised celery*
> 15 *ml spoon* [1 *tablespoon*]   *juice of* 1 *lemon*
>   *Worcester sauce*

1 Squeeze all tomatoes through fine sieve.
2 Add Worcester sauce, bruised celery, half-pint of cold water, lemon juice and strain.
3 Season and mix well; serve chilled.

Note. Orange juice and pineapple juice may also be served chilled, as for grapefruit juice.

FISH AND FISH PRODUCTS

148 Anguille fumée – Smoked eel

1 Skin. Slice in thin fillets.
2 Dress on a ravier.
3 Serve with lemon and sour cream or horse-radish sauce.

CAVIAR

The most renowned caviar comes from the delta of the Volga in the Caspian Sea – the area known as the Astrakan. The species are:

Beluga – Supreme quality: large grained and slightly salty.
Ocietrova Malossol – Small grained and less costly.
Secruga Malossol – Two-thirds of the price of Beluga.

149 Caviar

To serve:
1 See that it is in a perfectly fresh condition. (Caviar is perishable and loses its quality on ageing.)
2 Encrust it in ice and use a bone or ivory spoon for service.
3 Accompany the dish with: finely-chopped onions, halves of lemon, slices of rye bread or toast; or Blinis – small pancakes of buckwheat (Recipe 1095). (Sour cream may also be served with Blinis.)

HARENGS – HERRINGS

150 Bismarck herrings

Ingredients as for Marinade (Recipe 128).

1 Bone fresh herrings and sprinkle them with salt; leave over night.
2 Wash off surplus salt by letting cold water run over them for 2 hours.
3 Place the boned herrings flat in crocks with marinade (Recipe 128) including sliced onions, mustard seed, bay-leaves, peppercorns, chillies, sliced lemon and sliced salt-cucumbers and 250 ml (½ pint) water.
4 Store in a cool place for a few days and keep well covered.

151 Rollmops

1 Prepare as Bismarck herring (Recipe 150).
2 Roll herring around a slice of salt cucumber (or dill pickle) and a little mustard seed.
3 Secure in position with cocktail stick or small skewer.

152 Soused herrings

1 Pour marinade (Recipe 127) over the gutted fish.
2 Bake in dish in the oven till cooked.

Note. Trout or mackerel can be treated in the same way.

153 Smoked herring fillets in oil

If prepared canned fillets are not used, the following is an alternative:

4 *large kippers*	6 *peppercorns*
1 *bay-leaf*	250 *ml* (½ *pt*) *oil*

1 Place kippers on stove upside-down for a few minutes to remove skin.
2 Ease the bones out with the fingers.
3 Store the flesh in earthenware terrines with bay-leaves and peppercorns interspersed among the fillets.
4 Pour over the oil and leave over night.

154 Salade de poisson – Fish salad

1 Use left-over fish of firm texture.
2 Cut into small cubes.
3 Add the same amount of cold, boiled, sliced or diced potatoes and a few pieces of peeled and seeded tomatoes.
4 Bind with tomato-flavoured mayonnaise.

155 Sardines à l'huile – Sardines (canned) in oil

To serve:
1 These may be served direct from the tin.
2 May also be served dressed fanwise on a ravier with the tails pointing one way.
3 Serve a little oil on top and garnish with parsley.

156 Saumon fumé – Smoked salmon

| 250 g (½ lb) smoked salmon | 2 lemons | 15 g (½ oz) capers |

1 Slice salmon very thinly.
2 Garnish with capers, parsley sprigs and half-lemons.
3 Serve with brown bread and butter. Moulin (peppermill) and cayenne should be 'en place'.

157 Truite fumée – Smoked trout

| 4, 200 g (6 oz) trout | 2 lemons | 125 ml (¼ pt) sour cream |

1 Skin both sides of the trout.
2 Garnish with slices of lemon and parsley.
3 Serve separately, from sauce-boat, acidulated cream or sauce raifort (Recipe 99).

158 Thon à l'huile – Tunny fish in oil

To serve:
1 Remove from can and slice thickly.
2 Garnish with onion rings and dress with a little salad oil.

159 Pickled left-over white fish, salmon, etc.

1 If the fish has been fried or meunière remove brown coating.
2 Arrange the fish in a dish, season, add some sliced onions and cover with vinaigrette.

CHARCUTERIE: CURED OR SMOKED
MEATS AND SAUSAGES

160 Saucisson (Salami) – Smoked or prepared sausage

To serve:

1 Sausage of French type such as Saucisson de ménage, Saucisson de ménage fumé, Saucisson d'Arles, Saucisson de Lyons, etc., and Italian type such as Salami di Milano: slice thinly and dress the slices overlapping on a salver.
2 Types such as Mortadella (Italian) and Andouille de Vire (French): these slices should be slightly thicker, because of their larger diameter.
3 Saucisson à l'ail (Garlic sausage) and Leberwurst (Liver sausage): here again slices should be thicker because of the softer texture.

161 Jambon cru – Raw, salt ham

161a Jambon fumé – Smoked ham (such as Jambon de Bayonne – Bayonne ham)

Cut very thin: serve with lettuce, tomato and gherkin.

161b Jambone de Parme – Parma ham

This is served in a similar style to 161a (as is Bayonne ham).

162 Jambon cru au melon

Cured and smoked hams for eating without further preparation, other than slicing, may also be accompanied by melon. Parma ham is especially served in this style.

Other Smoked and Cured Meats. Westphalia ham, Bundnerfleisch (Swiss cured) dried beef-fillet, bœuf fumé Hamburg, smoked fillet of pork, smoked tongue and similar hams are similarly served thinly-sliced with gherkin and parsley sprig garnish.

EGGS

163 Œufs à la mayonnaise – Egg mayonnaise

1 Cold hard-boiled eggs.
2 Cut into halves and dress on a bed of shredded lettuce.
3 Coat with mayonnaise thinned to coating consistency and garnish with capers, anchovies, and lettuce hearts.
4 Sprinkle a little paprika on top for decoration if desired.

164 Plovers' eggs

Seldom encountered in post-war service; these are served hard-boiled within a 'nest' – usually of mustard and cress.

PÂTÉS AND TERRINES

165 Foie gras or pâté de foie gras

1 Serve from terrine embedded in ice.
2 Warm toast or brioche normally accompanies.
3 Chopped hard-boiled egg may also be served.

165a Chaud-froid de foie gras en caisses

½ tin natural foie gras	*250 ml (½ pt) aspic*	*blanched chervil*
30 ml (1 tbsp.) sherry	*jelly*	*leaves*
125 ml (¼ pt) white	*(Recipe 122)*	*4 small soufflé cases*
chaud-froid	*1 truffle*	*90 g (3 oz) fine*
(Recipe 134)		*Russian salad*

1 Remove foie gras from tin and trim all fat. Cut into slices the same size as the soufflé cases.
2 Mask with chaud-froid and decorate with truffle and chervil.
3 Place a small quantity of Russian salad in the bottom of each case, place the foie gras on top.
4 Serve a suitable salad separately.

165b Darioles de foie gras Vatel

4 fluted dariole moulds	*250 ml (½ pt) aspic*	*1 white of hard-*
125 g (¼ lb) foie gras	*(Recipe 122)*	*boiled egg*
		1 small truffle

1 Mask the dariole moulds with aspic jelly, decorate the sides and bottom with decorative cuts of truffle and egg white.
2 Work the foie gras into a purée and pipe into each dariole mould, cover with aspic jelly.
3 Set on ice until required. Turn out and serve with salad.

165c Médallions de foie gras

1 Slices of foie gras decorated and coated with aspic.
2 May also be served with warm brioche or hot on toast.

166 Pâté de foie – Liver pâté

750 g (1½ lb) chicken	*1 sprig thyme*	*125 ml (¼ pt) fresh*
livers	*2 bay-leaves*	*cream (or*
250 g (½ lb) lean pork	*seasoning*	*fromage frais or*
30 g (1 oz) chopped	*120 g (¼ lb) melted*	*quark)*
onions	*butter (or sunflower*	
	margarine)	

1 Dice the pork and fry gently in pan.
2 Add the onions and colour slightly.
3 Add the thyme, bay-leaf and chicken livers and fry the livers till cooked.
4 Season, pass through fine mincer and rub through a sieve.
5 Allow to go cold, place in basin and blend in the melted butter and cream.

167 Pâté de jambon – Ham pâté

750 g (1½ lb) lean cooked ham	2.5 ml (spoon [½ teaspoon] paprika	125 ml (¼ pt) fresh cream (or
250 g (¼ lb) melted butter (or sunflower margarine)	125 ml (¼ pt) cold Béchamel (Recipe 51)	fromage frais or quark) seasoning

1 Mince the ham finely and rub through a sieve.
2 Place in a basin, add the béchamel and paprika and beat well.
3 Place the basin on ice and gently beat in the butter and cream. Season.

168 Pâté maison – Pâté in the style of the house

1 kg (2 lb) chicken livers	60 g (2 oz) finely chopped onion	500 g (1 lb) streaky bacon
250 g (½ lb) lean pork	seasoning	1 sprig thyme
250 g (½ lb) lean bacon	2 bay-leaves	1 glass brandy
1 clove, crushed garlic		2 eggs

1 Dice the lean ham and pork and fry with the chopped onions and herbs.
2 Add chicken livers. Fry until cooked and season.
3 Pass through a fine mincer and then rub through a sieve.
4 Bind with the eggs and add the brandy.
5 Line a casserole with the streaky bacon and place the mixture in overlapping the bacon on top.
6 Place on lid and cook in the oven in a bain-marie slowly.
7 Allow to get cold and slice as required.

169 Terrine à la Bonne femme

500 g (1 lb) lean pork (diced)	2 boned grouse (diced) seasoning	1 sprig thyme 1 broken bay-leaf
500 g (1 lb) veal (diced)	60 g (2 oz) chopped onions	1 glass Madeira
1 boned hare (diced)	15 g (½ oz) chopped parsley	1 glass white wine
1 filleted chicken (diced)		

1 Fry meat and game in a little butter to stiffen but not to cook.
2 Mix in the onions and herbs; season.
3 Place the mixture in a terrine, and add the Madeira and white wine and put aside until next day.
4 Place in the oven with cover and cook slowly.
5 When cooked, allow to get cold and finish off with a good game aspic.

169a Mousse de macquereau fumée – Smoked mackerel mousse

240 g (8 oz) smoked mackerel, free from bone and skin	125 ml (¼ pt) double cream (or fromage frais or non-dairy creamer)	seasoning chopped parsley and chervil
62 ml (⅛ pt) aspic jelly		

1 Ensure that the mackerel is completely free from skin and bones.
2 Place with required seasoning and herbs in food processor to mince finely.
3 Remove from food processor, place in a basin, add warm aspic jelly, stir over a basin of ice until setting point.
4 Stir in the lightly whipped cream (or fromage frais).
5 Place in suitable mould. Allow to set in refrigerator.

Smoked trout or smoked salmon may be used in place of mackerel.

169b Chicken and vegetable terrine

240 g (8 oz) raw chicken breast, diced
2 egg whites
250 ml (½ pt) double cream
500 g (1 lb) leeks

120 g (4 oz) thin French beans (optional)
120 g (4 oz) carrot
120 g (4 oz) courgettes
120 g (4 oz) large open mushrooms
salt

1 Liquidize the chicken with the egg whites and salt until smooth.
2 Chill thoroughly on ice or in a refrigerator.
3 Keeping the mixture on ice, gradually beat in the cream.
4 Blanch and refresh the light green of leek and drain on a cloth.
5 Top and tail beans, cook for 5 minutes and refresh.
6 Peel and cut carrot into strips the same thickness as the beans. Cook for 5 minutes and refresh.
7 With a small knife lightly scrape and blanch the courgettes. Cut into strips.
8 Peel and wash the mushrooms and cut into strips. Keep raw.
9 Line a suitably sized terrine with leeks.
10 Pipe on a layer of one-third of the chicken farce.
11 Neatly add a row of beans and mushrooms, alternating.
12 Pipe on a second third of the chicken farce.
13 Neatly add the courgettes and carrots.
14 Pipe on remainder of the chicken farce.
15 Completely cover with the remaining leeks.
16 Cook in a bain-marie in the oven at 180°C (350°F, Reg. 4) for approximately 45 minutes.
17 Leave to set when cooked; then turn out carefully and cut one thick slice per portion.
18 Serve cold with a tomato coulis (fresh tomato sauce, Recipe 34a).

Note. Half the chicken farce can be mixed with spinach purée to give colour variation. Variations of vegetable terrine can include ham instead of chicken farce, coarse duxelle, asparagus, artichokes, courgettes, etc.

VEGETABLE HORS-D'ŒUVRE

Only a few examples of vegetable hors d'œuvre are given. These illustrate the typical preparation of vegetables for use as hors-d'œuvre.

General points
(i) Cut and shape vegetables with care to ensure uniformity and daintiness.
(ii) Before adding sauce or dressing, drain the vegetables well to ensure that all moisture is removed – this facilitates the adherence of the dressing and prevents its dilution.

170 Artichauts à la vinaigrette – Whole artichokes vinaigrette

1 Trim and cook for 20 minutes in salted water with lemon juice.
2 Remove centre part (the choke) and dress on a serviette.
3 Serve separately with a sauce-boat of vinaigrette.

Asparagus or asparagus tips may be similarly served.

171 Fonds d'artichauts à la grecque – Artichokes in à la grecque marinade

Trim and cut artichoke bottoms into quarters.
2 Cook until tender in à la grecque marinade (Recipe 129). Allow to go cold.

Mushrooms, button onions, celeriac (cut into jardinière) and other vegetables may be prepared in this style.

172 Betterave – Beetroot (pickled)

1 Cook in pan or steamer until tender.
2 Remove skin carefully.
3 Leave whole or slice.
4 When cold, cover with spiced vinegar (Recipe 131).
5 May be served sliced or diced and mixed with cream for hors-d'œuvre.

173 Choux rouge – Red cabbage (pickled)

1 Select firm cabbage of good colour.
2 Remove the hard mid-rib and shred the cabbage finely.
3 Sprinkle the shreds with coarse salt and leave for a day.
4 Drain. Pack into jars.
5 Cover with cold, spiced vinegar (Recipe 131), add a few juniper berries.
6 Tie a paper over each jar.
7 May be used after 4 hours' pickling.

174 Mais à la crème – Creamed sweetcorn

Remove the ears from the cooked sweetcorn and mix the grains with cream.

175 Corn on the cob (Hot sweetcorn)

As an appetizer course.

1 Boil the whole sweetcorn for 20 minutes in salt water containing a little milk.
2 Melted butter is served separately.

176 Piment à la provençale

1 Remove seeds and shred.
2 Cook in basic à la grecque marinade (Recipe 129) with equal parts of tomato concassé and one crushed clove of garlic; season.
3 Allow to cool.

SALADS FOR HORS-D'ŒUVRE

177 Salade de céleri–rave – Celeriac salad

1 Wash celeriac and peel.
2 Cut into thin slices with the mandolin and then cut into fine julienne.
3 Place in salted water to which lemon juice has been added.
4 Drain, mix with mayonnaise (Recipe 110) and season.

178 Salade de concombres – Cucumber salad

1 Peel thinly.
2 Slice very thinly and sprinkle with a little salt and vinegar.
3 Garnish with chopped parsley.

179 Salade de haricots blancs – Haricot bean salad

1 Soak beans for 12 hours – rinse.
2 Cook with plenty of water with a carrot, onion piqué and bouquet garni. Season.
3 When cooked allow to go cold and drain from liquor.
4 Add some finely chopped onion and season with vinaigrette (Recipe 118) and chopped parsley.
5 Serve on a ravier and garnish with a little sliced gherkins.

Flageolets and other types of beans may be similarly prepared.

180 Salade de haricots verts et tomates – French bean and tomato salad

1 Use small French beans. Top and tail.
2 Cook in boiling salt water and refresh.
3 Mix with vinaigrette (Recipe 118). Season.
4 Heap in the centre of a salad bowl.
5 Surround with blanched, sliced tomatoes.

181 Salade de pommes de terre – Potato salad

1 Steam potatoes in jacket.
2 When cold peel and dice.
3 Mix with finely-chopped onions, mayonnaise and a little chopped parsley. Season.

For half the mayonnaise, whipped fresh cream, fromage frais or yogurt may be substituted.

For flavour and garnish variations, sprinkle with chopped chives or mix in chopped mixed herbs (say parsley, chervil, basil, dill).

Note. Alternatively, potato salad may be mixed with vinaigrette (Recipe 118).

181a Salade cressonnière – Potato and watercress salad

500 g (1 lb) small cooked potatoes	1 hard-boiled egg
1 bunch watercress	chopped parsley or mixed fresh
4 tbsp. vinaigrette (Recipe 118)	herbs

1 Cut potatoes into 2 mm (⅛ in) slices.
2 Mix with picked watercress leaves and vinaigrette.
3 Dress in serving dish.
4 Sprinkle with sieved hard-boiled egg and chopped parsley.

182 Salade de piment – Pimento salad

1 Blanch and skin.
2 Remove seeds and shred.
3 Mix with vinaigrette (Recipe 118).

183 Salade russe – Russian salad

120 g (4 oz) carrots	1 tbsp. vinaigrette
60 g (2 oz) turnips	125 ml (¼ pt) mayonnaise or
60 g (2 oz) French beans	natural yogurt
60 g (2 oz) peas	salt, pepper

1 Peel and wash the carrots and turnips.
2 Cut into ½ cm (¼ inch) dice or batons.
3 Cook separately in salted water.
4 Refresh and drain well.
5 Top and tail the beans.
6 Cut in ½ cm (¼ inch) dice, cook, refresh and drain well.
7 Cook the peas, refresh and drain well.
8 Mix all the well-drained vegetables with vinaigrette and then mayonnaise.
9 Correct the seasoning.

183a Coleslaw

125 ml (¼ pt) mayonnaise (or	60 g (2 oz) carrot
natural yogurt with adjusted	30 g (1 oz) onion (optional)
seasoning)	salt, pepper
240 g (8 oz) white (or Chinese)	
cabbage	

1 Trim off the outside leaves of the cabbage.
2 Cut into quarters. Remove the centre stalk.
3 Wash the cabbage, shred finely and drain well.

4 Mix with a fine julienne of raw carrot and shredded raw onion. To lessen harshness of raw onion, blanch and refresh.
5 Bind with mayonnaise sauce, natural yogurt or vinaigrette.

183b Salade de viande – Meat salad

290 g (8 oz) cooked lean meat
  (well-cooked braised or boiled
  meat is ideal)
30 g (1 oz) gherkins
60 g (2 oz) cooked French beans
60 g (2 oz) tomatoes

7 g (¼ oz) chopped onion or chives
  (optional)
1 tbsp. vinaigrette
chopped parsley or mixed fresh
  herbs
salt, pepper

1 Cut the meat and gherkins in ½ cm (¼ inch) dice.
2 Cut the beans into ½ cm (¼ inch) dice.
3 Skin tomatoes, remove seeds.
4 Cut into ½ cm (¼ inch) dice.
5 Mix with remainder of the ingredients, blanching the onions if required.
6 Correct the seasoning.
7 Dress neatly in a ravier.
8 Decorate with lettuce leaves, tomatoes and fans of gherkins.

184 Salade de tomates – Tomato salad

1 Blanch and slice thinly.
2 Season; marinate with vinaigrette (Recipe 118).
3 Garnish with sliced onions and chopped parsley.

185 Radis – Radishes

1 Wash well and trim green part.
2 Cut the end into tulip shape.
3 Serve on crushed ice.

186 Riz – Rice (for hors-d'œuvre)

1 Prepare ordinary rice pilaff (Recipe 366).
2 Garnish with diced pimentoes and peas and diced, cooked chicken's liver.
3 Season with vinaigrette (Recipe 118).

Italian pastas (macaroni, etc.) may be similarly treated.

FINGER HORS-D'ŒUVRE AND SNACKS

These small items served at parties and buffet receptions may accompany aperitifs before any meal (whether luncheon, dinner or supper). Typically they include:

187 Bouchées

Hot savoury puff pastry patties with fillings incorporating shellfish (lobster, crab, shrimp) oyster, salmon, mushroom.

Bouchée fillings are numerous as bouchées are served both hot and cold. They may be served as cocktail savouries or as a first course, a fish course or as a savoury. All fillings should be bound with a suitable sauce, for example:

Mushroom	–	chicken velouté or Béchamel
Shrimp	–	fish velouté, Béchamel or curry
Prawn	–	fish velouté, Béchamel or curry
Chicken	–	chicken velouté
Ham	–	chicken velouté, Béchamel or curry
Lobster	–	fish velouté, Béchamel or mayonnaise
Vegetable	–	mayonnaise, natural yogurt, fromage frais, quark or Béchamel

188 Carolines and Duchesses, Eclairs

Both Carolines and Duchesses are used as appetizers. The former are small éclairs shaped like the letter 'C' and are 3 cm (1½ inches) long. The latter are small éclairs, of customary shape, also 3 cm (1½ inches) long. Both may be filled with various purées, i.e. cheese, ham or liver. They are then coated with chaud-froid, according to the filling, and finished with aspic.

189 Barquettes, Croustades, and Tartelettes

Some savouries may be served either as hot appetizers (at a cocktail reception) or as the last course of an evening meal. Tartlettes or barquettes made from thinly rolled short paste and cooked blind in small tins are of this kind. They may also be used (when filled with a vegetable purée, for example) to garnish main dishes. Otherwise fillings similar to those in bouchées, Carolines etc. (as above) are suitable, as are:

Examples of fillings
   Shrimps in curry and ginger sauce.
   Chicken livers in demi-glace or devilled sauce.
   Mushrooms in Béchamel, suprême or aurora sauce.
   Poached soft roes with devilled sauce.
   Poached soft roes covered with cheese soufflé mixture and baked.

Prepare the filling separately and neatly place it in them.
Warm through the cooked tartlettes or barquettes before service.
Garnish with a sprig of parsley.

190 Cassolettes

These can also be garnished with appetizer fillings. They are made by using a special iron mould, dipped into batter and deep-fried until crisp.

191 Canapés

Savoury finger toasts (or fried fingers of bread), or alternatively savoury biscuits or shaped savoury short pastry, covered with items such as thinly sliced charcuterie (salami, ham, tongue), smoked salmon, caviar (or lumpfish roe), sardines, eggs.

192 Hot savouries

Chipolatas (hot, small sausages), skewered bacon rolls cooked under the salamander with such fillings as prunes, oyster, chicken liver. Fried goujons of fish, fried fish balls.

193 Cold savouries

Celery segments filled with cheese spread, game chips, gaufrette potatoes.

194 Bridge rolls and sandwiches

Always small in size and cut, either open or closed.

FARCES AND MOUSSES

The finer forcemeats in this section, normally prepared in the larder, are not to be confused with hot stuffings such as those served with roast duck prepared in the English style. Stuffings are more appropriately included in Chapters 6 and 7.

PANADAS

Panadas are preparations that form the thickening or binding of forcemeat. They are not necessary for all forcemeats and the most delicate do not need a panada. There are three types of panada:

195 Bread panada

500 *ml* (1 *pt*) *milk*   250 *g* (½ *lb*) *breadcrumbs*

Pour boiling milk over the breadcrumbs and cook until all the milk has been absorbed and the mixture has become too thick to adhere to the spatula.

196 Flour panada

250 *ml* (½ *pt*) *water*   60 *g* (2 *oz*) *butter* (*or*   150 *g* (5 *oz*) *sifted*
                                        sunflower   *flour*
                                        margarine)

1 Boil the water with the butter; then add the sifted flour.
2 Cook together until the mixture no longer sticks to the spatula.

197 Frangipane panada

90 g (3 oz) flour   90 g (3 oz) melted butter
4 egg yolks   ½ pint milk

1 Blend together flour, egg yolks, melted butter and milk.
2 Mix well, strain and bring slowly to the boil.
3 Allow to cook slowly for 5 minutes stirring frequently.

Note. All panadas must be allowed to become cold before use after cooking. Butter the surface to prevent a crust forming while cooling.

198 Godiveau – Poached veal forcemeat balls

500 g (1 lb) veal   4 eggs
1 kg (2 lb) beef fat   350 ml (14 fluid oz)
                                         iced water
                                         seasoning

1 Remove sinews from veal and fat.
2 Mince finely in a food processor.
3 Season; add eggs one at a time and mix well.
4 Allow to stand in cool place.
5 Add the iced water to required consistency.
6 Shape in balls by means of two spoons and poach gently.

199 Quenelles – Poached forcemeat balls

This is the name given to completed forcemeats that are shaped to the required size by means of two spoons – or by moulding with the hands. The forcemeat for quenelles is made by mixing a panada with the required ingredients. Finely pounded chicken or fish, etc. may be used. Quenelles are used to garnish soups, sauces, and vol-au-vents, etc.

200 Farce fine de porc – Fine pork forcemeat

250 g (½ lb) lean pork   Seasoning of salt, ground mace,
250 g (½ lb) veal   pepper
250 g (½ lb) pork fat   1 glass brandy

1 Macerate the meats in the brandy for 1 hour.
2 Pass through a fine mincer, rub through sieve, and season.

201 Mousse de jambon – Cold ham mousse

480 g (1 lb) lean cooked ham   320 ml (⅔ pt) half-beaten cream (or
165 ml (⅓ pt) cold velouté   fromage frais, quark, yogurt or
  (Recipe 26) (or mayonnaise)   non-dairy creamer)
125 ml (¼ pt) aspic jelly
  (Recipe 122)

1 Mince ham finely and pound in the mortar with the velouté.
2 Rub through fine sieve.

3 Place mixture in a bowl of ice.
4 Gradually beat in the cream and the aspic jelly. Season.
5 Place mixture in an aspic-lined mould or soufflé dish.

Note. Mousse of chicken, fish, etc. can be made by using the same quantities as above: substitute chicken or fish for ham and use a chicken or fish velouté. A hot fish mousse and mousseline is included in the fish recipes (Chapter 5).

COLD COOKERY

This *Compendium* of recipes does not, of course, aim to cover work such as meat dissection and the preparation of small cuts, poultry, and fish. Dishes listed below, however, typify the actual cold cookery carried out in the larder but it should also be noted that many of the meat, poultry, game, and fish dishes from other chapters, when cold, can be treated by the chef responsible for cold preparations and buffets. Cold dishes are also included in Chapters 4, 5 and 6.

FISH

See Chapter 5 for court-bouillon (fish poaching liquors) and the poaching of fish.

202 Saumon poché froid – Cold salmon

See notes below.

203 Poaching whole salmon

5 *kg (10 lb) salmon*   9 *litre (2 gal.) approx. court-*
salt   *bouillon (Recipe 371)*

1 Prepare by gutting and scaling. Trim off fins.
2 Remove intestines and gills, clear blood from backbone and clean out head.
3 Wash well and tie into shape.
4 Place in a salmon kettle, cover with court-bouillon.
5 Under a lid, bring slowly to the boil, skim, then simmer gently for 10 minutes.
6 Allow to go cold with lid on.
7 When cold, skin both sides. Garnish and serve (see notes following Recipe 204).

204 Poaching a large piece

1¼ *kg (2½ lb) cleaned salmon*   1 *large lettuce*
1 *litre (1 qt) cold court-bouillon*   ½ *cucumber*
   (*Recipe* 371)   240 *g (8 oz) tomatoes*
250 *ml (½ pt) mayonnaise or*
   green sauce

1 Cook the salmon whole in the court-bouillon.
2 Allow to cool thoroughly in the cooking liquid to keep it moist.
3 If required to be served in portions, divide into four even portions, or if eight are required, remove centre bone and cut each darne in half.
4 Except when whole, remove the centre bone, also the skin and brown surface flesh. Dress neatly on a flat dish.
5 Peel and slice cucumber and neatly arrange a few slices with each portion.
6 Garnish with quarters of lettuce and quarters of tomatoes. Serve the sauce in a sauceboat separately.
7 Poaching darnes of salmon – see Chapter 5 and Recipe 427.

Notes
1 *Yields and cooking.* Half a kilo (1 lb) uncleaned salmon yields 2–3 portions. Salmon is obtainable in weights from 3½ kg to 15 kg (7–30 lb). Size is important in selection, and depends on whether the salmon is to be cooked whole or cut in darnes. Any size salmon may be cooked whole, but for darnes a medium-sized salmon is more suitable (see Recipe 427).
2 *Approximate simmering time guide:*
3½ kg (7 lb) – 15 minutes
7 kg (14 lb) – 20 minutes
10½ kg (21 lb) – 25 minutes
14 kg (28 lb) – 30 minutes
3 For cold service always allow the salmon to remain in the court-bouillon until cold.
4 *Decorations, garnish and accompaniments.* It is no longer fashionable to coat salmon with chaud-froid (Recipes 134 or 136) nor with mayonnaise (Recipe 110) cohered with aspic, whether the fish is whole or in a piece, or in darnes or tronçons. Food-poisoning risks associated with chaud-froid and aspic have also been noted earlier (p. 42).
   Garnish is nowadays kept simple: sliced cucumber, lettuce, tomato quarters or slices, egg (sliced or stuffed), and lemon quarters are among items selected. Mayonnaise sauce (or an alternative such as sauce verte) is served in a separate sauceboat.

205 Truite saumonée froide – Cold salmon–trout

1 Scale, gut and trim fins.
2 Poach gently in court-bouillon (Recipe 371) and allow to go very cold.
3 Proceed as for salmon.

HAM, VEAL, AND BRAWN DISHES

206 Ham

To boil:
1 Soak in cold water overnight.
2 Cook for approximately 4 hours.
3 Allow to go cold in its own cooking-liquor.
4 Remove skin and trim.
5 Coat with chaud-froid (Recipe 134); decorate, and glaze with aspic (Recipe 122).

Note. Many may not approve of coating ham with chaud-froid but the alternative method of carving the fat decoratively is tending to disappear. For economical service the fat may be plainly coated with brown breadcrumbs.

207 Brawn

½ pickled pig's head	*1 carrot*	*bouquet garni*
120 g (4 oz) cooked	*1 onion*	*peppercorns*
bacon	*2 cloves*	
1 hard-boiled egg		

1 Wash the head in several waters, remove brains, veins and bone splinters.
2 Cook the head in saucepan with enough water to cover. Add a little salt, onion piqué, bouquet garni and peppercorns. Cook 2 hours.
3 Skim frequently. Remove meat from bones and reduce liquor with bones.
4 Cut the meat and bacon in small dice.
5 Slice the egg and decorate the bottom of charlotte mould.
6 Fill the mould with the pig's head and bacon. Press lightly.
7 Add a reduced pint of the liquid.
8 Place in a refrigerator to set for 12 hours.
9 Warm mould in warm water before turning out.

208 Veal and ham pie (cold)

750 g (1½ lb) nut-veal	*seasoning*	*8 leaves soaked*
750 g (1½ lb) thickly	*30 g (1 oz) finely*	*gelatine*
sliced raw ham	*chopped onions*	*15 g (½ oz) chopped*
[0.5 cm (¼ inch)	*500 g (1 lb) streaky*	*parsley*
thick]	*bacon*	*Puff paste*
4 hard-boiled eggs		*(Recipe 994)*

1 Cut veal into 0.5 cm (¼ inch) thick escalopes.
2 Line the pie-dish with the streaky bacon.
3 Build the pie by adding alternate layers of ham, veal and gelatine.
4 Place in the middle a line of hard-boiled egg, onions, and chopped parsley.
5 Season each layer.
6 Cover with puff paste and decorate.
7 Cook, and when cold, fill with aspic jelly (Recipe 122).

BEEF DISHES

209 Langue de bœuf froide – Cold ox-tongue

1 If pickled, or salted, soak in cold water overnight and boil in water.
2 When cooked, skin, remove bones, and press.

210 Pièce de bœuf rôtie froide – Joint of cold roast beef

1 Remove chine bone.
2 Trim rib-bone ends.
3 Glaze with brown aspic (Recipe 122 with colouring).
4 Garnish as desired.

POULTRY AND GAME DISHES

211 Suprême de volaille en chaud-froid – Cold suprême of chicken

1 Poach chicken gently and when cold, carefully remove the suprêmes.
2 Make a farce by rubbing through a sieve equal parts of foie gras (or chicken liver pâté) and white meat of chicken.
3 Spread a layer of farce on the top of each suprême.
4 Coat each suprême with chaud-froid (Recipe 134) and decorate with truffles (or garnishing paste) and glaze with aspic jelly (Recipe 122).
5 Serve with small darioles of salade à la russe (Recipe 183) cohered with aspic jelly.

212 Galantine de volaille – Chicken galantine

one 2.5 kg (5 lb) chicken	*90 g (3 oz) pork fat*	*2 whole truffles*
750 g (1½ lb) fine pork or veal forcemeat (Recipe 195)	*½ glass sherry*	*(optional; or garnishing paste)*
	90 g (3 oz) ham	*2 gherkins*
	15 g (½ oz) pistachio nuts	*salt*
90g (3 oz) tongue	*1 hard-boiled egg*	*pepper*

1 Skin the bird completely without holes.
2 Take off the suprêmes and cut into fingers.
3 Bone out the legs and pass through fine mincer and rub through sieve and add to the pork forcemeat.
4 Spread the skin on a damp cloth and place a layer of forcemeat in the centre. Cut the ham, tongue and gherkins into strips and marinate in sherry. Then garnish each layer of farce with fillets of chicken, tongue, ham, fresh fat pork, egg quarters, gherkin strips, pistachio nuts and truffles.
5 Roll up, tie in damp cloth and cook in chicken stock (Recipe 11), allowing 20 minutes per 600 g or lb).
6 When cooked let it cool slightly; re-tie and press under a board.
7 When cold, remove cloth and string; coat with chaud-froid (Recipe 134); decorate, and glaze with aspic (Recipe 122).

213 Raised grouse pie

Pie mould 15 cm × 10 cm (5½" × 4")	*250 g (½ lb) chicken livers*	*1 glass of brandy*
750 g (1½ lb) hot-water paste (Recipe 997)	*seasoning*	*30 g (1 oz) finely chopped onions*
5 old grouse	*750 g (1½ lb) pork sausage-meat*	*500 g (1 lb) streaky bacon*

1 Line the pie mould with paste and see there are no cracks.
2 Reserve enough paste for the cover and decoration.
3 Line the inside with streaky bacon.
4 Remove the supremes from the grouse and soak in brandy.
5 Bone the legs and mince finely with the sausage-meat, liver and onions.

6 Place in layers of sausage-meat on the bacon, then the raw grouse fillets.
7 Continue until the pie is full, making sure the last layer is one of sausage-meat filling.
8 Cover with paste and decorate; egg-wash and bake in oven.
9 When cold, fill with game aspic (Recipe 122 with game stock).

SALADS TO ACCOMPANY MAIN DISHES

Examples of salads, mostly 'single' ones, suitable for hors-d'œuvre, tray or trolley raviers, have been listed earlier in the hors-d'œuvre section. The ingredients for salads served with cold meat, fish, poultry, pies, and game are capable of infinite variations and permutations. Such mixed salads are commonly of the à la française (French salad) type included below. Many salads are, however, suitable (and correct) for service with hot roasts, particularly poultry and game. Plain lettuce and other green stuffs are customarily dressed with vinaigrette (Recipe 118).

Substitutes for mayonnaise
Where mayonnaise is used, up to half the quantity may be replaced by fromage frais or yogurt, with adjustment of seasoning and acidity (by vinegar, lemon or lime juice).

214 à la française

Lettuce hearts, beetroot, tomatoes, hard-boiled eggs, dressed with vinaigrette and chopped tarragon.

215 à l'allemande

Diced apples, potatoes, gherkins, smoked herrings, onions, chopped parsley, vinaigrette-dressed, decorated with beetroot.

216 Carmen

Pimentos, dice of chicken, peas, rice, dressing of vinaigrette with mustard and chopped tarragon.

217 Chicago

Tomatoes, asparagus tips, French beans, slices of foie gras, julienne of carrots, mushrooms, mayonnaise sauce.

218 à la cressonnière

Slices of potatoes, watercress leaves sprinkled with parsley and hard-boiled eggs.

219 Dalila

Bananas, apples, julienne of celery, and mayonnaise.

220 à l'égyptienne

Rice pillaf with chicken livers, ham, mushrooms, pimentos, peas, served in artichoke bottoms.

221 à l'indienne

Rice, asparagus, julienne of pimentos, dice of apples, and curried cream-dressing.

222 à la japonaise

Dice of fresh fruit, mixed with acidulated cream, served with fresh lettuce or in half an orange.

223 Mimosa

Half-lettuce hearts garnished with orange fillets, grapes, bananas, and acidulated cream.

224 à la niçoise

French beans, tomatoes, potatoes, anchovies, olives, capers, lettuce, vinaigrette dressing.

225 à la tourangelle

Julienne of potatoes, French beans, flageolets beans, mayonnaise with cream, and chopped tarragon.

226 Waldorf

(a) Diced celeriac, apples, walnuts dressed with thin mayonnaise; or
(b) Celery, apples, bananas, walnuts, served in scooped-out apples.

3 Soups

CLASSIFICATION of the different types of soup can be effected in more than one way; witness the naïve waiting enquiry 'thick or clear'? It may be simple and convenient to group them as follows:

Classification of soups

Consommés – Clear soup of refined type, mainly used for dinner (and late supper) service.

Bouillons and broths – Clear soup of natural liquor base. Clear in the sense of being unthickened, but with garnishes and ingredients possibly clouding the clarity. Such soups tend to be used for luncheon or family supper purposes.

Bisques and chowders – Fish soups suitable for luncheon and dinner.

Purées – Vegetable soups with the ingredients themselves providing most or all of the thickening. These are mainly used for luncheon service.

Creams and veloutés – This group includes purées finely finished with cream, and high-quality thickened cream soups (veloutés) such as chicken. They are suitable for dinners, though possibly not so widely used as consommés for formal functions.

Unclassified – Including thickened brown and soups of foreign origin. Savoury or meaty soups such as kidney, oxtail, mulligatawny, are often chosen for luncheon service.

Cold soups – Soups suitable for service cold are chiefly found among the clear soups (Consommé and Bortsch for example) and creams. Cold fruit soups are not included.

Bread accompaniments with soup

Flutes – Thin slices from French bread of long, thin flute-shape and size, yielding small neat ovals or roundels for drying or toasting.

Croûtons or sippets – Small dainty dice of bread tossed in butter or oil to a golden brown and seasoned.

CONSOMMÉS

227 Clarified consommé [to yield 1 litre (1 quart)]

1.5 *litre* (1½ *qt) cold stock* (*Recipes* 6 or 7)	250 *g* (½ *lb) mirepoix* (*Recipe* 2 *but omit pork*)	1 *small bay-leaf* 6 *peppercorns, salt* 1 *chicken carcase*
350 *g* (¾ *lb) minced lean shin of beef*		2 *egg whites*

1 Roast the chicken carcase and vegetable in a little oil.
2 Mix minced beef and egg whites thoroughly with a little cold stock. See note on clarification.
3 Drain the bones free of fat and place in a large thick-bottomed saucepan.
4 Add the clarification (minced beef, etc.) and gradually add the cold stock until all is well mixed.
5 Put the pan to boil and stir often to prevent burning.
6 When boiling draw to the side (or reduce heat) and simmer for 1 hour.
7 Carefully remove all fat and strain gently through muslin into another pan.
8 Reboil and remove all grease with kitchen paper. Adjust seasoning.

Note. For clarification:
(i) Use the meat of old animals. This gives better flavour. The stock should be free of all fat. See the egg whites and minced shin of beef are mixed well. Damp the muslin before straining.
(ii) When straining consommé, dip ladle gently in at the side to avoid the breaking up of the clarification mixture.

227a Simplified consommé [to yield 1 litre (1 quart)]

500 *ml* (1 *pt) cold white stock*(*Recipe* 6)	250 *g* (½ *lb) minced shin of beef*	60 *g* (2 *oz) each sliced carrot, leek and celery*
1 *litre* (1 *qt) hot brown stock* (*Recipe* 7)	2 *egg whites* ½ *onion*	6 *peppercorns, parsley stalks*
1 *tbsp. oil*	1 *small bay-leaf seasoning*	

1 Mix minced beef thoroughly with the cold white stock. (See note on clarification.)
2 Brown onion, carrot, leek and celery in oil, drain and add to the minced beef with the remaining ingredients.
3 Stir into the hot brown stock.
4 Bring to boil and stir often to prevent burning.
5 When boiling, reduce heat and simmer for 1 hour.
6 Strain gently through muslin into another vessel.
7 Reboil, remove all grease and adjust for seasoning.

228 Consommé de volaille – Chicken consommé [to yield 1 litre (1 quart)]

1 *kg* (2 *lb) roast chicken carcase*	250 *g* (½ *lb) mirepoix* (*omitting pork*) (*Recipe* 2)	375 *g* (¾ *lb) minced shin of beef*
2 *litre* (2 *qt) fonds de volaille, cold* (*Recipe* 11)	*seasoning* 2 *egg whites*	120 *g* (4 *oz) cooked chicken*

1 Mince the shin of beef, chop the carcases and add the egg whites.
2 Place this in a thick saucepan and mix well with the cold chicken-stock.
3 Add the vegetable and bring to the boil, stirring frequently.
4 When boiling, add the fowl which has been browned in the oven.
5 Simmer for 1½ hours; strain through muslin and season; bring to the boil and remove all fat with greaseproof paper.

229 Game consommé (pheasant) [to yield 1 litre (1 quart)]

2 *litre* (2 *qt*) *fonds de gibier, cold* (*Recipe* 12) 1 *pheasant*	2 *egg whites* 30 *g* (1 *oz*) *diced mushrooms*	250 *g* (½ *lb*) *mirepoix* (*omitting pork*) (*Recipe* 2)

1 Bone the pheasant; mince finely and combine with the egg whites and ½ litre (1 pint) of cold game-stock; mix well.
2 Roast the pheasant bones and mirepoix in the oven until golden brown.
3 Place the bones, mushrooms, and minced pheasant in a large saucepan and gradually mix with remaining cold game-stock.
4 Bring to the boil stirring frequently.
5 Draw to the side and reduce heat and simmer for 1 hour.
6 Strain through muslin.
7 Remove all fat.

Note. If the flavour is to be of venison, rabbit or hare, allow 500 g (1 lb) of the appropriate meat for each litre (quart).

230 Consommé au fumet de céleri – Celery-flavoured consommé [to yield 1 litre (1 quart)]

1.5 *litre* (1½ *qt*) *chicken consommé* (*Recipe* 228)	500 *g* (1 *lb*) *blanched celery celery salt*

1 Cut the celery into small pieces.
2 Add the consommé while clarifying.
3 Garnish with bâtons of cooked celery.

231 Consommé à la tomate (base for consommé Carmen) – Tomato-flavoured consommé [to yield 1 litre (1 quart)]

30 *g* (1 *oz*) *blanched pimentoes* 2 *litre* (2 *qt*) *consommé de volaille* (*Recipe* 228)	125 *ml* (¼ *pt*) *tomato purée* 15 *ml* (*spoon* [1 *tablespoon*] *boiled rice*	125 *g* (¼ *lb*) *diced tomatoes* (*peeled*)

1 While clarifying 2 litres (2 quarts) of chicken consommé add the tomato purée to give a pink colour.
2 Strain the consommé in the usual way.
3 Garnish with tomatoes, rice, and pimento.

232 Consommé à la madrilène [to yield 1 litre (1 quart)]

2 *litre (2 qt) consommé de volaille (Recipe 228)* 500 *g (1 lb) blanched celery*	125 *ml (¼ pt) of tomato purée* 125 *g (¼ lb) diced, peeled tomatoes*	30 *g (1 oz) blanched pimento* 30 *g (1 oz) vermicelli* 15 *g (½ oz) shredded sorrel*

1 While clarifying 2 litres (2 quarts) chicken consommé add the tomato purée and celery to give celery flavour.
2 Strain and garnish with the tomato and diced pimento, vermicelli, and julienne of sorrel.

Note
(i) Cook the vermicelli in a little consommé for 15 minutes.
(ii) Sweat the sorrel in a little butter (or gently poach in water).
(iii) This soup may be served cold.
(iv) For cold madrilène add 15 g (½ oz) leaf gelatine soaked in water to 1 litre (1 quart) strong consommé; strain and garnish.

233 Consommé au vin – Consommé with wine

Consommé au madère	Comsommé au vin de Chypre
Consommé au marsala	Consomme au vin de Malvosie
Consommé au porto	

Add 250 ml (½ pint) of the chosen wine at the last minute, before service, to 1 litre (1 quart) of consommé.

234 Consommé aux nids d'hirondelles – Swallows' nest consommé [to yield 1 litre (1 quart)]

2 *litre (2 qt) chicken consommé (Recipe 228)*	2 *swallows' nests*

1 Prepare and strain 2 litres (2 quarts) chicken consommé.
2 Soak nests in cold water for 24 hours.
3 Remove any feathers from the nest.
4 When nests are clean drain well.
5 Place the nests in the consommé and simmer for 50 minutes.

Note. The gummy parts of the nest will have melted in the consommé, giving this consommé its characteristic consistency and flavour. There will only remain visible those portions which constitute the framework of the nest and resemble cooked vermicelli.

234a Consommé sous la cendre – Consommé under a puff pastry cap

For this presentation, allow the consommé (Recipe 228 but see notes below) to cool rapidly and place in individual consommé cups. Cover each cup with a round of puff pastry. Egg wash the pastry. Place in the oven at approximately

200°C (400°F) for about 10 minutes until golden brown. This also allows time for the consommé to reach sufficient heat for service.

Note. Any good, well-clarified consommé may be used, including those with tomato (madrilène), celery (au fumet de céleri), truffle-flavoured (truffé) or with varying garnishes. In all such cases the title may be amended approximately. This style of service sous croûte was popularized when Bocuse served a Consommé Valery Giscard d'Estaing at a luncheon at the Elysée Palace shortly after that French President took office.

235 Consommé froid en gelée – Cold consommé [to yield 1 litre (1 quart)]

A note in Recipe 232 for Consommé madrilène, indicates that a cold version may be made by adding 15 g (½ oz) soaked leaf-gelatine to 1 litre (1 quart) of strong consommé, followed by straining and in that case, garnishing. Other suitable consommés, for example, 'au porto', may be similarly prepared for cold service.

SELECTED CONSOMMÉ GARNISHES

Vegetables for garnishing consommés should be blanched and cooked in a little consommé au point (just cooked) so as not to cloud the clear soup. A vast number of garnishes exist in addition to those listed below.

Bretonne – Fine julienne of celery, leek and chervil.

Brunoise – Fine dice of mixed vegetables (carrots, turnip, leek, celery).

Carmen – Tomate consommé (Recipe 231) with diamonds of tomato, red pepper and rice.

Caroline – Diamonds of Royale (unsweetened egg-custard) chiffonnade of chervil and rice.

Célestine – Fine julienne of thin, cooked savoury pancake (also brunoise of truffle when costing permits). The consommé may be given slight 'body') with tapioca thickening.

Cheveux d'anges – Fine vermicelli; grated Parmesan cheese is served separately.

Clear oxtail soup – Infusion of turtle herbs, garnish small sections of oxtail, bâtons of vegetables (carrots, turnip, celery). Sometimes lightly lié with fécule.

Demidoff – Mixed spring vegetables, macédoine cut with tiny, fines herbes-flavoured quenelles (Recipe 199).

Diane – Game consommé (Recipe 229) with Madeira. Lean game-flesh in julienne, brunoise of truffle.

Du Barry – Tiny cauliflower sprigs, chiffonnade of chervil, Royale roundels, slight tapioca thickening.

Julienne – Fine julienne of mixed vegetables (carrots, leek, celery), with peas, chervil, and sorrel chiffonade.

Monte Carlo – Consommé de volaille (Recipe 228) with coin-size (one penny) shaped garnish of carrots, turnips and truffle (optionally with rolled, stuffed pancakes sliced in rings).

Niçoise – Consommé madrilène (Recipe 232). Diced tomato, French beans and potato.

Olga – Port flavoured. Julienne of gherkin, celeriac, carrot and leek.

Orge perlé – Pearl barley.

Portugaise – Tomato flavoured.

Printanier – Small parisienne spoon-scooped balls of carrots and turnip with peas.

Quenelles – With quenelles flavoured as desired.

Royale – Unsweetened egg custard cut into dice or diamonds. (See Recipe 236 below.)

Solange – Pearl barley, julienne of chicken, small square of lettuce.

236 Ordinary Royale (for consommé garnish)

250 *ml* (½ *pt*) *clear consommé (boiling)*	1 *whole egg*
	3 *egg yolks*
15 *g* (½ *oz*) *chervil leaves or stalks (optional)*	2.5 *ml spoon* [½ *teaspoon*] *salt*

1 Make an infusion of the consommé and chervil.
2 Strain the infusion.
3 Beat all the eggs in a basin with a whisk, pour over the infusion, add seasoning.
4 Strain through a fine chinois or muslin.
5 Butter some dariole moulds, pour in the mixture, poach in a bain-marie in the oven, taking care it does not boil. (Approximate cooking time, small moulds, 15 minutes.)
6 When cooked allow to cool, trim and cut into diamond shapes or as desired.

Note. This basic Royale may be varied by colouring with vegetable purées and by introducing other flavours, e.g. chopped tarragon, parsley, basil or chives infused in the consommé before straining.

CLEAR SOUPS

The following clear soups are akin to consommés and have a similar place on menus; in some instances their service at luncheon is appropriate.

236a Bortsch à la russe [to yield 1 litre (1 quart)]

> 250 ml (½ pt) beetroot juice*
> one 2 kg (4 lb) duck
> 2 litre (2 qt) fonds blanc (Recipe
>   6)
> 125 ml (¼ pt) sour cream
> 250 g (½ g (½ lb) boiling beef
> 12 small duck patties†
>
> 180 g (6 oz) parsley stalks
> 2 egg whites
> 120 g (4 oz) mirepoix
> 30 g (1 oz) julienne carrots
> 30 g (1 oz) julienne cooked beetroot
> salt, pepper

1 Roast the duck on the mirepoix.
2 Remove the flesh from the carcase.
3 Chop the carcase, add to the cold stock with the mirepoix of vegetables.
   Add the egg white, mix well.
4 Add seasoning and parsley stalks.
5 Add the beef and 125 ml (¼ pt) of the beetroot juice; simmer until the
   beef is tender.
6 Remove beef, cut into small dice. Cut the breast of duck in julienne.
   Reserve both for garnish.
7 Strain the soup through muslin.
8 Cook the julienne of carrot in a little stock. Add to the soup.
9 Add the julienne of cooked duck and beetroot.
10 Serve with a sauceboat of sour cream and beetroot juice, plus the small
   duck patties made from the remaining cooked duck.

237 Petite marmite [to yield 1 litre (1 quart)]

> 1 litre (1 qt) strong beef
>   and chicken
>   consommé (Recipes
>   227 and 228)
> 120 g (¼ lb) carrots
> 120 g (¼ lb) turnips
> 120 g (¼ lb) leeks
>   (white)
>
> 60 g (2 oz) diced lean
>   boiled beef
> 60 g (2 oz) white
>   cabbage
> 30 g (1 oz) julienne of
>   celery
>
> 8 slices beef-bone
>   marrow
> 1 sauceboat toasted
>   croûtons
> 120 g (¼ lb) cooked
>   chicken-dice or
>   winglets

1 Turn the carrots and turnips very small.
2 Shred the cabbage and leeks into julienne.
3 Cook the carrots, turnips, leeks, cabbage and celery in a little consommé
   until tender.
4 Add the garnish to the consommé and the beef and chicken.
5 Just before service add the marrow.
6 Serve in earthenware marmite pots accompanied by toasted croûtons.
   (Grated Parmesan cheese may be offered in a sauceboat.)

238 Petite marmite à la béarnaise [to yield 1 litre (1 quart)]

As Recipe 237, adding: 15 g (½ oz) cooked rice
                        30 g (1 oz) julienne-cooked potatoes

* *Beetroot juice* – Obtain by grating and squeezing raw beetroot.
† *Duck patties* – Made from a forcemeat of duck covered in puff paste, approximately
1½ cm (¾ inch) diameter.

239 Poule au pot

A variation of Petite marmite, Recipe 237, plus a fowl cooked in the stock and garnished in the same way.

240 Potage à la tortue clair – Clear turtle soup [to yield 1 litre (1 quart)]

750 ml (1½ pt) chicken consommé (Recipe 228)	120 g (¼ lb) dried turtle-meat	1 packet turtle herbs (Recipe 240a)
750 ml (1½ pt) beef consommé (Recipe 227)	30 g (1 oz) fécule (or arrowroot)	250 ml (½ pt) Madeira wine

Adjuncts: *Cheese straws (Recipe 1188), lemon.*

1 Soak the dry turtle-meat in water for at least 24 hours.
2 Mix the two consommés and cook the turtle while in the clarifying stage.
3 When the turtle is cooked, remove and cut into small dice.
4 Strain the consommé, bring to the boil and add the diluted fécule (or arrowroot).
5 Make an infusion of the turtle herbs in 250 ml (½ pint) of the strained consommé. (This infusion should stand for 10 minutes.)
6 Strain the infusion into the consommé, garnish with the diced turtle-meat; add the Madeira. Reboil and remove all grease.

240a Turtle herbs – dried

Basil	Sage	Thyme
Marjoram	Rosemary	Coriander
6 peppercorns	1 bay-leaf	

Tie in a muslin bag and use 7 g (¼ oz) total of dried herbs to 1 litre (1 quart) of turtle consommé.

BOUILLONS

Petite marmite and Poule au pot (see Recipes 237 and 239) may be considered refined forms of bouillon. The following examples typify the unthickened, natural liquor in which meat and poultry have been simply cooked and from which bouillons originate. This type of soup is suitable for luncheon. Originally, en famille, the boiled meat from the bouillon constituted a main course or further meal.

241 Bouillon de volaille [to yield 1 litre (1 quart)]

one 2.5 kg ((5 lb) old chicken	1 onion clouté	3 litre (3 qt) cold water
500 g (1 lb) chopped veal-bones	2 whole carrots	30 g (1 oz) vermicelli
250 g (½ lb) minced lean beef	250 g (½ lb) leeks	

1 Blanch the veal bones and clean and truss the fowl.
2 Mix the beef with the cold water and add the fowl.
3 Bring to the boil and remove all scum.
4 Add the vegetables whole.
5 Simmer till the fowl is cooked.
6 Remove all fat; strain through muslin.
7 Season and garnish with cooked vermicelli.

242 Bouillon aux œufs [to yield 1 litre (1 quart)]

As above, Recipe 241, with two fresh eggs beaten and strained into 1 litre (1 quart) bouillon, but do not use vermicelli.

243 Croûte au pot [to yield 1 litre (1 quart)]

1 Prepare Petite marmite, Recipe 237, and similarly garnish but omit the meat and chicken garnish.
2 Serve in marmite pots.

Note. The service of croûtons differs in that they are first dipped in a little stock fat and dried off in the oven.

244 Pot-au-feu [to yield 1 litre (1 quart)]

1 kg (2¼ lb) boiling beef	125 g (4 oz) baton (or turned) turnips
2 litre (2 qt) beef consommé (Recipe 227)	125 g (4 oz) small batons of celery
1 onion clouté	125 g (4 oz) white cabbage cut into paysanne
125 g (4 oz) baton (or turned) carrots	125 g (4 oz) leek cut into paysanne
1 bay-leaf	seasoning

1 Blanch the beef, place in the consommé with the onion clouté and bay-leaf. Bring to the boil and gently simmer until cooked. Remove. Cut into small dice.
2 Remove the onion clouté and bay-leaf from the consommé, add the rest of the vegetables, gently simmer until cooked.
3 Skim, add the diced beef. Correct seasoning.
4 Serve with toasted sliced flutes of bread (croûtes de flûte).

BROTHS AND GARNISHED UNTHICKENED SOUPS

The following soups have a base of broth or unthickened liquor. Garnishes in some instances, particularly heavy ones, do have the effect of slight thickening or clouding. These were traditionally regarded as luncheon soups.

In all recipes for 'unpassed' soups, vegetable quantities are of prepared weights.

245 Cocky Leeky [to yield 1 litre (1 quart)]

2 *litre* (2 *qt*) *chicken stock*   250 *g* (½ *lb*) *Julienne white leek*
(*Recipe* 11)   1 *bouquet garni*
30 *g* (1 *oz*) *boiled rice*   *one* 2 *kg* (4-*lb*) *chicken*
12 *stewed prunes*

1 Joint the chicken as for sauter.
2 Fry the chicken to a golden colour in butter.
3 Add the chicken to the stock.
4 Boil and skim; add bouquet garni and simmer till the chicken is cooked.
5 Strain the liquid.
6 Cut the chicken in small pieces.
7 Stew the leeks in butter, pour the stock over and cook for 20 minutes.
8 Add the boiled rice and chicken to the soup; remove all fat and season.
9 Prunes are heated in a little stock and added before service.

246 Cocky Leeky – Simplified recipe [to yield 1 litre (1 quart)]

2 *litre* (2 *qt*) *white chicken*   250 *g* (8 *oz*) *julienne of white of leek*
   consommé   250 *g* (8 *oz*) *julienne of cooked*
30 *g* (1 *oz*) *boiled rice*   *breast of chicken*
12 *soaked prunes cut into batons*

1 Garnish the boiling consommé with the rice, prunes, leek and chicken.
2 Correct the seasoning.

247 Minestrone [to yield 1 litre (1 quart)]

60 *g* (2 *oz*) *fat bacon*   60 *g* (2 *oz*) *leeks*   45 *g* (1½ *oz*) *rice*
1 *clove, crushed garlic*   *toasted croûtons*   1 *bouquet garni*
60 *g* (2 *oz*) *broken*   (*flutes*)   60 *g* (2 *oz*) *onions*
  spaghetti   240 *g* (½ *lb*) *tomato*   60 *g* (2 *oz*) *cabbage*
30 *g* (1 *oz*) *fresh or*   *concassé*   1.5 *litre* (1½ *qt*)
  frozen peas   10 *ml* (spoon [1   *white stock*
60 *g* (2 *oz*) *carrots*   *dessertspoon*]   30 *g* (1 *oz*) *grated*
60 *g* (2 *oz*) *turnips*   *tomato purée*   *Parmesan cheese*
60 *g* (2 *oz*) *celery*   30 *g* (1 *oz*) *French*
60 *g* (2 *oz*) *potato*   *beans* (*cut into*
   diamonds)

1 Dice the bacon to extract the fat.
2 Add the vegetables (cut into paysanne), and garlic, and sweat under cover.
3 Add the stock; boil and skim.
4 Add the bouquet garni and simmer for 20 minutes.
5 Add the tomato purée and tomato concassé, spaghetti, rice and French beans and peas.
6 Simmer for a further 15 minutes.
7 Skim off all fat; remove bouquet garni and season.
8 Serve with cheese and croûtons; do not strain.

248 Mutton broth [to yield 1 litre (1 quart)]

Prepare as Scotch broth, Recipe, 253, but halve the quantities of vegetable garnish.

249 Potage à la bonne-femme [to yield 1 litre (1 quart)]

1 *litre* (1 *qt*) *fonds blanc* (*Recipe* 6)	350 *g* (¾ *lb*) *white of leek* (*paysanne*)	720 *g* [1½ *lb* (*net*)] *diced potato*
125 *ml* (¼ *pt*) *fresh cream* (*or milk or skimmed milk*)	1 *bouquet garni seasoning*	120 *g* (4 *oz*) *butter* (*or sunflower margarine*)

1 Sweat the potatoes and leeks in 60 g (2 oz) butter under cover.
2 Moisten with the fond blanc. Boil and skim. Add bouquet garni and simmer until the vegetables are cooked.
3 Remove bouquet garni and all fat.
4 Season; add the cream (or milk) and blend in the butter (or margarine).
5 Sprinkle a little fresh, chopped parsley on the top before service.
6 Served toasted flutes separately or thin slices of toasted, French bread; do not strain.

Note. To the above a liaison of 1 egg yolk and 125 ml (¼ pt) of cream may be added. The cream should be warmed before adding. When this is done, the soup ceases to be an unthickened type.

250 Potage cultivateur [to yield 1 litre (1 quart)]

60 *g* (2 *oz*) *diced, salted pork*	60 *g* (2 *oz*) *turnips*	1 *litre* (1 *qt*) *white stock* (*Recipe* 6)
60 *g* (2 *oz*) *carrots*	60 *g* (2 *oz*) *celery*	1 *bouquet garni*
60 *g* (2 *oz*) *onions*	90 *g* (3 *oz*) *potatoes*	15 *ml* (spoon
90 *g* (3 *oz*) *leeks*	60 *g* (2 *oz*) *butter* (*or margarine*) *seasoning*	[1 *tablespoon*] *chopped parsley*

1 Blanch and refresh the pork and fry off.
2 Cut the vegetables into paysanne and sweat in butter under cover.
3 Moisten with the stock, boil, skim; add the bouquet garni and simmer till the vegetables are cooked.
4 Remove the bouquet garni and all fat.
5 Adjust the seasoning, add the fried pork and sprinkle with chopped parsley.

Note. The vegetables should retain their shape in cooking.

251 Potage à la fermière [to yield 1 litre (1 quart)]

1 *litre* (1 *qt*) *fonds de volaille* (*Recipe* 11)	60 *g* (2 *oz*) *celery*	1 *bouquet garni seasoning*
60 *g* (2 *oz*) *butter*	90 *g* (3 *oz*) *leeks*	15 *ml* (spoon
60 *g* (2 *oz*) *carrots*	90 *g* (3 *oz*) *potatoes*	[1 *tablespoon*]
60 *g* (2 *oz*) *turnips*	60 *g* (2 *oz*) *onions*	*chopped parsley*
	60 *g* (2 *oz*) *cabbage*	

1 Cut the cabbage into julienne and the rest of the vegetables into paysanne.
2 Sweat the vegetables in butter under cover.
3 Add the fond de volaille, boil and skim; add the bouquet garni.
4 Simmer till the vegetables are cooked; remove bouquet garni.
5 Remove all fat and season.
6 Sprinkle with fresh chopped parsley.
7 Serve toasted flûtes.
Note. The vegetables must retain their shape and not be in the purée.

252 Potage paysanne [to yield 1 litre (1 quart)]

1.25 *litre* (1¼ *qt*) *white stock* (*Recipe* 6)	15 *g* (½ *oz*) *chervil leaves*	1 *bouquet garni*
30 *g* (1 *oz*) *fresh peas*	60 *g* (2 *oz*) *carrots*	60 *g* (2 *oz*) *turnips*
30 *g* (1 *oz*) *French beans* (*cut into diamonds*)	90 *g* (3 *oz*) *butter* (*or margarine*)	60 *g* (2 *oz*) *onions*
30 *g* (1 *oz*) *flageolets*	15 *ml* (*spoon* [1 *tablespoon*] *chopped parsley*	60 *g* (2 *oz*) *leeks*
		60 *g* (2 *oz*) *celery*
		60 *g* (2 *oz*) *potatoes*
		seasoning

1 Cut the vegetables into paysanne and sweat in butter under cover.
2 Add the white stock. Boil, skim and add the bouquet garni.
3 Simmer until the vegetables are cooked. They must retain their shape when cooked.
4 Remove bouquet garni and all fat; season.
5 Sprinkle with parsley and chervil leaves before service.
6 Do not strain.

253 Scotch broth [to yield 1 litre (1 quart)]

1.5 *litre* (1½ *qt*) *water* [*or white stock* (*Recipe* 6) *from mutton bones*]	90 *g* (3 *oz*) *brunoise of celery*	90 *g* (3 *oz*) *brunoise of leek*
350 *g* (¾ *lb*) *scrag of mutton or lamb*	60 *g* (2 *oz*) *finely diced onions*	30 *g* (1 *oz*) *barley*
120 *g* (4 *oz*) *brunoise of carrots*	30 *g* (1 *oz*) *dried peas*	2 × 15 *ml spoon* [2 *tablespoons*] *chopped parsley*
60 *g* (2 *oz*) *brunoise of turnips*	60 *g* (2 *oz*) *diced cabbage*	*seasoning*

1 Soak, in separate dishes, the barley and peas in cold water.
2 Boil the water with the scrag of mutton; remove all scum.
3 Add the barley, peas and cook for 20 minutes.
4 Add all the vegetables and simmer till cooked and the meat tender.
5 Cut the meat into small dice.
6 Remove all fat; season, add the diced meat.
7 Sprinkle with chopped parsley.
Note. In some cases of high-quality service, the broth may be finished with light cream.

254 Soupe à l'oignon gratinée à la française – Brown onion soup (French style) [to yield 1 litre (1 quart)]

1 *kg (2 lb) sliced*	21 *g (¾ oz) flour*	*toasted flûte*
onions	120 *g (4 oz) butter*	*croûtons*
1.5 *litre (1½ qt) fonds*	90 *g (3 oz) grated*	*seasoning*
brun (Recipe 7 or 8)	*Gruyère (or*	
1 *clove crushed garlic*	*alternative cheese)*	

1 Fry onions and garlic in the butter to light-golden colour.
2 Blend in the flour and cook for about 3 minutes.
3 Moisten with the stock (good consommé is even better) and simmer till the onions are cooked.
4 Carefully remove all fat and season lightly from the pepper mill, and with salt.
5 Pour the soup into earthenware bowls and spread on the toasted flûtes neatly.
6 Sprinkle Gruyère cheese on top and set to brown in the oven or under salamander.
7 Do not strain.

255 Soupe au pistou – French style vegetable soup with basil and garlic paste

60 *g (2 oz) dried haricot beans*	2 *tbsp. olive oil*
120 *g (4 oz) white of leek finely*	120 *g (4 oz) carrot*
shredded	120 *g (4 oz) courgettes*
60 *g (2 oz) turnip*	120 *g (4 oz) broad beans*
60 *g (2 oz) French beans, cut into*	4 *tomatoes (skinned, deseeded and*
2.5 *cm (1 inch) lengths*	*chopped)*
60 *g (2 oz) tomato purée*	60 *g (2 oz) macaroni*
1 *litre (1 qt) vegetable (or bone)*	*seasoning*
stock	

1 Soak the haricot beans for approximately 8 hours.
2 Place the beans in a pan of cold water, bring to the boil and gently simmer for approximately 20 minutes. Refresh and drain.
3 Heat two tablespoons of oil in a suitable pan, add the white of leek and sweat for 5 minutes.
4 Add the carrot and turnip (both cut into brunoise) and cook for a further 2 minutes.
5 Add the haricot beans. Cover with vegetable stock and add the remaining ingredients.
6 Correct the seasoning and consistency of the soup and serve with the pistou (see below), which is stirred in. (The pistou may be served separately for the customer to do this.)

Note. The vegetable garnish may be varied (in some versions simply diced runner beans, diced potatoes, tomato concassé and a little vermicelli in a strong, clear stock).

The pistou has the following ingredients:

30 g (1 oz) basil	1 clove of garlic
60 g (2 oz) concassé tomato	4 tbsp. olive oil
60 g (2 oz) Gruyère cheese (optional)	peppermill

1 Make a purée of the basil, garlic and tomato (in a food processor if available).
2 Gradually add the oil until well-mixed and emulsified.
3 Finish with a light seasoning from the peppermill.

Note. This also is variable. Some, as in the Niçoise version, use tomato purée and omit the cheese. The base can be equally variable (according to region), in effect aillade (see Recipe 119) with the addition of concassé tomato and grated Gruyère cheese to complete the purée.

UNCLASSIFIED SOUPS

The following soups may have thickened brown stock or be of foreign origin.

256 Hare soup [to yield 1 litre (1 quart)]

1.5 litre (1½ qt) estouffade (Recipe 8)	30 g (1 oz) parsley stalks	125 ml (¼ pt) tomato purée
1 hare	60 g (2 oz) carrot (diced)	bouquet garni
250 ml (½ pt) port wine		125 ml (¼ pt) Madeira wine
60 g (2 oz) celery (diced)	60 g (2 oz) butter (or margarine)	
60 g (2 oz) flour		

1 Cut up the hare retaining the blood and liver.
2 Add the vegetables to the hare and pour on the port wine and stand for 12 hours.
3 Remove the hare and vegetables and fry off in the fat; add the flour and make a brown roux; when cooked, blend in the tomato purée.
4 Moisten with stock and the port wine from the hare; boil and skim; add bouquet garni.
5 Simmer one hour or until the hare is cooked well.
6 Beat the blood with a little water and add to the soup; simmer for a few minutes.
7 Strain, adjust the seasoning and add the Madeira wine.

Note. The soup may be finished with 30 ml spoon (2 tablespoons) of cream.

257 Mulligatawny [to yield 1 litre (1 quart)]

120 g (4 oz) chopped onion
1 chopped clove of garlic
60 g (2 oz) butter, margarine or
  sunflower oil
60 g (2 oz) flour (white or
  wholemeal)
30 g (1 oz) Madras curry powder
30 g (1 oz) tomato purée
salt

1 litre (1 qt) brown stock
30 g (1 oz) chopped apple
7 g (¼ oz) ground ginger
30 g (1 oz) chopped chutney
30 g (1 oz) desiccated coconut
15 g (½ oz) cooked rice (white or
  wholegrain)

1 Lightly brown the onion and garlic in the fat or oil.
2 Mix in the flour and curry powder. Cook for a few minutes, slightly browning.
3 Mix in the tomato purée. Cool slightly.
4 Gradually add boiling stock, stirring well between each addition.
5 Add remaining ingredients; season with salt.
6 Simmer for 30–45 minutes.
7 Liquidize, pass through a strainer.
8 Return to a clean saucepan and reboil.
9 Correct seasoning and consistency.
10 Add the rice. Serve.

Note. The soup may be finished with a little cream (up to 125 ml), milk or natural yogurt.

258 Potage queue de boeuf lié – Oxtail soup [to yield 1 litre (1 quart)]

½ oxtail
60 g (2 oz) oil or beef dripping
120 g (4 oz) chopped onion
1 clove of garlic
bouquet garni
120 g (4 oz) carrot and turnips for
  garnish

120 g (4 oz) carrot and turnips
60 g (2 oz) flour, white or
  wholemeal
30 g (1 oz) tomato purée
1½ litre (3 pt) brown stock
seasoning

1 Cut the oxtail into pieces through the natural joints.
2 Quickly fry in hot oil or fat until lightly browned.
3 Add the chopped onion and crushed garlic, carrot and turnips. Brown well.
4 Add flour, mix and cook until brown. Cool.
5 Mix in tomato purée.
6 Gradually add boiling stock. Skim.
7 Add bouquet garni and seasoning. Simmer for 3–4 hours.
8 Remove bouquet garni and oxtail.
9 Pass the soup through a fine strainer.
10 Remove flesh from oxtail and liquidize with the soup.
11 Return to a clean saucepan, reboil, correct seasoning and consistency.
12 Garnish with a small cooked dice of carrot and turnip cooked in a little salt water.
13 Finish soup with 2 tablespoons of sherry or Madeira wine.

259 Soupe aux rognons – Kidney soup [to yield 1 litre (1 quart)]

> 60 g (2 oz) beef dripping or
>   sunflower oil
> 60 g (2 oz) flour, white or
>   wholemeal
> 30 g (1 oz) tomato purée
> 1½ litre (3 pt) brown beef stock
>
> seasoning
> 240 g (8 oz) ox kidney
> 120 g (4 oz) diced carrot
> 120 g (4 oz) diced onion
> bouquet garni

1 Melt the fat in a saucepan. Mix in the flour. Cook to a brown roux. Cool slightly.
2 Mix in tomato purée.
3 Gradually add boiling stock. Stir well.
4 Remove skin and gristle from kidney. Cut into ½ cm (¼ inch) dice.
5 Quickly fry the kidney in hot fat until brown, add the carrot and onion, and fry together. Drain well, add to the soup.
6 Add bouquet garni and seasoning.
7 Simmer approximately 2½ hours. Skim well.
8 Remove bouquet garni. Pass soup through a fine strainer and liquidize.
9 Return to a clean pan and reboil.
10 Correct seasoning and consistency, and serve.
11 The soup may be garnished with a small dice of kidney (a little brunoise of vegetable may sometimes be included).

BISQUES AND CHOWDERS

Bisques are made of high-quality fish (usually shellfish) and are thick soups. Chowders, developed in America, are also thick soups owing their consistency to potatoes and biscuit crumbs. Bisques and chowders differ from the thin-liquor fish-soup stews in being thick and because they are normally made of shellfish.

260 Bisque d'écrevisse – Crayfish bisque [to yield 1 litre (1 quart)]

> 3 dozen crayfish
> 12 anchovy fillets
> 120 g (4 oz) butter
> 15 litre (1½ qt) fish
>   stock (Recipe 374)
>
> 125 ml (¼ pt) white
>   wine
> 125 ml (¼ pt) brandy
> 90 g (3 oz) fine
>   mirepoix (Recipe 2)
>
> 90 g (3 oz) rice,
>   Carolina
> bouquet garni
> 12 crushed
>   peppercorns
> 125 ml (¼ pt) cream
> juice of ½ lemon

1 Pound the crayfish and retain 12 tails for garnish.
2 Fry the mirepoix in butter, add the pounded crayfish and cook till a red colour; flame with brandy.
3 Add the fish stock, boil and skim; add the rice, bouquet garni, crayfish tails and white wine.
4 Simmer till the rice is cooked and very soft.
5 Liquidize in a food processor, then pass through a fine strainer (or rub through a tammy).

6 Reboil; season with lemon juice, salt and cayenne pepper.
7 Blend the cream and 30 g (1 oz) butter.
8 Garnish with the diced crayfish tails.

Note. Other bisques such as Bisque de crevettes (Shrimp) and Crabes (Crab) maybe, are prepared in the same way as the above.

261 Bisque de homard – Lobster bisque [to yield 1 litre (1 quart)]

one 750 g (1½ lb) *raw lobster*	60 ml (⅛ pt) *cognac*
120 g (4 oz) *fine mirepoix*	1.25 *litre* (2½ pt) *fish stock*
(*Recipe* 4)	(*Recipe* 374)
125 ml (¼ pt) *white wine*	*bouquet garni*
120 g (4 oz) *butter* (*or sunflower*	30 g (1 oz) *tomato purée*
margarine)	125 ml (¼ pt) *cream*
6 *crushed peppercorns*	*juice of* ½ *lemon*
90 g (3 oz) *flour*	*salt, cayenne pepper*

1 Split the lobster down the back.
2 Cut the body in half and the tail into three to four pieces.
3 Crack the claws.
4 Heat the butter or margarine in a suitable pan, add a little oil; quickly fry the lobster until it turns bright red.
5 Add the mirepoix, fry together.
6 Add the brandy, flame, burn off the alcohol.
7 Add the flour. Cook for 2–3 minutes.
8 Add the tomato purée.
9 Moisten with white wine and stock. Mix well.
10 Bring to boil, skim. Add bouquet garni. Simmer for a maximum of 20 minutes.
11 Remove the lobster, take out the meat and dice finely for garnish. Remove bouquet garni.
12 Chop the lobster shells, add to the soup and liquidize together. Pass through a strainer.
13 Place in a clean pan.
14 Bring to boil. Correct seasoning and consistency.
15 Finish with lemon juice, cream and 30 g (1 oz) butter.
16 Add lobster garnish. Serve.

The soup may also be finished with lobster butter (lobster eggs purée with butter, added to the soup at the last minute).

262 Clam chowder [to yield 1 litre (1 quart)]

18 *clams*	4 *diced white of leek*	15 g (½ oz) *fines*
500 g (1 lb) *small diced*	6 *water biscuits or*	*herbes*
potatoes	*cream crackers*	125 ml (¼ pt) *cream*
250 g (½ lb) *diced*	60 g (2 oz) *butter* (*or*	(*or yogurt*)
onions	*sunflower*	60 g (2 oz) *fat*
1 *litre* (1 qt) *fish stock*	*margarine*)	*pickled pork*
(*Recipe* 374)		

1 Open clams and gently poach in 500 ml (1 pint) of fish stock; when cooked cut into small dice.

2 Sweat the diced pork, onions, and leeks in butter; add the potatoes and sweat under cover for a further few minutes.

3 Moisten with fish stock and the cooking liquid from the clams.

4 Simmer gently until the vegetables are cooked; add the clams, cream, fines herbes, water biscuits (broken into small pieces); season.

263 New England chowder

This may be made by adding 250 g (½ lb) tomato concassé and a pinch of saffron to the ingredients of Recipe 262.

Note. Other white fish such as cod and haddock may be used in chowder-making.

Fish-soup stews. Bouillabaisse, the celebrated fish-soup stew of the Marseilles coast, is so truly regional that it is unlikely to be featured in good establishments outside its own area, but recipes for it, for matelotes, and for waterzoi are given in Chapter 5 (Recipes 455 to 458). For other fish soups of this kind, culinary encyclopaedias or speciality food books should be consulted.

THICKENED SOUPS: PURÉES, CRÈMES, AND VELOUTÉS

Purées and crèmes

Starchy vegetables such as haricot beans, lentils, and potatoes when purée-d in soups, usually act as self-thickeners. Soups made from these vegetables need no further thickening ingredient.

Other vegetables like carrots, pumpkins, turnips, celery and leaf greens do need an additional thickening agent as their own purées do not cohere at all. To effect coherence in this kind of vegetable purée, either potatoes or rice may be added: 90 g (3 oz) rice or 300 g (10 oz) potato per 500 g (1 lb) of vegetables.

Both these soups, self-thickened or with added rice- or potato-thickening, are correctly designated purées. For simple service, they may be prepared and served without a cream finish. Fromage frais, quark, non-dairy creamer or milk may also be used in lieu of cream.

Vegetable crèmes

In some instances purées may be called crèmes. Examples are Crème d'orge (Cream of barley) and, when the vegetable purée is specially named, St-Germain, for green-pea purée. The word crème (hence Crème St Germain) is commonly used when the purée has been given a cream finish (but see the following paragraph on crèmes).

Veloutés and crèmes

Basic veloutés for sauces have already been described in Chapter 1. Veloutés as soups are similar to other veloutés and, by the same token, differ from purées in that they require a thickening element, a roux. For soup veloutés 90 g (3 oz) of white roux per litre (quart) of the liquid to be thickened is used. Veloutés may be made with a vegetable content, e.g. velouté Crécy (carrot purée, roux-cohered) in conjunction with stock or white consommé (or fish stock for a fish velouté). For a velouté de volaille (chicken velouté) and derivatives, thickened white chicken consommé is the dominant element.

Generally, proportions for a velouté soup are ½ basic velouté (as appropriate); ¼ purée (of the appropriate main ingredient characterizing the soup); ¼ stock or white consommé used to dilute the mix of purée and velouté to the correct consistency.

Finishing veloutés

Correct finishing of velouté is effected with a liaison of beaten egg yolks and cream, using 3 yolks and ⅕ pint (100 ml) cream per 1 litre (1 quart) of soup.

Crèmes – creams

Cream soups, other than simple purées given a cream finish, are prepared similarly to veloutés with these differences:

(i)   Whatever the nature of the soup, Béchamel is used instead of velouté.
(ii) Milk is used to dilute and achieve correct consistency instead of stock or consommé.
(iii) Creams are finished with cream. They do not require egg yolk.

Note. An exception is tomato soup which, when not cream-finished, might correctly be designated velouté de tomates for it is roux-thickened. Yet when cream-finished this soup is invariably called crème de tomate – Cream of Tomato Soup (Recipe 290).

General comments. Although there are these differences between purées, veloutés and creams, the use of crème or cream as a common designation for soups made with a cream finish is now so widespread as to constitute accepted usage. What remains important is to use good methods and recipes for the type of soups desired.

Stock and consommé

In many of the recipes of master chefs of past generations, white consommés or chicken consommés were specified as the liquid base for most of the thickened soups in the following recipes. For vegetable, farinaceous, and pulse soups, good fonds blanc or good fonds de volaille are nowadays used for this purpose. The term white consommé did not, in any case, have the significance of the clarified consommés or clear soups and simply implied high-quality fonds or stock. Obviously, where white stock is to be used in cream or velouté of chicken, the white stock can be reinforced with chicken (bones and carcase).

THICK VEGETABLE SOUPS

The vegetable soups in this section include veloutés, purées and crèmes. Farinaceous soups of corn, barley and, of course, the pulses, have been grouped under the broad heading of 'vegetable'.

264 Potage ambassadeurs [to yield 1 litre (1 quart)]

30 g (1 oz) white of leek (cut into julienne)	15 g (½ oz) shredded lettuce
15 g (½ oz) shredded sorrel	1 litre (1 qt) Crème St-Germain (Recipe 287)

1 Stew the lettuce and sorrel in butter.
2 Cook the leek in fonds blanc (Recipe 6).
3 Add the garnish to litre (1 qt) St-Germain.

Note. This soup can also be made by using dried-pea purée (Recipe 284).

265 Crème Argenteuil (Crème d'asperges) – Cream of asparagus [to yield 1 litre (1 quart)]

60 g (2 oz) onions or white of leek	60 g (2 oz) flour
60 g (2 oz) celery	1 litre (1 qt) chicken stock
60 g (2 oz) butter or sunflower margarine	seasoning
	bouquet garni
500 g (1 lb) asparagus, fresh or frozen	125 ml (¼ pt) cream (or yogurt)

1 Sweat the sliced onions and celery in the butter or margarine without colouring.
2 Remove from heat, add the flour and return to heat, cooking without colouring.
3 Cool, gradually add the boiling stock, stir to the boil.
4 Add chopped asparagus, bouquet garni and seasoning.
5 Simmer for approximately 40 minutes. Remove bouquet garni.
6 Liquidize carefully.
7 Return to a clean saucepan, correct seasoning and consistency. Pass through a fine strainer if necessary.
8 Finish with cream or yogurt.

This soup may be garnished with blanched chervil or mint and small cooked asparagus tips.

266 Crème de céleri – Cream of celery [to yield 1 litre (1 quart)]

60 g (2 oz) sliced onions or white of leek	1 litre (1 qt) chicken stock
300 g (10 oz) celery	bouquet garni and seasoning
60 g (2 oz) butter or sunflower margarine	125 ml (¼ pt) cream (or natural yogurt)
60 g (2 oz) flour	60 g (2 oz) fine dice of cooked celery for garnish

1 Cook the vegetables in the butter or margarine without colouring.
2 Add flour, cook for 2 minutes without colouring.
3 Add the boiling stock, stir to the boil.
4 Add bouquet garni and seasoning.
5 Simmer for approximately 40 minutes.
6 Remove bouquet garni. Liquidize, then pass through a coarse strainer.
7 Return to a clean pan.
8 Reboil, correct seasoning and consistency.
9 Finish with cream (or yogurt).

Garnish with a fine dice of cooked celery.

267 Crème de champignons – Cream of mushroom [to yield 1 litre (1 quart)]

120 g (4 oz) onion, leek and celery	240 g (8 oz) white mushrooms
60 g (2 oz) butter or sunflower margarine	bouquet garni seasoning
60 g (2 oz) flour	125 ml (¼ pt) cream (or natural
1 litre (1 qt) chicken stock	yogurt)

1 Cook the onion, leek and celery in the butter or margarine without colouring.
2 Mix in the flour and continue to cook without colour.
3 Cool, add boiling stock. Stir to the boil.
4 Add washed and chopped mushrooms, bouquet garni and seasoning.
5 Simmer for approximately 10 minutes. Skim.
6 Remove the bouquet garni. Liquidize. Pass through a medium strainer.
7 Reboil, correct seasoning and consistency.
8 Finish with cream (or natural yogurt).

This soup may be garnished with a fine dice of mushroom cooked in a little lemon juice.

268 Purée or Crème Condé [to yield 1 litre (1 quart)]

300 g (10 oz) red beans	120 g (4 oz) chopped onions	90 g (3 oz) butter (or margarine)
500 ml (1 pt) red wine		
500 ml (1 pt) white stock (Recipe 6)	120 g (4 oz) diced carrots	125 ml (¼ pt) cream (or yogurt)
	bouquet garni	seasoning

1 Soak the beans in water for 6 hours.
2 Sweat the carrots and onions in butter, add the beans and sweat for a further 2 or 3 minutes.
3 Moisten with the wine and stew for about 15 minutes; add the white stock and bouquet garni and continue to cook until puréed.
4 Liquidize (or rub through a fine sieve); reboil and check for consistency (adjust with stock as necessary); season.
5 Blend in the cream and 30 g (1 oz) butter; serve with sippets.

269 Purée or Crème Crécy – Cream of carrot soup [to yield 1 litre (1 quart)]

750 g (1½ lb) thinly sliced carrots	2.5 ml spoon [½ teaspoon] sugar	60 g (2 oz) rice, Carolina
90 g (3 oz) finely chopped onions	1.5 litre (1½ qt) white stock (Recipe 6)	125 ml (¼ pt) fresh cream
90 g (3 oz) butter	1 sprig thyme	1 bay-leaf

1 Place the onions, carrots, thyme, bay-leaf, sugar, in a small saucepan with butter and stew until tender.
2 Add the white stock; boil, skim and add the rice.
3 Cook gently till a purée. Remove bay-leaf.
4 Liquidize; season and finish with cream and 30 g (1 oz) butter (or margarine and yogurt).

270 Crème or Purée à la cressonnière – Watercress and potato cream or purée soup [to yield 1 litre (1 quart)]

60 g (2 oz) butter or sunflower margarine	500 g (1 lb) potatoes
60 g (2 oz) onions	1 bunch watercress
60 g (2 oz) white of leek	bouquet garni
1 litre (1 qt) chicken stock	seasoning
125 ml (¼ pt) cream (or boiled milk or natural yogurt)	

1 Cook the onions and leek in the butter or margarine without colouring.
2 Add the stock and the peeled, washed, diced potatoes. Bring to boil.
3 Add the chopped watercress, bouquet garni and seasoning.
4 Simmer for approximately 30 minutes. Remove bouquet garni.
5 Liquidize, pass through a medium strainer.
6 Place in a clean pan. Bring to the boil.
7 Correct seasoning and consistency. Finish with 125 ml (¼ pt) cream (or boiled milk or natural yogurt).

Garnish with blanched watercress leaves.

271 Crème d'orge – Cream of barley soup [to yield 1 litre (1 quart)]

30 g (1 oz) white celery	1.5 litre (1½ qt) chicken stock (Recipe 11)	30 g (1 oz) butter (or sunflower margarine)
240 g (½ lb) pearl barley		
125 ml (¼ pt) cream (or fromage frais or yogurt)		seasoning

1 Wash barley and soak in lukewarm water for 2 hours.
2 Drain and add 750 ml (1½ pint) of chicken stock and celery. Cook gently under cover until a purée for approximately 2½ hours.
3 Dilute with the other 750 ml (1½ pint) of chicken stock, liquidize and pass through a strainer.
4 Reheat, season, blend in the cream and butter.
5 Adjust consistency with boiled milk.

272 Crème Du Barry – Cream of cauliflower soup [to yield 1 litre (1 quart)]

1 *litre (1 qt) white stock*	60 g (2 oz) flour	60 g (2 oz) onions
(Recipe 6)	75 g (2½ oz) butter (or	(diced)
375 ml (¾ pt) milk	sunflower	60 g (2 oz) white of
500 g (1 lb) cauliflower	margarine)	leek (diced)
125 ml (¼ pt) cream	seasoning	bouquet garni
(warm) (or yogurt,		
fromage frais or		
quark)		

1 Wash cauliflower and remove faded leaves.
2 Break into small sections (retaining some small pieces for garnish which should be cooked separately).
3 Blanch the remainder of the cauliflower.
4 Sweat the leeks and onions in the butter and make a white roux with the flour.
5 Moisten with the stock and milk; add the blanched cauflower, boil and skim; add bouquet garni.
6 Simmer until the cauliflower falls into a purée.
7 Liquidize and pass through a strainer; reboil, correcting consistency with boiled milk, adjust seasoning and add the small pieces of cauliflower; blend in the cream (or alternative) with 15 g (½ oz) butter (optional).

273 Purée or Crème Esaü [to yield 1 litre (1 quart)]

Prepare as Cream of lentil (Recipe 278), garnished with 60 g (2 oz) boiled rice.

274 Purée or Crème flamande – Brussels sprouts and potato purée [to yield 1 litre (1 quart)]

1.5 *litre (1½ qt) white*	120 g (4 oz) diced white	125 ml (¼ pt) cream
stock (Recipe 6)	of leek	(or fromage frais
500 g (1 lb) Brussels	90 g (3 oz) onions	or quark)
sprouts	bouquet garni	90 g (3 oz) butter
500 g (1 lb) diced	1 egg yolk	(or sunflower
potatoes (net)		margarine)

1 Trim and blanch the sprouts.
2 Stew them in 60 g (2 oz) butter until tender.
3 Sweat the onions and leeks and moisten with the stock.
4 Add the stewed sprouts, boil and skim; add the bouquet garni.
5 Simmer until all the ingredients are in a purée and liquidize.
6 Reboil, adjust the seasoning and consistency. Finish with cream (or alternative).
7 Blend in 30 g (1 oz) butter (optional).
8 Serve soup sippets separately.

If the consistency is too thick, adjust with boiled milk (or stock).

275 Crème florentine – Cream of spinach soup [to yield 1 litre (1 quart)]

500 g (1 lb) shredded spinach	250 ml (½ pt) fonds de volaille (Recipe 11)	30 g (1 oz) butter (or sunflower margarine)
750 ml (1½ pt) Béchamel (Recipe 51)	125 ml (¼ pt) fresh cream (or fromage frais)	seasoning

1 Wash spinach well.
2 Boil in salt water 10 minutes; squeeze out all moisture.
3 Add the spinach to the Béchamel and correct consistency with stock.
4 Simmer for about 25 minutes.
5 Liquidize.
6 Re-boil; season and blend in the butter and the cream.

276 Purée or Crème Freneuse – Turnip and potato purée [to yield 1 litre (1 quart)]

250 g (½ lb) finely chopped onions	1.5 litre (1½ qt) white stock (Recipe 6)	125 ml (¼ pt) cream (or fromage frais, yogurt)
500 g (1 lb) diced turnips	250 ml (½ pt) milk	
375 g (¾ lb) diced potatoes	120 g (4 oz) butter (or sunflower margarine)	bouquet garni seasoning

1 Sweat the onions in 90 g (3 oz) butter but do not colour.
2 Add the diced turnips and potatoes and sweat under cover for 10 minutes.
3 Moisten with stock, boil and skim; add bouquet garni and cook until purée-d.
4 Liquidize and adjust consistency with boiled milk.
5 Reboil, season, blend in the cream and 30 g (1 oz) butter (optional).
6 Serve with sippets.

277 Crème Judic [to yield 1 litre (1 quart)]

2 medium lettuce	250 ml (½ pt) white stock (Recipe 6)	60 g (2 oz) butter (or sunflower margarine)
750 ml (1½ pt) Béchamel (Recipe 51)	250 ml (½ pt) cream (or yogurt)	

Garnish (optional): *Roundels of lettuce leaves spread with poached quenelle forcemeat* (Recipe 199), using chicken.

1 Wash lettuce, remove faded leaves.
2 Shred lettuce into coarse julienne.
3 Stew the lettuce until tender in 30 g (1 oz) butter.
4 Add the stock, Béchamel and seasoning.
5 Bring to the boil, simmer for 20 minutes.
6 Liquidize, pass through a medium strainer.
7 Correct seasoning and consistency.
8 Finish with cream (or yogurt).
9 Garnish if desired.

278 Crème de lentilles – Cream of lentils [to yield 1 litre (1 quart)]

300 g (10 oz) lentils	1.5 litre (1½ qt) white	125 ml (¼ pt) fresh
60 g (2 oz) diced	stock (Recipe 6)	cream (or yogurt)
onions	60 g (2 oz) bacon	60 g (2 oz) butter
60 g (2 oz) diced	bones	(or margarine)
carrots	bouquet garni	seasoning

1 Wash the lentils and drain.
2 Sweat the onions and carrots in 30 g (1 oz) butter, add the lentils and allow to sweat under cover for 5 minutes.
3 Add the stock, boil and skim.
4 Add the bouquet garni and cook the lentils until puréed.
5 Liquidize (and, optional, rub the whole through a fine sieve).
6 Reboil, adjust the consistency and seasoning.
7 Blend in the cream and the remaining butter.
8 Serve with sippets.

279 Potage or Crème Longchamps [to yield 1 litre (1 quart)]

1 litre (1 qt) purée	30g (1 oz) vermicelli	15 g (½ oz) chervil
St-Germain		leaves
(Recipe 287)		

1 Poach vermicelli in stock.
2 Blanch chervil leaves.
3 Add the above garnish to 1 litre (1 quart) purée St-Germain.

280 Crème de maïs – Cream of sweetcorn soup [to yield 1 litre (1 quart)]

180 g (6 oz) sweetcorn	125 ml (¼ pt) cream or natural
750 ml (1½ pt) Béchamel	yogurt
(Recipe 51)	125 ml (¼ pt) chicken stock
seasoning	(Recipe 11)
	30 g (1 oz) butter or margarine

1 Boil the corn in salted water for 20 minutes.
2 Place the cooked sweetcorn in the chicken stock and Béchamel.
3 Liquidize.
4 Pass through a medium strainer. Bring to the boil.
5 Correct seasoning and consistency.
6 Finish with cream or natural yogurt.

281 Crème Washington – Cream of sweetcorn [to yield 1 litre (1 quart)]

120 g (4 oz) onion, leek and celery	300 g (10 oz) frozen sweetcorn
60 g (2 oz) butter or sunflower	bouquet garni
margarine	seasoning
1 litre (1 qt) chicken stock	
125 ml (¼ pt) cream or natural	60 g (2 oz) flour
yogurt	

1 Cook the onions, leek and celery in the butter or margarine without colouring.
2 Mix in the flour and continue to cook without colouring.
3 Cool, add boiling stock. Stir to the boil.
4 Add the frozen sweetcorn, bouquet garni and seasoning.
5 Simmer for approximately 20 minutes.
6 Remove bouquet garni. Liquidize, pass through medium strainer.
7 Reboil, correct seasoning and consistency.
8 Finish with cream or natural yogurt.

282 Crème Palestine – Cream of Jerusalem artichoke [to yield 1 litre (1 quart)]

120 g (4 oz) sliced onions, leek and celery	1 litre (2 pt) chicken stock
240 g (8 oz) washed, peeled Jerusalem artichokes	bouquet garni
	seasoning
60 g (2 oz) butter or sunflower margarine	125 ml (¼ pt) warm cream (or yogurt)
60 g (2 oz) flour	

Garnish: *blanched chervil or toasted, flaked almonds*

1 Cook the onions, leek and celery in the butter or margarine without colouring.
2 Add the flour, cook for 2 minutes without colouring.
3 Add the boiling stock. Skim well.
4 Add the diced Jerusalem artichokes, bouquet garni and seasoning.
5 Cook for approximately 40 minutes.
6 Liquidize, pass through a medium strainer.
7 Correct seasoning and consistency.
8 Finish with warm cream (or yogurt). Garnish with blanched chervil or toasted flaked almonds.

283 Crème or Purée parmentier – Potato cream purée soup [to yield 1 litre (1 quart)]

As for Crème cressonière but omit the watercress. (For a purée soup omit the cream (or yogurt) but finish with a little boiled milk [125 ml (¼ pt)].

284 Purée de pois – Pea soup [to yield 1 litre (1 quart)]

240 g (8 oz) dried green split peas	1 whole onion
1½ litre (3 pt) white stock or water	60 g (2 oz) bacon trimmings (optional)
bouquet garni	
30 g (1 oz) green of leek	seasoning
1 whole carrot	60 g (2 oz) butter or margarine

1 Soak the peas overnight if necessary.
2 Place in a saucepan, cover with stock or water.
3 Bring to the boil, skim.

4 Add remainder of ingredients. Season.
5 Simmer until tender.
6 Remove bouquet garni, carrot and bacon.
7 Liquidize.
8 Pass through a medium strainer.
9 Place in a clean pan, reboil, correct seasoning and consistency. Skim if necessary.
10 Serve with croutons.

Note. For fresh-pea purée see Recipe 287 (St Germain)

285 Potage potiron – Pumpkin soup [to yield 1 litre (1 quart)]

120 g (4 oz) chopped onion	chopped parsley
960 g (2 lb) pumpkin, peeled, seeded, chopped	60 g (2 oz) flour
	500 ml (1 pt) milk
120 g (4 oz) butter or margarine	125 ml (¼ pt) cream
500 ml (1 pt) white stock (Recipe 6)	60 g (2 oz) grated cheese
	salt and pepper

1 Sweat the onion and pumpkin in half the butter for a few minutes.
2 Add the stock and simmer until cooked.
3 Make a white sauce with the remaining butter, flour and milk.
4 Add to the pumpkin, blend and pass through sieve or liquidize.
5 Season, bring to the boil and finish with cream, cheese and parsley.

286 Purée or Crème soissonnaise – Haricot bean soup [to yield 1 litre (1 quart)]

500 g (1 lb) haricot beans	125 ml (¼ pt) cream (or yogurt)	seasoning
2 whole carrots	250 ml (½ pt) milk	1.5 litre (1½ pt) fonds blanc
1 onion clouté	30 g (1 oz) butter (or margarine)	(Recipe 6)
60 g (2 oz) bacon bones		

1 Soak beans and wash off.
2 Cook the beans with the stock and vegetables until purée stage.
3 Liquidize.
4 Rectify the consistency with boiled milk (or stock).
5 Adjust seasoning; blend in the cream and 30 g (1 oz) butter.
6 Serve soup sippets separately.

287 Crème St-Germain – Cream of fresh pea-soup [to yield 1 litre (1 quart)]

500 g (1 lb) shelled peas	125 ml (¼ pt) cream (or yogurt or fromage frais)	pinch of sugar
30 g (1 oz) green of leek		pinch salt
	250 ml (½ pt) water	60 g (2 oz) shredded lettuce
1 sprig mint	500 ml (1 pt) white stock (Recipe 6)	90 g (3 oz) butter (or margarine)

Garnish: 30g (1 oz) cooked peas

1 Sweat the leeks and lettuce in 60 g (2 oz) butter.
2 Add the peas, mint, water and stew until tender.
3 Liquidize (and rub through a fine sieve if desired).
4 Adjust the consistency with white stock and season.
5 Blend in the cream and butter.
6 Serve with soup sippets.

Note
(i) Quick-frozen peas are suitable in making this soup.
(ii) Variants of St-Germain by adding further garnish are:
Crème Lamballe with cooked tapioca; *Crème Longchamps* with cooked vermicelli and chiffonade of sorrel.
(iii) *Crème St-Germain* may be made by replacing stock with an equal quantity of Béchamel; adjust consistency, when finishing, with white stock.

Further thick cream soups. The following are not typical vegetable purées or cream soups nor may they be readily classified among the conventional veloutés.

288 Crème Germiny [to yield 1 litre (1 quart)]

1 *litre* (1 *qt*) *chicken consommé*	4 *egg yolks*
(*Recipe* 228)	30 *g* (1 *oz*) *cooked sorrel* (*julienne*)
125 *ml* (¼ *pt*) *cream*	*cheese straws* (*Recipe* 1188)
60 *g* (2 *oz*) *butter*	

1 Sweat the sorrel in 30 g (1 oz) butter.
2 Boil the consommé.
3 Beat egg yolks and cream (liaison).
4 Add the liaison to the consommé and mix well; reduce heat.
5 Blend in the remaining butter and season.
6 Serve cheese straws separately.

289 Crème portugaise [to yield 1 litre (1 quart)]

1 *litre* (1 *qt*) *cream of tomato*	30 *g* (1 *oz*) *plain boiled rice*
(*Recipe* 290)	

1 Basic Cream of tomato soup garnished with plain boiled rice.
2 Serve a sauceboat of soup sippets.

290 Crème de tomate – Cream of tomato soup [to yield 1 litre (1 quart)]

1.5 *litre* (1 *or* 1½ *qt*) *white stock*	60 *g* (2 *oz*) *flour*
(*Recipe* 6)	60 *g* (2 *oz*) *butter* (*or sunflower*
30 *g* (1 *oz*) *bacon rind* ⎤	*margarine*)
60 *g* (2 *oz*) *carrots* ⎬ *mirepoix*	10 *ml* (spoon [1 *dessertspoon*) *sugar*
60 *g* (2 *oz*) *onions* ⎦	125 *ml* (¼ *pt*) *cream* (*or fromage*
bouquet garni	*frais or yogurt*)
750 *g* (1½ *lb*) *fresh tomatoes or*	*seasoning*
190 *ml* (¼ *pt*) *of tomato purée*	*sippets*

1 Sweat off the diced bacon-rind in 30 g (1 oz) butter.
2 Add the mirepoix and colour slightly.
3 Add the flour and make a blond roux.
4 Mix the tomatoes with the roux.
5 Add the stock and mix well, boil and skim.
6 Add the bouquet garni and simmer 1 hour at the side of the stove or over low heat.
7 Add the sugar and strain through a fine chinois.
8 Adjust the seasoning, add the cream (or alternative), blend in the butter (optional).

Note
(i)   Check for colour and consistency and if using fresh tomatoes add 15 ml spoon (1 tablespoon) of tomato purée.
(ii) Tomato soup, as distinct from Cream of Tomato soup is simply the foregoing without cream-finish.
(iii) When using fresh tomatoes (as against canned purée) the lesser quantity of stock will be required.
(iv) For a distinctive flavour, omit the sugar and add a gatric (see below).

291 Gatric

    10 *ml* (1 *dessertspoonful*) *sugar*   70 *ml* (⅛ *pt*) *vinegar*

Mix the sugar and vinegar together. Cook to a light caramel, and add to the tomato soup.

CHICKEN VELOUTÉS AND CREAMS

Note. Among the following cream-soup examples, the first soup (Crème Derby) is not typical and may be regarded as a speciality soup.

292 Crème Derby [to yield 1 litre (1 quart)]

1.5 *litre* (1½ *qt*) *chicken stock* (*Recipe* 11)	125 *ml* (¼ *pt*) *cream* (*or fromage frais or yogurt*)	15 *g* (½ *oz*) *boiled rice*
60 *g* (2 *oz*) *rice*	120 *g* (4 *oz*) *butter*	18 *small chicken-quenelles* (*Recipe*
15 *g* (½ *oz*) *curry powder*	120 *g* (4 *oz*) *flour* *bouquet garni*	199, *using chicken meat*)
	60 *g* (2 *oz*) *diced truffle*	30 *g* (1 *oz*) *butter* (*or margarine*)

1 Make a blond roux.
2 Blend the curry powder with the roux.
3 Moisten with stock and mix well.
4 Boil, skim then add bouquet garni.
5 Wash the rice then add to the velouté.
6 Simmer until the rice is well cooked.
7 Strain, reboil, blend in the butter and cream. Season.
8 Garnish with the quenelles, boiled rice and truffles.

Note. Soak the rice in cold water for about 1 hour before adding.

293 Velouté de volaille 1 (basic recipe) – Chicken velouté soup [to yield 1 litre (1 quart)]

1.5 litre (1½ qt) white chicken stock (Recipe 11)	150 g (5 oz) butter
	120 g (4 oz) flour
60 g (2 oz) julienne cooked chicken	bouquet garni
	seasoning
125ml (¼ pt) cream ⎱ for liaison	
3 egg yolks ⎰	

1 Make a blond roux with 120 g (4 oz) butter and the flour.
2 Moisten with chicken stock.
3 Boil, skim, add bouquet garni.
4 Simmer, reducing to 1 litre (1 quart).
5 Strain, season; blend in remaining butter, egg yolks and cream.
6 Garnish with the julienne of chicken.

293a Velouté de volaille 2 (basic recipe) – Chicken velouté soup [to yield 1 litre (1 quart)]

120 g (4 oz) onion, leek and celery	120 g (4 oz) raw chicken meat
60 g (2 oz) butter or sunflower margarine	bouquet garni
	seasoning
1 litre (1 qt) chicken stock	125 ml (¼ pt) cream, natural
30 g (1 oz) diced cooked chicken meat	yogurt, fromage frais or quark
60 g (2 oz) flour	

1 Cook the vegetables in the butter or margarine without colouring.
2 Add the flour, cook to blond roux.
3 Gradually add the boiling stock.
4 Add the diced raw chicken meat.
5 Add bouquet garni and seasoning.
6 Simmer for approximately 40 minutes.
7 Remove bouquet garni.
8 Liquidize, pass through a medium strainer.
9 Place into a clean pan, reboil, correct for seasoning and consistency.
10 Finish with butter (optional) and/or a liaison of 1 egg yolk and cream, or, for the health-conscious, a little yogurt, fromage frais or quark.

294 Velouté Agnès-Sorel [to yield 1 litre (1 quart)]

1 litre (1 qt) chicken velouté (Recipe 293a)	75 g (2½ oz) butter
	125 ml (¼ pt) cream
240 g (8 oz) fresh mushrooms	seasoning
3 egg yolks	

Garnish
30 g (1 oz) cooked white meat of chicken
30 g (1 oz) cooked fresh tongue
30 g (1 oz) julienne mushrooms

1 Chop the mushrooms, add to the boiling velouté.
2 Liquidize, pass through a fine strainer.
3 Correct seasoning and consistency.
4 Finish with a liaison of yolks of egg and cream.
5 Add the garnish and serve.

Alternatively, for the health-conscious, omit the egg yolks and cream and finish with fromage frais, natural yogurt or quark.

295 Velouté Artois [to yield 1 litre (1 quart)]

250 ml (½ pt) purée
  haricot beans
50 ml (1 pt) chicken
  velouté (Recipe
  293a)
250 ml (½ pt) white
  stock (Recipe 6)

5 ml spoon [1
  teaspoon] blanched
  chervil leaves
30 g (1 oz) butter (or
  sunflower
  margarine)

120 ml (¼ pt) cream
  (or fromage frais,
  yogurt or quark)
30 g (1 oz) julienne
  of vegetables
seasoning

1 Mix haricot bean purée with the chicken velouté.
2 Simmer until the velouté is well flavoured with the beans.
3 Adjust consistency with the white stock.
4 Strain; blend in butter and cream.
5 Season, garnish with the cooked julienne and chervil leaves.

Note. To make haricot-bean purée, soak overnight in cold water 180 g (6 oz) haricot beans. Wash off and cook in a little stock until soft, then place in processor until purée.

296 Velouté Crécy [to yield 1 litre (1 quart)]

1.5 litre (1½ qt)
  chicken velouté
  (Recipe 293a)
125 ml (¼ pt) cream

bouquet garni
90 g (3 oz) butter (or
  sunflower
  margarine)

750 g (1½ lb) thinly
  sliced carrots
pinch sugar

1 Stew the carrots in 60 g (2 oz) butter and sugar until tender.
2 Melt the butter and add the flour to make a white roux.
3 Moisten with the chicken stock, add the sliced carrots and bouquet garni; boil, skim and simmer for 1 hour.
4 Remove bouquet garni, liquidize, reheat, adjust the seasoning, blend in the remaining butter, garnish with 30 g (1 oz) brunoise of cooked carrots and finish with cream.

297 Velouté Dame-Blanche [to yield 1 litre (1 quart)]

1 litre (1 qt) basic
  velouté de volaille
  (Recipe 293a)
15 g (½ oz) diced,
  cooked chicken

60 g (2 oz) butter (or
  sunflower
  margarine)
15 g (½ oz) pearl,
  Japanese sago or
  tapioca

18 chicken quenelles
  (Recipe 194)
125 ml (¼ pt) cream
  (or fromage frais,
  yogurt or quark)

1 Cook the pearls in a little consommé.
2 Add the pearls, diced, cooked chicken and quenelles to basic velouté.
3 Finish with cream and butter.

COLD SOUPS

298 Gazpacho – Chilled tomato, pimento and garlic soup [to yield 1 litre (1 quart)]

500 *ml* (1 *pt*) *tomato juice*	1 *clove of garlic*	1 *tbsp. lemon juice*
120 *g* (4 *oz*) *tomato concassé*	15 *g* (½ *oz*) *equal amounts chopped chive, parsley,*	*and/or wine vinegar*
120 *g* (4 *oz*) *cucumber, peeled and diced*	*chervil*	1 *tbsp. olive oil seasoning*
30 *g* (1 *oz*) *chopped pimento*	60 *g* (2 *oz*) *chopped Spanish onion*	*iced water*

1 Using cold bowls, crush and mix (or liquidize) the chervil, chives, garlic and parsley with salt and pepper from the mill.
2 Add the pimento, cucumber and tomato with a little iced water.
3 Beat the oil in slowly, alternating with vinegar and/or lemon juice.
4 Place in the cool to chill.
5 Correct the consistency with iced water, recheck seasoning and serve chilled (often in individual chilled soup bowls or plates). Garnish with a little finely sliced Spanish onion and cucumber.

Gazpacho is usually accompanied by a sauce boat of white breadcrumbs or trimmed pieces of white bread.

299 Vichyssoise or Crème Vichyssoise – Chive and potato soup [to yield 1 litre (1 quart)]

30 *g* (1 *oz*) *butter* (*or margarine or sunflower oil*)	125 *ml* (¼ *pt*) *cream* (*or fromage frais or natural yogurt*)
60 *g* (2 *oz*) *onion*	250 *ml* (½ *pt*) *milk*
½ *litre* (1 *pt*) *fond de volaille* (*chicken stock Recipe* 11)	*bouquet garni*
480 *g* (1 *lb*) *peeled potatoes*	60 *g* (2 *oz*) *white of leek*
finely chopped chives	*salt* (*about* ½ *tbsp.*)

1 Peel the onion. Thoroughly wash the leek.
2 Finely slice the onion and the white of leek [to yield 60 g (2 oz) sliced white of leek].
3 Melt the butter (or margarine) in a thick bottomed pan.
4 Add the onion and leek and cook for a few minutes with the lid on until just beginning to acquire colour.
5 Add the peeled, washed, sliced potatoes and bouquet garni.

6 Season. Simmer for approximately 30 minutes.
7 Remove the bouquet garni. Skim.
8 Liquidize the soup. (Rub through a very fine strainer if desired for finer finish.)
9 Return to a clean pan, add the milk, reboil, correct seasoning and consistency.
10 Finish with cream and garnish with chopped chives. Serve chilled.

299a Crème Vichyssoise à la Ritz

For this variant, replace 250 ml (½ pt) of the chicken stock in the Vichyssoise recipe with two tablespoons fine tomato concassé, made up to 250 ml (½ pt) with strained tomato juice.

299b Crème d'oseille glacé – Chilled cream of sorrel

Add 2 tablespoons of chopped sorrel, cooked without colouring butter to 1 litre (1 quart) Vichyssoise (Recipe 299).

4 Eggs, Pastas and Rice

EGGS, pastas or pâtes italiennes, and rice are linked together because traditionally they were prepared by the chef entremettier (vegetable cook) and still generally occupy a similar position on the menu as a preliminary course.

Pâtes italienne and rice are also used as a garnish or to accompany main dishes.

EGGS

Egg dishes are used as a preliminary course (like pâtes and rice) chiefly at luncheons, with the exception of omelettes. These are sometimes chosen by guests as main-course items for light luncheons and, of course, sweet omelettes (listed among the sweets in Chapter 8) may also be prepared by the entremettier in kitchens with large brigades. For easy reference, the styles in this section are listed alphabetically, and examples of cold egg dishes, normally prepared in the larder, are also included here.

300 Œufs brouillés – Scrambled eggs

1 Use a thick-bottomed saucepan.
2 For 3 eggs, melt 15 g (½ oz) butter in the pan.
3 Beat the eggs and season (some add a little milk, up to 2 tablespoons).
4 With the pan on the stove or over moderate heat, add eggs and stir constantly with a wooden spoon.
5 Avoid fierce heat, as this tends to coagulate the egg too much and too rapidly, thus forming lumps in the mixture.
6 Finish with 30 g (1 oz) butter and a 15 ml spoon [1 tablespoon] of cream.
7 The eggs, when cooked, should have a soft, creamy consistency.

301 Œufs brouillés aux cannelons

8 *eggs*	62 *ml* (⅛ *pt*) *cream*
4 *puff paste* (*Recipe* 994) *cornets*	*parsley*
60 *g* (2 *oz*) *butter*	

1 Make eggs as Recipe 300.
2 Fill cornets with the egg.
3 Arrange cornets on dish points inwards.
4 Garnish with parsley.

302 Œufs brouillés Aumale

8 eggs
120 g (¼ lb) diced
   tomatoes

120 g (¼ lb) diced
   kidney, sautéd and
   lié with Madeira
   sauce (Recipe 44)

60 g (2 oz) butter
   (or margarine)
62 ml (⅛ pt) cream

1 Cook eggs as for Recipe 300.
2 Mix tomatoes and kidney and use as garnish to top the mounded egg.

303 Œufs brouillés Yvette

8 eggs
62 ml (⅛ pt) cream
60 g (2 oz) butter

4 tartlet cases
8 asparagus tips (diced)
8 crayfish tails (diced)

4 slices truffle (see 4
  below)
62 ml (⅛ pt) Nantua
  sauce
  (Recipe 391)

1 Cook eggs as for Recipe 300.
2 Mix in asparagus and crayfish.
3 Place eggs in tartlet cases.
4 Top with slice of truffle (may be omitted owing to cost).
5 Cordon of sauce round the egg.

303a Piperade – Basque-style scrambled and garnished eggs

8 eggs beaten
570 g (1¼ lb) sliced onions
570 g (1¼ lb) tomato concassé
4 sliced red peppers (or equivalent
  in smaller green ones)

2 tbsp. olive oil or lard (pur porc
  fat), according to preference
pinch marjoram
salt, peppermill

1 Heat the oil in a sauté pan and cook the onions till gold (but not brown) colour.
2 Add the peppers and continue to cook till soft.
3 Add the tomatoes, cover the pan with lid and cook until nearly purée.
4 Add the beaten eggs and stir as for scrambled egg.
5 Often served with a thin slice of Bayonne ham.

304 Œufs durs – Hard-boiled eggs

Cook as for Œufs mollets (Recipe 313) but for 10 minutes cooking time. It is not necessary to specify œufs durs on menu, as the garnish denotes this fact.

305 Œufs à la tripe

4 hard-boiled eggs
250 ml (½ pt) cream sauce
  (Recipe 63)

60 g (2 oz) sliced onions
30 g (1 oz) butter
chopped parsley

1 Cook onions in butter without colouring.
2 Add onions to the sauce.

3 Heat eggs and slice into rounds.
4 Coat bottom of china dish with sauce.
5 Place eggs on top.
6 Coat eggs with sauce, sprinkle with chopped parsley and serve.

306 Œufs farcis Chimay

4 *hard-boiled eggs*	120 *g* (¼ *lb*) *duxelles*	250 *ml* (½ *pt*)
30 *g* (1 *oz*) *grated*	(*Recipe* 101)	*Mornay sauce*
cheese		(*Recipe* 58)

1 Halve each egg lengthwise.
2 Sieve yolks.
3 Mix yolks with duxelles and pipe into each half-egg.
4 Coat with mornay sauce.
5 Sprinkle with cheese and glaze in hot oven.

307 Scotch eggs

4 hard-*boiled eggs*	250 *g* (½ *lb*) *breadcrumbs*
500 *g* (1 *lb*) *savoury minced meat*	60 *g* (2 *oz*) *flour* (*seasoned*)
(*or sausage-meat*)	1 *egg for egg-wash*

1 Divide the meat into four portions.
2 Wrap meat round the floured egg.
3 Flour, egg-wash, and crumb each egg.
4 Fry in deep fat for 8 minutes.
5 Serve with fried parsley and tomato sauce (Recipe 34).

308 Œufs en cocotte – Eggs en cocotte (basic method)

Note. A special glazed earthenware cocotte is used, normally white inside, green or brown outside.

1 Heat and butter the cocotte.
2 Have ready a flat saucepan of hot water.
3 Break the egg into cocotte and season.
4 Lay cocotte in saucepan of hot water which should come only half-way up the cocotte.
5 Place saucepan on the stove and bring water to the boil.
6 Cover with a lid and draw to side of the stove.
7 Allow to simmer until the white of the egg is set and creamy and the yolk glossy.
8 Owing to condensation, it may be necessary to pour off water which may gather on top of the egg.

309 Œufs en cocotte à la bergère

1 *tablespoon melted*	30 *g* (1 *oz*) *butter* (*or*	60 *g* (2 *oz*) *minced*
meat glaze	*margarine*)	(*or finely diced*),
(*Recipe* 13)	60 *g* (2 *oz*) *sliced*	*cooked mutton*
4 *eggs*	*mushrooms cooked*	*lié with demi-glace*
	in butter	(*or well-reduced*
		stock)(*Recipe* 29)

1 Place garnish in bottom of cocotte.
2 Break eggs on top of garnish.
3 Cook eggs as Recipe 308.
4 Serve with cordon of meat glaze round the egg.

310 Œuf en cocotte à la reine

4 *eggs*
60 *g (2 oz) creamed, minced*
  chicken
60 *g (2 oz) butter*
62 *ml (⅛ pt) fresh cream*

1 Place chicken in bottom of cocotte.
2 Break eggs on top of chicken.
3 Cook eggs as described in Recipe 308.
4 Serve with cordon of cream on top of eggs.

311 Œuf en cocotte à la bordelaise

4 *eggs*
30 *g (1 oz) butter*
4 *slices poached beef-marrow*
125 *ml (¼ pt) sauce bordelaise*
  (Recipe 35)

1 Place slices of marrow in bottom of cocotte.
2 Break eggs on top of the marrow.
3 Cook eggs as Recipe 308.
4 Serve with cordon of sauce on top of eggs.

312 Œuf en cocotte Petit-Duc

4 *eggs*
45 *g (1½ oz) butter*
8 *asparagus tips cut in*
  half crosswise
125 *ml (¼ pt) sauce*
  Périgueux
  (Recipe 45)

1 Heat the asparagus in butter.
2 Garnish the bottom of cocotte with the asparagus.
3 Break eggs on top of the garnish and cook as Recipe 308.
4 Serve with cordon of sauce on top of the eggs.

313 Œufs mollets – Soft-boiled eggs

General points:
1 For mollet, the eggs are boiled sufficiently (3½ to 4½ minutes according to size) to set the whites leaving the yolks soft and creamy. The shell can thus be removed without breaking the egg.
2 Allow plenty of boiling water, roughly 750 ml (1½ pints) to two eggs, so that the water-temperature is only slightly lowered when the eggs are inserted. This allows quick return to boiling point and thus more accurate timing.
3 For large quantities of eggs use a wire basket in the boiling water. Convenient for insertion, this also ensures even cooking-time as they may be lifted out simultaneously.

4 When cooked, place the eggs immediately in a basin of cold running water until thoroughly cold. Shell the eggs carefully, taking care not to break them.
5 When required for use, reheat in salted hot water.

314 Œufs mollets Halévy

4 *eggs*
4 *tartlet cases*
125 *ml* (¼ *pt*) *tomato sauce*
  (*Recipe* 34)
2 *tomatoes concassé, hot*
10 *ml spoon* [½ *tablespoon*]
  melted meat glaze (*Recipe* 13)

15 *ml spoon* [1 *tablespoon*] *minced*
  (*or finely diced*), *creamed*
  chicken
125 *ml* (¼ *pt*) *suprême sauce*
  (*Recipe* 61)

1 Heat shelled, mollet eggs in hot water.
2 Garnish one half of the bottom of tartlet case with tomato and the other half with chicken-mix.
3 Place eggs on top of the garnish.
4 Coat one half of egg with tomato sauce.
5 Coat the other half with suprême sauce.
6 Divide the colours by means of a cordon of meat glaze.

315 Œufs mollets Argenteuil

250 *ml* (½ *pt*) *cream sauce* (*Recipe*
  65) *with purée of green*
  asparagus tips

4 *eggs*
4 *tartlet cases*
12 *asparagus tips*
30 *g* (1 *oz*) *butter*

1 Heat eggs in salted, hot water.
2 Place asparagus tips in buttered dish and heat in oven.
3 Garnish bottom of tartlets with asparagus tips.
4 Place eggs on top of garnish.
5 Coat eggs with cream sauce and serve very hot.

316 Œufs mollets à la florentine

4 *eggs*
4 *tartlet cases*
120 *g* (¼ *lb*) *cooked leaf spinach*
30 *g* (1 *oz*) *butter*

250 *ml* (½ *pt*) *Mornay sauce*
  (*Recipe* 58)
15 *g* (½ *oz*) *grated cheese*

1 Heat eggs in salted, hot water.
2 Melt butter in pan and heat seasoned spinach.
3 Place spinach in bottom of tartlet cases.
4 Place eggs on top of spinach.
5 Coat eggs with sauce.
6 Sprinkle cheese on sauce and glaze under salamander.

317 Œufs mollets Mornay

Ingredients and method are the same as florentine but without the spinach.

318 Œufs mollets à l'indienne

4 *eggs*	250 *ml* (½ *pt*) *curry*	30 *g* (1 *oz*) *boiled*
4 *tartlet cases*	*sauce* (*Recipe* 32 *but*	*rice*
	strained)	

1 Heat eggs in hot, salted water.
2 Heat rice and dry.
3 Place rice in bottom of tartlets.
4 Place egg on top of rice.
5 Coat egg with curry sauce.

319 Œufs pochés – Poached eggs

General points:
1 Have ready a sauté-pan, containing salted water, acidulated with vinegar [1 teaspoon vinegar per 250 ml (½ pint) water].
2 Bring water to the boil and break eggs, one at a time, over the water when it is boiling.
3 Allow to simmer. The white should envelop the yolk completely, taking the shape of the raw egg.
4 Cook for 3 minutes.
5 Trim ragged edges before serving.
6 To remove taste of vinegar, place eggs in a separate pan of hot, salted water.

Garnishes for œufs mollets may be applied to œufs pochés.

320 Œufs pochés Bénédictine – Poached eggs Bénédictine

4 *poached eggs*	90 *g* (3 *oz*) *York ham*
2 *muffins, halved, toasted and*	4 *tbsp. Hollandaise sauce*
buttered	(*Recipe* 70)

1 On the split, freshly toasted muffin place an equal-sized roundel of York (or Virginia) ham.
2 Lay on the poached egg.
3 Coat each with Hollandaise sauce.

Note. The above version, popularized in the USA, is now the most common, but the French serve this dish with poached eggs laid on truffle-garnished brandade (salt cod paste) and coated with cream sauce, or, similarly coated, in a tartlet case or on a croûton.

321 Œufs sur le plat – Oven-baked buttered eggs

General points:
1 For this a special china fireproof dish is used. There are two sizes. The smaller for one egg, the larger to hold two.

2 Place dish on top of stove and add a piece of butter.
3 Allow to melt, just simmer slightly. Use enough butter just to cover the bottom of the dish.
4 Add the egg carefully, seasoned with salt and pepper and allow to set slightly on the bottom. Then place in the oven to finish cooking.
5 The white should be just set and the yolk glossy.
6 Garnish is placed on the white part of the egg and if sauce is required, a cordon is placed round the egg. In some cases the garnish is placed directly in the dish, then the egg is added on top. Cook in the usual manner.

322 Œufs sur le plat Bercy

4 *eggs*
4 *grilled chipolata sausages*

125 *ml* (¼ *pt*) *tomato sauce*
  (*Recipe* 34)
30 *g* (1 *oz*) *butter*

1 Cook the eggs as Recipe 321.
2 Garnish with sausage.
3 Cordon with tomato sauce.

323 Œufs sur le plat chasseur

4 *eggs*
60 *g* (2 *oz*) *chicken's liver*

62 *ml* (⅛ *pt*) *chasseur sauce*
  (*Recipe* 38)
30 *g* (1 *oz*) *butter*

1 Cook eggs as Recipe 321.
2 Sauté livers and cohere with chasseur sauce.
3 Garnish egg with livers and cordon of sauce.

324 Œufs sur le plat Cluny

4 *eggs*
125 *ml* (¼ *pt*) *tomato sauce*
  (*Recipe* 34)

4 *small* 3 *cm* (1½ *in*) *long chicken-croquettes* (*Recipe* 725, *using chicken instead of beef*)

1 Cook eggs as Recipe 321.
2 Garnish with chicken croquettes.
3 Finish with cordon of tomato sauce.

325 Œufs sur le plat Omar-Pasha

4 *eggs*
30 *g* (1 *oz*) *butter*

30 *g* (1 *oz*) *grated*
  Parmesan cheese

60 *g* (2 *oz*) *finely*
  chopped onions

1 Sweat the onions in butter and place in buttered egg-dish.
2 Break eggs over the onions.
3 Sprinkle cheese on the eggs.
4 Cook in hot oven until slight gratin forms.

326 Œufs sur le plat Meyerbeer

4 *eggs*	125 *ml* (¼ *pt*) *sauce*	30 *g* (1 *oz*) *butter*
4 *lambs' kidneys*	*Périgueux*	
	(*Recipe* 45)	

1 Cook eggs as Recipe 321.
2 Garnish with grilled kidney.
3 Coat kidney with sauce and cordon of sauce round the egg.

327 Œufs sur le plat miroir

4 *eggs*	30 *g* (1 *oz*) *butter*	62 *ml* (⅛ *pt*) *cream*

1 Place eggs in dish and cover with cream.
2 Then cook as Recipe 321.

OMELETTES

General points:
(i)   To be successful, use the omelette pan only for making omelettes.
(ii)   A new pan may be 'seasoned' by half-filling it with oil. Heat on the stove, and allow it to lie warm for two hours.
(iii) After use, wipe the pan with a dry cloth or paper. On no account should water be used for cleaning.

Omelettes fourrées
These are omelettes with a filling or an interior garnish. Otherwise the garnish or flavouring is added to the egg (e.g. fines herbes).

Sweet omelettes
In a large kitchen brigade, sweet omelettes are made (as are all omelettes) by the chef entreméttier. (For sweet omelettes, see Chapter 8.)

Flat omelettes
Most omelettes are oval plump shapes (see Recipe 336) but Spanish omelette and similar kinds are prepared flat and round to cover the plate.

328 Omelette nature – Plain omelette

1 For each à la carte omelette, place 3 eggs (2 for table d'hôte service) in a bowl; season with salt and pepper.
2 Place pan on stove with oil or butter and heat. Pour off any surplus before adding the eggs.
3 Beat eggs in the bowl with a fork just sufficiently to incorporate yolks with the white.
4 Pour eggs into pan and shake briskly using a rotary movement. The fork may be used to loosen any egg which may stick to the sides of the pan.
5 Now loosen all round edges and fold side nearest into centre. Tap the handle sharply and the further side will come over the edge of the pan. Fold this into the centre.

6 Tilt the pan and turn out the completed omelette.

7 The degree of cooking depends on customer's requirements; 'baveuse' means very soft and sloppy inside.

8 When dished, omelettes may be brushed with melted butter to enhance appearance.

329 Omelette aux fines herbes

Prepare as plain omelette with the addition of chopped parsley.

330 Omelette à la turque (Omelette aux foies de volaille) – Chicken liver omelette (4 portions)

120 g (4 oz) trimmed chicken livers	125 ml (¼ pt) jus lié (Recipe 30) or reduced brown stock
30 g (1 oz) butter (or sunflower margarine)	seasoning chopped parsley

1 Prepare a basic folded omelette (Recipe 328).
2 Cut an incision down the centre.
3 Cut the liver into neat dice or slices, season.
4 Fry quickly in the butter or margarine. Drain.
5 Bind with the jus lié or reduced stock.
6 Place a spoonful in the omelette where the incision has been made. Sprinkle with chopped parsley.

331 Omelette à l'andalouse (fourrée)

8 eggs	60 g (2 oz) butter	250 g (½ lb) onions sliced in rings
125 g (¼ lb) diced pimentos	125 g (¼ lb) diced tomatoes	

1 Heat tomatoes and pimentos in butter.
2 Divide garnish into four.
3 Make separate omelettes and fill with garnish.
4 Dish and surround omelette with fried onion rings (oignons frits à la française, Recipe 871).

332 Omelette aux champignons – Mushroom omelette

8 eggs	250 g (½ lb) sliced mushrooms cooked in butter
60 g (2 oz) butter	

1 Heat mushrooms in pan.
2 Pour in eggs and make omelette.
3 May be decorated with turned mushroom on top.

333 Omelette aux rognons – Kidney omelette

2 sheep's kidneys	125 ml (¼ pt) jus lié (Recipe 30) or reduced brown stock
30 g (1 oz) butter (or sunflower margarine)	chopped parsley
seasoning	

1 Skin the kidneys, remove the gristle and cut into small dice. Season.
2 Quickly fry in the butter or margarine for 2–3 minutes, drain and discard the liquid.
3 Bind with the jus lié (or reduced stock).
4 Make the basic omelette (Recipe 328) with an incision in the top, fill with the kidneys. Sprinkle with chopped parsley. Serve.

334 Omelette au parmesan – Parmesan-cheese omelette

8 *eggs*   60 *g (2 oz) grated Parmesan cheese*
60 *g (2 oz) butter (or margarine)*

1 Add Parmesan cheese to eggs; cook omelette.
2 Sprinkle cheese on top.

Note. Cheese omelettes using other varieties of cheese may be similarly prepared.

335 Omelette aux pointes d'asperges (fourrée) – Asparagus-tip omelette

8 *eggs*	12 *asparagus tips*	60 *g (2 oz) butter*
6 *diced asparagus-tips*	*heated in butter (or margarine)*	*(or sunflower margarine)*

1 Mix diced tips with eggs.
2 Make omelette in usual manner.
3 Cut omelette lengthwise.
4 Fill cavity with tips.

336 Omelette Clamart (fourrée)

250 *g (½ lb) petits pois à la*   60 *g (2 oz) butter (or sunflower*
française (Recipe 882)   *margarine)*
8 *eggs*

1 Make omelette as described in Recipe 328.
2 Before folding fill with some peas.
3 Dish and make a cavity lengthwise in omelette.
4 Fill cavity with remaining peas.

337 Omelette espagnole – Spanish omelette

To the basic egg mixture (Recipe 328) add:

30 *g (1 oz) tomato concassé*   7 *g (¼ oz) pimento julienne*
30 *g (1 oz) sliced onions cooked in*   *pinch of chopped parsley*
butter (or sunflower margarine)
or olive oil without colouring

Cook and serve flat.

Note. Some add garlic and vary the garnish to include, for example, cooked peas and potato.

338 Omelette lyonnaise – Onion omelette

8 *eggs*	125 *g* (¼ *lb*) *sauté onions*
60 *g* (2 *oz*) *butter*	*seasoning*

Heat onions in pan and add beaten eggs, and make omelette as Recipe 328.

339 Omelette Parmentier – Potato omelette

8 *eggs*	180 *g* (6 *oz*) *diced*	*chopped parsley*
60 *g* (2 *oz*) *butter*	*potatoes, 0.5 cm*	
	cubes, cooked in	
	butter	

1 Add parsley to eggs.
2 Add potatoes to eggs in pan.
3 Finish and dish in usual fashion (Recipe 328).

340 Omelette à la paysanne

8 *eggs*	250 *g* (½ *lb*) *breast of bacon diced*
180 *g* (6 *oz*) *diced potatoes cooked*	*and cooked*
in butter	60 *g* (2 *oz*) *shredded sorrel stewed*
	in butter

Prepare as flat omelette (Recipe 337).

COLD EGGS

Examples of dishes are listed below but note the following general points for preparing cold eggs, particularly poached eggs:

(i)   Drain eggs well and trim.
(ii) Coat well with sauce.
(iii) Decorate finely.
(iv) Have aspic nearly at setting point when glazing.
(v)   Use the appropriate type of aspic.

341 Œufs à la russe

4 *hard-boiled eggs*	30 *g* (1 *oz*) *butter*	62 *ml* (⅛ *pt*)
250 *ml* (½ *pt*) *aspic*	125 *g* (¼ *lb*) *Russian*	*mayonnaise*
(*Recipe* 122)	*salad* (*Recipe* 183)	(*Recipe* 110)

1 Slit the eggs lengthwise.
2 Remove and pass yolks through sieve, mix with the butter, and season.
3 Pipe (using star tube) the yolk mixture into the egg whites.
4 Decorate and glaze with aspic.
5 Cohere some Russian salad with aspic and mayonnaise and set in a fancy mould.
6 When the mould is set, place on a round flat dish and garnish with the stuffed eggs.

342 Œufs pochés à la niçoise

4 *poached eggs*	250 *ml* (½ *pt*) *aspic*	90 *g* (3 *oz*) *cooked,*
125 *ml* (¼ *pt*)	(*Recipe* 122)	*diced French*
mayonnaise	4 *croustades*	*beans*
(*Recipe* 110)	(*Recipe* 189)	90 *g* (3 *oz*) *small,*
62 *ml* (⅛ *pt*) *cold*		*diced potatoes*
tomato sauce		0.5 *cm cubes*
(*Recipe* 34)		

1 Mix the tomato sauce and mayonnaise.
2 Cohere sauce with 62 ml (⅛ pint) aspic jelly at setting point.
3 Mix the French beans and potatoes with the sauce and leave a spoonful at the bottom of each croustade.
4 Coat each egg with the sauce and decorate and coat with aspic.
5 Place each egg on a garnished croustade.

343 Œufs moscovites

4 *hard-boiled eggs*	250 *ml* (½ *pt*) *aspic*	30 *g* (1 *oz*) *caviar*
8 *anchovy fillets*	(*Recipe* 123)	[*or* 30 *g* (1 *oz*)
4 *artichoke bottoms*		*lump fish-roe*]

1 Cut both ends off the eggs to imitate barrels.
2 Remove the centre with a round cutter.
3 Surround the top and base with anchovy fillets to resemble iron hoops.
4 Fill the centre with caviar.
5 Place each egg on artichoke bottoms and glaze with aspic.

PÂTES ITALIENNES AND NOODLES

Dry pâtes
Pastas, from past'asciutta – dry pasta, are used in Italy, their country of origin as a preliminary course to a meal, normally luncheon.

Besides the familiar spaghetti and macaroni there are many shapes and sizes, from the thread-like spaghettini (even finer than vermicelli) to zite – the fatter hollow tube which is larger than macaroni. Some of the tubes are grooved like millerighe, or grooved and curved like maniche. For fettucini, a strip pasta similar to nouille is used. Lasagne is a broader, crinkle-edged flat, ribbon pasta; lasagne matassa has a bundle shape. These are but a few; there are many more pastas including shell, ribbon, bow, and wheel shapes, and so on.

Basically, all these varieties are prepared in a similar way – in boiling water – followed by the appropriate dressing of sauce, grated cheese, butter, and so on.

Fresh pâtes
In addition there are fresh pastas (nouille types as distinct from dry) of which canneloni, ravioli, tagliatelle, tortellini are familiar examples. Lasagne and similar varieties are also made fresh.

Noodles – nouilles
Nouilles, the French term for noodles, are long fresh pâte strips. These and other pâtes were used in Chinese cuisine before they were introduced to the western world.

General rules for cooking pâtes Italiennes
(i)   Have a large pan with plenty of fast-boiling salted water.
(ii) Add pâtes only when water boils rapidly and stir immediately to prevent cohesion.
(iii) While cooking may be hastened by covering the pan, adjust heat to avoid boiling over.
(iv) Strain immediately after cooking.

Modes for preparing spaghetti, macaroni and other Italian pastes are interchangeable. In addition to the sauces for dressing pâtes referred to in the recipes below, include Chasseur (Recipe 38), Lyonnaise (Recipe 43), and meat and chicken sauces generally.

MACARONI, NOODLES, AND SPAGHETTI

344 Macaroni au gratin

250 ml (½ pt) Mornay sauce (Recipe 58) little grated nutmeg	180 g (6 oz) macaroni 30 g (1 oz) grated Parmesan cheese	21 g (¾ oz) butter (or olive oil) seasoning

1 Boil macaroni for 20 minutes in plenty of fast-boiling salted water and drain.
2 Toss in butter (or oil) and season.
3 Mix with Mornay sauce.
4 Sprinkle with cheese and gratin.

345 Macaroni à la italienne

180 g (6 oz) macaroni 62 ml (⅛ pt) cream 30 g (1 oz) Parmesan cheese	a little crushed and chopped garlic 21 g (¾ oz) butter (or olive oil) salt

1 Boil macaroni for 20 minutes in plenty of fast-boiling salted water.
2 Drain and toss in butter (or oil) with a little garlic, and season.
3 Stir in the cream and add a little cheese.
4 Serve the remainder of the cheese separately.

346 Macaroni à la napolitaine

125 ml (¼ pt) tomato sauce (Recipe 34) 30 g (1 oz) grated Parmesan cheese	a little garlic, crushed and chopped seasoning 180 g (6 oz) macaroni	62 ml (⅛ pt) cream 120 g (¼ lb) tomato concassé 21 g (¾ oz) butter (or olive oil)

1 Boil macaroni as Recipe 344.
2 Drain and toss in butter (or oil) with garlic and seasoning.
3 Add tomato concassé, half the cheese, and mix in the cream and seasoning.
4 Serve with a cordon of tomato sauce, but serve cheese separately.

Note. For à la carte service, plain macaroni is often sent to the dining-room with tomato concassé, tomato sauce and grated cheese served separately and placed before the guest.

347 Nouilles au beurre – Noodles with butter

250 g (½ lb) sifted flour	*4 yolks*
1 whole egg	*30 g (1 oz) milk*
15 ml spoon [1 dessertspoonful]	*1.25 ml spoon [¼ teaspoon] salt*
olive oil	

1 Sift flour and salt.
2 Make a bay and add all remaining ingredients.
3 Mix to a smooth dough.
4 Roll out in 2 thin pieces of 6 × 25 cm (3 by 12 inches) and let paste rest for 3 hours.
5 To cook cut into thin strips of 3 mm (⅛-inch) wide.
6 Cook in plenty of boiling salted water for 18 minutes.
7 Drain, toss in butter.

Note. Noodles may also be served like pastas in styles such as Milanaise, Napolitaine, Niçoise, etc., or as a garnish (with, for example, Hungarian goulash).

348 Nouilles à la niçoise

180 g (6 oz) nouilles	*a little crushed chopped*	*15 g (½ oz) grated*
(Recipe 347)	*garlic*	*Parmesan cheese*
30 g (1 oz) thinly sliced	*125 g (¼ lb) tomato*	*seasoning*
onion	*concassé*	
30 ml (1⁄16 pt) olive oil		

1 Boil and drain nouilles (Recipe 347).
2 Fry off the onions in oil. Add tomato concassé and garlic.
3 Add the nouilles, season, and add cheese.

349 Spaghetti au parmesan

180 g (6 oz) spaghetti	*30 g (1 oz) grated*	*60 g (2 oz) butter*
(unbroken)	*Parmesan cheese*	*seasoning*

1 Cook spaghetti in plenty of fast-boiling water for 18 minutes.
2 Drain well and toss in butter; season and mix in Parmesan cheese.

350 Spaghetti bolognese

30 g (1 oz) finely
   chopped shallots
1 clove chopped garlic
100 g (4 oz) tomato
   concassé

Sauce
125 g (¼ lb) finely
   chopped fillet-beef
62 ml ((⅛ pt) jus lié (or
   reduced stock)
   (Recipe 30)

62 ml (⅛ pt) tomato
   sauce (Recipe 34)
30 g (1 oz) butter
   (or olive oil)
seasoning

1 Fry off the shallots in butter.
2 Add the meat and brown.
3 Add the tomato concassé and garlic.
4 Moisten with the tomato sauce and demi-glace.
5 Simmer until the meat is cooked, and season.

Note. The sauce may be served separately or in the centre of the spaghetti. (For guéridon (side-table) service one sauceboat of tomato concassé and another of sauce may be sent to the restaurant for combining with the pasta at table.) Macaroni, ravioli and noodles can be served in the same way.

351 Spaghetti à la milanaise

180 g (6 oz) long spaghetti
15 g (½ oz) julienne ham
7 g (¼ oz) julienne truffles

15 g (½ oz) julienne tongue
15 g (½ oz) julienne cooked
   mushrooms

Prepare as napolitaine (Recipe 346) plus the julienne of ham, tongue, mushroom and truffles.

CANNELONI AND RAVIOLI

352 Canneloni à l'italienne

ravioli pasta (Recipe 353)
filling italienne (Recipe 355)
125 ml (¼ pt) jus lié (Recipe 30)

30 g (1 oz) butter or olive oil
30 g (1 oz) Parmesan

1 Cut the ravioli paste in squares 6 cm × 6 cm (3 by 3 inches).
2 Cook the paste for 18 minutes.
3 Drain – spread on the stuffing and roll.
4 Butter a dish well, place the canneloni on it and pour on the jus lié; sprinkle with cheese.
5 Bake in moderate oven for 10 minutes.

353 Pâte à ravioli – Ravioli pasta

250 g (½ lb) flour
37 g (1¼ oz) oil

1.25 ml spoon [¼ teaspoon] salt
95 ml (3¾ fluid oz) water

1 Sift flour and salt.
2 Make pliable dough with the oil and water.
3 Divide into halves and roll out into 2 very thin oblongs of paste.

FILLINGS FOR RAVIOLI AND CANNELONI

354 Florentine filling

30 g (1 oz) finely chopped shallots *1 egg yolk*	*250 g (½ lb) chopped spinach* *seasoning*	*1 crushed clove of garlic*

Mix all the ingredients and season.

355 Italienne filling

90 g (3 oz) braised beef *pinch of mixed herbs* *30 g (1 oz) cooked brains (optional)*	*125 g (¼ lb) chopped cooked spinach* *seasoning*	*1 chopped garlic clove* *1 egg yolk*

Mix all the ingredients and season.

RAVIOLIS

356 Ravioli à la florentine

Paste and filling as Recipes 353 and 354	*250 ml (½ pt) thin Mornay sauce (Recipe 58)*	*30 g (1 oz) butter* *30 g (1 oz) grated Parmesan cheese*

1 Cook, drain, toss in butter or olive oil.
2 Coat with Mornay sauce.
3 Sprinkle with cheese and brown.

357 Ravioli à l'italienne

125 ml (¼ pt) tomato sauce *30 g (1 oz) Parmesan cheese*	*30 g (1 oz) butter* *Paste and filling (Recipes 353 and 355)*

1 Having prepared the paste, lay one thin sheet of paste on marble slab.
2 Use a plain tube and pipe the garnish 2 cm (1 inch) apart in rows.
3 Egg-wash in between each piece and garnish.
4 Lay the other sheet of paste evenly on top.
5 Cut between each piece of garnish with the rotella or small round cutter.
6 Cook in boiling, salted water for 15 minutes; drain, toss in butter, coat with tomato sauce, sprinkle with Parmesan cheese and brown.

GNOCCCHI AND POLENTA

Gnocchi (noques, the French term, is sometimes used) are, in effect, tiny dumplings and come from the Italian cuisine. They are usually made either from semolina (the hard grains of wheat remaining in the sieve after milling) or from a potato and flour mix. French chefs make a paste that is virtually the same as choux paste (Gnocchi Parisienne, Recipe 358). Egg is normally the binding agent for all types though potato gnocchi may be made without it. These basic gnocchi are known as Romaine (semolina); Piedmontaise (potatoes and flour); Parisienne (water and flour and eggs – a choux paste).

Polenta is similar to semolina (Romaine) gnocchi but made with water instead of milk. Let it harden, cut into wedges and fry with garlic and onions. In some parts maize or buckwheat flour or semolina is boiled in saffron water and served in wedges from the plainly-boiled mass. In Corsica, a kind of Polenta is made with chestnut flour.

358 Gnocchi à la pariesienne – Paris style (basic choux type)

75 g (2½ oz) flour	2 eggs	125 ml (¼ pt) water
15 g (½ oz) grated	250 ml (½ pt) thin	60 g (2 oz) butter
Parmesan cheese	Mornay sauce	pinch salt
	(Recipe 58)	

1 Melt butter in water.
2 Boil – rain in flour with salt and mix to a smooth paste.
3 Cool; blend in eggs one at a time.
4 Place paste in savoy bag with plain tube.
5 Pipe into boiling salted water using a wet knife to cut into small pieces during the piping process.
6 Poach gently for 10 minutes; drain, sauté lightly in butter and season.
7 Cover with Mornay sauce; sprinkle with cheese and gratinate.

Note. Spatzelli, a Swiss species, is prepared in the same way as Gnocchi Parisienne except that a small plain tube is used. Spatzelli is used as a garnish for Hungarian goulash.

359 Gnocchi à la piedmontaise – Piedmont style (basic potato gnocchi)

250 g (½ lb) potato	30 g (1 oz) butter	1 egg yolk
125 g (¼ lb) cooked	15 g (½ oz) flour	15 g (½ oz)
chicken purée	seasoning	Parmesan cheese

1 Dry-mash the potatoes.
2 Mix with chicken purée and flour.
3 Bind with egg yolks and season.
4 Roll on a fork.
5 Poach in boiling salted water for 5 minutes.
6 Toss in butter, sprinkle with Parmesan cheese.

Tomato sauce (Recipe 34) may be served.

360 Gnocchi à la romaine – Roman style (basic semolina gnocchi)

500 ml (1 pt) milk	1 clove crushed garlic	15 g (½ oz) grated
45 g (1½ oz) butter	a little grated nutmeg	cheese (Parmesan
250 ml (½ pt) Mornay	180 g (6 oz) semolina	and Gruyère)
sauce (Recipe 58)	1 egg yolk	1.25 ml spoon [¼
		teaspoon] salt

1 Boil milk with the garlic, salt and nutmeg.
2 Rain in the semolina and mix smoothly.
3 Cook on the side of stove for about 12 minutes.
4 Cool slightly and beat in egg yolks.
5 Turn out on a greased dish 1 cm (½ inch) thick.
6 Allow to go cold and cut into crescent shapes with a 3-inch cutter.
7 Sauté lightly in butter, cover with sauce, sprinkle with Parmesan cheese and brown.

Note. Tomato sauce (Recipe 34) may be used in place of Mornay.

361 Gnocchi à l'italienne

500 g (1 lb) potatoes	*30 g (1 oz) Parmesan cheese*
15 g (½ oz) flour	*seasoning*
1 egg yolk	

1 Dry-mash potatoes.
2 Season and bind with egg yolks and flour.
3 Allow to go cold, roll on a fork 2 cm (1 inch) long.
4 Poach gently in boiling salt water for 4 minutes.
5 Drain and sauté in butter; season and sprinkle with Parmesan cheese, and gratinate.

Note. Other well-known styles of gnocchi are Florentine (potato, egg, and flour gnocchi with spinach and cooked ham); and Valdostana (also a potato, egg, and flour type with butter and Parmesan cheese).

RICE

Rice, and rice dishes belong to the same category on menus as Italian pastas.

General rules for cooking rice:
(i)   Clean thoroughly without washing, picking out any impurities by hand.
(ii) Cook in large, open saucepan with plenty of free boiling water.
(iii) Add rice gradually to the boiling water.
(iv) Refresh and strain immediately the rice is cooked.

Types of rice
Those most frequently used in the kitchen are:

(i)   Patna – Long-grained for Indian pilaffs.
(ii) Piedmont – Italian rice for risotto dishes.
(iii) Carolina – Sweet dishes: very white, soft-cooked.
(iv) Rice flour – Milled from broken grains.

Patna and Piedmont rice are used for boiling (including pilaff and risotto dishes) and served with savoury dishes; they are also used to garnish soup. Carolina rice is largely confined to sweet cookery.
    The different types are judged by their origin, shape, size, colour, and the shine of the grains of rice. A top-quality rice can be recognized by the large-sized grains and their glossy and transparent appearance. Good grains

should not boil to pieces within 20 minutes but cheap kinds cook floury-white and quickly boil away. Using the best and most suitable types, approximate cooking times range from 12 minutes (for boiling 'al dente' or firm 'to the teeth') to 15 minutes for soup garnish and risotto, and to 18 to 20 minutes for pilaff. Sweet-milk rice is usually boiled softly (from 25 minutes to 30 minutes).

362 Riz nature – Plain boiled rice

180 g (6 oz) *Patna or Piedmont*   2.5 *litre* (½ gallon) *water*
   rice   *salt*

1 Cook for 18 minutes in boiling salt water (according to general rules above).
2 Refresh and drain.

Note. See Riz indienne, Recipe 365.

363 Riz créole

45 g (1½ oz) *tomato concassé*   30 g (1 oz) *sliced cooked*
15 g (½ oz) *diced pimentos*   *mushrooms*

Add to the basic pilaff (Recipe 366) all the above as garnish.

364 Riz à l'égyptienne

30 g (1 oz) *diced*   30 g (1 oz) *diced fried*   30 g (1 oz) *cooked*
  cooked mushrooms   *chicken's liver*   *ham*

Mix all the ingredients and add to the basic rice pilaff (Recipe 366).

365 Riz à l'indienne

180 g (6 oz) *Patna rice*

1 Cook for 15 minutes in 2.5 litre (½ gallon) of boiling salt water.
2 Strain and dry on a serviette.
3 Keep warm in the oven.

PILAFF AND RISOTTO

The difference between a pilaff and risotto is that in the former grains are firmer and well separated whereas a risotto has softer grains and denser mass.

366 Riz pilaff – Pilaff (alternative spellings: Pilau, Pillaw)

45 g (1½ oz) *finely chopped*   60 g (2 oz) *butter (or sunflower*
  onions   *margarine)*
fonds blanc (white stock) twice the   1 *small bouquet garni*
  volume of rice   375 *ml* (¾ *pt) white stock*
180 g (6 oz) *Patna rice*   *(Recipe 6) or fish stock when pilaff*
                                   accompanies fish

1 Sweat the onions in 30 g (1 oz) butter (or alternative).
2 Add the rice and sweat for 2 or 3 minutes.
3 Moisten with twice the volume of boiling stock, season lightly.
4 Add bouquet garni; boil and cover with greased paper.
5 Place lid on top and cook in moderate oven 150°C (300°F) for 18 to 20
  minutes (when all stock will have been absorbed).
6 Remove bouquet garni, adjust seasoning and fork-in 30 g (1 oz) of butter.

Note. All grains of rice must be separate.

367 Rizotto – Riz italienne (Rice, Italian style)

180 g (6 oz) Piedmont rice	30 g (1 oz) finely chopped onions	1 small bouquet garni
500 ml (1 pt) fonds blanc (white stock) (Recipe 6)	30 g (1 oz) butter (or sunflower margarine)	15 g (½ oz) grated Parmesan cheese

1 Sweat the onions in butter (or alternative).
2 Wash the rice, and sweat for 2 or 3 minutes.
3 Add bouquet garni and 500 ml (1 pint) stock.
4 Add a little salt, boil and draw to the side of the stove and simmer till very
  soft and all stock has evaporated; stir frequently with wooden spatula.
5 When cooked, fork in 15 g (½ oz) of grated Parmesan cheese.

368 Rizotto à la milanaise

180 g (6 oz) Piedmont rice	30 g (1 oz) butter (or sunflower margarine)
15 g (½ oz) sliced raw mushrooms	1 small bouquet garni
500 ml (1 pt) fonds blanc (Recipe 6)	pinch saffron
30 g (1 oz) finely chopped onions	15 g (½ oz) grated Parmesan cheese
60 g (2 oz) tomato concassé	

Cook rice as Recipe 367 but infuse the saffron with a little boiling water and
add the infused liquor during the cooking together with mushrooms and
tomato concassé.

369 Rizotto à la piémontaise

15 g (½ oz) diced pimentos	7 g (¼ oz) diced truffle (optional)	15 g (½ oz) sliced, raw mushrooms

As Recipe 367, garnished with the additional ingredients. If using fresh
pimentos stew in 30 g (1 oz) of butter till tender.

5 Fish

FISH cookery (apart from the fish preparation and cold dishes of the garde manger) was, in traditional kitchens, separated from other sections and under the control of the chef poissonnier, or fish cook. Fish dishes must also be created from culinary basics or fonds de cuisine and, in many instances, from sauces containing fish or sauces specially created to accompany fish. Therefore, this section begins with the fonds de cuisine, sauces, and mise-en-place for fish cookery.

BASIC PREPARATIONS

Court-bouillon. If the delicate flavours of fish are to be preserved and enhanced, the liquor in which they are poached should be prepared with care so as to match the fish to the sauce with which it will be dressed. This liquor is called a court-bouillon and is a dilution of water with either vinegar, white or red wine with aromatics and flavouring. Also used as a fish poaching-liquor, bouillon au lait, or milk stock, is a simple dilution of milk and salted water in roughly, equal parts, particularly when white fish is prepared in 'light' style or for invalids.

When fish is actually presented 'au-court-bouillon' then care must be taken to ensure that vegetable ingredients are attractive and intact: for example, for onions use button onions, and carrots should appear in neatly sliced roundels.

370 Court-bouillon blanc – White court-bouillon

2 *litre* (2 *qt*) *water*	1 *sliced onion*	250 *ml* (½ *pt*) *milk*
1 *bay-leaf*	*juice of* 1 *lemon*	1 *teaspoon salt*
30 *g* (1 *oz*) *parsley stalk*	6 *peppercorns*	

1 Boil and simmer ingredients together for 10 minutes.
2 Strain and use for plainly boiled white fish.

371 Court-bouillon ordinaire – Ordinary court-bouillon

5 *litre* (5 *qt*) *water*	60 *g* (2 *oz*) *salt*
375 *ml* (¾ *pt*) *malt vinegar*	60 *g* (2 *oz*) *parsley stalks*
24 *ground peppercorns*	1 *sprig thyme*
360 *g* (¾ *lb*) *carrots*	2 *bay-leaves*
500 *g* (1 *lb*) *onions*	

1 Slice the onions and carrots thinly.
2 Place the vegetables and the rest of the ingredients in the water.
3 Simmer for 20 minutes.
4 Strain and use as required.

Used for lobster, shellfish, trout and salmon.

372 Court-bouillon au vin blanc – White wine court-bouillon

500 *ml* (1 *pt*) *dry, white wine*   7 *g* (¼ *oz*) *salt*
500 *ml* (1 *pt*) *boiled water*   6 *peppercorns*
60 *g* (2 *oz*) *sliced onions*   30 *g* (1 *oz*) *thinly-sliced carrots*
1 *bouquet garni*

1 Allow the boiled water to cool before using.
2 Add ingredients, bring to the boil and simmer for ½ hour.
3 Strain through muslin or fine strainer.

Used for fresh-water fish and white fish.

373 Court-bouillon au vin rouge – Red wine court-bouillon

50 *ml* (1 *pt*) *red wine*   1 *bouquet garni*   6 *peppercorns*
500 *ml* (1 *pt*) *water*   15 *g* (½ *oz*) *parsley*   60 *g* (2 *oz*) *thinly-*
60 *g* (2 *oz*) *sliced*   *stalks*   *sliced carrots*
   onions   7 *g* (¼ *oz*) *salt*

1 Use boiled, cooled water.
2 Boil and simmer all ingredients for ½ hour.
3 Strain through muslin or fine strainer.

Used for fresh-water fish.

FISH STOCK AND BASICS

Stock, essence, glaze, and velouté are as essential for the preparation of fish dishes as are the fonds or basics listed in Chapter 1 for other types of dishes.

374 Fumet de poisson – Fish stock [to yield 10 litres (2 gallons)]

5 *kg* (10 *lb*) *white*   150 *g* (5 *oz*) *parsley*   1 *bouquet garni*
   fish-bones and   *including stalks*   240 *g* (½ *lb*) *butter*
   trimmings   750 *g* (1½ *lb*) *sliced*   10 *litre* (10 *qt*) *cold*
1 *lemon*   *onions*   *water*

1 Butter the bottom of a saucepan.
2 Place in sliced onions and washed parsley.
3 Lay the fish-bones and trimmings (preferably of sole, whiting or turbot) on these aromatics and squeeze over the juice of 1 lemon.
4 Cover saucepan and allow to sweat.
5 Pour over the cold water.
6 Bring to the boil, skim, and simmer for 20 minutes.
7 Strain through muslin or fine strainer.

375 Essence de poisson – Fish essence

Reduce fumet de poisson (Recipe 374) by open boiling and evaporating by one-half.

376 Glace de poisson – Fish glaze

1 Reduce 8 litres (8 quarts) fumet de poisson or 4 litres (4 quarts) essence de poisson (Recipes 374 and 375) to 250 ml (½ pint).
2 Pour into jars when still hot; the fish glaze should be of a thick syrupy consistency.

377 Velouté de poisson – Fish velouté [to yield 1 litre (1 quart)]

120 g (4 oz) flour	1.5 litre (1½ qt) fish stock
120 g (4 oz) butter	(Recipe 374)
	6 crushed peppercorns

1 Melt butter and add flour to make a blond roux (Recipe 24).
2 Allow roux to cool, add the boiling fish stock and mix smoothly with wooden spoon.
3 Boil; skim; add the peppercorns and continue to simmer slowly over moderate heat until reduced to 1 litre (1 quart).
4 Strain through muslin or fine strainer; butter the surface to prevent the formation of a skin.

SAUCES FOR FISH

The fish-sauce recipes which follow have been arranged alphabetically. Those, in addition to the fumet and fonds (basics) introducing this section, that are generally considered basic are sauces vin blanc, vin rouge, Nantua and normande.

Most frequently 'en-place' in the chef poissonnier's bain-marie or used by him are Béchamel derivatives (e.g. sauces Mornay, anchois, and shrimp sauce prepared in the English style) together with other sauces from Chapter 1 such as hollandaise, and glace de viande (for meunière treatments). Butter, including beurre fondu, noir and noisette, is also required.

378 Sauce anchois – Anchovy sauce

500 ml (1 pt) sauce normande (Recipe 394)	90 g (3 oz) anchovy butter (Recipe 400)	30 g (1 oz) filleted anchovy

1 Blend the anchovy butter into the sauce normande.
2 Wash the anchovy fillets and cut into small dice.
3 Garnish the sauce with diced anchovy.

379 Anchovy sauce – English-style (Béchamel derivative)

500 ml (1 pt) Béchamel	30 g (1 oz) butter
(Recipe 51)	65 ml (⅛ pt) cream
15 ml spoon [1 tablespoon]	seasoning
anchovy essence	

1 Blend the anchovy essence into Béchamel.
2 Add the butter and cream and mix well.
3 Season and strain.

380 Sauce Bercy

30 g (1 oz) finely	125 ml (¼ pt) cream	90 g (3 oz) butter
chopped shallots	30 g (1 oz) finely	125 ml (¼ pt) fish
375 ml (¾ pt) fish	chopped herbs	stock
velouté (Recipe 377)	(tarragon, chervil,	(Recipe 374)
125 ml (¼ pt) white	parsley)	juice of ½ lemon
wine		

1 Sweat off the shallots in a little butter.
2 Add the fish stock and white wine and reduce to one-third.
3 Pour on the fish velouté and reduce the total liquid to 250 ml (½ pint).
4 Blend in the cream and butter, season and garnish with the fine herbs.

Note. A Bercy reduction, a combination of shallots, parsley, white wine, and fish stock, is commonly required in fish-cookery. Bercy sauce is sometimes referred to as fines-herbes sauce. *N.B.* For large numbers add a little sabayon 2 eggs per litre (quart), also add a little whipped cream, this gives a quick glaze; a useful method for banquets.

381 Sauce bourguignonne

45 g (1½ oz) maniéd	30 g (1 oz) finely	1 sprig thyme
butter (Recipe 19)	chopped shallots	12 crushed
500 ml (1 pt) red wine	seasoning	peppercorns
1 bay-leaf	60 g (2 oz) butter	5 ml spoon [1
		teaspoon] meat
		glaze (Recipe 13)

1 Sweat off shallots and peppercorns in 30 g (1 oz) butter.
2 Add the aromatics, pour on the wine and reduce to 250 ml (½ pint).
3 Thicken the liquid with the maniéd butter and work in the meat glaze.
4 Season and strain, blend in the butter.

Note. It is trade practice to add a little half-glaze to this type of sauce when making the reduction. Use 250 to 500 ml (½ to 1 pt) of red wine.
  Bourguignonne sauce can be used for egg dishes as well as fish.

382 Sauce Cardinal I

500 *ml* (1 *pt*) *Béchamel* (*Recipe* 51)	125 *ml* (¼ *pt*) *cream*	2 × 15 *ml spoon* [2 *tablespoons*]
250 *ml* (½ *pt*) *fish* *fumet* (*Recipe* 374)	90 *g* (3 *oz*) *lobster* *butter* (*Recipe* 402)	*brandy* *seasoning*

1 Reduce Béchamel and fish fumet to 500 ml (1 pint).
2 Blend in the cream, lobster butter, brandy. Season.

383 Sauce Cardinal II

250 *ml* (½ *pt*) *fish* *fumet* (*Recipe* 374)	*seasoning*	125 *ml* (¼ *pt*) *cream*
250 *ml* (½ *pt*) *lobster* *sauce* (*Recipe* 386)	250 *ml* (½ *pt*) *Béchamel* (*Recipe* 51)	2 × 15 *ml spoon* [2 *tablespoons*]
	60 *g* (2 *oz*) *butter*	*brandy*

1 Reduce fish fumet, Béchamel, lobster sauce to 500 ml (1 pint).
2 Blend in cream, butter and brandy; season.
3 If required for glazing, add 125 ml (¼ pint) of sauce Hollandaise.

384 Sauce aux crevettes – Shrimp sauce (English style)

500 *ml* (1 *pt*) *Béchamel* (*Recipe* 51)	60 *g* (2 *oz*) *shelled* *shrimps*	125 *ml* (¼ *pt*) *cream* *seasoning*
125 *ml* (¼ *pt*) *fish stock* (*Recipe* 374)	60 *g* (2 *oz*) *shrimp* *butter* (*Recipe* 401)	

1 Add cream, fish stock to Béchamel and reduce to 500 ml (1 pint).
2 Blend in shrimp butter.
3 Garnish the sauce with the shelled shrimps tossed in butter.
4 Adjust the seasoning.

385 Sauce genevoise

240 *g* (½ *lb*) *fine* *mirepoix* (*Recipe* 4)	1 *bouquet garni*	180 *g* (6 *oz*) *butter*
½ *bottle red wine*	500 *ml* (1 *pt*) *fish stock* (*Recipe* 374)	1 *glass brandy*
500 *ml* (1 *pt*) *jus lié* (*or* *reduced brown* *stock*) (*Recipe* 30)	500 *g* (1 *lb*) *salmon-* *head and/or bones*	2 × 15 *ml spoon* [2 *tablespoons*] *anchovy essence*

1 Sweat off the mirepoix in 60 g (2 oz) butter.
2 Add the salmon-head and bones and stew with lid on for 20 minutes.
3 Add the jus lié (or reduced brown stock), fish stock, and simmer.
4 Strain the liquid through a fine chinois.
5 Add the red wine to the strained sauce and reduce to 375 ml (¾ pint).
6 Add the anchovy essence, pass through a muslin or fine strainer, season and blend in the butter, add brandy.

386 Sauce homard – Lobster sauce (using cooked lobster)

500 g (1 lb) lobster	12 crushed	90 g (3 oz) flour
shell cooked	peppercorns	125 ml (¼ pt)
(including coral and	1 bouquet garni	brandy
spawn)	1.25 l (2½ pt) fish stock	90 g (3 oz) butter
180 g (6 oz) fine	(Recipe 374)	60 g (2 oz) tomato
mirepoix (Recipe 4)	125 ml (¼ pt) white	puree
½ clove crushed garlic	wine	salt
240 g (½ lb) tomato		
concassé		

1 Chop and crush the lobster shell, coral and spawn.
2 Sweat off the shells in the butter.
3 Add the mirepoix and garlic and sweat on.
4 Add the flour to make a roux and continue to cook for a few minutes.
5 Now mix in thoroughly, the tomato purée and fresh tomatoes.
6 Blend in the stock and white wine, stirring to a smooth sauce.
7 Bring to the boil, skim, add crushed peppercorns and bouquet garni.
8 Simmer for 1 hour on side of stove.
9 Strain, add brandy, and season.

386a Sauce homard – Lobster sauce (using live lobster)

480 g (1 lb) live lobster	125 ml (¼ pt) double	1 litre (2 pt) fish
120 g (4 oz) butter (or	cream (or fromage	stock
sunflower	frais)	125 ml (¼ pt) dry
margarine)	60 ml (⅛ pt) brandy	white wine
60 g (2 oz) onion	60 g (2 oz) tomato	bouquet garni
60 g (2 oz) carrot	purée	seasoning
250 ml (½ pt) fish		
velouté		

1 Wash the live lobster.
2 Cut in half lengthwise, the tail and the carapace.
3 Discard the sac from the carapace, clean the trail from the tail and wash all the pieces.
4 Crack the claws and the four claw joints.
5 Melt the butter or margarine in a suitable saucepan.
6 Add the lobster and the carrot and onion cut into mirepoix.
7 Lightly colour over a fierce heat for a few minutes.
8 Add the brandy and flame.
9 Remove from heat, add the tomato purée, white wine, fish stock, seasoning and bouquet garni. Bring to the boil.

10 Stir, allow to simmer for approximately 15–20 minutes.
11 Remove lobster pieces, remove meat from the shell. (The lobster meat is either retained for a fine dice to garnish the sauce or used for other dishes.)
12 Crush the shells, return to the sauce and continue to simmer for a further 15–20 minutes.
13 Remove bouquet garni, pound the shells and sauce in a food processor. Add the velouté.
14 Pass through a fine strainer.
15 Return to a clean pan, reboil, correct seasoning, finish with cream or fromage frais.

Note. Lobster brakes are normally used for this sauce. The sauce may also be finished with lobster butter and may be alternatively thickened with 30 g (1 oz) of arrowroot in place of the velouté. Rice flour is also occasionally used as a thickening.

387 Sauce Joinville

500 ml (1 pt) normande sauce
  (Recipe 394)
60 g (2 oz) crayfish butter*
15 ml spoon [tablespoon] brandy
60 g (2 oz) shrimp butter
  (Recipe 401)

15 g (½ oz) diced shrimp-tails
15 g (½ oz) diced, cooked
  mushrooms
22 g (¾ oz) diced truffles (optional)

1 Blend in the butter to the finished normande sauce.
2 Heat the shrimps, mushrooms and truffles in a 15 ml spoon (1 tablespoon) brandy and add to the sauce as a garnish.
3 Adjust the seasoning.

388 Sauce à la marinière

30 g (1 oz) finely chopped shallots
30 g (1 oz) fines herbes
375 ml (¾ pt) fish velouté
  (Recipe 377)
juice of ½ lemon
90 g (3 oz) butter

125 ml (¼ pt) mussel stock or
  Recipe 374 using mussels
125 ml (¼ pt) white wine
125 ml (¼ pt) cream ⎫
2 egg yolks   ⎬ liaison

24 bearded cooked mussels
30 g (1 oz) diced shrimp-tails

* Crayfish butter is made in the same way as shrimp butter (Recipe 401).

1 Sweat off the shallots in 30 g (1 oz) butter.
2 Add the mussel stock and wine and reduce to one-third.
3 Pour in the fish velouté and reduce to 250 ml (½ pint).
4 Draw to the side of the stove and blend in butter and liaison.
5 Add the fines herbes; season and garnish with the mussels and shrimps.

Note. This must not be confused with the classic recipe for moules (mussels) marinière.

389 Sauce matelote

500 *ml* (1 *pt*) *jus lié*	*cayenne pepper*	1 *bay-leaf*
(*Recipe* 30)	120 *g* (4 *oz*)	6 *crushed*
30 *g* (1 *oz*) *chopped*	*mushrooms*	*peppercorns*
shallots	250 *ml* (½ *pt*) *fish stock*	250 *ml* (½ *pt*) *red*
120 *g* (4 *oz*) *butter*	(*Recipe* 374)	*wine*
1 *sprig thyme*		

1 Sweat off peppercorns and shallots in 30 g (1 oz) butter.
2 Add wine and bay-leaf, thyme, fish stock and make a reduction.
3 Pour on the jus lié and simmer to 375 ml (¾ pint).
4 Season and strain through tammy-cloth.
5 Add a pinch of cayenne pepper and blend in butter.

390 Sauce matelote (white)

12 *cooked button-onions*	125 *ml* (¼ *pt*) *cream*
12 *small turned mushrooms*	250 *ml* (½ *pt*) *white wine*

Same method as Recipe 389 using fish velouté (Recipe 377) instead of half-glaze and white wine instead of red wine.

Note. Garnish the sauce with button onions and mushrooms cooked (à blanc) and finish off sauce with a little cream.

391 Sauce Nantua I

t1m12t2m12.6

500 *ml* (1 *pt*) *Béchamel*	30 *g* (1 *oz*) *diced prawns*
(*Recipe* 51)	90 *g* (3 *oz*) *crayfish butter* (*as*
250 *ml* (½ *pt*) *cream*	*Recipe* 401, *using crayfish*)
1 *glass sherry*	

1 Reduce Béchamel and cream by one-third to 500 ml (1 pint).
2 Pass through a fine chinois (strainer).
3 Blend in crayfish butter and sherry.
4 Season, garnish with diced prawns.

392 Sauce Nantua II

250 *ml* (½ *pt*) *Béchamel*	250 *ml* (½ *pt*) *cream*
(*Recipe* 51)	90 *g* (3 *oz*) *butter*
250 *ml* (½ *pt*) *lobster sauce*	1 *glass sherry*
(*Recipe* 386)	30 *g* (1 *oz*) *diced prawns*

1 Reduce Béchamel, cream and lobster sauce by one-third to 500 ml (1 pint).
2 Strain through fine strainer.
3 Blend in butter and sherry.
4 Season, garnish with diced prawns.

393 Sauce Newburg

1 kg (2 lb) raw lobster	1 glass Madeira	240 g (½ lb) tomato
125 ml (¼ pt) oil	1 glass brandy	concassé
120 g (¼ lb) fine	240 g (8 oz) butter	500 ml (1 pt) fish
mirepoix (Recipe 2)	250 ml (½ pt) cream	stock
125 ml (¼ pt) white	1 bouquet garni	(Recipe 374)
wine		

1 Divide the head of the lobster into two and remove the creamy parts and blend these well with 60 g (2 oz) butter.
2 Divide the tail into 4 thick slices.
3 Place the oil and 30 g (1 oz) butter into a thick saucepan and fry the head and tail to a fine red colour; flame with brandy.
4 Add the mirepoix and tomato concassé and sweat under cover for a few minutes.
5 Moisten with the wine and fish stock; add the bouquet garni; cook with lid on for 20 minutes.
6 Remove the lobster, reboil sauce, add the cream and finish off by adding the creamy parts of the lobster.
7 Strain through a fine chinois; add the Madeira; season and blend in the remainder of the butter.

Note. The sauce may be garnished with a small dice of cooked lobster-meat.

394 Sauce normande

1 litre (1 qt) fish velouté	5 egg yolks
(Recipe 377)	250 ml (½ pt) cream
125 ml (¼ pt) mushroom liquor	cayenne pepper
juice of ½ lemon	salt and pepper
250 ml (½ pt) fish stock	125 ml (¼ pt) oyster liquor
(Recipe 374)	120 g (4 oz) butter (or margarine)

1 Place in a thick-bottomed pan the following: fish velouté, mushroom liquor, fish stock, lemon juice, oyster liquor.
2 Reduce by one-third on a quick fire (brisk heat).
3 Beat up the egg yolks and cream and add to the sauce – draw to the side of the fire (reduce heat).
4 Blend in the butter, season and pass through muslin-cloth.

395 Sauce portugaise

120 g (4 oz) butter	480 g (1 lb) tomato concassé
85 ml (⅙ pt) olive oil	165 ml (⅓ pt) white wine
¼ clove crushed garlic	60 g (2 oz) finely chopped shallots
15 ml spoon [1 tablespoon] fish	375 ml (¾ pt) thin tomato sauce
glaze (Recipe 376)	(Recipe 34)
7 g (¼ oz) chopped parsley	

1 Lightly colour the shallots in the oil and add the garlic.
2 Make a reduction of the wine.
3 Add tomato concassé and sweat for a few minutes.
4 Add the tomato sauce, simmer for a few minutes and draw to the side of the stove (reduce heat); add fish glaze.
5 Thicken with butter (optional), adjust seasoning, and add parsley.

395a Rouille – Red pepper sauce

1 *pasteurized egg yolk (optional)*	8 *cloves chopped, crushed garlic*
250 *ml* (½ *pt*) *olive oil*	2 *cooked pimentos (or canned),*
1 *chilli pepper*	*depipped, drained and dried*
2 *slices crustless white bread*	*tabasco or harissa to taste (if*
(either crumbed, or soaked and	*required to replace or agument*
squeezed dry)	*the chilli pepper)*
salt	*pinch saffron (optional)*

1 Blend together the chilli, garlic, egg yolk and oil.
2 Add pimentos, bread crumbs (or soaked, squeezed bread) to achieve spreading consistency.
3 Adjust seasoning by adding tabasco (or harissa) to degree of hotness required, and salt to taste.

Notes

1 There are many variations of this mix.
2 Today (because of the concern regarding raw egg) hard-boiled egg yolk often replaces fresh egg yolk formerly used in starting the blend in mayonnaise style.
3 A potato cooked in the fish soup, drained and dried may also be used as substitute for some or all of the bread.
4 Ingredients and flavourings may be varied (garlic, red peppers, increased or reduced and basil, thyme and savory used to augment flavour).
5 Traditionally served with Bouillabaisse (Recipe 455) and now also with other fish soups or stews and fish grills.

396 Sauce au vin blanc I – White wine sauce

375 *ml* (¾ *pt*) *fish velouté (Recipe 377)*	*lemon juice*	30 *g* (1 *oz*) *finely chopped shallots*
125 *ml* (¼ *pt*) *white wine*	*salt*	125 *ml* (¼ *pt*) *cream*
120 *g* (4 *oz*) *butter*	250 *ml* (½ *pt*) *fish fumet (Recipe 374)*	*cayenne pepper*

1 Reduce the shallots, white wine and fish stock to one-third pt.
2 Add the fish velouté and cream, reduce the total sauce to 375 ml (¾ pint).
3 Blend in the butter and add the seasoning.

397 Sauce au vin blanc II

375 *ml* (¾ *pt*) *fish velouté (Recipe 377)*	250 *ml* (½ *pt*) *fish fumet (Recipe 374)*
125 *ml* (¼ *pt*) *white wine*	30 *g* (1 *oz*) *chopped shallots*
120 *g* (4 *oz*) *butter*	3 *egg yolks* } *liaison*
lemon juice	125*ml* (¼ *pt*) *cream* }
salt and pepper	*cayenne*

1 Reduce the shallots, white wine and fish stock to one-third pt.
2 Add the fish velouté and reduce to 250 ml (½ pt).
3 Draw to side of the fire, blend in butter, liaison, and season.

398 Sauce Sabayon au vin blanc III – White wine Sabayon Sauce

4 *egg yolks*   15 *ml spoon* [1 *tablespoon*] *fish*
                                      fumet (*Recipe* 374)

1 Beat the egg yolk and fish stock to ribbon stage (forming a sabayon) in
  bain-marie.
2 Add this sabayon to Recipe 396.

Note. If this method is used, no hollandaise is required; but when Sauce au
vin blanc is required for large parties, use Recipe 396 with equal parts of
sauce hollandaise (Recipe 70). This combination is recommended, as the
sauce does not relax and can stand until needed.

399 Sauce vin rouge – Red wine sauce

15 *g* (½ *oz*) *fine mirepoix*   *pinch cayenne pepper*
   (*Recipe* 4)   500 *ml* (1 *pt*) *jus lié* (*Recipe* 30) *or*
250 *ml* (½ *pt*) *red wine*   *reduced stock or demi-glace*
5 *ml spoon* [1 *teaspoon*] *anchovy*   (*Recipe* 29)
   essence   120 *g* (4 *oz*) *butter* (*or margarine*)

1 Fry, to golden colour, mirepoix in 30 g (1 oz) butter.
2 Add wine and reduce by half.
3 Moisten with demi-glace and reduce total liquid to 375 ml (¾ pint).
4 Strain the sauce, season and finish with butter, anchovy essence and
  cayenne pepper.

Note. For a red wine sauce for meat, see Sauce bordelaise (Recipe 35).

BUTTERS FOR FISH

A fish cook makes use of melted and noisette butter; and uses beurre noir
(particularly with raie [skate]; the compound butters such as beurre maître
d'hôtel (Recipe 89); and beurre vert (tinted with spinach juice). Beurre
manié is used to thicken a sauce that is too thin. The following are three
examples of beurres composés (compound butters) with fish itself in their
composition.

400 Beurre d'anchois – Anchovy butter

120 *g* (4 *oz*) *butter*   15 *ml spoon* [1   *juice of* ½ *lemon*
4 *anchovies*   *tablespoon*] *anchovy*   *cayenne pepper*
                                   essence

1 Pound the butter and anchovies in a mortar.
2 Add the lemon juice and anchovy essence and cayenne pepper; mix well.
3 Roll in greased paper or aluminium foil and keep in refrigerator till
  required.

401 **Beurre de crevettes** – Shrimp butter

120 g (4 oz) shrimps   120 g (4 oz) butter   juice of ½ lemon

1 Shell the shrimps
2 Pound lemon juice, butter, and shrimps in mortar.
3 Rub through a medium sieve.
4 Roll in greaseproof paper or aluminium foil and keep until required.

402 **Beurre de homard** – Lobster butter

1 *lobster shell, coral and spawn*   *pinch cayenne pepper*
180 g (6 oz) butter

1 Pound the lobster shell, coral and spawn in with the butter and cayenne.
2 Cook slowly in double boiler till all the butter rises to the top.
3 Strain and butter through a chinois.
4 Allow to cool and reserve for use.

Salpicons. As well as the salpicons listed in Chapter 1 (Recipes 103–9), there are those especially suited for use in fish dishes. Examples are the shrimps, mushrooms, and truffle, sweated in butter and cohered with Sauce Suprême for fish dishes; e.g. Joinville (see Recipe 387); and the salpicon used in Sole Otéro (Recipe 449).

TYPES OF FISH

A wide range of fish dishes may be prepared by using basic cooking methods (i.e. poaching, grilling, pan-frying and deep-frying) with the accompaniment of sauces in this and preceding chapters. The main types of fish are:

Fresh-Water Fish include those from river and lake such as fresh-water bream, carp, perch, pike, salmon, trout, sturgeon.

Sea-Water Fish may be further sub-divided into:
    Round oily fish – such as herrings and mackerel.
    White round – such as cod, haddock, whiting.
    Flat white – such as brill, lemon sole, plaice, sole, halibut, turbot.
    Shellfish – comprising (a) *Crustacea* such as: crab, crayfish, lobster, prawns, shrimps, scampis. (b) *Molluscs* such as: clams, oysters, mussels, scallops (in this category, snails, though not true fish, may conveniently be considered).
    Frogs (grenouilles) – although these do not belong to this category – are included.

CUTS OF FISH

Although small fish such as trout and lemon sole are often cooked whole, and large ones such as turbot and salmon may similarly be presented in their entirety, fish is frequently cut into steaks or filleted and cut into portions. These are named as follows:

Sole (with application to similar flat fish)
Délice – folded fillet.
Filets – fillets: lightly flatten with bat and cook flat.
Goujons or en goujons – gudgeon cut: thin strips of fillet for deep-frying or meunière.
Mignon: fillet folded as a cornet (triangular fold as for paper piping-bag).
Paupiette: flattened fillet, coated with fish farce and rolled; usually poached.
Plié – folded: flattened and folded in two.
Suprême: alternative name for fillet.

Salmon, turbot, and similar, larger fish
Côtelette: a fish cutlet or steak with bone. (Alternative name for tronçon).
Darne: a straight cut through the bone (and correctly from the middle) to yield the finest cut of round fish, such as salmon.
Escalope: thin slice from fillet.
Médaillon: a medallion-shaped portion from larger fillets.
Suprême: a fillet (or portion of large fillet).
Tronçon: a steak cut with bone.

TREATMENT OF FROZEN FISH

Generally, portioned frozen fish should not be defrosted prior to cooking and especially not defrosted for poaching, boiling and grilling. But if portioned fish is to be deep fried *à l'anglaise* (pané, crumbed) it is advantageous to defrost partially to make the portion flexible enough to be crumb or batter treated.

Bulk-packed frozen fish of larger varieties, i.e. large cod or other white fillets, may require just sufficient defrosting to enable separation and cutting to take place.

In all cases where some defrosting is indicated, normal defrosting in room temperature and *never* by immersion in warm water should be employed.

All methods for fresh fish in the following recipes may be applied to frozen fish.

METHODS OF COOKING FISH

403 Poisson bouilli – Boiled fish

Fish can be boiled in salted water (or in salted and vinegared water) but it is preferable to use a court-bouillon (Recipes 370–73), which should be pre-prepared, and the ingredients boiled together for 10 minutes. Larger, whole fish are usually covered with cold court-bouillon (or cooking-liquor), brought to boil and simmered gently so that outer parts do not flake away. Small fish and small cuts of fish are, however, plunged into already boiling liquor. For plainly boiled white fish use a court-bouillon (Recipe 370) for cooking-liquor. Soak the fish in a little cold, salted water before boiling.

Use the following general guide for boiling fish, but always test to check: when fish is cooked, a skewer or fork will easily detach flesh from bone cleanly.

Boiling for hot service
(i) Simmer large whole fish (e.g. turbot and brill) for 20 minutes (approximately).

(ii) Simmer small cuts of fish for 10 to 15 minutes (approximately).
(iii) For cuts of salmon see Recipe 427.

Boiling for cold service
(i) Simmer whole large fish (e.g. turbot) and cuts for 5 minutes after coming to boil, then cover closely and cool in own liquor.
(ii) For whole salmon see Recipe 490.

404 Poisson poché – Poached fish

Mise-en-place

finely chopped shallots	*lemon juice*	*butter*
fish stock	*greased kitchen-paper*	

1 Butter a shallow fish-dish.
2 Sprinkle on the shallots.
3 Lay fish flat on top.
4 Half cover with fish stock.
5 Cover with greased paper.
6 Poach in moderate oven.

405 Poisson braisé – Braised fish

Braising is generally applicable to whole or sliced salmon, sturgeon, turbot or trout.

Mise-en-place

aromatics	*carrots*	*onions*
wine	*fish stock*	*seasoning*

1 Place the seasoned fish on a bed of vegetables and aromates.
2 Moisten with red or white wine and fish stock.
3 The liquid should cover ¾ of the fish.
4 Cook under cover and baste frequently.
5 Drain well reserving the liquor as the sauce is made from its reduction.

406 Baked fish

Applicable to whole fish, plain or stuffed, and to cuts.
1 Butter a dish and place fish on top.
2 Cover with greased paper or aluminium foil.
3 Baste frequently with butter.

407 Poisson frit à l'anglaise – Fried fish (English style)

Mise-en-place

flour	*white breadcrumbs*	*parsley*
egg-wash	*lemon*	

1 Pass prepared fish through flour, egg-wash, and breadcrumbs.
2 Deep fry, serve with lemon and fried parsley.

Frying temperature. Between 175°C (350°F) and 190°C (375°F) according to speed of heat recovery.

Time. About 3 minutes for fillets of average size.

Note. Add a little oil to egg-wash.

408 Poisson frit à la française – Fried fish (French style)

Mise-en-place

seasoned flour   *lemon*   *parsley*
milk

1 Marinate the fish in milk.
2 Pass through seasoned flour.
3 Deep fry in oil.
4 Garnish with lemon and parsley.

409 Poisson Orly

Mise-en-place

instant marinade (*Recipe* 125) *butter coating*
tomato sauce (*Recipe* 34)   *parsley*

1 Marinate fish for 1 hour.
2 Pass through flour
3 Dip in batter.
4 Fry in deep oil or fat.
5 Garnish with fried parsley.
6 Serve tomato sauce separately.

Shallow- or pan-fried Fish. Shallow-frying is suitable for small round fish or slices of larger ones.

410 Poisson à la meunière

Mise-en-place

seasoned flour   *lemons*   *butter for beurre*
oil   *chopped parsley*   *noisette*
                    (*Recipe* 82)

1 Pass fish through seasoned flour.
2 Shallow fry both sides in hot oil.
3 Garnish with slices of lemon.
4 Finish with beurre noisette, chopped parsley and lemon juice.

Note. All round fish must be ciselé first.

411 Poisson doré – gilded

Mise-en-place

seasoned flour   *clarified butter*

1 Pass fish through seasoned flour.
2 Shallow fry both sides in clarified butter.
3 Season and serve on hot dish.

412 Poisson grillé – Grilled fish

Mise-en-place

oil   *seasoned flour*   *butter*

1 If fish is whole, ciseler.
2 Pass through seasoned flour.

3 Brush both sides with oil.
4 Cook both sides under grill and baste with butter.
5 Serve on dish without d'oyley or paper; garnish with lemon and parsley.

Suitable sauces: *Parsley butter, devil, piquante, béarnaise.*

FISH DISHES FOR HOT SERVICE

The recipes below are intended to act as examples of main treatments. With rare exceptions dish names and methods may be applied to more than the fish chosen. For example, place (plie) may be prepared, like sole, en goujons or as Goujons de plie. Indeed most methods cited for sole may be used for turbot and other white fish, and recipes for cod (cabillaud) may equally be applied to fresh haddock (aiglefin or aigrefin).

Some cold-service recipes appear at the end of this chapter, but cold fish (including herrings and mackerel) are dealt with in Chapter 2, 'Cold Preparations', and further fish dishes are among breakfast dishes.

All recipes are for 4 covers except modes for large whole fish.

BLANCHAILLES – WHITEBAIT

413 Blanchailles diablées – Devilled whitebait

500 g (1 lb) whitebait	*240 g (½ lb) seasoned*	*7 g (¼ oz) cayenne*
250 ml (½ pt) milk	*flour*	*pepper*
	60 g (2 oz) salt	*deep fat*

1 Soak whitebait in milk. Defrost frozen ones first.
2 Drain well and place a little at a time in the seasoned flour.
3 Sieve well on cane sieve.
4 Deep fry until golden brown and crisp.
5 Drain well and dust with a combination of salt and cayenne pepper.
6 Dress on serviette and garnish with quarters of lemon and fried parsley.

Note. Ample dredging-flour (used freshly each time) is essential if the whitebait are to remain separate and not stick together; therefore, also avoid cooking too many at one time. Strain fat after use.

414 Blanchailles frites or Blanchailles frites au citron – Fried whitebait with lemon

Basically as Recipe 413 but without the use of cayenne pepper.

CABILLAUD – COD

415 Cabillaud à la meunière

four 180 g (6-oz)	*125 ml (¼ pt) oil*	*125 g (¼ lb) butter*
darnes of cod	*7 g (¼ oz) chopped*	*noisette*
8 lemon slices	*parsley*	*(optional)*
		(Recipe 82)

1 Cook as Recipe 410.
2 Remove skin and centre bone.
3 Garnish with lemon slices.
4 Coat with beurre noisette (optional) and sprinkle with chopped parsley.

416 Cabillaud poché

four 180 *g* (6-*oz*) *darnes of cod* 12 *potatoes, medium size*	1 *litre* (1 *qt*) *white court-bouillon* (*Recipe* 370)	4 *lemon slices* *sprigs of parsley*

1 Wash the cod steaks.
2 Place in boiling court-bouillon.
3 Simmer for approximately 10 minutes.
4 Drain, garnish with slices of lemon and boiled 'turned' potatoes.
5 Pour a little of the cooking-liquid over before service.
6 Decorate with sprigs of parsley.

416a Cod roe à la meunière

750 *g* (1½ *lb*) *cod roe* 750 *ml* (1½ *pt*) *court-bouillon* (*Recipe* 371)	120 *g* (¼ *lb*) *butter* *chopped parsley* 120 *g* (¼ *lb*) *seasoned flour*

1 Place roe in cold court-bouillon.
2 Bring slowly to the boil.
3 Allow to cool in its own liquor.
4 Cut in thick slices.
5 Pass through seasoned flour.
6 Cook à la meunière (Recipe 410).

Cod roe may also be sliced after boiling and served cold for hors-d'œuvre in marinade or vinaigrette.

LOTTE – MONKFISH

417 Lotte à la sauce vin blanc et herbes – Monkfish with white wine and herb sauce

480–720 *g* (1–1½ *lb*) *prepared monkfish* 15 *g* (½ *oz*) *chopped parsley, chervil, tarragon and chives*	125 *ml* (¼ *pt*) *fish stock* 125 *ml* (¼ *pt*) *dry white wine* 120 *g* (4 *oz*) *butter* (*or sunflower margarine*)

1 Cut the monkfish into 8–12 pieces.
2 Place into a buttered dish, season, sprinkle with half the herbs.
3 Add fish stock and white wine. Cover with buttered greaseproof paper and poach gently.
4 Remove fish, drain well, keep warm.
5 Strain off cooking liquor, reduce to a glaze.
6 Montez au beurre (or margarine). Correct seasoning, add remainder of the herbs.

LOUP DE MER – SEA WOLF (or SEA BASS, BAR or SEA PERCH)

418 Loup de mer grillé au fenouil – Grilled sea bass with fennel

> four 360–480 g (12 oz–1 lb) sea
>   bass
> 60 g (2 oz) fennel sprigs
>
> seasoning
> oil for grilling

1 Scale, trim, gut and wash the fish.
2 Cut 3–4 incisions on either side. Season.
3 Pack the stomach cavities with fennel.
4 Brush with oil and grill.
5 Serve sprinkled with chopped fennel and quarters of lemon.

Note. A little Pernod may be flamed and poured over the fish before service.

418a Suprêmes de loup de mer au vert de laitue – Sea bass fillets with lettuce
leaves

> 720 g (1½ lb) sea bass fillets
> 30 g (1 oz) chopped shallots
> 62 ml (⅛ pt) dry white vermouth
> 1 egg yolk
> 60 g (2 oz) flour
> 2 round lettuce
>
> 62 ml (⅛ pt) white wine
> 62 ml (⅛ pt) whipping cream
> 60 g (2 oz) butter (or sunflower
>   margarine)
> 1 tbsp. oil (for frying)

1 Skin fillets, portion, season and pass through seasoned flour.
2 Gently brown fillets in a frying pan with butter and oil.
3 Wash and blanch lettuce, refresh, drain.
4 Wrap the outer leaves round the sea bass fillets.
5 Butter a shallow dish, spread with shallots, lay on top the flattened lettuce
  hearts; next lay on the fillets, which have been wrapped in lettuce leaves.
6 Add the white wine and vermouth. Cover with a buttered pan and lid.
  Bake in the oven at 170°C (325°F) for approximately 10 minutes.
7 When cooked, drain the bass fillets. Arrange on a serving dish with the
  lettuce hearts underneath the fish.
8 Pour the cooking liquor into a saucepan, reduce rapidly to a glaze.
9 Beat the cream and egg yolk in a separate basin; gradually add this to the
  glaze.
10 Return to the heat but do not boil. Mount with butter whisking
  continuously. Correct seasoning.
11 Pour the sauce over the fish and serve.

MERLAN – WHITING

419 Merlan frit en colère – Fried whiting en colère

> 4 medium whiting
> 2 lemons
> fried parsley
>
> 2 beaten eggs
> 240 g (½ lb) white
>   breadcrumbs
>
> deep oil for frying
> 120 g (¼ lb)
>   seasoned flour

1 Trim fins and remove eyes.
2 Skin both sides starting from head.
3 Place tail through eyes.
4 Four, egg, and crumb.
5 Deep fry; drain and season; dress on dish-paper; garnish with lemon and fried parsley.

420 Merlan a l'anglaise – Whiting, English style

4 medium whiting
60 g (2 oz) clarified butter
120 g (¼ lb) parsley butter
   (Recipe 89)

240 g (½ lb) fine white breadcrumbs
120 g (¼ lb) seasoned flour
2 beaten eggs

1 Split the whiting from head to tail along the back without separating the fish.
2 Remove the backbones, leaving the fillets joined and lying flat.
3 Pass through seasoned flour, then egg and breadcrumbs.
4 Shallow fry both sides in clarified butter (see note below).
5 Serve spread with parsley butter (with optional garnish: slices of peeled lemon dipped in chopped parsley).

Note. To reduce fat absorption, some chefs brush with melted clarified butter or oil and grill both sides.

421 Merlan St-Germain

four 180 g (6-oz) whole
   whiting
240 g (½ lb) white
   breadcrumbs

120 g (¼ lb) melted
   butter
240 g (1 lb) pommes
   noisette (Recipe 903)

125 ml (¼ pt) sauce
   béarnaise
   (Recipe 71)
seasoning

1 Remove fins and scales, open down back, gut and remove backbone; leave head on and remove eyes.
2 Melt the butter; season fish lightly, dip fish in melted butter then in breadcrumbs.
3 Place on a buttered tray, sprinkle the fish with melted butter and grill gently until golden brown.
4 Dish (no paper or d'oyley) and surround with roasted noisette potatoes.
5 Garnish heads with sprigs of parsley and serve sauce béarnaise separately. (A thread of béarnaise may be piped down the centre of each fish.)

Note. This method can be applied to sole, smelts and fresh haddock. (Sole are kept whole with black skin removed, gutted and with head left on.)

422 Merlan farci – Stuffed whiting

4 medium whiting
120 g (4 oz) chopped parsley
120 g (4 oz) white breadcrumbs
pinch of mixed herbs

180 g (6 oz) clarified butter
   (Recipe 84)
1 egg
30 g (1 oz) finely chopped onions

1 Trim fins and eyes from fish.
2 Sweat the onions in butter to golden brown.
3 Mix onions, crumbs, parsley and herbs and bind with egg; season.
4 Place equal parts of stuffing into the flap of the fish.
5 Bake in a buttered dish approximately 15 minutes.
6 Garnish with lemon and sprigs of parsley.

Note. Haddock is frequently prepared in the same way.

RAIE – SKATE

423 Raie au beurre noir – Skate with black butter

1 kg (2 lb) skate	juice of 1 lemon
30 g (1 oz) capers	7 g (¼ oz) chopped parsley
2 × 15ml spoon [2 tablespoons]	500 ml (1 pt) court-bouillon
vinegar	(Recipe 370)
120 g (¼ lb) butter	

1 Soak skate overnight.
2 Cut into 4 equal portions.
3 Cook in court-bouillon for 10 minutes.
4 Skin both sides when cooked.
5 Make a beurre noisette (Recipe 82) very brown and add the vinegar, capers and lemon juice.
6 Pour over the skate and sprinkle with chopped parsley.

Note. Skate is also deep-fried or meunière. In such cases, skin before cooking.

ROUGET – RED MULLET

Red Mullet is normally cooked without being gutted or 'drawn'; hence its popular designation 'woodcock of the sea'.

424 Rouget en papillote – Red mullet in paper

four 250 g (8-oz) red mullet	seasoning
60 g (2 oz) finely chopped	125 ml (¼ pt) jus lié (Recipe 30) or
mushrooms	demi-glace (Recipe 29) or
15 g (½ oz) butter	reduced stock
4 sheets greaseproof paper	8 slices of boiled ham
250 ml (½ pt) oil	

1 Prepare by cleaning, scaling, and removing the eyes; then grill the mullet.
2 Sweat mushrooms in butter, mix with the demi-glace and season.
3 Cut the paper (or aluminium foil) into large heart-shapes using full sheet for each one.

4 Oil both sides of the paper.
5 Place 1 slice of ham on one side of each heart then lay the mullet on top and coat each with sauce; lay another slice of ham on each one.
6 Seal both sides of the paper together.
7 Set the paper containing the fish on silver dishes containing hot oil and place in oven to rise.

425 Rouget grillé – Grilled red mullet

four 250 g (8-oz) red mullet	*fried parsley*
120 g (¼ lb) shrimp butter	125 ml (¼ pt) oil
(Recipe 401)	4 lemons
120 g (¼ lb) seasoned flour	

1 Clean and remove scales and eyes.
2 Ciseler, flour, and brush with oil and season.
3 Grill both sides and baste during cooking process.
4 Garnish with shrimp butter, lemons, and fried parsley.

426 Rouget à la livournaise

four 250 g (½-lb) red mullet	15 g (½ oz) finely chopped shallots
240 g (½ lb) tomato concassé	120 g (¼ lb) butter
125 ml (¼ pt) fish stock	salt
(Recipe 374)	seasoning
4 g (⅛ oz) julienne truffle	peppermill
(optional)	cayenne

1 Remove scales, eyes, and gut.
2 Butter oval fish-plaque.
3 Sprinkle with chopped shallots.
4 Place the melted butter on top.
5 Cover the fish with tomato concassé.
6 Pour over the fish stock and add a little seasoning.
7 Cover with greased paper, bring to boil.
8 Oven-bake for approximately 15 minutes.
9 When cooked, remove from liquid and keep warm.
10 Reduce the cooking-liquor to one-third and enrich with butter and truffles and adjust seasoning.
11 Coat the sauce over the well-drained fish and glaze.

SAUMON – SALMON

For boiled salmon, i.e. poaching whole fish or large pieces see Recipes 203 and 204.

427 Darne de saumon pochée – Poached salmon middle-cut steak

1 *litre* (1 qt) court-bouillon	*four* 180 g (6-oz) slices of salmon
(Recipe 371)	360 g (¾ lb) potatoes
salt	¾ sliced cucumber

1 Wash and remove all blood.
2 Place in boiling court-bouillon.
3 Simmer gently for 5–7 minutes.
4 Before service remove skin and bone in the centre.
5 Garnish with boiled, turned potatoes and sprigs of parsley.
6 Serve hollandaise sauce (Recipe 70) or beurre fondu and slices of cucumber.

428 Darne de saumon grillée, sauce béarnaise

four 180 g (6-oz) slice
salmon
sprigs parsley
125 ml (¼ pt) oil

120 g (¼ lb) parsley
butter (Recipe 89)
120 g (¼ lb) seasoned
flour
¼ sliced cucumber

4 lemon slices
125 ml (¼ pt) sauce
béarnaise
(Recipe 71)

1 Wash salmon of all blood.
2 Pass through seasoned flour.
3 Brush both sides with oil, season.
4 Grill both sides slowly and baste.
5 Remove skin and centre bone.
6 Garnish with parsley butter and lemon slices.
7 Dress on silver dish without d'oyley and garnish with springs of parsley.
8 Serve béarnaise sauce and sliced cucumber separately.

429 Darne de saumon Chambord

four 180 g (6-oz) darnes of salmon
250 ml (½ pt) red wine
16 glazed button onions
4 fish quenelles (Recipe 461)
4 slices of truffles (optional)

4 turned mushrooms
15 g (½ oz) beurre manié
(Recipe 19)
4 fried soft roes
60 g (2 oz) butter seasoning

1 Braise salmon in red wine (Recipe 405).
2 When cooked, drain, remove skin and centre bone.
3 Reduce cooking-liquor by half and thicken with beurre manié.
4 Blend in butter and seasoning.
5 Garnish the salmon with the mushrooms and coat with sauce.
6 Set to glaze.
7 Garnish with the soft roes meunière, quenelles and glazed onions.
8 Garnish each darne with a slice of truffle (optional).

430 Côtelette de saumon Pojarski – Salmon cutlets

375 g (¾ lb) raw fillet salmon
salt and pepper
2 beaten eggs
120 g (¼ lb) seasoned flour
120 g (¼ lb) white breadcrumbs

120 g (¼ lb) clarified butter
(Recipe 84) or oil
125 ml (¼ pt) milk
breadcrumbs for coating

1 Mince the salmon finely.
2 Soak the 125 g (½ lb) breadcrumbs in milk and squeeze out all the moisture.

3 Mix the bread with the salmon and season.
4 Shape into cutlets.
5 Flour, egg, and crumb.
6 Shallow fry in oil or clarified butter.

431 Salmon fishcakes – See Recipes 1204 and 1205.

SARDINE

431a Sardines fraîches à la sauce tomate – Fresh sardines with tomato sauce

480–720 g (1–1½ lb) *large fresh*   480 g (1 lb) *tomato concassé*
sardines   *seasoning*
180 g (6 oz) *finely sliced onions*   *chopped parsley*
62 ml (⅛ pt) *dry white wine*

1 Scale, gut, wash and dry the sardines.
2 Shallow fry rapidly in oil both sides. Remove from pan.
3 Sweat the onion in the same pan without colouring them.
4 Add wine, reduce by two-thirds, add tomatoes, seasoning and reduce by half.
5 Pour the sauce into an earthenware dish, arrange sardines on top.
6 Cook for 5–7 minutes in the oven at 220°C (425°F) and serve sprinkled with chopped parsley.

SOLE

Treatment and recipes for sole may be applied to other white fish, even the small cuts of larger fish such as brill and turbot. Especially may lemon sole (limande) be prepared as Dover sole. Plaice (plié) is generally grilled, deep-fried or meunière. Except in obvious cases (such as Colbert) the following methods may be used for fillets (filets) as well as whole sole. When fillet of sole is required, remove black and white skin before filleting.

432 Sole Colbert

four 360 g (¾ lb) *Dover soles*   2 *lemons*
120 g (¼ lb) *parsley butter*   2 *eggs for egg-wash*
  (*Recipe* 89)   *drainers*
120 g (¼ lb) *seasoned flour*   *fried parsley*
480 g (1 lb) *white breadcrumbs*   *deep fat*

1 Trim fins, remove eyes and gut.
2 Remove black skin and scrape white skin.
3 Make incision along back-bone (or spine) on the skinned side; with filleting knife partially detach on that side the two fillets from the centre; fold back in 2 flaps to form a 'purse'.
4 Break centre bone, thus exposed, in 3 places.
5 Paner and place between 2 spikers taking care to keep flaps open.
6 Fry in deep fat; when cooked, remove centre bone.

7 Fill with sliced parsley butter.
8 Present on a dish-paper, flap side uppermost; garnish with fresh parsley
   and half lemon.

433 Sole Doria

Four 360 g (¾ lb) Dover soles   15 g (½ oz) chopped parsley
120 g (¼ lb) seasoned flour   125 ml (¼ pt) oil
60 g (2 oz) butter   cucumber
12 slices peeled lemon

1 Remove fins, eyes, gut, remove black skin and scrape white skin.
2 Peel cucumber and cut into small sections and turn like small olives.
3 Cook the turned cucumber in a little salted water and butter.
4 Pass the sole through the seasoned flour and shallow fry in oil,
   white-skinned side first.
5 Place the sole on a silver dish and garnish each one with a row of turned
   cucumbers down the centre; complete the garnish with slices of lemon and
   a little chopped parsley.
6 Coat with beurre noisette (Recipe 82).

434 Goujons de sole frits

500 g (1 lb) filleted sole   500 g (1 lb) white   2 eggs for egg-wash
240 g (½ lb) seasoned   breadcrumbs   2 lemons
    flour

1 Cut each fillet into 4 or 5 strips, 6 cm (3 inches) long.
2 Flour, egg-wash, and crumb and roll each strip.
3 Fry in deep fat.
4 Drain and season.
5 Serve on a dish-paper, garnish with lemon and fried parsley.

435 Sole au gratin

four 360 g (¾ lb) Dover soles   125 ml (¼ pt) white wine
30 g (1 oz) finely chopped shallots   1 lemon
16 cooked mushrooms   120 g (¼ lb) butter
7g (¼ oz) chopped parsley   375 ml (¾ pt) gratin sauce
120 g (¼ lb) white breadcrumbs   (Recipe 436)
120 g (4 oz) sliced, raw
    mushrooms

1 Prepare the soles as for Colbert (Recipe 432).
2 Place a walnut-size piece of butter under each fillet.
3 Place the sole on a well-greased china dish with some finely chopped
   shallots and a little gratin sauce.
4 Garnish each sole with 4 cooked mushrooms and surround with 15 g (½ oz)
   sliced mushrooms.
5 Pour over each sole the white wine and coat with gratin sauce (Recipe
   436).

6 Pour a little melted butter over the sole and sprinkle with breadcrumbs and bake in a moderate oven.

7 Serve the sole on the same dish and before service squeeze a little lemon juice on top and sprinkle with chopped parsley.

436 Gratin sauce (for fish au gratin)

30 g (1 oz) finely chopped shallots　　*240 g (½ lb) finely chopped*
250 ml (½ pt) jus lié (Recipe 30) or　　　*mushrooms*
*　　well-reduced stock*　　　　　　　　*15 g (½ oz) butter*

1 Sweat the shallots in butter.
2 Wash and squeeze the mushrooms and chop finely.
3 Add the mushrooms to the butter and cook for a few minutes.
4 Moisten with the jus lié and simmer for approximately 10 minutes.
5 Add a little chopped parsley and season.

437 Sole grenobloise

Prepare as Sole Doria (Recipe 433) using 60 g (2 oz) capers in place of cucumbers.

438 Sole grillée

four 360 g (¾ lb) Dover soles　　*125 ml (¼ pt) oil*
120 g (¼ lb) parsley butter　　　*2 lemons*
120 g (¼ lb) seasoned flour

1 Trim fins, remove eyes and gut.
2 Remove black skin and scrape white skin.
3 Pass through seasoned flour and brush both sides with oil.
4 Grill black-skin side first and turn over and grill the other side slowly.
5 Garnish with parsley butter and half lemons; do *not* serve on dish-paper or d'oyley.

439 Goujons de sole Murat – Method 1

12 pieces fillet sole　　　　　*480 g (1 lb) diced potatoes*
4 artichoke bottoms　　　　　*7 g (¼ oz) chopped parsley*
60 g (2 oz) butter　　　　　　*juice of ½ lemon*
120 g (¼ lb) seasoned flour　*125 ml (¼ pt) oil*

1 Cut the sole into goujons (Recipe 434); thickly slice (or halve) the artichoke bottoms.
2 Roll in seasoned flour.
3 Toss in hot oil à la meunière (Recipe 410).
4 Sauter the diced potatoes and artichoke bottoms in butter (see note below).
5 Mix the sole, artichoke bottoms and potatoes together and toss in butter.
6 Season, add lemon juice.
7 Sprinkle with chopped parsley and/or garnish with 4 rindless lemon slices dipped in chopped parsley.

440 Goujons de sole Murat – Method 2, using cooked (or canned) artichoke bottoms

1 Follow Recipe 439, No. 1.
2 Follow Recipe 439, No. 2.
3 Toss in hot oil à la meunière (Recipe 410) and transfer to (and keep warm in) a suitable serving dish.
4 Sauté the diced potato.
5 Thickly slice the artichoke bottoms.
6 Cook the butter in a pan to noisette stage.
7 Add lemon juice, potatoes and artichokes, allow to heat through, and pour over the goujons.
8 Sprinkle with chopped parsley and/or garnish with four peeled, lemon slices dipped in chopped parsley.

441 Sole Waleska

four 360 g (¾-lb) *Dover soles*	250 ml (½ pt) fish stock (Recipe 374)
500 ml (½ pt) Mornay sauce	15 g (½ oz) grated Parmesan cheese
(Recipe 58)	62 ml (⅛ pt) cream
juice of ½ lemon	60 g (2 oz) butter
8 slices cooked lobster	4 slices truffle (optional)

1 Prepare sole for poaching.
2 Grease tray with butter.
3 Place on sole, white side up.
4 Add fish stock and lemon juice.
5 Cover with greased paper. Bring to boil, and then cook in moderate oven for 15 minutes.
6 Drain, remove side-bones and keep warm.
7 Reduce cooking-liquid to a glaze and add to Mornay sauce.
8 Garnish each sole with sliced lobster.
9 Finish sauce with cream and butter; season.
10 Coat the sole, sprinkle with cheese, and brown under the grill.
11 Garnish with slices of truffle (optional).

WINE-BASED SOLE DISHES

Glazing sole bonne femme and other white wine sauce fish dishes
Many chefs now adapt the original method of glazing. Some believe the traditional way to be too rich, others that results are less certain, being over-dependent on skill and experience. In addition to butter (or in substitution for some of it) cream and egg yolk are thus increasingly considered acceptable.

One alternative Sole bonne femme method, advanced by S. Fortin (as practised by him before World War II in Paris Prunier and in Chez Letessier, Avenue Victo Hugo) in the *Journal of the Hotel & Catering Institute* (Summer, 1951. Ed. John Fuller), but which at the time of publication evoked disagreement, may be summarized as follows:

1 Butter a sauteuse, lay in very finely chopped shallots, sliced mushrooms, the sole fillets, salt, pepper, chopped parsley, white wine and fish fumet, and cook.
2 Transfer fillets to serving dish and keep warm.
3 Very quickly reduce the liquor by about half ('your experience should be your guide', said M. Fortin).
4 Add fish velouté, shaking the sauteuse vigorously on full heat until it is blended with the reduced liquor.
5 Add a spoonful of double cream, bring back to boil and monter au beurre.
6 Finally, shake into the sauce a spoonful of sauce hollandaise (or sauce divine), immediately nap over the fillets and gild under a salamander.

Subsequently other chefs in the *Journal* correspondence disagreed, some deploring any departure from the Escoffier method of cooking in their fish velouté and white wine, subsequent reduction and monter au beurre. However, the latest Cracknell and Kaufmann translation adds a note referring to restaurants with regular demand having *en place* 'a fish sauce already thickened with egg yolks and enriched with butter'. One correspondent advocated reduction of cooking liquor, addition of cream and monté au beurre. (Fortin accepted this latter but with the addition of a little glace de poisson and hollandaise.)

It thus appears that individual chefs will develop their own favoured ways of ensuring reliable glazing of white wine sauces compatible with customers' current taste.

442 Sole au vin blanc

four 360 g (¾-*lb*) *Dover soles*
125 *ml* (¼ *pt*) *white wine*
125 *ml* (¼ *pt*) *fish stock*
  (*Recipe* 374)
125 *ml* (¼ *pt*) *fish velouté*
  (*Recipe* 377)

juice of ¼ *lemon*
30 g (1 *oz*) *finely chopped shallots*
8 *fleurons* (*Recipe* 1024)
120 g (¼ *lb*) *butter*
125 *ml* (¼ *pt*) *cream* ⎱ *liaison*
2 *egg yolks* (*optional*) ⎰

1 Trim fins, remove eyes, gut.
2 Remove black skin, scrape white skin.
3 Grease tray with butter, sprinkle with shallots.
4 Place sole, white skin uppermost, on top.
5 Pour on wine, fish stock and lemon juice,, cover with greased paper and place in moderate oven for 15 minutes.
6 Remove sole, trim side-bones and keep warm.
7 Reduce cooking-liquid by half, add fish velouté and reduce until it coats a wooden spoon.
8 Remove from fire and add the cream or the liaison with yolks (if used).
9 Thicken with butter and season.
10 Place a little sauce on bottom of dish.
11 Coat remainder of sauce over fish.
12 Garnish with fleurons.

Note. Method also applies to Filet de sole (Sole fillets).

432 Sole Bercy

four 360 g (¾-lb) Dover soles   125 ml (¼ pt) fish velouté
15 g (½ oz) chopped parsley   (Recipe 377)
30 g (1 oz) finely chopped shallots   120 g (¼ lb) butter
125 ml (¼ pt) fish stock   juice of 1 lemon
   (Recipe 374)   125 ml (¼ pt) cream } liaison
125 ml (¼ pt) white wine   2 egg yolks (optional) }

1 Prepare soles for poaching.
2 Grease tray with butter and shallots.
3 Place sole on top, white side up.
4 Add wine, fish stock, lemon juice and parsley.
5 Cover with greased paper, bring to boil, then cook in moderate oven for 15 minutes.
6 Drain, remove side bones and keep warm.
7 Reduce cooking liquor by half and add fish velouté; reduce further until it will coat back of spoon; add parsley.
8 Draw to side of fire, thicken with butter, add cream (and beaten egg yolk if desired). Coat fish and glaze.
9 Alternative to 8, a liaison may be used prior to glazing.

444 Sole à la bonne femme

four 360 g (¾ lb) Dover soles   15 g (½ oz) chopped parsley
30 g (1 oz) finely chopped shallots   juice of 1 lemon
180 g (6 oz) sliced mushrooms   125 ml (¼ pt) fish stock
125 ml (¼ pt) white wine   (Recipe 374)
125 ml (¼ pt) fish velouté   120 g (¼ lb) butter
   (Recipe 377)   125 ml (¼ pt) cream } liaison
salt   2 egg yolks (optional) }
cayenne pepper

1 Trim fins, remove eyes, gut and remove black skin, scrape white skin.
2 Grease fish-pan, sprinkle with shallots.
3 Lay sole on the top, sprinkle with parsley and sliced mushrooms.
4 Moisten with fish stock, white wine and lemon juice; season.
5 Cover with greased paper.
6 Boil and cook in moderate oven for 15 minutes.
7 Drain and trim off side bones. Keep warm.
8 Reduce cooking-liquid by half.
9 Add fish velouté and reduce.
10 Thicken with butter. Finish with cream and beaten egg yolk, if desired.
11 Coat the fish with the sauce and glaze.

444a Sole Boistelle (or Sole aux champignons)

1 As for Bonne femme (Recipe 444); do not glaze.
2 Garnish with fleurons (puff paste, Recipe 1024).

445 Sole à la dieppoise

Four 360 g (¾ lb) Dover soles	30 g (1 oz) finely chopped shallots	62 ml (⅛ pt) white wine
125 ml (¼ pt) fish velouté (Recipe 377)	30 g (1 oz) bearded, cooked mussels	15 g (½ oz) shrimp tails
8 turned mushrooms	juice of 1 lemon	120 g (¼ lb) butter
4 g (⅛ oz) chopped parsley	8 fleurons Puff paste (Recipe 1024)	62 ml (⅛ pt) cream
		125 ml (¼ pt) fish stock (Recipe 374)

1 Trim fins, remove eyes, gut and remove black skin, scrape white skin.
2 Grease fish-pan with butter, sprinkle with shallots; lay sole on top, white skin uppermost.
3 Moisten with fish stock, wine and lemon juice; cover with greased paper, boil and cook in moderate oven for 15 minutes.
4 Drain sole, remove side fins, and keep warm.
5 Reduce cooking-liquid by half, add the fish velouté and shrimp tails and mussels; reduce further till the sauce coats the back of a spoon.
6 Add the cream and the chopped parsley.
7 Thicken with butter (montez au buerre) and season.
8 Place a little sauce on bottom of serving dish; place the soles on top, white side uppermost.
9 Do *not* glaze; garnish each sole with turned mushrooms and cover completely with the sauce.
10 Garnish with fleurons.

446 Filet de sole Duglére

two 750 g (1½ lb) Dover soles	1 finely chopped shallot	juice of ½ lemon
125 ml (¼ pt) fish velouté (Recipe 377)	240 g (½ lb) (net) tomato concassé	90 g (3 oz) butter
½ oz) chopped parsley	125 ml (¼ pt) fish stock (Recipe 374)	62 ml (⅛ pt) white wine
		62 ml (⅛ pt) cream

1 Remove both skins and fillet.
2 Wash bones and make 250 ml (½ pt) fish stock; reserve 125 ml (¼ pt) and make the other 125 ml (¼ pt) into fish velouté.
3 Grease tray with butter and sprinkle with shallots and lay on the sole.
4 Sprinkle the tomato concassé on top, add the fish stock, wine and lemon juice, and parsley.
5 Cover with greased paper and place in the oven approximately 15 minutes.
6 Drain sole and keep warm.
7 Reduce cooking-liquid by half and add the strained fish velouté.
8 Add the cream; thicken with butter; season and add a little chopped parsley.

9 Place a little of the sauce in the bottom of the dish; place the sole on top and cover completely with the remainder of the sauce; do *not* glaze.

Note. For whole sole method see Sole au vin blanc (Recipe 442).

447 Sole Marguéry

four 360 g (¾-*lb*) *Dover soles*	16 *bearded, cooked mussels*
125 *ml* (¼ *pt*) *white wine*	30 g (1 *oz*) *finely chopped shallots*
125 *ml* (¼ *pt*) *fish velouté*	4 *fleurons* (*Recipe* 1024)
(*Recipe* 377)	125 *ml* (¼ *pt*) *cream* ⎫ *liaison*
30 g (1 *oz*) *shelled shrimps*	2 *egg yolks* (*optional*) ⎭
125 *ml* (¼ *pt*) *fish stock*	120 g (¼ *lb*) *butter*
(*Recipe* 374)	*juice of* ½ *lemon*

1 Trim fins, remove eyes and gut.
2 Remove black skin, scrape white skin.
3 Grease tray with butter, add shallots.
4 Place sole on top, white side uppermost.
5 Add wine, lemon juice, and fish stock.
6 Cover with greased paper, bring to boil, then cook in moderate oven for 15 minutes.
7 Drain and remove side-bones; keep warm.
8 Reduce cooking-liquid by half and add fish velouté; reduce further until the sauce covers the back of a spoon.
9 Draw to side of fire (add liaison if used) and thicken with butter (montez au beurre), and season.
10 Garnish the centre of each sole with shrimps and mussels tossed in butter.
11 Cover with sauce and glaze.
12 Garnish with fleurons.

448 Sole Véronique

four 360 g (¾ *lb*) *Dover soles*	30 g (1 *oz*) *finely chopped shallots*
125 *ml* (¼ *pt*) *fish stock*	125 *ml* (¼ *pt*) *cream* ⎫ *liaison*
(*Recipe* 374)	2 *egg yolks* (*optional*) ⎭
30 *ml* (¹⁄₁₆ *pt*) *curaçao*	120 g (¼ *lb*) *butter*
120 g (¼ *lb*) *white grapes*	*juice of* ½ *lemon*
125 *ml* (¼ *pt*) *fish velouté*	
(*Recipe* 377)	

1 Prepare soles for poaching.
2 Grease tray with butter; add shallots.
3 Place sole on top, white side up.
4 Add wine, fish stock, and lemon juice.
5 Cover with greased paper, bring to boil, then cook in moderate oven for 15 minutes.
6 Drain, remove side-bones and keep warm.

7 Reduce cooking liquor by half, add fish velouté and reduce further until it coats the back of spoon; draw to side of fire, thicken with butter, add cream and beaten egg yolk, if desired and season.
8 Garnish centre of sole with blanched, de-pipped grapes.
9 Cover with sauce and glaze.

449 Paupiette de sole Otéro

4 *large baked potatoes*	8 *paupiettes of sole*	62 *ml (⅛ pt) brandy*
30 *g (1 oz) diced,*	4 *slices of truffle*	125 *ml (¼ pt)*
cooked lobster	*(optional)*	*lobster sauce*
250 *ml (½ pt) fish stock*	30 *g (1 oz) shelled*	*(Recipe 386)*
(Recipe 374)	*shrimps*	15 *g (½ oz) grated*
250 *ml (½ pt) Mornay*	120 *g (¼ lb) diced,*	*Parmesan cheese*
sauce (Recipe 58)	*cooked mushrooms*	62 *ml (⅛ pt) cream*
	60 *g (2 oz) butter*	

1 Bake the potatoes, remove the tops and make the interior into pommes duchesse (Recipe 909).
2 Pipe the edge of each potato with a star tube and brown lightly.
3 Toss the lobster, mushrooms and shrimps in a little butter and mix with the brandy and lobster sauce.
4 Place a little of this mixture into the bottom of each potato.
5 Poach the sole in fish stock, covered with greased paper, in a moderate oven for 15 minutes.
6 Drain the sole well and keep warm.
7 Reduce the cooking-liquor to a glaze and combine it with Mornay sauce; finish the sauce with cream and butter.
8 Place the sole into potato and cover with the sauce.
9 Sprinkle with cheese, and brown.
10 Garnish with a slice of truffle (optional).
11 Serve on a serviette with sprig of parsley.

TRUITE – TROUT

450 Truite grillée – Grilled trout

four 240 *g (8 oz) trout*	4 *slices lemon*
125 *ml (¼ pt) oil*	15 *g (½ oz) seasoned flour*
120 *g (4 oz) parsley butter*	*sprig parsley*
(Recipe 89)	

1 Clean and ciseler trout.
2 Pass through seasoned flour.
3 Brush both sides with oil and season.
4 Grill both sides (approximately 6 minutes).
5 Garnish with lemon slices and sprig of parsley.
6 Serve parsley butter separately.

451 Truite Cléopatra

> *four* 240 *g* (*8-oz*) *trout*   4 *slices lemon*
> 15 *g* (½ *oz*) *chopped parsley*   *juice of* ¼ *lemon*
> 30 *g* (1 *oz*) *shelled shrimps or*   4 *soft roes*
>   *prawns*   15 *g* (½ *oz*) *capers*
> 120 *g* (¼ *lb*) *butter*

1 Cook trout as for meunière (Recipe 410).
2 Garnish with shrimps, capers, and soft roes (cooked as meunière).
3 Finish with beurre noisette (Recipe 82), lemon juice, and parsley.

452 Truite Belle-Meunière

> *four* 240 *g* (*8-oz*) *trout*   125 *ml* (¼ *pt*) *oil*   4 *soft roes*
> 15 *g* (½ *oz*) *chopped*   120 *g* (¼ *lb*) *butter*   *juice of* ¼ *lemon*
>   *parsley*   4 *turned mushrooms*   *flour*
> 4 *blanched tomatoes*   8 *slices lemon*

1 Clean and ciseler trout.
2 Cook as for meunière (Recipe 410).
3 Garnish with cooked mushrooms and soft roes, meunière, and quartered, skinned tomatoes with pips removed.
4 Finish off with slices of lemon on top of trout, beurre noisette (Recipe 82), lemon juice and parsley.

Note. Garnish should be arranged neatly on top of each trout.

453 Truite saumonée – Salmon trout

Salmon trout may be prepared as above recipes or as for salmon.

TURBOT AND OTHER WHITE FISH

Other of the larger white fish include: Turbotin – Baby turbot (known as chicken turbot); Barbue – Brill; Flétan – Halibut. For the cuts commonly used for such larger, flat fish proceed as follows:

> Tronçon (steak cut) – divide fish down the middle (through bone) and cut into 180 g (6 oz) steaks (with bone).
> Filet or Suprême (fillet) – fillet then skin fish on *both* sides and cut into 120 to 180 g (4 to 6 oz) portions.

Note. Many of the treatments given for sole may be applied.

454 Turbot poché à la hollandaise

> *four* 180 *g* (*6-oz*)   *sprigs parsley*   4 *slices lemon*
>   *tronçons of turbot*   500 *ml* (1 *qt*) *white*   250 *ml* (½ *pt*) *sauce*
> 360 *g* (¾ *lb*) *small,*   *court-bouillon*   *hollandaise*
>   *turned potatoes*   (*Recipe* 370)   (*Recipe* 70)

1 Cut turbot into tronçons.
2 Soak in water for 2 hours.

3 Wash off and cook in boiling, white court-bouillon and simmer 10 minutes.
4 Remove skin and centre bone.
5 Garnish with boiled potatoes, lemon slices, and sprig of parsley.
6 Serve with a little of the cooking-liquor.
7 Hollandaise sauce is served separately.

FISH SOUPS OR STEWS

455 Bouillabaise – Method 1

1 *sliced French loaf*	120 g (¼ *lb*) *squid*	2 *cloves crushed*
120 g (¼ *lb*) *conger eels*	16 *crayfish*	*garlic*
120 g (¼ *lb*) *rascasses*	24 *mussels in shell*	120 g (¼ *lb*) *tomato*
(*hog-fish*)	240 g (½ *lb*) *julienne of*	*concassé*
240 g (½ *lb*) *John Dory*	*leek and onions*	good pinch saffron
240 g (½ *lb*) *whiting*	2 *bay-leaves*	250 *ml* (½ *pt*) *oil*
120 g (¼ *lb*) *red mullet*	*pinch of fennel*	250 *ml* (½ *pt*) *white*
		wine

1 Cut large fish leaving small fish whole (or cut all fish to pieces of regular size, 2 cm (1 inch) diameter).
2 Cook the leek and onions in oil; add the garlic, fennel, bay-leaves.
3 Add the fish and sweat under cover for a few minutes.
4 Add the tomato and moisten with the wine and a little fish stock.
5 Bring to the boil, add the mussels and saffron; cook approximately 15 minutes; season, using the peppermill liberally.
6 Serve in a large tureen with toasted slices of bread which have been piquéd with garlic.
7 Serve Rouille (Recipe 395a) separately.

456 Bouillabaisse – Method 2

1¼ kg (2½ *lb*) *assorted fish* (*see*	1 *tomato concassé* (*medium size*)
note below)	¼ *teaspoon chopped parsley*
1 *small onion, chopped*	1 *bouquet garni*
¼ *litre* (½ *pt*) *light fish stock*	15 g (½ *oz*) *beurre manié*
(*Recipe* 374)	(*Recipe* 19)
⅕ *litre* (⅖ *pt*) *white wine*	*mussels and other shellfish for*
1 *tbsp. olive oil*	*garnish*
4 *slices of olive-oil fried French*	*seasoning*
bread (*or as oven-dried croûtes*)	*pinch of saffron*
chopped white of 1 *leek*	10 g (⅓ *oz*) *crushed garlic*

Note. Fish for authentic Bouillabaise comes from the Mediterranean (Marseilles coastal area) but may be made outside that region with a mix of other fish. In Paris, for example, selection is made from: gurnard (gurnet), weever, conger eel, burbot, monkfish, John Dory, turbot and langouste (crawfish).

1 Sweat in oil the onion and leek.
2 Moisten with the fish stock, wine and tomato.
3 Add the garlic, bouquet garni, pinch of saffron and lightly season.
4 Bring to the boil and cook for 10 minutes.
5 Add those fish with firm flesh, such as conger and the langouste, all sliced into tronçons.
6 After 5 minutes, add (similarly sliced) the softer fleshed fish, together with the chopped parsley.
7 Continue to cook steadily for a further 15 minutes.
8 Then thicken with the beurre manié.
9 Service is in a tureen, deep dish or timbale, and usually this has the fried bread placed in the bottom first. (Note that some use plainly baked or toasted bread. Some serve the bread (fried or toasted) separately but soaked in the Bouillabaisse liquor.) Add all the fish and liquor with a surrounding garnish of open mussels and other shellfish. Serve Rouille (Recipe 395a) separately.

457 Matelote d'anguilles – Eel matelote

750 g (1½ lb) eels
20 glazed button onions
8 heart-shaped croûtons
250 ml (½ pt) red wine
8 cooked crayfish
15 g (½ oz) butter ⎱ for beurre
15 g (½ oz) flour ⎰ manié

60 g (2 oz) butter
8 whole, cooked mushrooms
30 g (1 oz) finely chopped shallots
1 bouquet garni
1 clove garlic
62 ml (⅛ pt) cream

1 Sweat the shallots.
2 Skin and section the eels and sweat under cover with the shallots for a few minutes.
3 Add a clove of crushed garlic.
4 Moisten with the red wine, add the bouquet garni and braise in the oven until tender.
5 Reduce the cooking-liquor and thicken with beurre manié. Season, add a little cream and blend in the butter.
6 Mix the eels with the sauce and garnish with mushrooms, onions, and crayfish.
7 Dip the end of the croûtons in chopped parsley.

458 Waterzoï

240 g (½ lb) carp
240 g (½ lb) pike
240 g (½ lb) eel
60 g (2 oz) thinly sliced carrots
120 g (¼ lb) small onion rings
125 ml (¼ pt) white wine

125 ml (¼ pt) fish stock
(Recipe 374)
bouquet garni
pinch sage
60 g (2 oz) butter
salt and pepper
8 slices buttered French bread

1 Cook the vegetables in the fish stock and white wine with the herbs until tender; season.
2 Cut the fish into sections in the bone and sweat under cover for a few minutes.
3 Pour over the liquid and cook.
4 Serve in a large soup-tureen and garnish the top with the bread.

MOUSSES, MOUSSELINES, AND QUENELLES OF FISH

These preparations are all made from the same basic *farce* (forcemeat) of fish (which may be, for example, brill, halibut, pike, salmon, scampi, sole, trout, turbot, whiting or other variety). Mousses are those of larger size in moulds for several covers. Mousselines are in individual portions (either piped meringue fashion or by tablespoons), and quenelles are smaller, either moulded with teaspoons or by piping into small balls.

459 Mousse de sole (or Mousse de merlan) – Sole (or whiting) mousse

240 g (½ lb) raw fillet-sole (or   250 ml (½ pt) fresh cream
    whiting)   seasoning
2 egg whites

1 Mince the fish finely (in a food processor).
2 Gradually add the beaten egg whites; season and pound until well bound.
3 Rub through fine sieve.
4 Place the mixture in a bowl on ice and ensure that the mix is well chilled.
5 Gradually add the previously chilled cream (if the cream is slightly warm the mixture will separate and curdle).
6 Place in a buttered mould and cook in bain-marie.

460 Mousselines de poisson

1 Prepare as for mousse (Recipe 459) but shape with a 30 ml spoon (2 tablespoons) and poach.
2 Mousselines are served, with the appropriate sauce, as a dish in themselves.

461 Quenelles (of fish)

Preparation as for mousses or mousselines (Recipes 459 and 460) but either (i) shape with teaspoons into smaller balls or ovals or (ii) pipe into small balls. Quenelles are used as component of or garnish to a dish.

SHELLFISH

General Points. Because shellfish begin to decompose swiftly after death, they are brought alive into the kitchen. For many fishes, particularly for cold service, shellfish are simply placed into boiling, salted water (or court-bouillon) and cooked, in the case of lobster, crab, langoustine, for approximately 20 minutes per 500 g (lb). Scampi, crayfish, prawns and shrimps take only up to 10 minutes, according to size. It is important not to over-cook for this toughens the flesh. As in the case of white fish, methods and recipes for shellfish are interchangeable particularly where similar types are concerned. Crustaceans may be accorded similar treatment in cooking and dressing, i.e. many methods are interchangeable.

Main crustaceans used in the kitchen are:

Shrimps – crevettes grises (often abbreviated to crevettes). Prawns – crevettes roses. Dublin Bay Prawns or Scampi – langoustine. Crayfish – écrevisses. Crayfish – langoustes. Lobsters – homards. Crabs – crabes.

Other shellfish treated in this chapter are:

Oysters (huitres) – Mussels (moules) – Scallops (coquilles St Jacques).

Similar methods may be applied to others, such as cockles (coques).

462 Crevettes roses frites – Fried prawns

500 *ml* (1 *pt*) *shelled prawns*	120 *g* (¼ *lb*) *flour*	*seasoning*
	2 *eggs*	*deep fat*

1 Four, egg and crumb.
2 Fry in deep fat.
3 Serve with Sauce tartare (Recipe 114).

463 Curried Prawns

1 Toss shelled prawns in butter, mix with curry sauce (Recipe 32).
2 Serve with plain boiled rice.

464 Ecrevisses – Crayfish

1 These are frequently cooked in court-bouillon (Recipe 370) for 15 minutes and are used for garnish.
2 They may also be prepared as Newburg or Américaine (Recipes 471 and 468).

COQUILLES ST-JACQUES – SCALLOPS

465 Coquilles St-Jacques Mornay – Scallops Mornay

4 *coquilles St-Jacques*	250 *ml* (½ *pt*) *mornay sauce*
240 *g* (½ *lb*) *duchesse potatoes*	(*Recipe* 58)
(*Recipe* 909)	30 *g* (1 *oz*) *grated Parmesan cheese*

1 Apply gentle heat to open coquille.
2 Remove fish and deep shell.

3 Cook the fish in court-bouillon (Recipe 371) approximately 5 to 10 minutes.
4 Surround each deep shell with duchesse potatoes.
5 Place a little sauce in the bottom of each shell, slice and lay fish on top.
6 Cover fish with sauce, sprinkle with Parmesan cheese.
7 Brown under grill.

466 Coquilles St-Jacques à la parisienne

4 *coquilles St Jacques*
4 *slices truffle (optional)*

250 *ml (½ pt) white wine sauce*
(*Recipe* 396)

1 Prepare as for Mornay (Recipe 465) but substitute white wine sauce for Mornay.
2 Glaze and garnish with slices of truffle.

467 Coquilles St-Jacques au lard – Scallops with bacon

8 *rolls bacon*
4 *coquilles St Jacques*
120 *g (¼ lb) butter*

15 *g (½ oz) chopped*
parsley
4 *lemon slices*

120 *g (4 oz) flour*
62 *ml (¼ pt) oil*

1 Blanch and cook the coquilles St-Jacques à la meunière (Recipe 410).
2 Garnish with roll of cooked bacon.
3 Finish off with chopped parsley, lemon slices and beurre noisette (Recipe 82).

HOMARD – LOBSTER

468 Homard à l'américaine – Lobster américaine

1.5 *kg (3 lb) raw lobster*
250 *ml (½ pt) fish stock*
(*Recipe* 374)
120 *g (¼ lb) brunoise vegetable*
(*Recipe* 750)
1.25 *ml spoon* [¼ *teaspoon*]
chopped tarragon
240 *g (½ lb) tomato concassé*
10 *ml spoon* [½ *tablespoon*]
tomato purée

125 *ml (¼ pt) white wine*
60 *g (2 oz) butter*
62 *ml (⅛ pt) oil*
1.25 *ml spoon* [¼ *teaspoon*]
chopped parsley
½ *bouquet garni*
240 *g (½ lb) rice for rice pilaff*
(*Recipe* 366)
½ *glass (30 ml (1⁄16 pt)) brandy*

1 Remove legs and claws from a washed lobster.
2 Crack the claws. Halve the lobster by cutting it lengthwise between tail and carapace.
3 Remove the trail and cut the tail through and across the shell into thick slices.
4 Discard the sac and pound with (or mix in food processor) equal quantity of butter (to produce lobster butter).
5 Fry the lobster in a sauté pan in the oil.
6 Add the brandy and flame.

7 Add the brunoise and half the parsley and tarragon and sweat under cover for 5 minutes.

8 Add the tomato concassé, fish stock and tomato purée; bring to the boil; add bouquet garni and cook under cover for 20 minutes.

9 Remove meat from the shells and keep warm; (in continental style the fish may also be left in shell for service).

10 Reduce the sauce and thicken with the lobster butter and season.

11 Dress the lobster in a timbale; decorate with the heads and strain sauce over with a coarse chinois (strainer). Sprinkle with remainder of parsley and tarragon.

12 Serve with rice pilaff.

469 Homard Cardinal

Four *half-lobsters*	*250 ml (½ pt) lobster*	*30 g (1 oz) grated*
1 *egg yolk* ⎫	*sauce (Recipe* 386)	*Parmesan cheese*
62 *ml (⅛ pt)* ⎬ *liaison*	15 *g (½ oz) diced*	*30 g (1 oz) butter*
cream ⎭	*truffles (optional)*	*4 sliced truffles*
60 *g (2 oz) cooked,*	1 *glass (30 ml (¹⁄₁₆ pt)*	*(optional)*
diced mushrooms	*brandy*	

1 Remove meat from shells.

2 Leave the meat from the claws whole but dice the remainder.

3 Sweat the lobster in butter and flame with brandy.

4 Mix the diced truffles and mushrooms with a little of the lobster sauce to form a salpicon.

5 Heat the shells and place the salpicon in the bottom.

6 Place the lobster inside the shell with the claws in the head part.

7 Add the egg yolks and cream to the remainder of the lobster sauce and coat each lobster.

8 Sprinkle with cheese and brown under grill.

9 Garnish each lobster with slice of truffle (optional).

10 Serve on d'oyley-covered dish with sprigs of parsley.

470 Homard Mornay

four cooked half-lobsters	*30 g (1 oz) butter*
500 ml (1 pt) Mornay sauce	*seasoning*
(Recipe 58)	1 *egg yolk* ⎫ *liaison*
30 g (1 oz) Parmesan cheese	62 *ml (⅛ pt) cream* ⎭

1 Remove meat from shells and leave the claw meat whole.

2 Cut the lobster into scallops and sweat the lobster in butter with the claws.

3 Add the egg yolks and cream into the mornay sauce.

4 Line the bottom of each shell with a little sauce.

5 Mix a little sauce with the lobster meat and fill in each shell, placing the claw part in the head.

6 Cover with the remainder of sauce.

7 Sprinkle with cheese and brown under grill.

8 Serve on d'oyley-covered silver dish and garnish with parsley.

471 Homard Newburg

1 kg (2 lb) cooked lobster	½ glass (30 ml (¹⁄₁₆ pt)) sherry	45 g (1½ oz) butter
1 egg yolk ⎫	250 ml (½ pt) lobster	180 g (6 oz) rice for
62 ml (⅛ pt) ⎬ liaison	sauce (Recipe 386)	pilaff
cream ⎭	4 slices truffle	(Recipe 366)
62 ml (⅛ pt) brandy	(optional)	

1 Cut the lobster head in half and the tail section in tronçons.
2 Remove meat from claws and tail sections.
3 Toss the lobster in butter and flame in the brandy, then add the sherry.
4 Add the lobster sauce and cook for about 5 minutes.
5 Add the liaison of egg yolks and cream; draw to side of stove (reduce heat).
6 Season and thicken with butter (montez au beurre).
7 Serve the lobster in a timbale and garnish with slices of truffle; serve also a timbale of rice pilaff.
8 Lobster Newburg may also be prepared by simply adding a liaison and omitting lobster sauce.

472 Homard Thermidor

four cooked half-lobsters	2.5 ml spoon [½ teaspoon] diluted mustard
250 ml (½ pt) Mornay sauce (Recipe 58)	30 g (1 oz) Parmesan cheese
30 g (1 oz) shallots (chopped)	1 egg yolk ⎫ liaison
62 ml (⅛ pt) white wine	62 ml (⅛ pt) cream ⎭
62 ml (⅛ pt) fish stock (Recipe 374)	15 g (½ oz) parsley
	30 g (1 oz) butter

1 Prepare lobster as for Mornay (Recipe 470).
2 Sweat the shallots in butter and make a reduction with the parsley, wine and fish stock; add to the Mornay sauce and blend in the diluted mustard; effect a liaison with the egg yolks and cream.
3 Pour a little sauce in bottom of each shell.
4 Sweat the lobster in butter and mix with a little of the sauce and fill in each half.
5 Coat with sauce; sprinkle with cheese and brown under the grill.
6 Serve as for Mornay.

HUITRES – OYSTERS

473 Huitres Mornay

24 oysters	250 ml (½ pt) Mornay sauce (Recipe 58)	30 g (1 oz) Parmesan cheese

1 Beard and cook the oysters for 3 minutes in a little fish stock (Recipe 374) and drain.

2 Wash the deep shells, place a little mornay sauce on the bottom of each one; place the oysters on top and coat with mornay sauce.
3 Sprinkle with cheese and brown.
4 Serve on silver with d'oyley and parsley.

474 Huitres à la florentine

Prepare as for huitres Mornay (Recipe 473) but place a little cooked leaf-spinach on the bottom of each shell.

MOULES – MUSSELS

475 Moules marinière

1 *kg (2 lb) mussels*	62 *ml (⅛ pt) fish stock (Recipe 374)*
30 *g (1 oz) finely chopped shallots*	*juice of ¼ lemon*
30 *g (1 oz) butter*	*cayenne pepper*
62 *ml (⅛ pt) cream*	62 *ml (⅛ pt) white wine*
15 *g (½ oz) flour* ⎱ *beurre*	
15 *g (½ oz) butter* ⎰ *manié*	

1 Wash and scrape the mussels well.
2 Place in a pan with the shallots, herbs, wine and fish stock.
3 Cook quickly under cover for 5 minutes.
4 Remove mussels; take off the beads and half the shell.
5 Place in a casserole to keep warm.
6 Decant the cooking-liquor to clean pan and reduce by half with a little cream.
7 Thicken slightly with the beurre manié and enrich the sauce with a little butter: season, add lemon juice and cayenne pepper.
8 Pour the sauce over.

SCAMPI (LANGOUSTINES) – DUBLIN BAY PRAWNS

476 Scampi frits – Fried scampi

500 *g (1 lb) scampi tails*	375 *g (¾ lb) white*	2 *eggs*
120 *g (¼ lb) flour*	*breadcrumbs*	

1 Cook the scampi in court-bouillon (Recipe 371) for a few minutes.
2 Allow to cool; drain.
3 Flour, egg, and crumb.
4 Fry crisp in hot fat; season and drain.
5 Serve with fried parsley, lemon, and sauce tartare (Recipe 114).

477 Scampi Germaine

500 *g (1 lb) scampi*	250 *ml (½ pt) sauce béarnaise*
240 *g (½ lb) riz pilaff (Recipe 366)*	*(Recipe 71)*
62 *ml (⅛ pt) cream*	

1 Cook the scampi in court-bouillon (Recipe 372).
2 Drain and mix with sauce béarnaise, add a little cream.
3 Serve with a border of rice pilaff.
4 Glaze under grill.

478 Scampi à la créole

500 g (1 lb) scampis	240 g (½ lb) riz pilaff	2 eggs
15 g (½ oz) curry powder	(Recipe 366)	120 g (¼ lb) flour
	375 g (¾ lb) white crumbs	

1 Cook scampi in court-bouillon (Recipe 371) and then cool.
2 Mix 7 g (¼ oz) curry powder with the crumbs.
3 Flour, egg, and crumb.
4 Mix the remainder of curry powder with rice pilaff.
5 Fry the scampi in deep fat.
6 Serve with a surround of rice with scampi in the middle.
7 Serve separately curry sauce in sauce-boat.

479 Brochette de scampi – Skewered scampis

4 rashers streaky bacon	7 g (¼ oz) sultanas
4 scampis	7 g (¼ oz) pimentos
2 thick slices cucumber	120 g (¼ lb) white breadcrumbs
120 g (¼ lb) riz pilaff (Recipe 366)	1 tomato
15 g (¼ oz) currants	125 ml (¼ pt) tomato sauce
3 mushroom caps	(Recipe 34)
2 bay-leaves (blanched)	30 g (1 oz) peas
pinch chopped chervil	

1 Blanch the scampis and refresh.
2 Roll the scampis in bacon.
3 Cut the cucumber into rounds about 1 cm (½ inch) thick and blanch.
4 Alternate the scampis, cucumber, bay leaves, tomato, mushrooms on a silver skewer, and brush with butter.
5 Roll the brochette in white-crumbs with chervil.
6 Brush with oil, and grill gently.
7 Serve on a bed of pilaff rice garnished with fruit, peas and pimentos, with a cordon of tomato sauce.

EDIBLE SNAILS

480 Escargots – Snails

1 Allow to 'desgorge' for 12 hours by soaking in water.
2 Marinate in wine and aromatics for 3 hours.
3 Gently simmer them in their own juice.
4 Remove from shells and trim.
5 Boil the shells with bicarbonate of soda for 30 minutes.
6 Return to shells.
7 Fill with beurre d'escargots (as for other beurres composés (compound butters)) using fines herbes, garlic and butter.

GRENOUILLES – FROGS

An alternative name for genouilles in the kitchen is nymphes; therefore, 'Cuisses de nymphes' is used instead of Cuisses de genouilles (frogs' legs). These, specially bred for table use, are prepared in many ways of which the following are examples:

481 Cuisses de nymphes aux fines herbes

1 Season; toss in butter with chopped shallots, chopped parsley and lemon juice.
2 Add beurre noisette (Recipe 82).

482 Cuisses de nymphes frites

1 Pass through seasoned flour.
2 Dip in batter.
3 Fry in deep fat.
4 Serve with green parsley and lemon.

483 Cuisses de nymphes au gratin

Poach and serve with Italienne Sauce (Recipe 42) and grated Parmesan cheese. (Remove feet.)

484 Cuisses de nymphes à la meunière

1 Pass in milk and flour.
2 Fry in butter, lemon juice, and chopped parsley.

485 Cuisses de nymphes à la poulette

1 Poach in white wine and fish stock (Recipe 374) and mushrooms.
2 Add fish veloute (Recipe 377).
3 Thicken with egg yolks and cream.

486 Cuisses de nymphes à la mode paysanne

Sauté in butter with garlic, concassé tomatoes, and chopped parsley.

487 Cuisses de nymphes en brochette

1 Thread on silver skewer with mushrooms.
2 When cooked, roll in white breadcrumbs containing chopped parsley and garlic.
3 Brown under grill.

FISH FOR COLD SERVICE

488 Salade de poisson – Fish salad

As main course

360 g (¾ lb) cooked *white fish free from skin and bone*	1 blanched tomato	7 g (¼ oz) capers
	4 anchovy fillets	4 stoned olives
	62 ml (⅛ pt) vinaigrette	seasoning
1 lettuce	(Recipe 118)	
1 hard-boiled egg		

1 Flake the fish and marinate with the vinaigrette and season.
2 Finely shred the outside leaves of lettuce retaining the heart.
3 Place the lettuce on the bottom of a large salad bowl; season.
4 Pile the fish neatly on top of the lettuce.
5 Decorate with criss-cross anchovies and capers.
6 Garnish with hearts of lettuce cut into quarters, quarters of egg and tomato in between the lettuce hearts.
7 Place the stoned olives neatly on top of the fish and sprinkle a little pepper.
8 Serve vinaigrette separately.

489 Mayonnaise de poisson – Mayonnaise of fish

Prepare as above, using same ingredients but coat the fish with mayonnaise sauce (Recipe 110). See also Recipe 492.

SALMON

490 Boiled Salmon

1 Cook the fish in a court-bouillon, whole, filleted or in cutlets.
2 Allow to cool in cooking liquor.
3 Remove, drain.
4 Flake the fish, taking care to remove all traces of bone, marinate with the vinaigrette and season well.
5 Finely shred the outside leaves of lettuce retaining the heart.
6 Place the lettuce on the bottom of a large salad bowl, season.
7 Pile the fish neatly on top of the lettuce.
8 Decorate with a trellis of anchovy fillets and capers.
9 Garnish with hearts of lettuce cut into quarters, quarters of hard boiled egg and tomato in between the lettuce hearts.
10 Place the stoned olives neatly on top of the fish and sprinkle a little paprika pepper.
11 Serve vinaigrette separately.
12 See also Recipes 202–205 and 427.

For Cold Service
1 Using a 5 kg (10-lb) salmon proceed as for hot salmon but simmer only for 10 minutes.
2 Then remove from the fire and allow to cool in its cooking-liquor under cover.
3 When cold, skin, and decorate.

SALMON WITH MAYONNAISE

Salmon mayonnaise (or Darne de saumon à la mayonnaise) differs from Mayonnaise de saumon which is shown in the two recipes for Salmon mayonnaise and Mayonnaise of salmon which follow. The difference applies when other fish are prepared in the same way.

491 Darne de saumon à la mayonnaise – Salmon mayonnaise

four 180 *g* (6-*oz*) *darnes of cold salmon*	125 *ml* (¼ *pt*) *mayonnaise sauce* (*Recipe* 110)	120 *g* (4 *oz*) *finely sliced cucumber* 750 *ml* (1½ *pt*)
1 *lettuce*	62 *ml* (⅛ *pt*) *vinaigrette*	*court-bouillon*
1 *hard-boiled egg*	(*Recipe* 118)	(*Recipe* 371)
1 *blanched tomato*		

1 Place the salmon in simmering court-bouillon (Recipe 371) for 5 minutes. Allow to cool in the liquor under tight cover.
2 Remove the skin and centre bone.
3 Dress neatly on a large flat oval dish.
4 Garnish round the sides with quarter-hearts of lettuce, well drained, egg and tomato (firm).
5 Garnish the top of the salmon with a few slices of cucumber marinated with vinaigrette and dress on a ravier with a little chopped parsley sprinkled on top.
6 Serve the mayonnaise sauce (which should be of stiff consistency) in sauceboat with the ravier of cucumber separately.

492 Mayonnaise de saumon – Mayonnaise of salmon

750 *g* (¾ lb *cooked salmon, free of skin and bone*	1 *hard-boiled egg* 1 *blanched tomato*	62 *ml* (⅛ *pt*) *vinaigrette* (*Recipe* 118)
1 *large lettuce*	4 *anchovy fillets*	7*g* (¼ *oz*) *capers*
90 *g* (3 *oz*) *thinly sliced skinned cucumber*	4 *stoned olives* *seasoning*	125 *ml* (¼ *pt*) *mayonnaise* (*Recipe* 110)

1 Flake the salmon and marinate in vinaigrette; season.
2 Finely shred the outer leaves of lettuce retaining the hearts.

3 Place the shredded lettuce on the bottom of a large salad-bowl, season lightly.
4 Pile the salmon neatly on top of the lettuce.
5 Coat the salmon evenly with 125 ml (¼ pt) sauce mayonnaise and place the remainder in a sauce-boat.
6 Decorate the top of the salmon with criss-crosses of anchovies, capers and the stoned olives.
7 Garnish the sides of the bowl with quarters of lettuce hearts, cucumber slices, hard-boiled egg and stoned olives.
8 Final presentation, dust the top of salmon with a little paprika or chopped lobster-coral: do *not* sprinkle with chopped parsley.

SHELLFISH
CRABE – CRAB

493 Dressed Crab

four 500 g (1-*lb*) *crabs*	125 *ml* (¼ *pt*) *mayonnaise*
4 *hard-boiled eggs*	(*Recipe* 110)
1 *lettuce*	2 *blanched tomatoes*

1 Cook crab in court-bouillon (Recipe 371) for 20 minutes and allow to cool.
2 Remove purse and claws and shred meat finely.
3 Mix the soft part with a little mayonnaise and breadcrumbs; season.
4 Dress each side of crab with this mixture and place meat in the centre.
5 Decorate with chopped hard-boiled egg.
6 Serve with French salad and sauce-boat of mayonnaise.

CREVETTES GRISES – SHRIMPS AND PRAWNS

494 Potted Shrimps (or Prawns)

375 *g* (¾ *lb*) *butter*	250 *g* (½ *lb*) *shelled*
nutmeg	*shrimps* (*or prawns*)
	seasoning

1 Melt the butter, add shrimps and season.
2 Fill into small pots and cover with clarified butter.

495 Cocktail de crevettes – Shrimp cocktail

240 *g* (½ *lb*) *peeled shrimps*	4 *slices lemon*
62 *ml* (⅛ *pt*) *whipped cream*	500 *ml* (1 *pt*) *mayonnaise*
15 *ml spoon* [1 *dessertspoon*]	(*Recipe* 110)
tomato ketchup	4 *stoned olives*
2.5 *ml spoon* [½ *teaspoon*]	4 *blanched tomatoes*
chopped parsley	1 *large lettuce* (*julienne*)
5 *ml spoon* [½ *dessertspoon*]	7 *g* (¼ *oz*) *finely chopped onions*
Worcester sauce	

1 Mix mayonnaise, onions, cream.
2 Add Worcester sauce, parsley and tomato ketchup.
3 Remove pips from tomatoes and rub through fine sieve.
4 Mix with sauce.
5 Add shrimps and season.
6 Place a little lettuce in the bottom of each glass. Serve in suitable goblets, which, if desired, may be rimmed with a little chopped parsley.
7 Place the shrimp mixture on top.
8 Garnish with olive and a little shredded lettuce, and slice of lemon dipped in parsley.

496 Crevettes roses – Prawns

Shell the tails of the prawns and hang over a goblet containing crushed ice.

HOMARD – LOBSTER

497 Demi-homard froid, Sauce mayonnaise – Cold half-lobster, sauce mayonnaise

4 *half lobsters (cooked)*   4 *hard-boiled eggs*
½ *sauce-boat mayonnaise*   1 *lettuce*
   (Recipe 110)   15 *g* (½ *oz) capers*
2 *blanched tomatoes*

1 Cut the whole lobster in half.
2 Remove the brain and intestines.
3 Fill the head part with capers and place the shelled claw on top.
4 Garnish with quarters of lettuce, tomatoes, and hard-boiled eggs.
5 Serve a sauce-boat of mayonnaise.

498 Mayonnaise de homard – Mayonnaise of lobster

1 *kg (2 lb) cooked lobster*   12 *capers*
8 *anchovy fillets*   2 *hard-boiled eggs*
4 *stoned olives*   2 *blanched tomatoes*
250 *ml* (½ *pt) mayonnaise*   1½ *lettuce*
   (Recipe 110)

1 Cut the lobster in two and the tail in sections. Break the claws and remove meat whole; also remove meat from the tail section.
2 Wash the lettuce well and shred one and cut the other into quarters.
3 Place the shredded lettuce in a large glass salad-bowl and season.
4 Place the lobster meat on top and coat with mayonnaise.
5 Decorate with the anchovies, olives, and capers.
6 Garnish the bowl with lettuce hearts, quarters of egg, tomato, and lobster claws.

499 Salade de homard – Lobster salad

1 Proceed as for Lobster Mayonnaise but do not coat the meat with mayonnaise sauce.
2 Serve vinaigrette (Recipe 118) separately from sauceboat.

Mayonnaise and Salads of Shellfish:
Other shellfish suich as langouste, langoustine, may be prepared as for lobster.

500 Cocktail de homard

Prepare as Recipe 495 but substitute lobster for shrimp; cut lobster into small dice.

HUITRES – OYSTERS

501 Huitres nature

Allow 6 oysters per person.

1 Serve on deep shell.
2 Present on a bed of crushed ice with lemon and parsley; and thinly-cut brown bread and butter.

LANGOUSTE – CRAYFISH

502 Langouste – Crayfish

1 Cook in court-bouillon (Recipe 371) for 20 minutes, allow to cool in its cooking-liquor.
2 May be used for cold dishes as for lobster.

6 Meat, Poultry and Game

THE arrangement of the contents of this section has been determined by the methods of cookery involved in the recipes rather than by the main items of meat (or bird) that are used. Such meat foods are, in a kitchen, organized in the classic French manner, prepared either by the roast cook (including the subordinate grillardin or grill cook), the saucier (sauce cook), or, in the case of cold dishes, the garde manger (larder chef).

As noted earlier in Chapter 2, many tasks involved in cold preparations have been eliminated or affected by the ever-increasing amount of pre-prepared and pre-portioned items now bought in from outside. These can replace much, if not all, of that work previously undertaken by larder and vegetable chefs. In large professional kitchens where there is still sectionalization (or up-dated parties) interdependence between specialist chefs may remain.

Although sections or parties within professional kitchens continue to change, it is convenient within this *Compendium* to group recipes for meat (including offal), poultry and game according to mode of cookery (roasting, boiling, etc.). This attempt to build a logical sequence has not slavishly followed traditional considerations. Ease of reference has been a further factor in determining arrangement. Possibilities exist for developing the recipe range in this section by the use of sauces (as in Chapter 1) and vegetable garnishes (as in Chapter 7).

ROASTING

True roasting is exposing food to the radiant heat of a fire; traditionally on a spit (therefore, à la broche is used as an alternative term for rôti – roasted) or by hanging in a Dutch oven. For 'spitted' roasts: all red meats should be properly 'set' by fierce heat and then, according to their size, exposed to the penetrating heat from a fire that has a little or no flame. For small game the fire should, however, have more flame than glowing embers. But for white meats, regulate the fire to allow the joint to cook and colour at the same time.

When roasting, aim at retaining all the juice. Today, this is usually done in the oven, by putting meat in a hot oven 200°C (400°F) for 10 minutes and then reducing the temperature to 180°C (360°F). The meat is basted frequently with fat. The joint should be raised out of the fat to prevent the meat from 'frying' and becoming hard. This may be done by using a trivet or by resting the joint on a bed of roughly-cut vegetables. Take care not to over-brown the vegetables otherwise a singed or acrid flavour will be given to the jus rôti (gravy), which is made later by deglazing in the roasting-tray.

Amount of Roasting. Beef, particularly, and also game and mutton are generally preferred rather underdone (saignant). Lamb, pork, veal and poultry are usually well cooked (bien cuit). Lamb may also be cooked pink.

Testing when done. Very underdone red meat remains resilient to pressure; when it is cooked adequately the meat should not resist finger pressure. In the case of white meats (including poultry), juice-flow when cooked should be clear or 'white'.

SUITABLE JOINTS FOR ROASTING

Beef	Pork	Veal	Lamb and Mutton
Fillet	Leg	Leg (Cuisse or	Best end
(Filet de bœuf)	(Cuisse de	Cuissot de veau)	(Carré)
Foreribs	porc	Loin (Longe)	Leg (Gigot)
(Première côte de	Loin	Shoulder	Saddle (Selle)
bœuf)	(Longe de	(Épaule)	Shoulder (Épaule)
Middle ribs	porc		
(Côte de bœuf)	Shoulder		
Sirloin	(Épaule de		
(Aloyau)	porc)		
Topside (Tranche			
tendre)			
Rump (Culotte de			
bœuf)			
Wing end (Côte			
de bœuf			

APPROXIMATE ROASTING TIMES FOR MEAT, GAME, AND POULTRY

Beef:	15 to 20 minutes per 500 g (lb) and 20 minutes over
Mutton:	25 minutes per 500 g (lb) and 20 minutes over
Lamb:	20 minutes per 500 g (lb) and 20 minutes over
Veal:	25 minutes per 500 g (lb) and 20 minutes over
Venison:	25 minutes per 500 g (lb) and 20 minutes over
Pork:	25 minutes per 500 g (lb) and 25 minutes over
Black game:	Total time ¾ hour
Hazel hen:	Total time ¾ hour
Quails:	Total time 10 minutes
Guinea fowl:	Total time ¾ hour
Hare:	Total time 1 hour
Rabbit:	Total time ¾ hour
Chicken:	15 minutes per 500 g (lb) (or 2.5 kg (5-lb) chicken: 1 hour)
Duck:	20 minutes per 500 g (lb) (or 2 kg (4-lb) duck: 1 hour)
Duckling:	15 minutes per 500 g (lb) (or 1.5 kg (3-lb) duckling: ¾ hour)

Turkey:	20 minutes per 500 g (lb)
Goose:	20 minutes per 500 g (lb)
Grouse:	Total time 20 to 25 minutes
Pheasant:	Total time ¾ hour
Partridge (young):	Total time 15 to 25 minutes
Woodcock (young):	Total time 15 to 20 minutes
Snipe:	Total time 10 to 15 minutes
Lark:	Total time 10 to 15 minutes
Wild Duck:	Total time 20 minutes to ¾ hour (roasted for à la presse, 12 minutes)

The above cooking times *are approximate*. Times must be adjusted according to the size, shape, thickness, and age of joints and birds. When roasting in convection ovens, cooking times may be slightly reduced.

Meats that are normally preferred underdone (beef and, sometimes, lamb) are roasted in a hot oven; small birds (particularly game) in a very hot oven; while well-roasted (bien cuit) meats and poultry are finished in a moderate temperature. To facilitate carving, allow underdone meat to 'rest' in a warm place for a few minutes.

As it is particularly relevant here, we are repeating the table of 'Oven Temperatures' that appears on page xii at the front of the *Compendium*.

OVEN TEMPERATURES

	Gas Mark	Degrees Celsius	Degrees Fahrenheit
Very cool	¼	115	240
	½	120	250
Cool	1	135	275
	2	150	300
Warm	2	150	300
	3	160	325
Moderate	3	160	325
	4	175	350
Moderately hot	5	190	375
	6	200	400
Hot	7	215	425
	8	230	450
Very hot	9	245	475

GARNISHES FOR ROASTS

Accompaniments and stuffings for roasts. In addition to the modes of presentation outlined in the recipes of this section, the following are customary accompaniments for roasts.

503 Meat garnishes

Beef: Yorkshire pudding, horse-radish sauce, unthickened gravy, watercress.
Lamb: Mint sauce or mint jelly, unthickened gravy, watercress (see also Mutton below).
Mutton: Onion sauce, red-currant jelly, unthickened gravy, watercress. (As today mutton is less commonly available, its garnishes (especially red-currant jelly) may also be offered with lamb.)
Pork: Sage and onion stuffing, apple sauce, unthickened gravy.
Veal: Lemon stuffing, baked or grilled bacon, jus lié (slightly-thickened gravy).

504 Poultry garnishes

Capon: As for chicken (or turkey).
Chicken and poussin: Grilled bacon, bread sauce, pommes chips (game chips), unthickened gravy, watercress.
Duck, duckling or goose: Sage and onion stuffing, apple sauce, unthickened gravy, watercress.
Guinea fowl: Croûtons, bread sauce, thin gravy, game chips, grilled bacon.
Pigeon: As for chicken.
Turkey: Bread sauce, Cranberry sauce, sausages, gravy, chestnut stuffing (or alternative stuffing).

505 Game garnishes

Venison: Red-currant jelly, sour cream, jus or jus lié (slightly thickened gravy).
Hare: Red-currant jelly, gravy, stuffing-balls.
Rabbit: Stuffing (sage and onion or lemon stuffing), bacon, jus lié or piquante sauce.

506 Game-bird garnishes

Grouse Partridge Pheasant Plover Ptarmigan Woodcock	Croûtons, gravy, game chips, fried breadcrumbs (and/or bread sauce), watercress. Farce au gratin (see Recipe 508 below).
Widgeon Wild duck	Orange salad, gravy, game chips, watercress, also fried breadcrumbs (and/or bread sauce).

507 Yorkshire pudding

> 120 g (¼ lb) flour   salt   62 ml (⅛ pt) water
> 2 eggs   62 ml (⅛ pt) milk

1 Gradually mix the eggs into the sifted flour and salt.
2 Add sufficient liquid until a beating consistency (that of cream) is achieved then beat well.
3 Allow the mixture to stand for at least half an hour before using.
4 Give a final beating before pouring into a roasting-tray of smoking fat (or oil). Cook in a hot oven for 25 minutes.

508 Farce au gratin – Poultry and game stuffing

> 240 g (½ lb) chicken livers   1 sprig thyme
> 120 g (¼ lb) fat bacon   60 g (2 oz) butter (or sunflower
> 30 g (1 oz) chopped onions   margarine)
> 1 bay-leaf   seasoning

1 Cut the bacon into small pieces and fry gently in butter; add herbs.
2 Add the onions and cook until golden brown.
3 Add the chicken livers, fry quickly and season.
4 Pass through a fine sieve then place in basin covered with buttered paper. (A little chopped truffle may be added to this farce.)

Note
(i) Farce au gratin is sometimes referred to as farce polonaise.
(ii) Also used for spreading on croûtons.

509 Chestnut stuffing

> 360 g (¾ lb) chestnuts   brown stock (Recipe 8)
> 60 g (2 oz) finely chopped suet   salt, pepper
> 30 g (1 oz) breadcrumbs   grated nutmeg

1 Slit, bake, peel, and coarsely-chop the chestnuts.
2 Add the finely chopped suet and mix well with the crumbs, add sufficient stock to moisten and season with salt, pepper, and nutmeg.

Used for turkey and other fowls. (Often with addition of 60 g (2 oz) pork sausage-meat.)

510 Forcemeat balls

Ingredients as Recipe 512.

1 Shape into the desired size of ball.
2 Flour, egg and crumb and deep-fry.

511 Oyster forcemeat

6 *large oysters*
60 *g (2 oz) white*
breadcrumbs
62 *ml (⅛ pt) white*
stock (Recipe 6)

pinch ground mace
7 *g (¼ oz) chopped*
parsley
grated zest of lemon

salt, pepper
1 *small egg*
21 *g (¾ oz) butter*

1 Beard and poach the oysters (with the beards) in stock.
2 Drain, remove the bears and chop the oysters.
3 Mix the oysters with the breadcrumbs, lemon, mace, parsley, and butter; add the oyster stock and season and bind with beaten egg.

Use for poultry (and fish).

512 Plain forcemeat

60 *g (2 oz) finely chopped beef*
suet
120 *g (4 oz) breadcrumbs*
7 *g (¼ oz) chopped parsley*
62 *ml (⅛ pt) milk*

2.5 *ml spoon [½ teaspoon] mixed*
herbs
salt, pepper
1 *small egg*

1 Mix all the ingredients.
2 Bind with beaten egg; milk and season.

Used for veal, mutton, rabbit. If used for poultry, e.g. turkey, incorporate 240 g (½ lb) pork sausagemeat.

513 Sage and Onion stuffing

2 *large onions*
7 *g (¼ oz) sage*
21 *g (¾ oz) fat*

62 *ml (¼ pt) brown*
stock (Recipe 8)
60 *g (2 oz)*
breadcrumbs

3 *g (⅛ oz) salt and*
pepper

1 Chop the onions finely and cook to golden colour in fat.
2 Add the brown stock and cook the onions.
3 Add the sage and white breadcrumbs, season and allow to cook for a few minutes at side of the stove.

Used for pork, duck, goose and rabbit.

514 Veal stuffing

60 *g (2 oz) chopped beef suet*
30 *g (1 oz) finely chopped cooked*
ham
60 *g (2 oz) breadcrumbs*
7 *g (¼ oz) chopped parsley*

2.5 *ml spoon [½ teaspoon] mixed*
herbs
½ *grated lemon zest*
salt, pepper
1 *egg for binding*

1 Mix all the ingredients.
2 Bind with the beaten eggs and season.

Used for chicken, turkey, rabbit, veal.

ROASTS OF BEEF

515 Contrefilet de bœuf rôti – Roast boned-sirloin of beef

1 This rather flat joint (the boned-sirloin without the fillet) is cooked quickly [15 minutes per 500 g (lb)] in a hot oven.
2 It is sometimes larded.

516 Filet de bœuf piqué à la bouquetière – Larded beef-fillet bouquetière

750 g (1½ lb) long-fillet beef	60 g (2 oz) butter seasoning	125 ml (¼ pt) sauce Madère (Recipe
90 g (3 oz) peas	½ wine-glass Madeira	44)
120 g (¼ lb) carrots	12 glazed button	60 g (2 oz) sliced
120 g (¼ lb) turnips	onions	vegetables
4 turned mushrooms	4 blanched tomatoes	(carrots and
	120 g (¼ lb) bacon fat	onions)

1 Turn and glaze all vegetables (except those to be minced).
2 Trim the fillet (i.e. remove all nerves).
3 Cut the fat bacon into strips and insert these into the fillet with the larding needle and tie up, and season.
4 Melt the butter in a suitable roasting tray and colour the fillet well on both sides.
5 Add the sliced vegetables and cook in a hot oven 190°C (375°F) for ½ hour, basting frequently.
6 When cooked, déglacer the pan with a little Madeira and add the sauce.
7 Garnish a silver dish with bouquets of the prepared vegetable, place the fillet in the centre; strain the sauce and serve it separately.

Note. Some chefs brush a little meat glaze over the fillet.

517 Roast forerib or sirloin of beef, and Yorkshire pudding

1 Remove surplus fat.
2 Remove the nerve and chine the vertebræ.
3 Tie up and place on roasting tray.
4 Cover with liquid fat (or oil) and season.
5 Place in hot oven 200°C (400°F) to seal; reduce heat to 190°C (375°F) and baste frequently (see cooking time).
6 When cooked pour away surplus fat from tray and retain residue, add brown stock, boil and season; remove all fat and strain for roast gravy.
7 Serve Yorkshire pudding (Recipe 507) as garnish.

ROASTS OF LAMB OR MUTTON

518 Carré d'agneau rôti, sauce menthe – Roast best end of lamb and mint sauce

4 pairs of cutlets, best end lamb	125 ml (¼ pt) mint sauce
1 bunch watercress	(Recipe 100)
250 ml (½ pt) brown stock	60 g (2 oz) dripping (or oil)
(Recipe 7 or 8)	8 cutlet frills

1 Prepare the carré by removing the vertebræ bone; trim off each cutlet end.
2 Roast by placing on a bed of vegetables and coating with fat (or oil) and seasoning.
3 Roast in hot oven basting frequently; reduce oven temperature when meat is sealed.
4 When cooked, place cutlet-frill on each cutlet and serve mint sauce and gravy separately.
5 Garnish with watercress.

519 Couronne d'agneau à la bouquetière – Crown of lamb bouquetière

750 g (1 lb) best end of lamb	90 g (3 oz) cooked peas
12 turned carrots	90 g (3 oz) cooked French beans
12 turned turnips	120 g (4 oz) butter
120 g (¼ lb) matignon (Recipe 3)	seasoning
4 turned mushrooms	12 button onions

1 Prepare best end of lamb as for roast carré of lamb.
2 Arrange the carrés in the shape of a crown and sew into position.
3 Place the crown on the matignon and also place a few potatoes in the centre of the crown in order to keep its shape when roasting.
4 Carefully baste during the roasting process; when cooked, garnish each cutlet end with a frill.
5 Glaze the carrots, turnips and onions and garnish the dish with bouquets of each vegetable.
6 Serve gravy separately.

520 Épaule d'agneau farcie – Roast stuffed shoulder of lamb

1.25 2kg (½ lb) shoulder of lamb	1.25 ml spoon [¼ teaspoon] mixed herbs
250 ml (½ pt) brown stock (Recipe 7 or 8)	7 g (¼ oz) chopped parsley
60 g (2 oz) carrots ⎱ mirepoix 60 g (2 oz) onions ⎰	1 small egg little milk
60 g (2 oz) breadcrumbs	1.25 ml spoon [¼ teaspoon] lemon rind
30 g (1 oz) chopped suet	seasoning

1 To make stuffing, mix breadcrumbs, suet, mixed herbs, lemon rind and parsley together, bind with the egg, milk and season.
2 Bone out the scapula and humerus-bone in the shoulder.
3 Place the stuffing in the centre and roll and tie.
4 Place the shoulder on the mirepoix in a roasting tray, cover with fat and season.
5 For the first 10 minutes the oven temperature should be 200°C (400°F); then reduce to 180°C (360°F); baste frequently.
6 When cooked, pour away surplus fat from roasting tray and add the brown stock to make the gravy; season and strain and remove all fat.
7 Garnish the shoulder with watercress; serve mint sauce and gravy separately.

521 Gigot d'agneau rôti à la boulangère – Roast leg of lamb boulangère

1.25 kg (2½-lb) leg of lamb	240 g (½ lb) sliced onions	250 ml (½ pt) white stock
500 g (1 lb) sliced potatoes	45 g (1½ oz) butter (or sunflower margarine)	seasoning

1 Prepare the leg of lamb as for roasting and season.
2 Seal the lamb in a hot oven and then finish cooking by placing it on a bed of boulangère potatoes (Recipe 937).
3 Serve lamb with the boulangère garnish.

522 Selle d'agneau rôtie – Roast saddle of lamb.

1 Skin the saddle and remove surplus fat and kidneys.
2 Trim and tie into shape and lightly score with a small knife.
3 Roast in the usual manner.
4 May be carved: (a) English style – cut as for noisettes; (b) French style – lengthwise.

NB. Short saddles are best for banquets.

ROASTS OF PORK, VEAL, AND VENISON

523 Roasts of pork

Cuisse de porc rôtie – Roast leg of pork
Longe de porc – Roast loin of pork

1 For cuisse (leg): remove pelvic bone. For longe (loin): score the skin and tie the meat.
2 Place in roasting tray and cover with a little good dripping (or oil), seal in hot oven; reduce heat and cook slowly, basting frequently.
3 Serve with crackling, sage and onion stuffing, apple sauce, and gravy.

Note. Épaule de porc – Shoulder of pork; though not a prime joint is also sometimes roasted.

524 Roasts of Veal

1 Joints of veal may be piqué, with strips of fat.
2 They are in any case normally covered with slices of back-fat and roasted on a bed of root vegetables with frequent basting. An example is:

525 Longe de veau rôtie chasseur – Roast loin of veal and sauce chasseur

1 Piqué the loin with fat bacon.
2 Roast on a bed of aromatics and serve sauce chasseur (Recipe 38) separately.

526 Hanche de venaison rôtie – Roast haunch of venison

1 Trim off a haunch of venison by removing chine-bone and the end of the knuckle.
2 Wrap well in greased paper to prevent fat from burning.
3 Roast for 2½ to 3 hours basting frequently.
4 Remove the paper, brush with butter to colour a good brown.
5 Dredge lightly with flour and continue to baste until it is well coloured.
6 Make a gravy with the residue from the pan plus any trimmings.
7 Serve red-currant jelly separately.
8 May also be served with chestnut purée.

Note. Venison should be well hung for at least 6 days before use.

527 Cuissot de chevreuil, sauce au cassis

½ *leg venison*
240 g (½ lb) *fat bacon*
1 *litre* (1 *qt*) *red wine marinade*
   (*Recipe* 126)
30 g (1 *oz*) *meat glaze* (*Recipe* 13)

15 *ml spoon* [1 *tablespoon*] *black-currant jelly*
125 *ml* (¼ *pt*) *sauce poivrade*
   (*Recipe* 47)
62 *ml* (⅛ *pt*) *port wine*

1 Carefully skin the leg of venison.
2 Piqué it evenly with the fat bacon.
3 Cover with the marinade and allow to marinate for 10 hours.
4 Roast it as for roast haunch and when cooked; garnish with watercress.
5 Remove all fat from the roasting tray and put the marinade liquid in the pan; reduce to 500 ml (1 pint), add the sauce poivrade, port, and black-currant jelly; reduce to correct consistency, season and strain.
6 Pour some of the sauce around the joint and serve remainder separately.

Note. Some chefs brush the roasted haunch with meat glaze for appearance.

ROASTS OF POULTRY

528 Trussing Poultry and Game

1 Remove winglets and feet.
2 Insert needle and string through winglets.
3 Press legs back and continue insertion of needle through the middle of leg at joint.
4 Pass needle diagonally towards the parson's nose and pull the string right through.
5 Pass the needle through a small piece of skin on the legs, and insert needle on the opposite side towards the middle of the other leg.
6 Pull string through and tie.

529 Poulet rôti au lard – Roast chicken with bacon

one 2 *kg (4-lb) chicken*	125 *ml* (¼ *pt*) *gravy* (*Recipe* 18)
120 *g* (¼ *lb*) *mirepoix* (*Recipe* 3)	240 *g* (½ *lb*) *game chips*
125 *ml* (¼ *pt*) *brown stock*	1 *bunch watercress*
(*Recipe* 8)	30 *g* (1 *oz*) *dripping* (*or oil*)
8 *slices bacon*	*salt, pepper*
125 *ml* (¼ *pt*) *bread sauce*	
(*Recipe* 96)	

1 Clean and truss the bird.
2 Place the fat in roasting tray and heat.
3 Season the chicken inside and outside and roll it in the hot fat.
4 Place it leg-side down first and add the mirepoix and place in oven 190°C (375°F); baste frequently.
5 Turn over on the other leg and continue basting.
6 Turn the chicken on its back and cook until golden brown.
7 Allow approximately 20 minutes per 500 g (lb) plus 20 minutes extra.
8 When cooked, remove string and keep hot.
9 Pour away surplus fat from roasting tray and rinse with brown stock; season, strain, and skim off fat.
10 Garnish the chicken with game chips, grilled bacon, and watercress.
11 Serve gravy and bread sauce separately.

530 Chapon rôti – Roast capon

Prepare and cook as chicken; garnish as chicken (or also with turkey accompaniments).

531 Dinde rôtie – Roast turkey (young turkey is designated Dindonneau)

one 2.5 *kg (5-lb) turkey*	*fat bacon*
480 *g* (1 *lb*) *turkey stuffing*	250 *ml* (½ *pt*) *bread sauce*
(*Recipe* 509)	(*Recipe* 96)
250 *ml* (½ *pt*) *brown stock*	*bacon rolls*
(*Recipe* 8)	240 *g* (½ *lb*) *chipolatas*

1 Pull sinews from legs (for ease of subsequent carving many chefs also carefully remove the wishbone) otherwise truss as Recipe 528.
2 Stuffing (see note below).
3 Cover with fat bacon and place in roasting tray with hot fat
4 Roast on the leg sides first then the back. Baste frequently.
5 Present with grilled chipolatas, bacon rolls and watercress.
6 Serve bread sauce, cooked stuffing and gravy separately.

Note. Because of probable bacterial growth and later inadequate heat penetration in roasting (especially in large birds such as goose and turkey), it is not advisable to cook the stuffing in the bird itself, ie not to use the traditional method of stuffing the crop and sewing the apron to the carriage. Alternatives include rolling the stuffing in oiled or greased aluminium foil and either baking for 15 minutes at 180°C (360°F) or steaming for approximately 20 minutes. Some chefs remove the drumsticks from the turkey (after drawing the sinews), bone and stuff them to roast for about 30 minutes at 180°C (360°F) to coincide with the service of the turkey.

532 Oie rôtie – Roast goose

one 2 to 2.5 kg (4 lb to 5 lb) goose	*60 g (2 oz) breadcrumbs*
15 g (½ oz) dripping (or oil)	*1 small egg*
9 sage leaves	*30 g (1 oz) chopped onions*
30 g (1 oz) chopped suet	*pepper, salt*

1 Pick, draw, and singe the goose.
2 Blanch the sage and onions together, strain, chop and mix with the crumbs, suet, and seasoning; bind with egg.
3 See note on Stuffing in Recipe 531 above. Truss the bird.
4 Roast in the usual way and baste frequently.
5 Serve with cress, gravy, stuffing and apple sauce.

533 Caneton rôti – Roast duck

Prepare, cook, and serve as for roast goose (Recipe 532).

ROAST GAME BIRDS

Note. Roast game birds are presented on croûtons prepared as follows:

534 Croûtons for game

1 Take bread slice of approximately 1.5 cm (¾-inch) thickness.
2 Cut to the size of the bird to be served.
3 Hollow out the top-centre slightly to form a 'bed'.
4 Fry to golden brown in clarified butter.
5 Spread the hollow part with farce au gratin (Recipe 508).

535 Bécasse flambée – Flamed woodcock

1 whole bird	*15 g (½ oz) foie gras*	*30 g (1 oz) butter*
¼ glass (30 ml) brandy	*(optional)*	*juice of ½ lemon*
125 ml (¼ pt) jus lié	*2 oblong croûtons*	*pinch cayenne*
(Recipe 30) or well-	*(Recipe 534)*	*farce au gratin*
reduced stock	*62 ml (⅛ pt) cream*	*(Recipe 508)*

1 Skewer with beak and do not clean.
2 Roast for 8 minutes.
3 Skin, remove legs, and breast.
4 Withdraw entrails.
5 Chop the carcase, entrails, and legs.
6 Sweat with butter under cover.
7 Add brandy and flame.

8 Add the estouffade and reduce.
9 Work in the cream, foie gras, and butter.
10 Strain, place the suprêmes on croûtons (as Recipe 534); coat with the sauce.
11 Serve salade Japonaise (Recipe 222).

536 Bécasse rôtie – Roast woodcock

4 *slices fat bacon*	240 *g* (½ *lb*) *game chips*	10 *ml spoon* [½
4 *oblong croûtons*	(*Recipe* 927)	*tablespoon*]
120 *g* (¼ *lb*) *white*	1 *bunch watercress*	*brandy*
breadcrumbs	250 *ml* (½ *pt*) *game*	60 *g* (2 *oz*) *farce au*
125 *ml* (¼ *pt*) *bread*	*stock* (*Recipe* 12)	*gratin*
sauce (*Recipe* 96)	4 *woodcock*	(*Recipe* 508)

1 Remove the gizzard and eyes.
2 Truss by piercing the legs with the beak.
3 Cover with the fat bacon and roast quickly in hot fat for 18 minutes.
4 Remove from pan, pour away any surplus fat and rinse with game gravy and brandy; season and strain.
5 Fry the croûtons in butter and spread with farce au gratin.
6 Dress on croûtons (Recipe 534).
7 Garnish with game chips and watercress.
8 Serve with the breadcrumbs tossed in butter, but serve gravy and bread sauce separately.

537 Bécassine rôtie – Roast snipe

Prepare as woodcock.

538 Caille rôtie – Roast quail.

Factors in selection and cooking:
1 Select quails white and very fat.
2 Remove gizzard only just before cooking.
3 Wrap them in buttered vine leaves and thin slices of bacon.
4 Roast in fast oven for 10 to 12 minutes.
5 Serve on toasted croûtons with half-lemon.
6 Serve their own gravy.

539 Caille rôtie aux raisins – Roast quail with grapes

4 *quails*	125 *ml* (¼ *pt*) *game stock*
4 *slices bacon*	(*Recipe* 12)
4 *large vine leaves*	120 *g* (¼ *lb*) *white grapes*
120 *g* (¼ *lb*) *farce au gratin*	
(*Recipe* 508)	

1 Clean the quails but draw only the gizzard and entrails, leaving heart and liver.
2 Blanch, peel, and stone the grapes, and stuff the quails with a mixture of farce au gratin and grapes.

3 Truss the quails and wrap in slices of bacon then in vine leaves.
4 Brush them with butter andd roast in very hot oven for 10 to 12 minutes.
5 Remove the vine leaves and bacon from quails and place quails on croûtons (as Recipe 534).
6 Serve lemon and roast gravy.

540 Caneton sauvage rôti – Roast wild duck

1 Roast quickly and keep underdone.
2 Allow 20 minutes full cooking time.
3 Garnish with lemon slices and watercress. Serve on croûtons (Recipe 534) with game gravy (Recipe 18).

541 Caneton sauvage à l'anglaise

This is prepared similarly but served with apple sauce.

542 Faisan rôti – Roast pheasant

1 *pheasant*	125 *ml* (¼ *pt*) *game*	1 *croûton* (*as*
120 *g* (¼ *lb*) *fine*	*stock* (*Recipe* 12)	*Recipe 534*)
mirepoix (*Recipe* 2)	1 *bunch watercress*	240 *g* (½ *lb*) *farce au*
125 *ml* (¼ *pt*) *bread*	8 *slices lean bacon*	*gratin*
sauce (*Recipe* 96)	240 *g* (½ *lb*) *game chips*	(*Recipe* 508)
1 *large slice fat bacon*		

1 Clean and truss; tie fat bacon over and around the pheasants.
2 Proceed to roast in the same manner as roast chicken (Recipe 529) until moderately underdone.
3 When cooked, remove string and fat bacon; pour away surplus fat from roasting tin and rinse with game stock; season and strain.
4 Dress the pheasants on the croûtons (spread with farce au gratin).
5 Garnish the birds with grilled bacon, game chips, and watercress.

543 Roast grouse

4 *young grouse*	120 *g* (¼ *lb*) *white*	120 *g* (¼ *lb*) *farce au*
4 *croûtons*	*breadcrumbs*	*gratin*
4 *slices fat bacon*	125 *ml* (¼ *pt*) *game*	(*Recipe* 508)
4 *slices lean bacon*	*stock* (*Recipe* 12)	125 *ml* (¼ *pt*) *bread*
1 *bunch watercress*	240 *g* (½ *lb*) *game chips*	*sauce* (*Recipe* 96)

1 Clean and truss; wrap with fat bacon and tie up.
2 Roast quickly until moderately underdone – approximately 25 minutes.
3 Remove bacon and string; pour away surplus fat from roasting tray and rinse with game stock; season and strain.
4 Sauté the croûtons in butter and spread with farce au gratin (Recipe 534).
5 Dress the grouse on each croûton with grilled bacon on top.
6 Garnish with game chips and watercress, and serve breadcrumbs tossed in butter, gravy, and bread sauce.

544 Perdreau rôti – Roast partridge
To prepare, use the same method as for roast grouse.

545 Pluvier rôti – Roast plover.
1 Proceed as for roast grouse but do not cover with fat bacon.
2 Cook in rapid oven until moderately underdone.
3 Serve only gravy and a little watercress.

546 Pintade rôtie – Roast guinea fowl
Prepare as for roast pheasant. (Guinea fowl being domestically reared is therefore not truly game but is prepared in a similar style.)

GRILLS

Grilling or broiling. Traditionally, grills are prepared on hot grids above a bright well-ventilated fire, preferably charcoal for cleanliness and flavour. But there are satisfactory modern substitutes such as gas- or electrically-heated radiants. Grilling is used for small cuts of meat, poultry, and fish: meat and poultry cuts are brushed with oil and seasoned; fish is also passed through seasoned flour. Meat is trimmed and also slightly flattened with a bat. Grilling times depend on meat thickness and guest's requirements.

Terms for degrees of grilling:
bient cuit – well cooked.
à point – medium (literally, 'to the point', i.e. just done).
saignant – underdone (literally 'bleeding', i.e. flows with red juice when cut).
au bleu – very underdone or rare (literally, 'blue' inside).
flared – burnt on the outside and raw inside.
   Beef cuts are normally preferred underdone rather than well-cooked through, lamb and mutton are generally liked à point or well cooked, and pork, well cooked.

BEEF GRILLS

Entrecôte (sirloin steak)	300 g (10 oz)	– A cut from the boned sirloin.
Entrecôte double	600 g (20 oz)	– A double-sized entrecôte.
Entrecôte minute	300 g (10 oz)	– An entrecôte batted flat.
Rumpsteak	240 g (8 oz)	– A steak from the boned rump.
Point steak	270 g (9 oz)	– Steak from the triangular piece of rump.
Porterhouse (T bone steak)	900 g (1¾ lb)	– A cut through sirloin, bone and fillet.
Chateaubriand	600 g (20 oz)	– A cut from head fillet (for 2 or more persons).

Filet (fillet)*	300 g (10 oz)	– A cut from middle fillet.
Tournedos	240 g (8 oz)	– A cut from middle fillet, the fat removed, circled with string (and sometimes, back fat) to keep round shape.
Côte à l'os	750 g (1½ lb)	– Cut from the wing-end with bone (equivalent to a large cutlet – for 2 or more).
Carpet-bag steak	600 g (20 oz)	– Double entrecôte, incised for six oysters as stuffing and sewn (piqué) with back-fat strips (for 2 or more).

LAMB GRILLS

Chop	300 g (10 oz)	– Cut from loin (half-saddle).
English chop	500 g (16 oz)	– Complete cut across saddle, including kidney skewered-in.
Cutlet	90 to 120 g (3 to 4 oz)	– From the best end.
Double cutlet	240 g (8 oz)	– 2 cutlets joined from best end.
Chump chop	300 g (10 oz)	– Cut from leg-end of loin.
Filet mignon	120 g (4 oz)	– Small fillet from inside saddle.
Kidneys		– 2 per portion, split open and skewered.
Noisette	90 g (3 oz)	– Cut from saddle.

PORK GRILLS

Chop	240 g (8 ooz)	– Cut from saddle.
Cutlet	200 to 240 g (7 to 8 oz)	– Cut from best end.
Fillets	180 g (6 oz)	– Under-cut from saddle.
Steak (gammon)	300 g (10 oz)	– Cut from gammon-slice.

MIXED GRILLS

A standard mixed grill is likely to consist of:

1 *lamb cutlet* 90 g (3 oz)	1 *pork sausage* 60 g (2 oz)
1 *lamb's kidney*	1 *bacon rasher* (*back*)

together with mushroom, tomato, pommes paille (straw potatoes) and watercress, but substitutions and/or additions may include lambs' or calves' liver, small tournedos, and parsley butter.

---

* An English-style fillet steak is not trimmed but grilled with its own surrounding fat.

VEAL

Except for veal kidneys, similar veal cuts to those of other meats listed above are normally sautéd, not grilled.

POULTRY GRILLS

Poussins and small chickens may be grilled (Recipes 561–5). Legs of chicken are also grilled from raw and, on occasion, cooked chicken-legs are coated with devilled mixture and grilled.

GRILLED BONES

Beef rib-bones, if sufficient meat is attached, may also be grilled. Bones from cooked rib-roasts may similarly be devilled for grilling.

DRESSING AND GARNISHING OF GRILLS

Accompaniments which may be served with grills include:

(i)   Sauces: Béarnaise, Choron, Chateaubriand, etc.
(ii) Butters: Montpeelier, garlic, hongroise, mustard, mâitre d'hôtel (parsley butter), etc.
(iii) Watercress (vert pré): and straw potatoes.

The use of these accompaniments determines the dish's menu title: e.g. Tournedos grillé béarnaise or Filet de bœuf grillé mâitre d'hôtel.

547 Other garnishes for grills:

Américaine: Grilled bacon, tomatoes with pommes paille.
Bouquetière: (Particularly for tournedos, Chateaubriand), glazed mixed olive-turned vegetables with sherry-flavoured jus lié as a separate sauce.
Continentale: Grilled mushrooms, tomatoes with pommes soufflées.
Garni: Grilled tomatoes, mushrooms, pommes paille, French fried onions (usually also sauce béarnaise).
Mirabeau: Spanish black olives within rolled anchovy-fillet, beurre d'anchois, pommes paille and watercress.
Tyrolienne: Grilled tomatoes, French fried (deep) onions, pommes paille, mâitre d'hôtel butter.

BEEF GRILLS

548 Entrecôte grillé au vert-pré – Grilled sirloin steak

four 300 g (10-oz) *entrecôte steaks*	240 g (½ lb) *straw potatoes*	1 *bunch watercress*
120 g (¼ lb) *parsley*	(*Recipe* 929)	62 *ml* (⅛ *pt*) *oil*
butter (*Recipe* 89)		*seasoning*

1 Brush with oil and season.
2 Place on hot grill and cook both sides, basting frequently.
3 Garnish with straw potatoes, watercress and parsley butter.

Note. Double and minute entrecôtes, tournedos, rump, and point steaks are similarly prepared.

549 Filet de bœuf grillé

In addition, this is accompanied by a piece of grilled suet. Cuts from the filet (including chateaubriand) are lightly batted before oiling and seasoning.

550 Chateaubriand

1 Originally and traditionally, a large fillet steak grilled between a sandwich of two, thin, inferior steaks later discarded, the chateaubriand is today plainly grilled as Recipe 548, accompanied by a piece of grilled suet and other appropriate grill garnishes.
2 It is 'finished' by carving at the guéridon (side-table service) by the waiter.

551 Porterhouse steak

This may be prepared and served (without grilled suet) as chateaubriand.

LAMB OR MUTTON GRILLS

552 Mixed grill

four 90 g (3-*oz*)	4 *slices back bacon*	4 *medium*
trimmed lamb cutlets	4 *small pieces lamb's*	*mushrooms*
4 *sheep's kidneys*	*liver*	4 *cutlet frills*
4 *whole tomatoes*	4 *sausages*	1 *bunch watercress*
parsley butter	*straw potatoes*	62 *ml* (⅛ *pt*) *oil*
(*Recipe* 89)	(*Recipe* 929)	*seasoning*

1 Remove skin from kidney, slit open and skewer; brush with oil, and season.
2 Similarly prepare the mushrooms and tomatoes for grilling (cultivated mushrooms need not be peeled).
3 Prick the sausage with a fork.
4 Dust the liver with a little seasoned flour.
5 Place each commodity on separate trays if grilling under salamander or direct on to an underfired or charcoal grill; season while cooking.

Presentation. Place the grilled mushrooms on top of the tomatoes, and arrange the cutlets (with frills on), sausages, liver, bacon, neatly on a silver dish. The kidney should be filled with parsley butter (Recipe 89) and served underdone. Garnish with watercress and straw potatoes. Brush with oil.

553 Chop d'agneau grillé – Grilled lamb chop

120 g (¼ lb) parsley butter	1 bunch watercress
(Recipe 89)	four 300 g (10 oz) chops
240 g (½ lb) straw potatoes	62 ml (⅛ pt) oil
(Recipe 929)	seasoning

1 Remove from the saddle the skin, kidneys and surplus fat.
2 Divide into two parts by cutting right through the vertebræ lengthwise.
3 Cut the saddle into chops 300 g (10-oz) each.
4 Brush both sides with oil, season and grill; approximate full cooking time 20 minutes.
5 Serve with parsley butter separately; garnish with straw potatoes and watercress.

554 Côtelette d'agneau grillée – Grilled lamb cutlet

120 g (¼ lb) parsley butter	1 bunch watercress
(Recipe 89)	eight 120 g (4 oz) cutlets
240 g (½ lb) straw potatoes	62 ml (⅛ pt) oil
(Recipe 929)	seasoning

1 Remove cutlets from the carré (best end) and well trim the cutlet bones.
2 Brush with oil, season and grill both sides.
3 Garnish each cutlet with a frill and the dish with straw potatoes and watercress.
4 Serve parsley butter separately.

555 Rognons de mouton grillés

240 g (½ lb) straw potatoes	seasoning
(Recipe 929)	8 sheep's kidneys
120 g (¼ lb) parsley butter	1 bunch watercress
(Recipe 89)	62 ml (⅛ pt) oil

1 Skin the kidney and cut lengthwise but not completely in half.
2 Skewer each one to remain open and to retain their shape.
3 Brush with oil and grill both sides and season; (kidneys are normally served underdone).
4 Garnish each one with parsley butter.
5 Serve watercress and straw potatoes.

PORK AND GAMMON GRILLS

556 Côtelettes de porc grillées, sauce Robert

Grill the cutlets and serve with sauce Robert (Recipe 49).

557 Grilled gammon steak

> *four* 180 g (*6-oz*)   *straw potatoes*   *watercress*
> *gammon steaks*   (*Recipe* 929)

1 Cut the fat with little slits all round.
2 Brush with oil and grill both sides.
3 Garnish with cress and straw potatoes.
4 Serve sauce diable (Recipe 40) separately.

558 Barbecued gammon

1 Dust a thick gammon rasher with mixed spice, sprinkle with brown sugar and grill.
2 Serve with grilled pineapple and piquante sauce (Recipe 46).

VEAL GRILLS

559 Rognon de veau grillé – Grilled veal kidney

> 4 *kidneys*   *straw potatoes*   *watercress*
> 120 g (*¼ lb*) *parsley*   (*Recipe* 929)   *seasoning*
> *butter* (*Recipe* 89)

1 Trim the kidneys leaving a slight layer of fat.
2 Cut in half, lengthwise, without separating the two halves.
3 Impale on a small skewer to keep shape.
4 Season with salt and pepper, brush with butter, and grill both sides; remove skewer before serving.
5 Garnish with parsley butter, watercress, and straw potatoes.

560 Rognon de veau grillé à l'américaine

> 4 *veal kidneys*   4 *rashers streaky bacon*
> 4 *tomato halves*   60 g (*2 oz*) *butter*

1 Remove skin and cut lengthwise in half, but not in two.
2 Skewer to keep open, season, brush with oil and grill both sides.
3 Wrap the streaky bacon round the tomatoes and grill.
4 Dress the kidney and tomato on a serving dish and finish with beurre noisette (Recipe 82).

POULTRY GRILLS

561 Preparation of chicken, poussin, and pigeon for grilling

1 Cut open from the back, spread out and flatten with the bat.
2 Remove the rib-bones and insert 2 skewers through the wings to keep flat.
3 Rub both sides with lemon juice and season with salt and pepper.
4 Immerse the bird in oil.

562 Chicken spatchcock

one 2 kg (4-lb) chicken	*125 ml (¼ pt) oil*	*1 bunch watercress*
120 g (¼ lb) white breadcrumbs	*9 gherkins*	*125 ml (¼ pt) diable or piquante sauce*
120 g (¼ lb) melted butter (or sunflower margarine)	*240 g (½ lb) straw potatoes (Recipe 929)*	*(Recipes 40 or 46)*

1 Prepare the chicken for grilling (Recipe 561).
2 Brush with melted butter and half-cook in oven.
3 Sprinkle both sides with white breadcrumbs, pour over melted butter and complete by grilling; baste frequently.
4 Serve on a silver flat and garnish with fanned gherkins, watercress and straw potatoes.
5 Serve sauce diable or piquante separately.

563 Poulet grillé à l'américaine

one 2 kg (4-lb) chicken	*8 bacon rashers*	*125 ml (¼ pt) devil sauce (Recipe 40)*
4 tomatoes	*240 g (½ lb) straw potatoes*	*4 mushrooms*
1 bunch watercress	*(Recipe 929)*	

1 Prepare as for chicken diable (Recipe 556) and garnish with grilled tomatoes, mushrooms, bacon, cress and straw potatoes.
2 Devil sauce is served separately.

564 Poulet grillé à la diable

one 2 kg (4-lb) chicken	*120 g (¼ lb) white breadcrumbs*	*1 bunch watercress*
8 slices bacon	*240 g (½ lb) straw potatoes*	*125 ml (¼ pt) oil*
½ tablespoon mustard seasoning	*(Recipe 929)*	*125 ml (¼ pt) devil sauce (Recipe 40)*
120 g (¼ lb) melted butter (or sunflower margarine)		

1 Prepare the chicken for grilling (Recipe 561).
2 Brush with diluted mustard and melted butter and half-cook in the oven.
3 Sprinkle both sides with breadcrumbs, pour over the melted butter and complete by grilling, basting frequently.
4 Serve on a silver flat, garnish the chicken with grilled bacon, watercress and straw potatoes.
5 Serve devil sauce separately.

565 Poulet grillé à la crapaudine

one 2 kg (4-lb) chicken	*4 grilled tomatoes*	*125 ml (¼ pt) sauce diable (Recipe 40)*
120 g (¼ lb) pommes paille (Recipe 929)	*1 bunch watercress*	
	4 grilled mushrooms	

1 Singe and clean chicken.
2 Do not remove winglets or feet.
3 Cut from the breast-top through rib-cage to the joint of the wing.
4 Pull the breast-bone up in the form of a hinge until the chicken lies flat in the shape of a frog or toad.
5 Bat the cut side to facilitate cooking and removal of bone when cooked.
6 Cook as for Chicken spatchcock (Recipe 562).
7 When cooked, decorate the tip of the breast with roundels of cooked egg and slices of stoned, black olives or stuffed olives, or garnishing paste or truffle to form two eyes.
8 Garnish the dish with grilled tomatoes and mushrooms, pommes pailles and watercress.
9 Serve sauce diable separately.

Note. Poussins may be treated in the same way.

BRAISING

Braising combines baking (or oven roasting) with stewing. Joints or pieces of meat are browned quickly in fat or oil in the oven and then moistened with stock and cooked slowly under cover. In the traditional brigade this cooking is undertaken by the chef saucier (sauce cook).

While many of the less costly cuts, if suitably prepared, may be braised the following are generally considered the most suitable joints for braising in the piece:

Beef – Rump, silverside, topside, thick flank, aitch bone
Mutton (or Lamb), Pork, and Veal – Leg, shoulder, breast

Poultry may be braised and the method is particularly suitable for game birds when they are older such as older partridge, pheasant or grouse. Offal including liver, heart, sweetbreads, and so on, are all used in braising.

GARNISHES

566 Garnishes for all braised joints

Examples of types of garnish and accompaniments used with braised joints of meat include:

Nemours: Noodles and Duchesse potatoes.
Badoise: Braised red cabbage, lean bacon, Duchesse potatoes.
Bourgeoise: Turned carrots, button onions, lardons.
Charollaise: Cauliflower Villeroy, croustades of turnip purée.
Clamart: Artichoke bottoms filled with purée of fresh peas, château potatoes.
Mercédes: Braised lettuce, grilled tomatoes and mushrooms, croquette potatoes.

Moderne: Cauliflower Mornay, stuffed tomato, Duchesse potatoes.
Richelieu: Braised lettuce, stuffed tomatoes, mushrooms, pommes château.
St-Florentin: Cèpes bordelaise, pommes St-Florentin.
Samaritaine: Timbales of rice, braised lettuce, Dauphine potatoes.
Soissonnaise: With braised haricots blancs.

567 Braised joints (red meat)

Both traditional (Procedure A) and more modern approaches (Procedure B) are outlined below.

Procedure A (traditional)
1 When meat cuts for braising are very lean, they may be piquéd, i.e., threaded by larding needle or daube needle with strips of fat placed regularly.
2 Meat is then placed in a marinade (Recipe 126) usually for 24 hours and turned at regular intervals: the acid action of the wine helps to tenderize while the mirepoix and aromatics impart flavour.
3 Place the joint in a braising-pan on the thickly sliced vegetables and aromatics (taken from the mirepoix); baste with a little fat (or oil) and roast with the lid off until the meat and vegetables are lightly coloured. This seals the meat fibres for juice and flavour retention. Pour over the marinade liquor and reduce it to a syrupy consistency (glaze); sprinkle the meat with flour and place in the oven.
4 When brown, remove from the oven and three-quarters cover the meat with brown stock; add concassé tomatoes, cover with tight lid and place to cook in a moderate oven; (if tomato purée is used instead of fresh tomatoes, add before the stock).
5 During cooking, baste and turn the meat in the sauce to prevent skin formation; when the meat is cooked, remove from the pan.

Sauce and garnish
Reduce the liquor until it is a sauce of the required consistency, skimming frequently to ensure a glossy finish. Strain and add the appropriate garnish. If the joint is to be served whole, it is glazed. This is done after it is cooked by placing the meat on a tray in the oven and sprinkling with the sauce until the joint is glossy. If the meat is to be presented carved, this process serves no purpose.

Alternative traditional thickenings:
1 Demi-glace: Moistening may also be done with jus lié (Recipe 30) or demi-glace (Recipe 29) instead of stock, in which case omit the flour before adding the sauce.
2 Fécule or Arrowroot: Another method is to use brown stock but omit the flour and thicken the sauce with fécule (cornflour or arrowroot) after the meat is cooked.

Procedure B (more recent alternative)
Today's chefs may adapt the foregoing as follows:
Omit sprinkling with flour and placing in the oven (as in Step 3 above).
Do not brown in the oven as in Step 4 above), but simply add tomato purée and brown stock before placing in the oven to cook.

Sauce and garnish
Adapt the procedure under that heading above by simply reducing the liquor, which may be very lightly thickened with fécule (arrowroot or cornflour).

568 Culotte de bœuf braisé à la jardinière – Braised beef jardinière

1 *kg (2 lb) beef*	*jardinière garnish (Recipe 755)*
500 *ml* (1 *pt*) *brown stock*	500 *ml* (1 *pt*) *marinade (Recipe 126)*
(*Recipe 7 or 8*)	

Note. Culotte is the top of rump cut. Other suitable joints are topside, silverside, and thick flank.

Procedure A (traditional)
1 Lard the beef and place in marinade for 12 hours, turning frequently.
2 Remove the beef from the marinade and place in braising-pan to seal off.
3 Add the vegetables from the marinade and dust meat with flour and place in the oven so that flour will brown.
4 Half cover with brown stock and the marinade liquor and add a little tomato purée and bouquet garni; cover with lid and baste frequently.
5 When the meat is cooked remove from the pan, reduce the sauce as may be required and strain through a fine chinois, being careful to remove all fat.
6 Slice thickly and serve with jardinière of vegetables tossed in butter.

Procedure B (modern adaptation)
Do not sprinkle with flour and brown in the oven (as in Step 3 above). After adding vegetables (as in Step 3), simply proceed to Step 4. When the meat is cooked, adapt Step 5 above so that the liquor is simply reduced and slightly thickened if desired with fécule (arrowroot or cornflour).

569 Bœuf braisé à la mode

1 Proceed as for braising with the addition of 1 calf's foot.
2 Garnish with diced calf's-feet meat and turned, glazed vegetables (bouquetière as Recipe 750).

570 Bœuf braisé à la bourguignonne

1 *kg (2 lb) topside beef*	500 *ml* (1 *pt*) *red-wine*	120 *g* (¼ *lb*) *diced*
240 *g* (½ *lb*) *button*	*marinade (Recipe*	*bacon*
onions	126)	4 *heart-shaped*
seasoning	240 *g* (½ *lb*) *button*	*croûtons*
	mushrooms	

Note. In the following recipe many modern chefs omit (in Step 2) dredging with flour and browning in the oven (singer au four), and (in Step 4) simply reduce the liquor and, if desired, slightly thicken with fécule (arrowroot or cornflour).

1 Lard the beef and place in a red-wine marinade for 12 hours.
2 Remove, drain and brown the meat in hot fat (or oil); dredge with flour and with the vegetable from the marinade place in the oven to brown.
3 Add the liquid from the marinade and sufficient brown stock to half cover the meat.
4 When cooked, remove meat and reduce the sauce as required; remove all fat and strain through a fine strainer (chinois); season.
5 May be served whole or sliced; garnish with glazed onions, mushrooms, fried diced bacon and heart-shaped croûtons.

571 Bœuf braisé à la bourgeoise

As Recipe 568 but with vegetable-garnish bourgeoise, Recipe 750.

572 Langue de boeuf braisée – Braised ox-tongue

½ ox-tongue	*360–500 g (¾–1 lb) carrots (to yield*
240 g (½ lb) button onions	*16 pieces carrots)*

1 Braise the tongue as for ordinary braising.
2 When two-thirds cooked surround with the carrots also two-thirds cooked, and the small onions browned in butter.
3 Simmer gently until cooked and remove all grease before service.

573 Braised pieces (white meat)

1 White meat for braising include not only joints of veal but also poultry (including turkey) and sweetbreads. Sweetbreads are first soaked in cold salted water to withdraw the blood (dégorger). Except for sweetbreads which must be blanched first, the joint or bird must be stiffened in butter (or oil or margarine).
2 Place the joint in a suitable braising-pan, lay it on the roots and aromatics, moisten with a little veal stock and reduce. Continue this process until a glaze is obtained. Then add enough veal stock to half-cover the joint and place in a moderate oven with a tight lid.
3 The meat requires constant basting while it cooks to prevent drying. As the stock is gelatinous it forms a coating on the surface and so prevents the juices escaping. It is for that reason the first stock must be reduced to a glaze before the final addition of the stock. The meat is known to be cooked when a clear liquid escapes if pricked with a needle.
4 White meats that are braised are always larded and glazed.

Sauce: The accompanying sauce is made by reducing the cooking-liquor and adding the appropriate wine and either jus lié, thin demi-glace or reduced brown stock for a brown sauce or velouté and cream (or fromage frais, yogurt or quark) for a white sauce.

574 Fricandeau de veau à la briarde – Leg fillet of veal briarde

1 *kg (2 lb) leg fillet of* *veal*	2 *lettuce*	360 *g (¾ lb) carrots*

1 Cook as for noix de veau florentine (Recipe 575).
2 Garnish with braised lettuce and new carrots à la crême.
3 Serve with the reduced cooking-liquor strained and all fat removed.

575 Noix de veau à la florentine – Cushion of veal with spinach

1 *kg (2 lb) veal*   500 *g (1 lb) spinach (in leaf)*

1 Piqué the cushion of veal with fat bacon.
2 Proceed to braise as for white braising (see notes on white braising).
3 Garnish with leaf spinach tossed in butter.
4 Serve with the reduced cooking-liquor, strained and free from fat.

576 Poitrine de veau farcie – Stuffed breast of veal

1 *kg (2 lb) veal*

Stuffing:		*salt and pepper*
240 *g (½ lb) fine* *sausage-meat*	7 *g (¼ oz) chopped* *parsley*	30 *g (1 oz) butter* 1 *small egg*
30 *g (1 oz) dry duxelles* *(Recipe* 101)	*tarragon and chives* *grated zest of ½ lemon*	

1 For the stuffing mix all ingredients.
2 Bone the thickest part of the veal-breast to form a pocket.
3 Place the stuffing in the pocket and sew up, taking care to remove string when cooked.
4 Braise the veal as for white braising; approximate time 3 hours.
5 Garnish with spinach (Florentine) or Jardinière or Bourgeoise.
6 Serve the reduced cooking-liquor as a sauce.

577 Rognonnade de veau braisée – Braised saddle, best end and kidneys of veal

1 Bone the loin and best end of veal in one piece.
2 Insert the veal kidneys along the length and tie with plenty of fat bacon to cover the outside.
3 Stiffen the veal in butter and colour lightly on both sides.
4 Now prepare a fine mirepoix (Recipe 2) and place the veal on top and add a little veal stock; cover and reduce this stock to a glaze, then half-cover with veal stock; baste well and frequently.
5 When cooked, reduce liquor, add a little cream and strain; season.
6 Garnish with turned mushrooms, and serve with a sauce-boat of cooking-liquid, and the sauce.
7 This dish can be presented whole or sliced.

578 Selle de veau braisée Metternich

1 Trim the saddle and remove the kidneys.
2 Cut sufficient slices of fat bacon to cover the top of the saddle and secure-firmly with string.
3 Slightly stiffen the saddle both sides in butter (or oil or margarine).
4 Now place the meat on a bed of aromatics and root vegetables in a pan just big enough to hold it. Moisten with a little stock and reduce to form a glaze; half-cover the meat with the veal stock and cook with lid on in a moderate oven and baste frequently.
5 When cooked, remove the fillets from the joints with care and cut into regular sized collops.
6 Spread over the saddle bone a few 15 ml spoons (tablespoons) of Béchamel (Recipe 51) flavoured with paprika.
7 Reconstruct the fillets on the saddle bone in such a way as to make them appear untouched and between the each collop insert a 5 ml spoon (teaspoon) of Béchamel and 2 slices of truffle (optional).
8 Cover the saddle completely with thin Béchamel sauce flavoured with paprika and set to glaze.
9 Serve separately: rice pilaff (Recipe 366) and a sauce-boat of the braising liquid.

BRAISING HAM

579 Jambon braisé au madère – Braised ham and Madeira sauce

1 Parboil the ham for ½ hour in boiling water.
2 Remove rind and trim off excess fat for an even appearance.
3 Stud with cloves.
4 Place the ham on a matignon (Recipe 4) in a suitable braising-pan.
5 Add 500 ml (1 pt) Madeira and cover two-thirds with brown stock and sprinkle a layer of brown sugar on top of the ham.
6 Set to cook in a moderate oven, basting frequently to give an even glaze.
7 When the ham is cooked and evenly glazed dé-glacer the pan with jus lié (Recipe 30) or demi-glace (Recipe 29), remove all grease and correct the seasoning. (Alternatively, to achieve a light, thin, coating sauce, reduce the cooking liquor by about one third).
8 Finish off the sauce with 60 g (2 oz) butter per pint (optional).
9 Suitable garnishes for ham include, spinach, braised lettuce, endives and vegetable purées.

580 Jambon braisé à l'alsacienne

Prepare with braised sauerkraut and Madeira sauce (Recipe 44).

581 Jambon braisé à la florentine

Prepare with purée of spinach and sauce Madre (Recipe 44).

BRAISING OF POULTRY AND GAME

582 Caneton braisé aux petits pois – Braised duckling and green peas

One 2 kg (4 lb) duckling
240 g (½ lb) button onions
180 g (6 oz) breast pork
500 ml (1 pt) demi-glace (Recipe
   29) (or jus lié Recipe 30 (thin))
480 g (1 lb) fresh peas

120 g (¼ lb) brown stock
   (Recipe 7 or 8)
bouquet garni
30 g (1 oz) butter (or margarine)
seasoning

1 Dice the pork into lardons and blanch.
2 Place butter in a braising-pan and brown the lardons and onions.
3 When browned, remove from the braising-pan and brown the trussed ducks in the residue fat.
4 Drain off the fat, add the jus lié or half-glaze and stock; boil and add the bouquet garni.
5 Cook under cover, basting frequently.
6 When half-cooked, add the onions, lardons and peas and continue cooking.
7 Skim all the fat from the sauce, check for seasoning and consistency.
8 Coat the ducks in the sauce and garnish.
9 Cooking should be in a moderate oven for 1 hour or according to quality of duck.

Note. Demi-glace or jus lié may be replaced by 1 litre good, brown stock (Recipe 7 or 8) and (at Step 7) reduced as may be required to create a light coating sauce.

583 Canard braisé à l'orange – Braised duck with orange

one 2 kg (4 lb) duck
500 ml (1 pt) jus lié (Recipe 30) or
   demi-glace (Recipe 29)
1 bouquet garni
2 oranges

120 ml (¼ pt) brown stock
   (Recipe 7 or 8)
½ lemon
30 g (1 oz) butter (or margarine)
seasoning

1 Brown the ducks in the braising-pan.
2 Cover the ducks with the jus lié or demi-glace and stock; boil and add bouquet garni.
3 Cook under cover in a moderate oven, basting frequently.
4 Cut into fine julienne th ' zest of 1 orange and ½ lemon, and blanch.
5 Extract the juice from the lemon and all the oranges.
6 When the ducks are cooked, remove all fat from sauce and reduce to the required consistency; strain through a fine strainer, add the orange and lemon juice; check for seasoning and consistency.
7 Add the julienne of orange and lemon at the last moment.
8 Glaze the ducks and coat with the sauce.
9 Surround the dish with orange sections.
10 Serve a sauce-boat of sauce.

Note. Alternatively omit the demi-glace or jus lié and use 1 litre brown stock (Recipe 7 or 8) and reduce if and as required (at Step 6) to yield a light, thin, gelatinous coating sauce.

584 Caneton braisé aux navets – Braised duckling with turnips

one 2 kg (4-lb) duckling	*2.5 ml spoon [½ teaspoon] sugar*
240 g (½ lb) button onions	*360 g (¾ lb) turned turnips*
500 ml (1 pt) jus lié (Recipe 30) or	*90 g (3 oz) butter (or margarine)*
demi-glace (Recipe 29)	*125 ml (¼ pt) white wine*
125 ml (¼ pt) brown stock	*seasoning*
(Recipe 7 or 8)	

1 Clean and truss the duckling.
2 Brown the duckling in 45 g (1½ oz) butter (or margarine or oil) in braising-pan.
3 Drain away the fat and rinse with white wine; add the jus lié or demi-glace and reduced brown stock.
4 Return the ducklings to this sauce, boil, skim and add bouquet garni.
5 Cover and braise gently in moderate oven, basting frequently.
6 Sprinkle the turnips with sugar and glaze to a light brown.
7 Cook the onions and glaze in butter.
8 When the ducklings are half-cooked transfer to a clean pan and add the garnish of turnips and onions.
9 Re-boil the sauce, remove all fat and strain over the ducklings and complete the cooking.
10 Present with the garnish of onions and turnips arranged round the birds.

Note. 1 litre brown stock (Recipe 6 or 7) may be substituted for the 500 ml jus lié or demi-glace and procedure adapted as in the the notes in the two preceding recipes.

585 Perdeau sur un lit de chou – Partridge on a bed of cabbage

4 young partridges and their livers	*1 kg (2¼ lb) Savoy cabbage*
4 rounds of French bread	*120 g (4 oz) lardons of bacon*
1 clove of garlic	*1 litre (1 qt) water*
4 thin slices streaky bacon	*30 g (1 oz) butter (or sunflower*
62 ml (⅛ pt) dry white wine	*margarine)*

1 Season the inside of the birds and put in each a slice of bread that has been rubbed with garlic and spread with liver purée.
2 Truss the birds, cover with slices of streaky bacon held in place with string.
3 Cut the cabbage in four, remove the tough centre stalk, wash well.
4 Blanch the cabbage leaves in boiling, salted water until limp. Refresh and drain.
5 Blanch and refresh lardons.
6 Smear the partridges with butter (or margarine), season and pot roast in a casserole for 15–20 minutes.
7 Remove the bacon slices, keep warm.
8 Deglaze the casserole with white wine and 2 tablespoons of water. Season.

9 Add to this the cabbage leaves lightly shredded with the lardons of bacon. Allow the cabbage to be immersed in the liquor.
10 Finally check the seasoning.
11 The partridges may be carved or served whole (or halved) on the bed of cabbage.

POÊLER

The process of poêler resembles that of pot-roasting. The cooking vessel, the poêlé, is a deep fireproof one in which the joint or bird to be cooked is placed ʼn a bed of mirepoix (the size of the cut varying according to the size of the ʼce). Joints and birds for roasting may be cooked in this manner and, even, s ʼ of the superior pieces may be poêlé.

. ˌ cocotte is, in effect, a poêlé so that when cooking (as distinct from simply dishing up) is 'en cocotte' then the method of cooking is poêler. These dishes are the responsibility of the chef saucier (sauce cook) in a traditional kitchen brigade.

586 Method of poêler

1 Butter a large pan or casserole and place a layer of raw mirepoix (Recipe 2) of vegetables on the bottom.
2 Place the meat or poultry on top of the vegetables and cover meat with plenty of butter (or margarine).
3 Place a lid on top and cook in a moderate oven, basting frequently with butter.
4 When the meat or poultry is cooked remove the lid to colour the meat.
5 Remove meat, add some good veal stock (Recipe 10) to the pan and simmer for 10 minutes.
6 Remove all grease and strain the sauce through a muslin.
7 Add the appropriate garnish.

587 Noix de veau poêlée – Cushion of veal poêlée

625 g (1¼ lb) veal cushion	1 bay-leaf	30 g (1 oz) celery
250 ml (½ pt) brown veal stock (Recipe 10)	30 g (1 oz) carrots	1 small sprig thyme
	30 g (1 oz) onions	seasoning
	90 g (3 oz) butter (or margarine)	

1 Bard the veal with fine slices of back fat and tie lightly with string.
2 Melt the butter in a casserole or small braising-pain and lay the aromatics and thick, sliced vegetables on the bottom.
3 Season the meat well, place on the bed of roots and baste well with melted butter.
4 Cover with a tight-fitting lid and place in a moderate oven to cook.
5 Baste often with butter, taking care not to brown the vegetables.
6 When veal is almost cooked, remove lid so that the joint may colour lightly.
7 Remove joint when cooked and remove string.
8 Add the brown stock to vegetables and simmer gently for 10 minutes.

9 Adjust seasoning, strain gravy through fine strainer, and remove all excess fat.
10 This joint is normally served with a vegetable garnish, i.e. florentine, bouquetière.
11 Gravy is served separately.

Note
(i) The veal may be piqué or larded. Larding is to be preferred as this helps to retain juice in the joint.
(ii) Other joints such as longe de veau (loin), épaule (shoulder) may, of course, be poêlé.

588 Caneton poêlé à la bigarade – Duck bigarade

one 2 kg (4-lb) duck	*15 ml spoon [1 tablespoon] vinegar*
3 oranges	*3 cubes of sugar*
½ lemon	

1 Clean and truss the duck.
2 Poêlé the duck (Recipe 578).
3 Cut into fine julienne the zest of 1½ oranges and ½ lemon, blanch.
4 Squeeze the juice from the oranges and lemon, reduce the braising-sauce until it is dense; strain.
5 Add the lemon and orange juice to bring the sauce to its normal consistency; add the vinegar and the dissolved sugar.
6 Garnish with the julienne of orange and lemon zest; check the sauce for seasoning and consistency; if the sauce is too thin, cohere with a little arrowroot.
7 Serve the duck in thin slices and garnish the duck with orange fillets and the sauce poured over.

589 Pigeon poêlé à l'anglaise

4 pigeons	*15 g (½ oz) chopped onions*
120 g (¼ lb) chicken livers	*9 slices lean bacon*
120 g (¼ lb) breadcrumbs	

1 Toss the onions, breadcrumbs and chicken's liver in butter and season.
2 Stuff the pigeons and truss.
3 Poêlé (as Recipe 578).
4 Serve with grilled bacon and gravy.

589a Poularde poêlée Chimay – Chicken (young fowl) poêlé

	For poêlé:	
240 g (½ lb) noodles	*60 g (2 oz) minced*	*60 g (2 oz) butter*
one 2 kg (4-lb) chicken	*carrots*	*1 bay-leaf*
15 g (½ oz) foie gras	*120 g (¼ lb) minced*	*125 ml (¼ pt) brown*
(optional)	*onions*	*veal stock*
62 ml (⅛ pt) cream	*30 g (1 oz) raw ham*	*(Recipe 10)*
⅛ glass (30 ml (1/16 pt))		
sherry		

1 Par-cook half the quantity of noodles and toss in butter, mix with cream and diced foie gras and season.
2 Stuff the chicken with this mixture.
3 Sweat off the ham and vegetables in butter and deglacer with sherry.
4 Truss the chicken and colour in butter; poêlé as in Recipe 586 adding the herbs and stock; cook under cover, basting frequently; when cooked remove the chicken; skim all fat from the sauce and thicken with a little arrowroot; season, and strain some over the chicken.
5 Sauté the remainder of the raw noodles and garnish.
6 Serve in a large casserole with some of the sauce, serving the remainder separately.

591 Poularde Souvaroff

one 2 kg (4 lb) chicken	*½ glass (60 ml (⅛ pt) Madeira*
240 g (½ lb) foie gras	*flour and water paste*
150 g (5 oz) diced truffles	*5 small white truffles*

1 Stuff the chicken with the foie gras and diced truffles.
2 Poêler the chicken (Recipe 586) but when three-quarters cooked, place in a large cocotte.
3 Déglacer the poêlé pan and reduce this liquor; season and strain over the chicken.
4 Cook the whole truffles in the sherry for 2 or 3 minutes and add these to the chicken.
5 Seal the lid well down with flour and water paste and continue cooking in the oven for 30 minutes approximately.
6 Serve the birds in the cocotte and do not break the seal until at the table.

Note. Pheasant, Faisan Souvaroff, may be similarly prepared. The high cost of this luxury dish may be reduced by substitution of other liver (pâté) for foie gras, and black garnishing paste for truffle.

592 Poulet en cocotte à la bonne femme – Chicken bonne femme

one 2 kg (4 lb) chicken	*120 g (¼ lb) butter (or*	*480 g (1 lb) potatoes*
240 g (½ lb) lardons	*sunflower*	*chopped parsley*
18 button onions	*margarine)*	

1 Truss the chicken and season.
2 Colour the chicken in butter in a large cocotte and continue cooking.
3 Add a garnish of cocotte potatoes (large olive-shape, château-cooked as Recipe 902), lardons and button onions fried in butter.
4 Sprinkle with a little chopped parsley before service.

593 Poulet en cocotte Champeaux

one 2 kg (4 lb) chicken	*500 g (1 lb) potatoes*
250 ml (½ pt) jus lié (Recipe 30) or	*125 ml (¼ pt) white wine*
demi-glace (Recipe 29) (or well-	*120 g (¼ lb) butter (or sunflower*
reduced brown stock)	*margarine)*
360 g (¾ lb) button onions	*seasoning*

1 Truss the chicken and season.
2 Colour the chicken in butter, add the white wine, jus lié (or alternatives above) and continue cooking.
3 Glaze the onions and fry the potatoes cut to large olive-size (cocotte) to golden brown; remove all fat from the sauce and season.
4 Garnish with the potatoes and onions.
5 Sprinkle a little chopped parsley before service.

594 Poussin à la polonaise

4 *single poussin*	*7 g (¼ oz) chopped parsley*
240 g (½ lb) *farce au gratin*	120 g (¼ lb) *butter*
(*Recipe* 508)	*juice of ½ lemon*
120 g (¼ lb) *white breadcrumbs*	2 *small hard-boiled eggs*

1 Stuff the birds with farce.
2 Poêler as Recipe 586.
3 Toss the breadcrumbs in butter until golden colour.
4 Pass the eggs through medium sieve and add to the crumbs.
5 Dress the poussin in a large cocotte and pour over the poêlé gravy.
6 Garnish with the egg and crumbs. Add beurre noisette (Recipe 82) and sprinkle with chopped parsley.

SAUTER AND FRYING

Deep-frying is applied to meat chiefly when it is compounded into croquettes and similar composite items. Calf's liver is sometimes thinly sliced, floured, egged and crumbed for deep-frying accompanied by fried parsley (foie de veau frit) and corned beef or cooked meat may be made into fritters.

Shallow-frying or sauté is, however, a common and important method of cooking meat, particularly the better small cuts which may be cooked either plain, or pané (breadcrumbed). Meat cuts, poultry and game dishes involving shallow-frying or sauté-ing are assigned to the chef saucier (sauce cook) in a large professional brigade.

Cuts for Sauter
(i)   Beef cuts used for sauter include: tournedos, entrecôte, rump and point steaks.
(ii) Lamb cuts so used are: noisettes, filet mignon and côtelettes. *Noisette* is literally a hazel-nut but in cookery it also means a small round piece of lean meat. A slice of boned loin of lamb about 2 cm (1 inch) thick, nicely trimmed and cut wedge-shape is a noisette.
(iii) Veal cuts for sauter include: escalope, grenadin médaillon, côtelette. *Grenadins de veau* are thick escalopes from the noix studded with truffles and fat. *Médaillons* are also cut from the noix, shaped as tournedos and can also be studded with truffles or back fat.
(iv) Port cuts such as escalope and côte may be treated similarly to veal in sauté-ing.
(v)   Chicken, particularly suprêmes are also dealt with by sauté-ing, plain, and pané (breadcrumbed).

GARNISHES FOR SAUTER

595 Garnishes for small cuts

These are largely interchangeable and include (particularly for tournedos sauté au beurre and dished on croûtons):

Arenberg – Tartlettes filled with carrots and spinach, slices of truffles (optional or use substitute), béarnaise sauce or sauce madère.

Baron Brisse – Sauce demi-glace, tomato concassé, artichoke bottoms, soufflèd potatoes, small balls of truffle.

Catherine – Sauce bordelaise, small pommes Macaire, marrow.

Chantecler – Sauce au porto (as Recipe 44 substituting port for madeira), julienne of truffles (optional or substitute garnishing paste), lamb's kidneys, cockscomb, tartelettes filled with asparagus heads.

Dauphine – Sauce madère, dauphine potatoes.

Duroc – Sauce chasseur, noisette potatoes.

596 Garnishes for entrecôtes

Also for other steaks sauté au beurre:

Cécilia – Sauce béarnaise, large-grilled mushrooms, asparagus tips, soufflés potatoes.

Champignons – Mushroom sauce, grilled mushrooms.

Hongroise – Sauce hongroise, plain-turned boiled potatoes.

Lyonnaise – Sauce lyonnaise.

597 Garnishes for noisettes

Also for filet mignon, and cutlets of lamb sauté au beurre; (for noisettes, serve on croûtons cut to size):

Marseillaise – Half-glaze sauce, small tomatoes filled with olives, garlic, anchovy fillets, copeaux potatoes.

Masséna – Sauce Périgueux, artichoke bottoms filled with sauce, slice of bone marrow on top.

Du Barry – Sauce au madère, small cauliflower covered with Mornay sauce.

Crécy – Sauce au madère, glazed carrots.

Clamart – Sauce madère, artichoke bottoms filled with green peas.

Fleuriste – Demi-glace sauce, halves of tomato filled with jardinière of vegetables.

Method of Sauter. Sauter literally means 'to jump', and describes the method of tossing meat in shallow, hot fat for frying. A jumping or tossing process is also used in some forms of shallow-frying such as vegetables: for example, pommes sautées. The same technique is used in meat cookery for dishes such as sauté de bœuf Strogonoff, or foie de volaille, rognons, etc.

Generally, however, in sauté-ing small cuts such as tournedos, escalopes, noisettes, and similar cuts, the pieces are simply laid in hot butter or oil (or a mixture of both) in a sauté-pan (plat à sauter or sautoir). For small thin pieces, rapid heat may be continued; for larger ones a moderate, steady heat is preferable. The correct plat à sauter has a handled cover used when larger

pieces are slowly finished or when sauce or deglazing liquor has been added.
Additionally, when several pieces, such as noisettes, are required together,
they may be assembled on the cover's flat surface and slid simultaneously
into the hot fat.

BEEF SAUTÉS

598 Bitok à la russe

300 g (10 oz) minced, raw veal (or
   topside of beef)
60 g (2 oz) finely-chopped onions
200 ml (⅜ pt) milk
480 g (1 lb) white breadcrumbs

seasoning
120 ml (¼ pt) sauce Smitane
   (Recipe 599)
1 egg yolk

1 Cook the onions to golden brown in a little butter.
2 Soak the breadcrumbs in milk and squeeze to remove all liquid.
3 Mix the meat, onions, breadcrumbs together and season; bind with egg
   yolks.
4 Scale into 90 g (3-oz) pieces, and shape like tournedos; dip in flour and
   sauté in clarified butter.
5 Coat with sauce Smitane.

599 Sauce Smitane

30 g (1 oz) finely-chopped onions
250 ml (½ pt) sour cream (or
   quark or yogurt)
30 g (1 oz) butter (or margarine)

juice of ¼ lemon
15 ml spoon [1 tablespoon]
   mushroom ketchup or essence
   (optional)

1 Fry the onions to golden colour in butter.
2 Add the cream and reduce by half.
3 Add the mushroom ketchup and lemon juice.
4 Garnish with a little butter, season; do not strain.

600 Filet de bœuf sauté Strogonoff

30 g (1 lb) fillet beef
30 g (1 oz) finely chopped shallots
¼ clove crushed garlic
juice of ½ lemon
pinch of tarragon

125 ml (¼ pt) cream
120 g (¼ lb) butter (or oil or
   margarine)
seasoning

1 Cut the fillet into rough julienne or small escalopes.
2 Cook the shallots to golden colour in butter in sauté pan.
3 Quickly sauté the escalopes in butter; drain and add to shallots.
4 Reduce the cream with the meat and shallots; add the tarragon, a squeeze
   of lemon juice, thicken with butter (montez au beurre); and season.

601 Filet de bœuf sauté à la minute hongroise

As Recipe 600 but dust meat with 7 g (¼ oz) paprika before sauté-ing.

602 Hamburger or Hamburg steak

500 g (1 *lb*) *minced rump or*
  topside of beef
60 g (2 *oz*) *finely chopped onions*
5 *eggs*
2 *large onions*

7 g (¼ *oz*) *chopped parsley*
120 g (¼ *lb*) *flour seasoning*
120 ml (¼ *pt*) *sauce piquante*
  (*Recipe* 46)
120 ml (¼ *pt*) *milk*

1 Cook the chopped onions to golden colour.
2 Mix the meat, onions and parsley together.
3 Bind with 1 whole egg and season.
4 Shape into rounds and scale at 90 g (3 oz) each.
5 Flour and sauté in oil (or clarified butter).
6 Place a fried egg on top of each hamburger and garnish the dish with French-fried onions.
7 Serve separately sauce piquante.

603 Tournedos Rossini

four 180 g (6 *oz*) *tournedos*
4 *round croûtons*
60 g (2 *oz*) *butter*
4 *medallions of foie gras*

4 *slices truffle*
120 ml (¼ *pt*) *Madeira*
125 ml (¼ *pt*) *jus lié* (*Recipe* 30) *or*
  demi-glace (*Recipe* 29)

1 Cook the tournedos in oil (or clarified butter (Recipe 84).)
2 When nearly cooked add the croûtons and cook to golden brown.
3 Remove the string and dress the tournedos on the croûtons.
4 Déglacer the pan with Madeira, add the jus lié (or well-reduced brown stock) and simmer.
5 Gently heat the foie gras and place on top of the tournedos.
6 Butter and adjust seasoning of sauce, strain over the tournedos and finish off with slice of truffle.

Note. For economy, substitutes may include, for truffle, black garnishing paste, and for foie gras, slices of parfait de foie gras or liver paste.

LAMB AND MUTTON SAUTÉS

604 Côtelette d'agneau Reform – Lamb cutlet Reform

eight 90 g (3 *oz*) *cutlets*
125 ml (¼*pt*) *sauce Reform*
  (*Recipe* 48)
240 g (½ *lb*) *white breadcrumbs*
7 g (¼ *oz*) *chopped ham*

7 g (¼ *oz*) *chopped tongue*
7 g (¼ *oz*) *chopped parsley*
62 ml (⅛ *pt*) *oil*
60 g (2 *oz*) *butter*

Garnish: 15 g (½ *oz*) *of cooked and julienne-cut: ham, tongue, gherkins, egg white, beetroot, truffles*

1 Add the chopped ham, tongue, and parsley to white breadcrumbs.
2 Trim and flatten the cutlets with the batte.
3 Pané the cutlets in flour, egg and prepared crumbs.
4 Sauté both sides of cutlet to golden brown gently in oil.
5 Toss the garnish in a little butter and dress the cutlets in the form of a crown.
6 Finish with beurre noisette (Recipe 82) and place a frill on each cutlet.
7 Serve the sauce Reform separately in sauceboat.

605 Epigramme d'agneau à la provençale

500 g (1 lb) breast of lamb	*125 ml (¼ pt) tomato sauce*
4 lamb cutlets	*(Recipe 34)*
4 small tomatoes	*1 small carrot*
240 g (½ lb) white breadcrumbs	*1 small onion clouté*
120 g (¼ lb) duxelles (Recipe 101)	*62 ml (⅛ pt) oil*
	seasoning

1 Cook the breast of lamb in water with a carrot and onion clouté.
2 When cooked, remove the bones and press; when cold, cut into diamond shapes, 4 cm by 4 cm (2 inches by 2 inches).
3 Pané the diamonds and cutlets and sauter gently in oil until golden brown.
4 Blanch the tomatoes and remove the seeds; stuff with the duxelles.
5 Arrange the cutlets and épigrammes neatly on a dish, garnish with the stuffed tomatoes, and finish with a beurre noisette (Recipe 82) (optional).
6 Serve tomato sauce (Recipe 34) separately.

606 Noisette d'agneau à la niçoise

8 noisettes [90 g (3 oz) each]	*180 g (6 oz) French beans*
4 small tomatoes	*seasoning*
125 ml (¼ pt) sauce au Madère	*360 g (¾ lb) château potatoes*
(Recipe 44)	*(Recipe 902)*
8 croûtons	

1 Cook château potatoes in oil (or butter or a combination of both) and drain.
2 Cook the French beans and arrange in small bouquets in serving dish.
3 Blanch the tomatoes and cook whole in butter.
4 Sauté the noisettes quickly in butter (or margarine); season.
5 Shallow fry the croûtons in oil.
6 Déglacer the noisette pan with sauce Madère.
7 Arrange the noisettes on the croûtons and arrange on the serving dish in the form of a crown.
8 Add the tomatoes and potatoes to dish.
9 Strain the sauce on the noisettes.
10 Sprinkle a little chopped parsley over the potatoes.

VEAL SAUTÉS

607 Côte de veau en cocotte – Veal cutlet in cocotte

four 300 *g* (10 *oz*) *veal cutlets*   240 *g* (½ *lb*) *diced mushrooms*
500 *g* (1 *lb*) *potatoes*   120 *g* (¼ *lb*) *butter*
12 *glazed onions*   *seasoning*

1 Dust cutlets with flour and season.
2 Sauté in oil (or clarified butter).
3 Toss the mushrooms in butter and cook the cocotte potatoes (cut to olive size) to golden brown.
4 Mix the onions, potatoes and mushrooms, sprinkling over cutlets when cooked.
5 Dress them in a large casserole and finish off with a beurre noisette (Recipe 82) (optional) and chopped parsley.

608 Côte de veau à la bonne femme

Prepare as Recipe 607 omitting mushrooms.
Veal cutlets may, of course, be prepared in similar style to veal escalopes.

609 Côtelette de veau Pojarski

500 *g* (1 *lb*) *veal fillet*   1 *egg white*   125 *ml* (¼ *pt*) *milk*
120 *g* (¼ *lb*) *white*   62 *ml* (⅛ *pt*) *cream*   *seasoning*
   breadcrumbs   *oil* (*or clarified butter*)
15 *g* (½ *oz*) *butter*

1 Remove all nerves from the veal, mince finely and pass through a sieve.
2 Pound the veal in a food processor (or mortar) and bind with the egg whites and beat in the cream.
3 Soak the crumbs in milk, squeeze out all moisture (panada).
4 Mix the veal and panada together and season and add 30 g (1 oz) butter.
5 Shape as cutlets, flour, egg and crumb.
6 Sauté both sides in oil (or clarified butter (Recipe 84).)

610 Fricadelles de veau

360 *g* (¾ *lb*) *lean veal*   1 *egg*
180 *g* (6 *oz*) *butter*   7 *g* (¼ *oz*) *salt*
75 *g* (2½ *oz*) *milk-soaked*   30 *g* (1 *oz*) *chopped cooked onions*
   breadcrumbs   *grated nutmeg*

1 Remove all fat and gristle from veal and mince very finely.
2 Squeeze all moisture from breadcrumbs and mix the veal, eggs, onions and breadcrumbs together with the butter; season.
3 Divide into portions approximately 100 g (3½ oz) each and shape into quoits.
4 Dust with flour and cook both sides in oil (or clarified butter).
5 Serve with sauce Robert (Recipe 49) separately.

611 Escalope de veau Holstein

four 180 g (6-oz) escalopes	240 g (¼ lb) butter
240 g (½ lb) white breadcrumbs	12 anchovy fillets
5 eggs	4 slices lemon

1 Flatten escalopes with the batte, flour, egg and crumb.
2 Sauté and garnish with lemon slices, fried eggs topped with a criss-cross of anchovies.
3 Finish with beurre noisette (Recipe 82) or serve surrounded with a little light jus lié.

612 Escalope de veau à la milanaise

four 180 g (6-oz) escalopes	62 ml (⅛ pt) tomato sauce
120 g (¼ lb) butter (or sunflower	(Recipe 34)
margarine)	60 g (2 oz) tomato concassé
4 lemon slices	15 g (½ oz) Parmesan cheese
360 g (¾ lb) white breadcrumbs	seasoning
180 g (6 oz) spaghetti	1 egg

7 g (¼ oz) each, julienne cooked: ham, tongue, mushroom, truffles (optional)

1 Soak the ham, tongue, and truffles in a little sherry.
2 Flour, egg, and crumb the escalopes.
3 Sauté in oil (or clarified butter and oil).
4 Cook spaghetti 18 minutes in boiling water and drain.
5 Toss in butter with the garnish, mix in tomato concassé and sauce, sprinkle in cheese; season.
6 Dress the garnish alongside of escalopes and garnish each escalope with lemon slices with a surrounding of sherry-flavoured jus lié or finish with beurre noisette (Recipe 82).

613 Escalope de veau à la napolitaine

	Garnish napolitaine:	
four 180 g (6 oz)	125 ml (¼ pt) tomato	15 g (½ oz)
escalopes	sauce (Recipe 34)	Parmesan cheese
180 g (6 oz) spaghetti		120 g (¼ lb) butter
		3 tomato concassé

1 Prepare and cook escalopes as Recipe 612.
2 Cook spaghetti 18 minutes in boiling water and drain.
3 Toss in butter, mix with tomato concassé and tomato sauce; season and sprinkle with cheese.
4 Dress the garnish alongside the escalopes with a slice of lemon on each escalope.
5 Place a thread of tomato sauce (cordon) around the dish; finish with beurre noisette (Recipe 82) or serve a light, tomato sauce separately.

614 Escalope de veau à la suédoise

four 180 g (6 oz) escalopes
250 ml (½ pt) cream
240 g (½ lb) sliced mushrooms
30 g (1 oz) finely chopped shallots

60 g (2 oz) butter (or margarine)
½ glass (⅛ pt) brandy
juice of ¼ lemon

1 Dust the escalopes with flour and season.
2 Sauté in butter and remove from pan.
3 Sweat the shallots, add the mushrooms, and sweat until cooked under cover, then add brandy.
4 Add the cream and reduce to half its quantity, draw to side of stove, add lemon juice and monter au beurre (as defined in glossary).
5 Season and coat sauce over the escalopes.

PORK SAUTÉS

615 Côtelette de porc à la charcutière – Pork cutlet charcutière

four 240 g (8 oz) pork cutlets
30 g (1 oz) finely chopped onions
250 ml (½ pt) jus lié (Recipe 30)
   (or demi-glace, Recipe 29, or
   well-reduced brown stock)
82 ml (⅙ pt) white wine

2.5 ml spoon [½ teaspoon] mustard
15 g (½ oz) meat glaze (Recipe 13)
30 g (1 oz) butter
15 g (½ oz) julienne of gherkins
seasoning

1 Trim and sauté the cutlets.

For the sauce:
2 Fry the onions gently without colouring in the sauté pan.
3 Add white wine and reduce.
4 Add jus lié or demi-glace and further reduce.
5 Add diluted mustard; season and garnish with gherkin julienne, and finish with meat glaze and butter (optional).
6 Serve sauce separately in sauce-boat.

616 Côtelette de porc à la flamande

four 240 g (8 oz) cutlets   seasoning
4 apple rings

60 g (2 oz) butter
   (or sunflower
   margarine)

1 Dust the cutlets with flour and season.
2 Partly fry both sides, place the apple rings on top and finish cooking in the oven.
3 Add a beurre noisette (Recipe 82) before serving (or serve separately a little jus or jus lié, possibly flavoured with a little Calvados).

617 Escalope de porc Zingara

4 *pork escalopes*
4 *slices cooked ham*
62 *ml* (⅛ *pt*) *white wine*
60 *g* (2 *oz*) *butter*
125 *ml* (¼ *pt*) *jus lié* (*Recipe* 30) *or*
  demi-glace (*Recipe* 29)

62 *ml* (⅛ *pt*) *tomato sauce*
  (*Recipe* 34)
30 *g* (1 *oz*) *julienne of cooked ham,*
  tongue, mushroom and truffle
  (*optional*)

1 Remove all nerves and sinews from the pork fillet and flatten with the batte.
2 Flour the escalopes and sauté in butter; cut the ham the size of the escalope.
3 Place the previously-heated ham on top of the escalope.
4 Deglaze the pan with the wine and add the jus lié (or reduced brown stock), tomato sauce and mushroom liquor (resulting from mushroom cooking); reduce for a few minutes.
5 Add the julienne of ham, tongue, mushrooms, and truffles; season and finish with butter (optional).
6 Surround the escalopes with the sauce.

618 Escalope de porc à la viennoise

4 *escalopes*
1 *hard-boiled egg*
4 *stoned olives*

7 *g* (¼ *oz*) *capers*
62 *ml* (⅛ *pt*) *oil*
4 *slices lemon*

12 *anchovy fillets*
4 *g* (⅛ *oz*) *chopped*
  parsley
120 *g* (¼ *lb*) *butter*

1 Prepare the escalopes, flour, egg, and crumb.
2 Sauté to golden colour in oil and butter.
3 Pass the egg yolks and the white separately through a medium sieve.
4 Arrange the eggs, parsley, and capers rainbow fashion on each side of the centre of escalopes.
5 Garnish each escalope with a criss-cross of anchovy fillets, olives, and slice of lemon.
6 Finish with beurre noisette (Recipe 82) (optional, or thread round a little jus or jus lié).
Note. Veal escalopes are similarly prepared.

OFFAL SAUTÉS

619 Brochettes de rognons – Skewered kidneys

8 *sheep's kidneys*
120 *g* (¼ *lb*) *lean bacon*
240 *g* (½ *lb*) *small*
  mushrooms

120 *g* (¼ *lb*)
  breadcrumbs
seasoning
30 *g* (1 *oz*) *melted*
  butter

120 *g* (¼ *lb*) *straw*
  potatoes
  (*Recipe* 929)
1 *bunch watercress*

1 Remove the skin from kidneys.
2 Cut into roundels 1 cm (one-third inch) thick.
3 Season kidneys and sauté quickly in butter.
4 Impalé them on skewers alternating them with 2 cm (1-inch) squares of blanched lean bacon and slices of sauté mushrooms.
5 Brush with melted butter, sprinkle with breadcrumbs and grill.
6 Serve on the skewer and garnish with straw potatoes and watercress.

620 Escalope de ris de veau à la maréchale – Escalope of sweetbread maréchale

4 *calves' sweetbreads*	16 *asparagus tips*
4 *slices truffle (optional)*	120 g (¼ *lb*) *butter*

1 Blanch the sweetbreads, skin and press.
2 Cut into escalopes and season.
3 Flour, egg, and crumb and sauté to a golden colour in oil (or clarified butter) (Recipe 84).
4 Garnish with asparagus tips and slices of truffle (optional).
5 Finish with beurre noisette (Recipe 82).

621 Foie de veau au lard – Liver and bacon

500 g (1 *lb*) *calves' liver*	30 g (1 *oz*) *flour*	*seasoning*
8 *slices back bacon*	30 g (1 *oz*) *butter*	

1 Skin the liver and cut into medium slices.
2 Dip in seasoned flour and fry both sides quickly in clarified butter.
3 Garnish with grilled bacon.
4 Finish with a thread of jus lié (or beurre noisette (Recipe 82)).

622 Foie de veau à la lyonnaise – Calves' liver lyonnaise

500 g (1 *lb*) *calves' liver*	250 ml (½ *pt*) *lyonnaise sauce (Recipe* 43)

Prepare and cook as for foie de veau au lard (Recipe 614), but omit the bacon and coat with Lyonnaise sauce.

623 Foie de veau aux fines herbes

Prepare as Recipe 615 but coat with the following sauce:

623a Sauce aux fines herbes or Sauce Bercy (for meat)

30 g (1 *oz*) *finely chopped shallots*	500 ml (1 *pt*) *jus lié (Recipe* 30) *or demi-glace (Recipe* 29) *or well-reduced brown stock*	15 g (½ *oz*) *fine herbs*
125 ml (¼ *pt*) *wine (white)*		120 g (¼ *lb*) *butter*
15 g (½ *oz*) *meat glaze (Recipe* 13)		*seasoning*

1 Sweat the shallots in 30 g (1 oz) of butter.
2 Make a reduction of white wine.
3 Add the jus lié and simmer for 10 minutes.
4 Add meat glaze and herbs.
5 Blend in the butter, adjust seasoning; do not strain.

624 Ris de veau sauté St-Germain – Calves' sweetbreads St Germain

1 kg (2 lb) calves' sweetbreads	250 ml (½ pt) sauce béarnaise
500 g (1 lb) pommes parisiennes	(Recipe 71)
(Recipe 904)	120 g (¼ lb) butter
250 g (½ lb) fresh-pea purée	7 g (¼ oz) cooked peas
	500 g (1 lb) glazed carrots

1 Blanch, trim, and sauté sweetbreads, basting frequently with butter.
2 Garnish bouquets of potatoes and carrots.
3 Serve sauce béarnaise and pea purée separately.
4 Finish with beurre noisette (Recipe 82) (or a thread of Madeira- or sherry-flavoured jus) and fried parsley.

625 Rognon de veau à la bordelaise

4 kidneys	120 g (¼ lb) sliced	15 g (½ oz) diced
250 ml (½ pt) sauce	cepes (if unavailable,	bone marrow
bordelaise	other types of	4 heart-shaped
(Recipe 35)	mushroom)	croûtons

1 Skin and cut the kidney into small escalopes.
2 Sauté quickly in oil or clarified butter and drain.
3 Mix the kidney with the sauce, marrow and cepes.
4 Garnish with the croûtons, the ends dipped in parsley.

626 Rognons sautés chasseur

8 sheep's kidneys	180 g (6 oz) mushrooms
125 ml (¼ pt) jus lié (Recipe 30) or	7 g (¼ oz) fines herbes
demi-glace (Recipe 29) or well-	7 g (¼ oz) chopped onions
reduced brown stock	30 g (1 oz) butter
7 g (¼ oz) meat glaze (Recipe 13)	125 ml (¼ pt) white wine
62 ml (⅛ pt) tomato sauce	120 g (¼ lb) tomato concassé
(Recipe 34)	

1 Skin and cut the kidneys into small escalopes.
2 Fry the kidneys quickly in oil or butter, drain and keep warm.
3 Sweat the onions in a sauté pan in butter, add the sliced mushrooms and make a reduction of the white wine.
4 Add the tomato concassé, moisten with the jus lié (Recipe 30) or demi-glace (or reduced brown stock) and tomato sauce and simmer for 10 minutes; skim, add the meat glaze and blend in the butter, add the fines herbes and season.
5 Mix the kidneys with the sauce and garnish with heart-shaped croûtons.

627 Rognons sautés Turbigo – Kidneys sautés Turbigo

8 *sheep's kidneys*	60 *g (2 oz) butter (or sunflower*
½ *glass (60 ml (⅛ pt) sherry*	*margarine)*
9 *heart-shaped croûtons*	120 *g (¼ lb) mushrooms*
30 *g (1 oz) finely chopped shallots*	*seasoning*
250 *ml (½ pt) jus lié (Recipe 30) or*	7 *g (¼ oz) chopped parsley*
demi-glace (Recipe 29) (or well-	9 *chipolatas*
reduced brown stock)	

1 Blanch and grill the chipolatas.
2 Remove the skin from kidney and cut into half lengthwise.
3 Remove stalks and wash the mushrooms. Cut into quarters and toss in butter.
4 Sauté the kidney quickly in oil or butter and drain.
5 Fry shallots in a little butter (or margarine) until golden brown.
6 Deglaze the pan with the sherry.
7 Add demi-glace and reduce by half; season and enrich with butter (optional).
8 Add the kidney and mushrooms to sauce.
9 Garnish with chipolatas, heart shaped croûtons (croûton ends dipped in parsley).

CHICKEN SAUTÉS

628 Sauté of chicken

1 Thoroughly clean the bird.
2 Cut off the legs, pull gently from the bird and cut each leg in two pieces at the join.
3 Cut off the wings (pinch up a piece of flesh between the thumb and forefinger before cutting).
4 Cut the body in half, cutting through rib cage.
5 Cut the breast diagonally across in two pieces.
6 Cut the base or undercarriage in three pieces.
7 This yields 8 pieces. The undercarriage pieces are cooked and used to build up the centre of the dish when serving, although not served as portions.
8 Place the pieces in a sauté pan with oil or clarified butter (Recipe 84).
9 Colour quickly and finish he cooking under cover. (White meat will cook before dark meat).

Notes
(i) Alternatively the wing, with trimmed wing-bone only, may be used as a suprême and legs may be boned and prepared as a separate dish. Pieces may be sautéd, plain, or panéd. Game birds may be similarly prepared.
(ii) To achieve light sauces, demi-glace (Recipe 29) may be replaced by thin jus lié (Recipe 30) or a well reduced brown meat stock (Recipe 10 or 7).

629 Typical Chicken Sauté Garnishes

Poulet sauté Beaulieu: Déglacer with white wine, add demi-glace garnish of artichoke bottoms, tomatoes, stoned olives, and cocotte potatoes.

Poulet sauté Bordelaise: Deglacér with red wine, add demi-glace garnish of shallots, quarters of artichokes, French fried onions, and sauté potatoes.

630 Typical Suprêmes Sautées Garnishes

Suprême de volaille Maréchale: Egg and crumb; garnish of asparagus tips, slice of truffle (or substitute or optional), beurre noisette.
Suprême de volaille Richelieu: Egg and crumb; garnish top with parsley butter and slice of truffle (or substitute or optional).
Suprême de volaille Maryland: Egg and crumb; add garnish Maryland.

631 Ballotine de volaille chasseur – Chicken ballotine chasseur

250 ml (½ pt) sauce chasseur (Recipe 38)	125 g (¼ lb) fine forcemeat (Recipe 200)	4 raw chicken-legs

1 Bone the legs neatly without cutting the drumstick.
2 Stuff with the forcemeat and sew up.
3 Sauté in oil and butter, remove the string and coat with sauce chasseur.

632 Poulet sauté archiduc – Chicken sauté archiduc

one 2 kg (4 lb) chicken
5 slices truffle (optional)
250 ml (½ pt) fresh cream
seasoning
½ glass 30 ml (⅟16 pt) brandy (or whisky)
90 g (3 oz) finely chopped onions

125 ml (¼ pt) chicken velouté (Recipe 27)
juice of ¼ lemon
120 g (¼ lb) butter (or sunflower margarine)
30 ml (⅟16 pt) Madeira

1 Joint the bird as for sauté (Recipe 628).
2 Fry in butter (or margarine) without colouring.
3 Add the onions, previously cooked in butter (or margarine), and complete the cooking of the chicken under cover.
4 When cooked, withdraw the pieces and keep hot.
5 Moisten the onions with brandy and reduce; add the cream and velouté and rub through fine chinois (strainer).
6 Finish the sauce with butter, Madeira, and lemon juice; pour sauce over chicken.
7 Decorate with slices of truffle (or garnishing paste or optional).

633 Poulet sauté à l'arlésienne

one 2 kg (4 lb) chicken
125 ml (¼ pt) white wine
240 g (½ lb) concassé tomatoes
1 egg-plant
1 large onion

190 ml (⅓ pt) jus lié or demi-glace (Recipe 29) (or reduced brown stock)
190 ml (⅓ pt) tomato sauce (Recipe 34)

1 clove chopped garlic
9 heart-shaped croûtons
7 g (¼ oz) chopped parsley

1 Cut the chicken as for sauté (Recipe 628), sauté in butter (or margarine) and remove from the pan when cooked.
2 Rinse the pan with the white wine and reduce; add garlic, tomato sauce, demi-glace and reduce by one-third.
3 Peel the egg-plant, cut into roundels, dip in flour, and deep-fry.
4 Slice the onions into rings and French-fry.
5 Toss the tomato concassé in butter (or margarine).
6 Season the sauce and finish with butter (optional).
7 Arrange the chicken neatly on a dish and coat with the sauce.
8 Garnish with alternate bouquets of tomato, onions, egg-plant, and croûtons.
9 Sprinkle a little chopped parsley on the chicken.

634 Poulet sauté chasseur

one 2 kg (4 lb) chicken
250 ml (½ pt) jus lié (Recipe 30)
* demi-glace (Recipe 29) (or well-*
* reduced brown stock)*
62 ml (⅛ pt) tomato sauce
* (Recipe 34)*
4 heart-shaped croûtons
chopped parsley

240 g (½ lb) tomato concassé
7 g (¼ oz) finely chopped onions
7 g (¼ oz) fines herbes
120 g (4 oz) mushrooms
90 g (3 oz) butter (or sunflower
* margarine)*
½ glass (30 ml (1/16 pt) brandy
* (optional)*
125 ml (¼ pt) white wine
15 g (½ oz) meat glaze (Recipe 13)

1 Cut the chicken as for sauté (Recipe 628); and season.
2 Sauter in butter until cooked; (the white meat will cook quicker than the darker flesh).
3 Sauté the chopped onions in the residue and rinse the pan with the white wine.
4 Add the sliced mushrooms and cook for a few minutes: then add the tomato concassé.
5 Add the 2 sauces, brandy, herbs, and meat glaze and reduce to 250 ml (½ pt); check the sauce for seasoning and consistency; enrich with a little butter.
6 Arrange the chicken neatly on the serving dish and coat with the sauce.
7 Garnish with the croûtons fried in oil and/or butter – the ends dipped in parsley. (Though not classic, these enhance the dish.)

635 Poulet sauté à la hongroise

one 2 kg (4 lb) chicken
30 g (1 oz) finely chopped onions
15 g (½ oz) paprika
180 g (6 oz) tomato concassé
120 g (¼ lb) rice (rice pilaff
* Recipe 366)*

125 ml (¼ pt) cream (or fromage
* frais, yogurt or quark)*
120 g (¼ lb) butter (or sunflower
* margarine)*

1 Cut the chicken as for sauté (Recipe 628), sauté in butter without colouring.

2 Withdraw from the sauté pan, sweat the onions, add the paprika and tomato concassé; replace the chicken and finish cooking under cover.
3 When the chicken is cooked, withdraw; add the cream (or alternative) to the sauce, enrich with butter, and season.
4 Mix a little cooked tomato concassé with the rice and arrange as a border.
5 Dress the chicken to the centre and coat with the sauce.

636 Poulet sauté Marengo

one 2 kg (4 lb) chicken
4 heart-shaped croûtons
4 French-fried eggs (deep fried)
4 slices truffle (optional)
62 ml (⅛ pt) oil
30 g (1 oz) butter (or sunflower margarine)
125 ml (¼ pt) white wine
4 crayfish cooked in court-bouillon (Recipe 371)

8 turned mushrooms
240 g (½ lb) tomato concassé
1 clove bruised garlic
4 stoned olives
250 ml (½ pt) jus lié (Recipe 30) or half-glaze (Recipe 29) (or well-reduced brown stock)
62 ml (⅛ pt) tomato sauce (Recipe 34)
chopped parsley

1 Cut as for sauté (Recipe 628); colour the pieces in oil and finish cooking under cover.
2 When cooked, pour away the oil; déglacé the pan with the white wine; add garlic, tomato concassé, half-glaze or jus lié (or well-reduced brown stock), tomato sauce, and reduce to correct consistency; season, add the chicken, and simmer for a few minutes at the side of the stove.
3 Dress the chicken in crown-shape, cover with the sauce.
4 Garnish with the cooked mushrooms, crayfish, olives, and French-fried eggs.
5 Complete the garnish with croûtons fried in butter – the ends dipped in parsley.

637 Poulet sauté Maryland

one 2 kg (4 lb) chicken
1 tin (240 g (8 oz)) sweetcorn
1 egg yolk
2 bananas
4 small grilled tomatoes
4 slices bacon

120 g (¼ lb) butter (or sunflower margarine)
125 ml (¼ pt) sauce Raifort (Recipe 99)
fried parsley
white breadcrumbs

1 Cut the chicken as for sauté (Recipe 628).
2 Flour, egg, and crumb; and sauté in clarified butter (Recipe 84) (or oil).
3 Drain the liquid from the sweetcorn; bind with egg yolks and a little flour; 8 small pancakes 0.5 cm (¼-inch) thick, 4 cm (2 inches) in diameter and fry.
4 Grill the bacon, bananas, and tomatoes.
5 Arrange the chicken on the centre of dish; garnish around neatly. Some chefs add 4 small croquette potatoes (Recipe 913)) and finish with beurre noisette (optional).
6 Decorate with fried parsley.
7 Serve creamed horse-radish sauce (Raifort) separately.

638 Suprême de volaille Maryland

Prepare as Recipe 637.

639 Suprême de volaille en papillote – Wing fillet of chicken en papillote

two 1.5 kg (3 lb) chickens
125 ml (¼ pt) sauce italienne
(Recipe 42)
4 slices cooked ham
30 g (1oz) flour

4 sheets greaseproof paper (or
aluminium foil)
seasoning
oil
120 g (¼ lb) butter

1 Cut the greaseproof paper into large heart-shapes and oil both sides.
2 Flour and season the suprêmes and sauter in butter (or oil and butter or sunflower margarine) to a golden colour.
3 Place a slice of ham on each side of the prepared paper; lay the suprême on top of the ham and a tablespoon of the sauce on top of each.
4 Fold the paper (or foil) over and seal securely.
5 Place in a hot dish containing oil and soufflé them for 2 or 3 minutes in a hot oven; serve in the papers (or foil).

640 Suprême de volaille à la maréchale

two 1.5 kg (3 lb) chickens
16 asparagus tips
120 g (¼ lb) butter

4 slices truffle (optional)
125 ml (¼ pt) jus lié (Recipe 30) (or
well-reduced brown stock, Recipe
10 or 7)

1 Remove the suprêmes from chicken.
2 Season, flour, egg and crumb; fry both sides in butter (or oil, or oil and butter or sunflower margarine)
3 Garnish with asparagus tips, thread of jus lié and beurre noisette (Recipe 82).
4 Decorate with slices of truffle (optional).

DUCK SAUTÉ

641 Aiguillettes de caneton au poivre verte – Fillets of duck with green peppercorns

four 225 g (8 oz) duck breasts
62 ml (⅛ pt) groundnut (arachide)
oil
125 ml (¼ pt) dry white wine
62 ml (⅛ pt) white stock (Recipe
6)
125 ml (¼ pt) jus lié (Recipe 30) or
well-reduced brown stock
(Recipe 8)

30 g (1 oz) butter (or sunflower
margarine)
250 ml (½ pt) double cream)
62 ml (⅛ pt) brandy
1 tbsp. wine vinegar
½ tbsp. caster sugar (for caramel)
62 ml (⅛ pt) port
15 g (½ oz) green peppercorns
3 dessert apples
seasoning
15 g (½ oz) diced red peppers

1 Remove the skin and the fat from the duck breast. Discard the fat; replace and tie on the skin.
2 Lightly cook the breasts in hot oil on top of the stove (or in the oven) until cooked and just pink.
3 Bring the white wine and brandy to the boil and reduce by two-thirds.
4 Add the white stock and the jus lié (or reduced brown stock). Simmer for 5 minutes. Add the cream, season and continue to reduce by one-third.
5 Make a caramel with the vinegar and sugar. Add to the reduced sauce. Add the green peppercorns and diced pimentos.
6 Prepare the garnish by peeling and coring the apples, cut into neat slices. Quickly fry the slices in butter.
7 Remove the skin from the duck breasts. Slice thinly across the grain.
8 Arrange the slices in a fan on individual plates. Sauce over, decorate with apples and serve.

642 Magrets de canard à l'Armagnac – Duck breasts with armagnac and burgundy

4 *duck breasts*	120 g (4 oz) *butter*
seasoning	60 g (2 oz) *finely chopped shallots*
60 g (2 oz) *butter* (*or margarine or*	60 ml (⅛ pt) *Armagnac*
oil)	250 ml (½ pt) *red Burgundy*

For garnish: *glazed button onions, turned* (*or diced*) *slices turnips, butter-fried mushrooms, freshly cooked leaf spinach*

1 Trim the duck breasts, season with salt and pepper.
2 Heat 60 g butter (or alternative) in a pan and gently cook the breasts on both sides until just pink.
3 Slice the breasts for service on a plate.
4 Add the shallots to the pan. Sweat in the residual fat then deglaze with the Burgundy and Armagnac.
5 Bring to the boil and reduce by half; enrich the resultant sauce carefully with remaining butter.
6 Correct the seasoning.
7 Coat the duck breasts with the sauce; garnish with the button onions, turnips and mushrooms fried in butter and freshly cooked leaf spinach.

SAUTÉS OF POULTRY OFFAL

643 Brochettes de foies de volaille – Skewered chicken livers

240 g (½ lb) *chicken livers*	240 g (½ lb) *straw potatoes*
120 g (¼ lb) *mushrooms*	(*Recipe* 929)
4 *bay-leaves*	1 *bunch watercress*
60 g (2 oz) *butter* (*or sunflower*	4 *skewers*
margarine)	120 g (¼ lb) *bacon*
120 g (¼ lb) *white breadcrumbs*	

1 Sauté the livers quickly in butter (or margarine).
2 Cut the bacon in pieces 2 cm (1 inch) square, 0.5 cm (¼ inch) thick, and blanch.
3 Cut the mushrooms into pieces of 2 cm (1 inch) and sauté in butter (or margarine).
4 Impale the liver, bacon, and mushrooms alternately on each skewer with a bay-leaf.
5 Brush over with melted butter (or margarine), sprinkle with crumbs, grill and baste.
6 Serve on the skewers and garnish with straw potatoes.

644 Foies de volaille sautés au vin rouge – Sauté of chicken livers in red wine

360 g (¾ lb) chicken livers	1 sprig thyme
125 ml (¼ pt) red wine	1 bay-leaf
250 ml (½ pt) jus lié (Recipe 30) or	90 g (3 oz) butter (or sunflower
demi-glace (Recipe 29) or	margarine)
reduced brown stock	7 g (¼ oz) meat glaze (Recipe 13)
45 g (1½ oz) finely chopped	
shallots	

1 Remove gall bladder and cut livers into 2 cm (1-inch) pieces.
2 Quickly fry in butter (or margarine) and drain.
3 Sweat the shallots in sauté pan and déglacer with red wine; add the jus lié (or alternative) and herbs and reduce by half; add the meat glaze.
4 Season, strain, and enrich with butter (optional); strain over the livers.

GAME SAUTÉ

645 Suprême de faisan voilé au porto – Breast of pheasant with port

4 breasts of pheasant	500 ml (1 pt) game	120 g (4 oz)
120 g (4 oz) of pork	stock (Recipe 12)	pheasant livers
back fat	200 ml (⅜ pt) white	4 large cap
180 g (6 oz) butter or	stock (Recipe 6)	mushrooms
margarine	120 g (4 oz) wild rice	seasoning
60 g (2 oz) finely		250 ml (½ pt) port
chopped onion		

1 Trim the breasts.
2 Gently fry the breasts in 60 g (2 oz) of the butter until coloured but still pink in the centre.
3 Remove the breasts and keep warm.
4 Deglaze pan with the port and reduce by two-thirds. Add the game stock. Continue to reduce until the liquid reaches the consistency of a light syrup.
5 Enrich the sauce with 90 g (3 oz) of the butter.
6 Pass the sauce through a fine strainer. Correct the seasoning.
7 Sauté the wild rice and onions in 30 g (1 oz) butter. Add 200 ml (⅜ pt) of boiling white stock and braise.
8 Serve the pheasant breasts on a bed of wild rice, mask with sauce. Garnish each breast with a sauté mushroom.

646 Râble de lièvre à l'allemande – Saddle of hare à l'allemande

2 saddles of hare	*120 g (¼ lb) butter (or sunflower*
250 ml (½ pt) fresh cream (or	*margarine)*
yogurt)	*15 g (½ oz) meat glaze (Recipe 13)*
500 ml (1 pt) red-wine marinade	*120 g (¼ lb) fat bacon*
(Recipe 124)	*seasoning*
	juice of ¼ lemon

1 Remove the skin and nerves from the saddles and piqué with fat bacon.
2 Place in the red-wine marinade for 2 days, turning frequently.
3 Remove the saddles and vegetables from the marinade and dry well.
4 Brown the saddles in butter (or margarine) and set to cook with the vegetables from the marinade.
5 When nearly cooked, remove the vegetables, pour in the cream and complete the cooking, basting with cream (or yogurt) frequently.
6 When cooked, remove the saddles, dress on a large entrée dish, and keep warm.
7 Reduce the cooking-liquor, add meat glaze, lemon juice and enrich with butter (optional); season.
8 Strain the sauce over the saddles.

BOILING AND POACHING

647 Boiling of meats

1 Boiling is cooking by immersion in boiling liquid; usually water or stock in the case of meats.
2 The boiling temperature of water is 100°C (212°F).
3 Once the boiling process is well started it is normal to reduce the heat so that meat is simmered (boiled very gently).
4 Most boiled meats and poultry dishes are the responsibility of the chef saucier (sauce cook) in a large kitchen brigade.

Cooking times. Boiling time varies according to the thickness of joints and is generally 20 minutes per 500 g (lb). Large joints of salt beef may take up to 25 or 30 minutes per 500 g (lb). For fowls allow 15 to 20 minutes per 500 g (lb) according to age; 2 kg (4-lb) to 2.5 kg (5-lb) birds will take from 1 to 1½ hours.

Quantities. As the cooking-loss when boiling meat may vary between 15 per cent to 20 per cent, this should be taken into account when estimating recipe quantities. Thus, for 8, 90 g (3-oz) portions of boiled silverside, 750 g (1½-lb) boneless meat will not suffice and at least 1 kg (2 lb) should be allowed. For larger joints the percentage-loss will be less and the net amount required will be nearer the portion's total weight.

648 Suitable boiling joints

While most of the cheaper cuts of meat and also older fowls and game may be boiled, the most suitable for plainer, boiled dishes are:

Beef	*Mutton*	*Pork*	*Bacon*	*Veal*
Silverside	Leg	Hand and spring	Gammon	Head (no
Brisket	Head (now not	Head and feet	Forehock	longer used for
Plate	used for safe	(for brawn)	Collar	health reasons)
	food reasons)			

Note. Lamb was not used for plain boiling when mutton was widely available but nowadays lamb is often substituted for scarcer mutton. Veal is seldom plainly boiled. Beef and pork joints are frequently pickled in brine.

649 Poaching

The method of poaching is used for fish and eggs and also for white meat, particularly poultry. In practice, poached poultry does not materially differ from boiled poultry; though, traditionally, flesh (for example fish-flesh) is actually half-steamed when poached as the piece is only partially covered with liquor and, once boiling is well started, it is covered by a lid (or, usually for fish, buttered paper) and finished in a moderate oven.

650 Garnishes

Garnishes and accompaniments for boiled pieces include:
Alsacienne: Sauerkraut (choucroute) with bacon and pommes vapeur.
Anglaise: Plainly-boiled vegetable garnish e.g., cabbage, carrot, turnip and boiled potato.
Flamande: Bacon, cabbage, carrot, turnip and potato.

651 Boiling fresh meat

1 Wipe the meat and remove any surplus fat.
2 Tie the meat in shape and place in sufficient boiling water or stock to cover.
3 Add whole vegetables to flavour the cooking liquor or stock.
4 Boil quickly for the first 10 minutes to seal and retain the meat juices.
5 Simmer until tender.

652 Boiling salt beef

1 Wash the salt beef in cold water to draw out salt.
2 Place in cold water, bring slowly to boiling-point and skim thoroughly.
3 Simmer gently: add mixed root-vegetables to flavour the cooking-liquor.

653 Boiled silverside of beef and dumplings

1 Silverside to be pickled (Recipe 132) at least 5 days.
2 Wash and cook as Recipe 652.
3 When cooked, garnish with turned carrots, turnips and small, whole onions. Some peas add colour if sought.
4 Cook the dumplings (Recipe 654) in the cooling-liquor.

654 Paste for dumplings

240 g (½ lb) strong flour   water to mix
7 g (¼ oz) baking power   salt
120 g (4 oz) suet

1 Skin and chop the suet finely using a little of the measured flour to prevent sticking (or use commercially prepared, including vegetable, suet).
2 Sift flour, baking powder and salt; mix all ingredients with cold water to form a slack dough.
3 Prepare in 60 g (2 oz) portions; cook for 20 minutes in the stock.

655 Boiled leg of mutton (or lamb when mutton unavailable) and caper sauce

1 For whole leg [approx. 3.5 kg (7 lb) or, if lamb, 2 kg (4 lb)] remove pelvic bone and tie up.
2 Soak in cold water overnight and wipe.
3 Place in cold water, bring to the boil removing scum; add a little salt and bouquet garni, onion clouté, and some whole vegetables.
4 Turn some carrots and turnips, and cook in some of the stock.
5 When the meat is cooked, garnish with the vegetables (some may add a few fresh peas for colour) and serve a little stock.

Note. Caper sauce, Recipe 62, should be made from the cooking-liquor. Parsley sauce is also suitable.

656 Boiled salt pork

1 Cook as for boiled, pickled beef.
2 Garnish with cabbage, butter beans, or pease pudding.

657 Boiled ham

1 For whole gammon [approx. 7 kg (14 lb)] soak overnight in cold water.
2 Saw a small piece off the knuckle-end.
3 Place in cold water with 2 apples clouté with cloves.
4 Simmer approximately 4 hours and allow to become cold in the cooking liquor.
5 Remove skin and trim.

Note. Cider, up to half the total quantity, may be added to the water for cooking.

BOILED AND POACHED POULTRY

658 Poularde bouillie à l'anglaise – Boiled chicken (English style)

one 2 kg (4 lb) chicken   240 g (½ lb) turned   240 g (½ lb) button
240 g (½ lb) raw ham   turnips   onions
240 g (½ lb) turned   1 white leek   125 ml (¼ pt)
    carrots   120 g (¼ lb) white   parsley sauce
                                 celery   (Recipe 68)
                                                            seasoning

1 Clean and truss chicken.
2 Cover the chicken with salted water; bring to boil and skim.
3 Add the ham and vegetables; simmer until tender.
4 When cooked, serve with a garnish of sliced ham and vegetables.
5 Serve the parsley sauce and cooking-liquor separately.

659 Poularde pochée au riz and sauce suprême

Fowls may be poached and served with pilaff rice (Recipe 366) and with sauce suprême (Recipe 61) made with the cooking-liquor.

660 Poularde pochée Stanley

one 2 kg (4 lb) chicken	*62 ml (⅛ pt) cream*
500 g (1 lb) onions	*45 g (1½ oz) cooked julienne*
45 g (1½ oz) julienne truffle	*mushrooms*
(optional)	*125 ml (¼ pt) chicken velouté*
2.5 ml spoon [½ teaspoon] curry	*(Recipe 27)*
powder	*120 g (¼ lb) rice*

1 Clean the chicken from the crop and remove the wish-bone.
2 Partly cook the rice as for pilaff (Recipe 366) and mix with the mushrooms and truffles.
3 Stuff the chicken (crop end) and truss.
4 Slice the onions, blanch, and add the curry powder.
5 Poach the birds with onions under cover; add a little stock.
6 When the chicken is cooked rub the onions and liquid through the tammy or fine sieve and add the chicken velouté.
7 Add cream and reduce to a good coating sauce.
8 Pass through a fine chinois, add a little cream and adjust seasoning.

For service:
(i) Remove the skin but leave the rice inside the birds.
(ii) Wings may be removed, breast-bone cut out and the wings replaced on top.
(iii) Napper with sauce.
(iv) Garnish top with a little julienne of truffles.

661 Poussin poché Derby

4 single poussins	*125 ml (¼ pt) veal stock (Recipe 9)*
120 g (¼ lb) rice	*seasoning*
45 g (1½ lb) diced foie gras or liver	*7 g (¼ oz) arrowroot*
paté	*½ glass champagne (or white wine)*
45 g (1½ oz) diced truffles	*60 g (2 oz) butter (or sunflower*
(optional)	*margarine)*
125 ml (¼ pt) cream	

1 Clean the poussins from the crop end and remove the wishbone.
2 Partly cook the rice as for pilaff (Recipe 366) and mix with the diced foie gras and truffles.

3 Stuff the birds and truss.
4 Poêler the poussins, basting frequently.
5 When the poussins are cooked, place on a suitable dish.
6 Deglaze the pan with white wine, reduce by half, moisten with the white stock. Reduce to 250 ml (½ pt) and lightly thicken with arrowroot if desired.
7 Correct seasoning and consistency. Pass through a fine strainer. Finish with cream (or alternatives).
8 Mask the poussins with this sauce and serve the remainder separately.

STEWING – ÉTUVER

662 Stewing of meats

Stewing is simmering meat in liquor; the term is normally applied to small cuts of meat, or poultry, when the resulting produce may be a stew, goulash, ragoût, braised steak, curry, or even, a sauté de bœuf.

Using terms like braised and sauté in such circumstances may be confusing but there are two main types of stewing:

(i) when the meat is first browned and,
(ii) when the meat is stewed either plain or blanched.

The first method, when the meat is browned, so resembles braising that the term, braised steak, may reasonably be used. For beef dishes, when the browning stage is one of sauter in hot fat, the term sauté is sometimes retained in the title despite the fact that the subsequent (and principal) form of cooking is stewing as, for example, in sauté de bœuf à la bourguignonne.

663 Étuver

Étuver virtually means to cook in the food's own juice using butter (possibly a little stock or other cooking-liquor) only to start the slow, oven-cooking which must be sealed under cover to prevent liquor from evaporating.

Almost all meats, game, and poultry can be stewed: if cuts are selected, it is so that the finest pieces can be reserved for roasting, grilling, and the quicker cookery processes.

664 En daube

Cooking 'en daube' is akin to braising, and involves cooking in a daubière, a lidded cooking-vessel that is usually a large earthenware stew-pan which is used for oven-to-table service. Mutton or beef can be treated en daube. In the case of beef:

1 Cut the topside of beef into squares of 6 cm by 2 cm (3 by 1 inch) thick.
2 Lard each piece with pieces of back-fat and roll in chopped parsley and crushed garlic.
3 Pickle for 1 hour in a mixture of brandy, white wine, and oil.

4 Place the meat with alternate layers of belly pork, sliced carrots, chopped onions, thyme, bay-leaves, tomatoes, stoned, black olives, bunch herbs; season as you go and then cover with pickle.
5 Seal the lid of the daubière with paste and set to cook in the oven for approximately 2 hours.

665 En casserole and en cocotte

Meats may, of course, be oven-stewed or braised, 'en cocotte' and 'en casserole'. There is sometimes confusion because sauté dishes can be presented or finished en cocotte without having been completely cooked in that vessel.

666 Blanquette

This is a stew or ragoût without colour and is made of white meats such as poultry, veal, or rabbit. For blanquettes the meat is blanched and the sauce is made from the stock in which the meat is cooked; the garnish is cooked separately.

667 Fricassée

The result is similar to a blanquette. The meat is cooked without colour, but in this case both the garnish and the meat are cooked in the sauce.

STEWED BEEF

668 Bifteck braisé à la bourgeoise – Braised steak bourgeoise

four 180 g (6 oz) *rump or topside*	500 ml (1 pt) *jus lié (Recipe 30) or*
30 g (1 oz) *flour*	*well-reduced brown stock*
30 g (1 oz) *dripping (or oil)*	120 g (¼ lb) *mirepoix (Recipe 2)*
30 g (1 oz) *boiled French beans*	12 *turned carrots*
cut into diamonds	12 *turned turnips*
bouquet garni	12 *button onions*
	30 g (1 oz) *tomato purée*

1 Fry off the steaks in fat (or oil).
2 Fry off mirepoix and add to meat; place all in braising-pan.
3 Dust the meat with flour and brown in the oven.
4 Add the tomato purée and brown stock; mix well.
5 Boil and skim; add bouquet garni and cook under cover in moderate oven.
6 When cooked, remove meat, reduce and strain sauce, adjust seasoning, and pour over meat.
7 Cook and glaze the vegetables and garnish.

669 Carbonnade de bœuf

750 g (1½ lb) *topside*	30 g (1 oz) *oil or butter*	250 ml (½ pt) *brown*
360 g (¾ lb) *thinly*	250 ml (½ pt) *beer*	*stock (Recipe 8)*
sliced onions	30 g (1 oz) *flour*	*seasoning*

1 Cut the meat free from fat and into small escalopes.
2 Roll in flour and sauté in oil.
3 Sweat the onions in butter (or margarine).
4 Prepare alternate layers of onions and meat in a casserole, seasoning each layer.
5 Pour over beer and brown stock.
6 Braise under cover in the oven.
7 Adjust the seasoning and remove all fat before serving; sprinkle with chopped parsley.

670 Goulash de bœuf à la hongroise – Hungarian goulash (of beef)

750 g (1½ lb) topside of beef	8 small, turned potatoes
360 g (¾ lb) diced onions	120 g (¼ lb) gnocchis parisienne
15 ml spoon [1 tablespoon]	(Recipe 358)
paprika	30 g (1 oz) flour
62 ml (⅛ pt) oil	bouquet garni
15 g (½ oz) butter (or margarine)	500 ml (1 pt) white stock (Recipe 6)
30 g (1 oz) tomato purée	seasoning

1 Remove fat from meat and cut into 2 cm (1-inch) cubes.
2 Roll in paprika and fry in oil.
3 Sweat the onions in butter (or margarine) in braising-pan.
4 Add the meat to onions, dust with flour, and brown in oven.
5 Blend in the tomato purée, pour on stock, and mix well.
6 Boil, skim, add bouquet garni and cook under cover in moderate oven.
7 Skim frequently during cooking, and 15 minutes before completion; add the blanched small, turned potatoes and allow them to finish cooking in the sauce (see Note 2 below).
8 Adjust seasoning and remove all fat.
9 Garnish with gnocchis parisienne; do not strain sauce.

Notes
(i) Hungarian goulash is also commonly made with veal.
(ii) Some use an equivalent quantity of parisienne potatoes. Some also do not finish potato cooking in the sauce but add freshly-boiled at step 9 with the gnocchis.

671 Kari de bœuf – Curried beef

750 g (1½ lb) topside or thick flank	60 g (2 oz) chopped apples	seasoning
30 g (1 oz) flour	15 g (½ oz) chutney	7 g (¼ oz) currants
bouquet garni	500 ml (1 pt) estouffade	7 g (¼ oz) sultanas
30 g (1 oz) curry powder	(Recipe 8)	15 g (½ oz) desiccated coconut
60 g (4 oz) chopped onion	30 g (1 oz) clarified butter (or oil)	125 ml (¼ pt) milk
120 g (¼ lb) rice	15 g (½ oz) tomato purée	

1 Remove fat from meat and cut into 2 cm (1-inch) cubes and fry off.
2 Sweat onions in a braising-pan, add meat and curry powder.
3 Dust with flour, and brown in oven.
4 Blend in the tomato purée, add stock, and mix well.
5 Boil, skim, add bouquet garni, and cook under cover in moderate oven.
6 Cook for approximately 1 hour; add chopped apple and chutney.
7 Soak the sultanas and currants in warm water for a few minutes; drain, and add these to the meat just before cooking is completed.
8 Soak the coconut in milk for a few minutes, squeeze out and add resulting liquid to the curry.
9 Adjust seasoning (including hot mango-kasundi) and remove surplus fat.
10 Serve with plainly-boiled rice, separately.

Accompaniments:
(i) Bombay Duck: This may be deep-fried or grilled (1 per portion).
(ii) Poppadums: These may be deep-fried or grilled (1 per portion).
(iii) Mango Chutney and/or
(iv) Lime Pickle (or similar Indian conserves).
(v) French-fried onion rings.
(vi) Sambals or Raviers: Diced apples, onion and tomato salad, bananas, sliced or diced, cucumber, yogurt sprinkled with nutmeg, grated coconut, lemon quarters (in lieu of limes).

Note. This is an anglicized type of curry dish derived also from adaptations evolved in British kitchens by French chefs or in the French kitchen and is given because of the possible demand for this version of 'curry'. See also Recipe 677 for curried lamb and Recipe 678 for a more traditional Indian method.

672 Paupiettes de bœuf farcies – Beef olives

750 g (1½ lb) topside of beef	120 g (¼ lb) finely minced steak
4 stoned olives	1 small egg
1.25 ml spoon [¼ teaspoon] mixed herbs	60 g (2 oz) fine mirepoix (Recipe 4)
	15 g (½ oz) chopped onions
500 ml (1 pt) jus lié (Recipe 30), demi-glace (Recipe 29) or well-reduced brown stock	1 bouquet garni
	15 g (½ oz) breadcrumbs
	30 g (1 oz) dripping (or oil)
7 g (¼ oz) chopped parsley	

1 Remove fat from meat and cut into 4 thin escalopes.
2 Beat them flat with the cutlet bat.
3 Mince the trimmings finely and combine with the 120 g (¼ lb) of minced steak and sweated onions.
4 Add the herbs and breadcrumbs; bind the mixture together with the egg; season.
5 Divide the stuffing equally; place in centre of each escalope with the stoned olive in the middle; roll and tie; shallow-fry briskly to colour.
6 Fry the mirepoix and place the olives and mirepoix in a suitable braising-pan.

7 Cover with jus lié (or alternatives); add bouquet garni, and braise in moderate oven.
8 When cooked, remove string and reduce sauce; adjust seasoning and strain over the olives.
9 Garnish; jardinière (Recipe 750) or rice pilaff (Recipe 366).

673 Sauté de bœuf à la bourguignonne – Beef sauté bourguignonne

750 g (1½ lb) topside of beef	1 bouquet garni
90 g (3 oz) diced onions	21 g (¾ oz) fat or oil
500 ml (1 pt) brown stock	9 small mushrooms
(Recipe 8)	120 g (¼ lb) lardons
125 ml (¼ pt) red wine	18 glazed button onions
30 g (1 oz) flour	8 heart-shaped croûtons
30 g (1 oz) tomato purée	15 g (½ oz) chopped parsley
1 clove chopped garlic	

1 Remove fat from meat and cut into 2 cm (1-inch) cubes.
2 Fry off meat in the fat, add the onions and garlic and place in braising-pan.
3 Dust with flour and brown in oven.
4 Add tomato purée and mix well; add wine and stock.
5 Boil, skim, add bouquet garni and cook under cover in moderate oven.
6 When cooked, remove meat, re-boil sauce and reduce; skim, season, and pour over meat.
7 Blanch the lardons and fry off.
8 Garnish meat with glazed onions and the cooked mushrooms.
9 Present with heart-shaped croûtons dipped in parsley.

674 Sauté de bœuf à la jardinière

750 g (1½ lb) topside of beef	30 g (1 oz) tomato purée
30 g (1 oz) dripping or oil	1 clove of crushed garlic
seasoning	1 bouquet garni
750 ml (¾ pt) brown stock	45 g (1½ oz) mirepoix (Recipe 2)
(Recipe 7 or 8)	

Garnish jardinière:

15 g (½ oz) French beans cut in diamond shape	30 g (1 oz) carrots ⎱ cut into bâtons
15 g (½ oz) peas	30 g (1 oz) turnips ⎰

1 Remove fat from meat and cut into 2 cm (1-inch) cubes; fry off in dripping.
2 Fry off mirepoix, drain, add to meat and place in braising-pan.
3 Dust with flour, and brown in oven.
4 Add tomato purée, crushed and chopped garlic and blend in stock.
5 Bring to boil and skim; add bouquet garni and season lightly; cover with lid.
6 Cook in moderate oven for 1½ hours' skim frequently.
7 When cooked remove meat from sauce.
8 Re-boil sauce, season, and strain over meat; garnish with jardinière of vegetables.

675 Scotch beef mince

500 g (1 lb) topside of beef
240 g (½ lb) finely chopped onions
4 heart-shaped croûtons
15 g (½ oz) dripping or oil

250 ml (½ pt) (approx.) white stock
(Recipe 6)
4 baked onions
seasoning

1 Remove fat and mince beef finely through medium cutter.
2 Sweat the onions in the dripping or oil.
3 Add the minced beef and sweat under cover.
4 Moisten with sufficient white stock or water to cover and slightly season.
5 Simmer until cooked, adjust seasoning.
6 Garnish with baked onions and heart-shaped croûtons having previously dipped the ends in chopped parsley.

The dish may be further garnished with dumplings (Recipe 654) or with a jardinière of vegetables (as in Recipe 674).

STEWS OF LAMB AND MUTTON

676 Irish stew

750 g (1½ lb) stewing lamb
240 g (½ lb) sliced celery
240 g (½ lb) sliced onions
120 g (¼ lb) cabbage (sliced)

240 g (½ lb) sliced leek
500 g (1 lb) sliced potatoes
8 turned potatoes
seasoning

1 Prepare 4 neck cutlets and 8 pieces of breast of lamb or mutton.
2 Blanch and refresh the meat.
3 Mix the onions, leeks, celery, and cabbage together; and season.
4 Cut the potatoes into roundels; divide into 2 equal portions and place on the bottom of a braising-pan, sprinkle half of the mixed vegetables on top and season.
5 Lay the meat neatly on top of the vegetables and season (some chefs add bouquet garni).
6 Cover the meat with the remainder of the vegetables and arrange the remainder of the sliced potatoes on top; season.
7 Cover with water, bring to the boil, cover and cook for approximately 1½ hours.
8 Arrange the turned potatoes on top and finish off the cooking under cover.
9 Remove all fat and sprinkle with chopped parsley (some include chopped celery leaves) before service.

Note. Some prefer to garnish with button onions and to pass the liquid with its softened potato content through a strainer to yield a very thin purée. Some chefs prefer vegetables cut into paysanne, others larger, turned pieces.

677 Kari d'agneau – Curry of lamb

See also note on ingredients below.

650 g (1¼ lb) lean lamb
90 g (3 oz) finely chopped onion
30 g (1 oz) to 20 g (⅝ oz) curry
  powder
30 g (1 oz) flour

30 g (1 oz) oil (or clarified butter)
bouquet garni
seasoning
500 ml (1 pt) brown stock
(Recipe 7)

1 Remove all fat from the lamb and cut into cubes.
2 Fry the lamb and onions to a golden brown in the oil (or butter).
3 Dredge the meat with the curry powder and mix well; dredge with the flour and cook in the oven for a few minutes.
4 Moisten with the stock and stir well; bring to boil, skim, and add the bouquet garni.
5 Cook in a moderate oven with lid on for approximately 1½ hours.
6 When cooked, remove all grease, check sauce for seasoning and consistency.
7 Serve plainly-boiled rice separately with mango chutney, Bombay duck and poppadums (see Recipe 671 for other accompaniments).

Note. Anglicized versions of curry include additional ingredients (some seldom or never used or used only in accompanying dishes such as pilaff on the Indian sub-continent): for example, 60 g (2 oz) chopped apple, 7 g (¼ oz) sultanas, 15 g (½ oz) dessicated coconut, 15 g (½ oz) mango chutney. In India itself there is a wealth of dishes and certainly no one dish that can be called 'curry' (or Kari).

678 Lamb or mutton curry (Indian style)

750 g (1½ lb) stewing lamb (or
  mutton)
2 small Spanish onions
60 g (2 oz) butter or margarine
  (vanaspati)
1 crushed bay-leaf
62 ml (⅛ pt) yogurt
30 g (1 oz) tomato purée

1 clove garlic
0.5 cm (¼ inch) cinnamon stick
salt, cayenne pepper
30 g (1 oz) curry powder (or to
  taste)
2–3 cloves
2–3 cardamom seeds

1 Finely slice the onions and sweat in butter for 10 minutes to a golden brown.
2 Add crushed garlic, curry powder, salt and cayenne pepper; continue to sweat for further 3 minutes.
3 Add tomato purée, mix well, then add yogurt.
4 Trim the meat of fat, cut into fairly small pieces and brown rapidly in sauté-pan.
5 Add the meat to the curry sauce, deglaze the pan with brown stock and add this liquor to the sauce.
6 Tie the cinnamon stick, cloves, cardamom seeds and bay-leaves in a muslin bag for easy removal before service.

7 Cover tightly and simmer on top of stove or cook in oven until meat is tender.

8 Serve plainly-boiled rice separately; for accompaniments see Recipe 671.

Notes

(i) Curry is improved by preparation in advance of service but must be cooled rapidly, kept under refrigeration and thoroughly re-heated before service. Surplus fat may be removed before re-heating, although correctly in Indian style this is a fatty dish, the surplus 'ghee' enjoyed in India does not accord with either Western taste or notions of healthy eating.

(ii) Chicken, rabbit, raw mince, and cooked meats can be curried in similar style.

679 Navarin d'agneau aux primeurs – Brown-lamb stew with spring vegetables

750 g (1½ lb) stewing lamb	30 g (1 oz) flour
240 g (½ lb) button onions	1 clove crushed garlic
240 g (½ lb) turned carrots	22 g (¾ oz) tomato purée
240 g (½ lb) turned turnips	seasoning
240 g (½ lb) turned potatoes	120 g (¼ lb) mirepoix (Recipe 2)
bouquet garni	30 g (1 oz) oil or dripping
500 ml (1 pt) brown stock (Recipe 7)	

1 Cut 4 neck cutlets and 8 pieces of breast of lamb 5 cm × 5 cm (2½ by 2½ inches), free from fat.

2 Put the dripping in a braising-pan and sauter the lamb to a golden brown.

3 Add the mirepoix to the meat and colour.

4 Pour off the fat and dust with the flour; place in oven to brown.

5 Remove from the oven, add the tomato purée and mix well; add the chopped garlic and moisten with the stock.

6 Bring to the boil and skim; add bouquet garni.

7 Simmer under cover in a moderate oven for approximately 1½ hours.

8 Sauter the button onions, carrots, turnips in butter (or margarine) to a golden brown and blanch the potatoes.

9 Remove the meat from the pan and place in a clean pan; add the sauté vegetables and turned potatoes.

10 Strain the sauce, correct the seasoning, consistency and colouring; dilute with a little stock, if necessary.

11 Add the sauce to the meat and vegetables; bring to the boil and simmer until the meat and vegetables are tender.

12 Remove all fat; dress on an entrée dish and arrange the garnish neatly; sprinkle with chopped parsley.

Note. Navarin d'agneau, similarly prepared, may be garnished jardinière or bouquetière.

680 Ragoût d'agneau aux haricots blancs – Haricot lamb

750 g (1½ lb) neck of lamb	30 g (1 oz) oil or dripping	Garnish:
120 g (¼ lb) diced onions	500 ml (1 pt) brown stock (Recipe 7)	120 g (¼ lb) haricot beans
120 g (¼ lb) diced carrots	15 g (½ oz) tomato purée	120 g (¼ lb) bacon bones
30 g (1 oz) flour	seasoning	1 whole carrot
	1 clove garlic	1 onion clouté

1 Soak the beans overnight in water and rinse.
2 Cover with cold water, bring to boil and skim.
3 Add the bacon bones, carrot and onion clouté, simmer until tender.
4 Strain off the stock and keep the beans hot until required.
5 Cut the lamb in pieces of 4 cm × 4 cm (2 by 2 inches) and remove surplus fat.
6 Put the oil or dripping in a braising-pan and fry the meat and vegetables until golden brown; drain off surplus fat.
7 Dust the meat and vegetables with flour and brown in the oven.
8 Remove from oven, add the crushed clove of garlic, tomato purée, and mix well.
9 Mix the brown stock and liquor from cooking the beans 500 ml (about 1 pint).
10 Boil and skim; add bouquet garni and cook under cover for approximately 2 hours in moderate oven.
11 When cooked, remove meat and place in clean pan.
12 Strain the sauce, correct for colour, seasoning and consistency, pour over the meat and garnish with cooked beans.

Note. Fried lardons may be included in the garnish.

VEAL

681 Blanquette de veau à l'ancienne

750 g (1½ lb) tendron of veal (or stewing veal)	bouquet garni
500 ml (1 pt) white stock (Recipe 6)	30 g (1 oz) flour
	seasoning
12 button mushrooms	30 g (1 oz) butter (or margarine)
12 button onions	62 ml (⅛ pt) cream ⎱ liaison
1 onion clouté	1 egg yolk ⎰
1 small carrot	heart-shaped croûtons

1 Cut the veal into approximately 90 g (3 oz) pieces.
2 Blanch and refresh.
3 Cover with stock, boil and skim; add onion clouté, carrot, bouquet garni and simmer gently for 1½ hours.

4 Prepare a white roux with the flour and butter (or margarine); strain the stock from the veal over roux and mix well; cook for 20 minutes.
5 Transfer the veal to a large casserole and add the onions and mushrooms which have been cooked à blanc.
6 Finish off the sauce with the liaison; add a few drops of lemon juice; adjust the seasoning and strain over the veal.
7 Garnish with croûtons.

Note. Having added the liaison do not reboil. In the case of blanquette, fillet of veal may be used.

682 Fricassée de veau à l'ancienne

750 1g (1½ lb) fillet of veal or
   boned shoulder
180 g (6 oz) button onions
60 g (2 oz) button mushrooms
bouquet garni
500 ml (1 pt) white veal stock
   (Recipe 9)

90 g (3 oz) butter (or margarine)
30 g (1 oz) flour
125 ml (¼ pt) cream ⎫
1 egg yolk   ⎬ liaison
heart-shaped croûtons ⎭
seasoning

1 Cut the veal into 60 g (2 oz) pieces.
2 Place the butter (or margarine) in a braising-pan and stiffen the veal without colouring.
3 Sprinkle the veal with flour and allow to cook for a few minutes.
4 Moisten with white stock and mix well; boil, skim, add bouquet garni and cook under cover in moderate oven.
5 Meanwhile turn the mushrooms and cook the onions à blanc (Recipe 757).
6 When the veal is cooked, transfer it to another pan and add the garnish.
7 Reduce the sauce and draw to side of stove; add the liaison of cream and egg yolks; season and strain over the veal.
8 Garnish with croûtons fried in oil and butter (or margarine); dip ends in parsley.

683 Goulash de veau à la hongroise

Prepare as Recipe 670 but using veal.

684 Jarret de veau (Osso Bucco) à la milanaise – Veal knuckles (Milan style)

1 kg (2 lb) veal knuckle
240 g (½ lb) tomato concassé
500 ml (1 pt) thin tomato sauce
   (Recipe 34)
1 clove crushed garlic
bouquet garni

125 ml (¼ pt) white wine
seasoning
grated zest of orange, chopped
   parsley
62 ml (⅛ pt) oil
120 g (¼ lb) finely chopped onions

1 With a saw cut the knuckles of veal in 8 slices, approximately 4 oz each.
2 Dust with flour and fry to golden brown in oil.
3 Remove veal from pan; sweat the onions and garlic in the remaining oil; swill with the white wine, and reduce.

4 Add the tomatoes and sweat for a few minutes; place the veal on top and moisten with the tomato sauce; bring to the boil and add the bouquet garni.
5 Cook under cover in a moderate oven and when cooked, degrease, adjust seasoning and sprinkle with chopped parsley and grated orange zest.
6 Serve a risotto milanaise (Recipe 368), separately.

685 Paupiette de veau à la financière

> *four* 280 g (7 oz) *veal escalopes*
> 180 g (6 oz) *fine forcemeat*
> (*Recipe* 195)
> 4 *slices of truffle* (*optional*)
>
> 8 *chicken quenelles* (*Recipe* 199 or
> 716)
> 4 *turned mushrooms*
> 4 *stoned olives*

1 Prepare 4 escalopes 8 cm (4 inches) long by 4 cm (2 inches) wide, and season.
2 Cover each with forcemeat and roll into scrolls; tie to keep shape.
3 Braise in manner of beef olives (Recipe 672).
4 Strain the sauce when cooked; garnish with mushrooms, olives, quenelles; pour over sauce and finish with slices of truffle (optional).

Note. Cockscombs and chicken kidneys once integrated in the garnish are now seldom encountered.

686 Sauté de veau Marengo

> 750 g (1½ lb) *breast of veal*
> 30 g (1 oz) *chopped onions*
> 360 g (¾ lb) *tomato concassé*
> 500 ml (1 pt) *jus lié* (*Recipe* 30) *or*
> *demi-glace* (*Recipe* 29) (*or well-*
> *reduced brown stock*)
>
> 125 ml (¼ pt) *white wine*
> *bouquet garni*
> 1 *clove crushed garlic*
> 250 ml (½ pt) *oil*

Garnish: 12 *glazed button onions*; 240 g (½ lb) *diced mushrooms*;
8 *heart-shaped croûtons*; *chopped parsley*

1 Cut the veal into 60 g (2 oz) pieces.
2 Fry in oil until golden.
3 Drain away all the oil and moisten with the wine and reduce; add the tomato concassé and the jus lié (or alternatives).
5 Bring to the boil, skim, add bouquet garni.
6 Cover and cook in moderate oven for 1½ hours.
7 Transfer the veal to another pan; add the mushrooms and onions, and cover with the strained sauce.
8 Cook for a further 15 minutes; remove all fat, and adjust seasoning.
9 Garnish with croûtons fried in oil and the ends dipped in parsley.

687 Tendrons de veau

1 Tendrons are cut from the breast of veal and are the extreme end of the ribs including cartilage of the sternum.

2 They are cut crosswise into pieces approximately 90 g (3 oz) each for use in dishes such as sauté de veau (Recipe 686 as above).

3 Breast of veal can be braised whole (see notes on white braising) as well as in smaller pieces.

CASSEROLE OR OVEN-STEWS OF LAMB, MUTTON, AND PORK

688 Chump Chop Champvallon

four 300 g (10 oz) *chump chops*	120 g (¼ lb) sliced *tomatoes*	240 g (½ lb) sliced *onion*
500 g (1 lb) sliced *potatoes*	250 ml (½ pt) white *stock (Recipe 6)*	60 g (2 oz) lard or *oil*
4 slices bacon	bouquet garni	seasoning

1 Trim the chump chops well and fry to golden colour in oil or lard.
2 Place a slice of tomato and bacon on the top of each chop.
3 Butter an earthenware dish and place on the bottom a layer of sliced potato, then another layer of onions.
4 Place the chops on this bed and another layer of onions and potatoes, seasoning each layer; add the bouquet garni.
5 Moisten well with seasoned stock and add a few knobs of butter.
6 Cook in a moderate oven.
7 Remove all grease before service and sprinkle with chopped parsley.

Note. There are alternative presentations of this dish, but this preparation has proved acceptable.

689 Lancashire hot-pot

500 g (1 lb) stewing lamb	500 g (1 lb) sliced onions
120 g (¼ lb) kidney	seasoning
625 g (1¼ lb) sliced potatoes	

1 Prepare 4 pieces of neck cutlets and 4 pieces of breast cut into 4 cm × 4 cm (2 by 2 inch) squares, and the kidney into smaller pieces.
2 Fry off the meat and kidney to a golden colour in a little oil or fat and drain.
3 Slice the potatoes into thin roundels.
4 Layer potatoes liberally on the bottom of a braising-pan and sprinkle with a layer of the sliced onions, and season.
5 Place the meat neatly on top of this layer and repeat layering to fill dish.
6 Finish by placing the remaining sliced potatoes neatly, in overlapping rows on top.
7 Add water or white stock to just below surface, and scatter a few knobs of butter or brush surface with melted butter (or margarine), and season.

8 Put in a moderate oven; when the potatoes are brown, cover with grease-proof paper (or aluminium foil) and allow to finish cooking – approximately 2½ hours.
9 Before service, remove all grease and sprinkle with chopped parsley.
10 Serve a bowl of pickled cabbage as a garnish.

Note. Oysters and other variants are added in some areas of Lancashire. Some do not fry off the meat, some do not include kidney.

690 Cassoulet de porc

750 g (1¼ lb) breast of pork	240 g (½ lb) pork or bacon rind
240 g (½ lb) haricot beans	120 g (¼ lb) breadcrumbs
1 small carrot	120 g (¼ lb) lardons
1 onion clouté	120 g (¼ lb) garlic sausage
4 casseroles	360 g (¾ lb) sliced bacon

1 Soak the beans and cook until tender with the carrot, onion clouté, and pork or bacon rind.
2 Dice the pork into 2 cm (1-inch) squares, fry to golden colour in oil or lard.
3 Blanch the lardons.
4 Line each casserole with sliced bacon and fill with alternate layers of beans, pork and bacon and the garlic sausage cut into thick slices.
5 Moisten each casserole with the haricot bean cooking-liquor.
6 Cover with breadcrumbs, baste frequently with some of the reserved haricot-bean liquor.
7 Approximate cooking-time, 1 hour in moderate oven.

691 Choucroûte garnie – Sauerkraut garnished

360 g (¾ lb) sauerkraut	2 peeled carrots
4 frankfurters	6 juniper berries (some also add, or
240 g (½ lb) shoulder bacon	substitute a pinch of caraway
120 g (¼ lb) bacon rind	seeds)
1 onion clouté	250 ml (½ pt) fonds blanc (Recipe
240 g (½ lb) garlic ham-sausage	6)
120 g (¼ lb) lard (or oil)	240 g (½ lb) turned potatoes
	bouquet garni

1 Line a thick-bottomed braising-pan with bacon rind.
2 Place the choucroûte on top and insert the onions and carrots in the middle with the piece of bacon.
3 Cut the lard into small pieces and place on top.
4 Add the stock and bouquet garni and juniper berries wrapped in muslin; cover with a tight-fitting lid and braise for approximately 1 hour in the oven.
5 Remove lid, place garlic sausage and the frankfurters on top.
6 Replace lid and continue to cook for a further 15 minutes.
7 Serve with plain boiled potatoes.

STEWS OF OFFAL

692 Foie de bœuf braisé à la bourgeoise – Braised ox-liver bourgeoise

500 g (1 lb) ox-liver	*500 g (1 lb) glazed onions*
250 ml (½ pt) jus lié (Recipe 30) or	*60 g (2 oz) flour*
demi-glace (Recipe 29) or good	*120 g (¼ lb) lardons*
brown stock	*chopped parsley*
120 g (¼ lb) glazed carrots	*30 g (1 oz) dripping or oil*

1 Remove all skin from liver and cut into 8 equal slices.
2 Dip each piece in flour and shallow-fry each piece in smoking fat.
3 Drain and cover with jus lié (or alternative) and cook under cover in the oven until tender.
4 Remove from pan and arrange the pieces neatly in an entrée dish.
5 Check the sauce for seasoning and consistency and strain over the liver.
6 Blanch and fry off the lardons in butter and strain.
7 Garnish the liver with bouquets of glazed vegetables and the lardons; sprinkle with chopped parsley.

693 Queue de bœuf braisée à la printanière – Braised oxtail printanière

1 kg (2 lb) oxtail	*500 ml (1 pt) brown stock*
bouquet garni	*(Recipe 7 or 8)*
240 g (½ lb) mire poix (Recipe 2)	*180 g (6 oz) glazed carrots*
30 g (1 oz) flour	*180 g (6 oz) glazed turnips*
30 g (1oz) tomato purée	*180 g (6 oz) glazed onions*
30 g (1 oz) dripping (or oil)	*seasoning*
	1 clove garlic, crushed and chopped

1 Remove all fat from oxtail and cut the thicker part into 4 cm (2 inch) sections.
2 In a braising-pan fry the tail sections and mirepoix to a golden brown; drain off surplus fat.
3 Sprinkle in the flour, and cook for a few minutes in the oven.
4 Add the tomato purée and garlic; mix well, and moisten with the stock.
5 Boil, skim, add bouquet garni, and cook under cover in a moderate oven until tender (usually not less than 3 hours).
6 When cooked remove the sections (discarding the bouquet garni) and place in clean pan.
7 Reduce the sauce; check for seasoning and consistency; strain over the tails.
8 Garnish with glazed vegetables.

694 Ris de veau – Calves' sweetbreads

1 Stews, or braisings, of sweetbreads may be prepared by applying white-braising principles (Recipe 573): before braising, soak the sweetbreads in cold water overnight to remove blood.
2 Blanch and refresh; trim and remove skin.
3 Piqué with fat bacon or truffles.

Garnish examples include:

695 Ris de veau à la bonne-maman

Garnish with large vegetable julienne and the reduced cooking-liquor.

696 Ris de veau aux champignons

Garnish with mushrooms and mushroom sauce.

697 Ris de veau à la financière

Garnish with salpicon financière (Recipe 103).

698 Ris de veau braisé Demidoff

1 *kg (2 lb) calves'*	30 *g (1 oz) bacon*	6 *small (button)*
sweetbreads	60 *g (2 oz) carrots*	*onions*
15 *g (½ oz) truffles*	60 *g (2 oz) turnips*	30 *g (1 oz) celery*
(optional)		

1 Cut the vegetables paysanne style (or with the demidoff knife into half-moon shapes) and the onions into roundels and stew in butter (or margarine).
2 Piqué the prepared sweetbreads with the bacon and truffles and white braise.
3 Add the garnish of carrots, turnips and button onions (already cooked glacé à blanc). (If available, 25 ml (1 fluid oz) of truffle essence may also be added to the braising sauce.)
4 Serve in a cocotte coated with the garnish and sauce.

699 Rognons de veau en cocotte

4 *veal kidneys*	120 *g (¼ lb) quartered*	10 *ml spoon [½*
120 *g (¼ lb) lardons*	*mushrooms*	*tablespoon]*
360 *g (¾ lb) potatoes*	120 *g (¼ lb) butter (or*	*sherry*
120 *g (¼ lb) glazed*	*margarine)*	125 *ml (¼ pt) veal*
button onions		*gravy (Recipe 10)*

1 Trim each kidney leaving a slight layer of fat round it.
2 Fry in butter (or margarine) in a large casserole; cook gently for 30 minutes, turning the kidneys frequently.
3 Blanch and fry lardons and place in the casserole with the cooked mushrooms and fried cocotte (turned to olive shape) potatoes.
4 Complete cooking for another 10 minutes, and at the last minute add veal gravy and sherry.

700 Tripe and onions

500 *g (1 lb) ox-tripe*	62 *ml (⅛ pt) cream,*	500 *g (1 lb) onions*
(prepared, i.e.	*fromage frais or*	22 *g (¾ oz) flour*
dressed)	*quark*	*seasoning*
500 *ml (1 pt) milk*	22 *g (¾ oz) butter (or*	
bouquet garni	*margarine)*	

1 Cut the prepared tripe into pieces 4 cm × 4 cm (2 by 2 inches).
2 Peel the onions, cut in half, slice thinly and blanch.
3 Add the onions to the tripe and pour over the milk; simmer gently with the bouquet garni.
4 Make a white roux with the flour and butter and when tripe is cooked make a sauce with the strained cooking-liquor.
5 Mix the tripe with the sauce and simmer for a few minutes at the side of the stove.
6 Season and finish with the cream (or alternative).
7 If the sauce is too thick, dilute with a little boiled milk.

STEWS OF POULTRY AND GAME

701 Coq au vin

2 kg (4 lb) chicken	seasoning
120 g (¼ lb) lardons ⎫	250 ml (½ pt) red wine
120 g (¼ lb) ⎪	60 g (2 oz) butter (or margarine)
mushrooms ⎬ garnish	heart-shaped croûtons
120 g (¼ lb) button ⎪	1 bay leaf
onions ⎭	1 spring thyme
15 g (½ oz) meat glaze	garlic
30 g (1 oz) (approx.) beurre-manié	

Note. This dish is traditionally made from a freshly-slaughtered bird, with the blood utilized in the sauce.

1 Clean the chicken, retain liver.
2 Cut as for sauté. (Chop the carcase.)
3 Colour chicken pieces and carcase in butter (or margarine) – withdraw from pan.
4 Cook off the garnish in the residue and reserve.
5 Replace the chicken and carcase pieces in the pan.
6 Add the garlic and herbs.
7 Cover with red wine and simmer until cooked.
8 Reduce the cooking liquid to half. Add the meat glaze.
9 Thicken with beurre-manié (formerly with the blood). Strain and season.
10 Dress the chicken in a cocotte, add the garnish and cover with sauce.
11 Chop and sauté the chicken liver in butter. Spread on croûtons and add to decorate dish or garnish with heart-shaped croûtons dipped in parsley.

702 Fricassée de volaille à l'ancienne

one 2 kg (4 lb) chicken	4 heart-shaped croûtons
240 g (½ lb) button onions	22 g (¾ oz) flour
120 g (¼ lb) turned mushrooms	120 g (¼ lb) butter (or margarine)
seasoning	375 ml (¾ pt) chicken stock
bouquet garni	(Recipe 11)
125 ml (¼ pt) cream ⎫ liaison	pinch chopped parsley
2 egg yolks ⎭	pinch chives

1 Cut the chicken (Recipe 628) as for sauté and the carcase into 3 equal parts.
2 Gently sauter in butter (or margarine) in a large sauteuse. Do not colour.
3 Dust the chicken with flour and cook a little.
4 Moisten with stock; mix well; add bouquet garni, and bring to boil and simmer under cover in moderate oven until half-cooked.
5 Cook the mushrooms and onions in a little stock and butter (or margarine).
6 Remove the chicken and place in a clean pan; add the mushrooms and onions, strain the liquor over, and continue the cooking.
7 When the chicken is cooked, add the liaison and season.
8 Dress the chicken neatly on a silver dish with the garnish around; decorate with heart-shaped croûtons dipped in parsley (or with fleurons (Recipe 1024)) and sprinkle with chopped parsley and chives.

703 Pigeon en compote – Stewed pigeon

2 young pigeons
125 ml (¼ pt) tomato sauce (Recipe 34)
12 button onions
240 g (½ lb) breast of pork
240 g (½ lb) mushrooms
375 ml (¾ pt) jus lié (Recipe 30), well-reduced stock or demi-glace (Recipe 29)
60 g (2 oz) butter (or margarine)
bouquet garni
62 ml (⅛ pt) white wine

1 Truss the pigeon; peel and quarter the mushrooms; cut the pork into lardons and blanch.
2 Fry the onions, mushrooms, and pork, in butter (or margarine) in the braising-pan; remove and set the pigeons to brown in same butter (or margarine).
3 When the pigeons are brown take them out and drain the fat from the pan; make a reduction of the white wine, add the jus lié (or alternative) and tomato sauce and return the birds.
4 Boil, skim, add bouquet garni and cook under cover, basting frequently.
5 When cooked, remove birds and garnish with onions, mushrooms, and pork.
6 Reduce the sauce to correct consistency, season, enrich with butter (optional) and strain.
7 Place the birds in a large cocotte and pour over the sauce; sprinkle with chopped parsley.

704 Salmis de faisan – Salmis of pheasant

1 pheasant
125 ml (¼ pt) red wine
6 ground peppercorns
1 bay-leaf
½ glass (62 ml (⅛ pt)) brandy
45 g (1½ oz) chopped shallots
190 ml (⅓ pt) jus lié (Recipe 30), well-reduced brown stock or demi-glace (Recipe 29)
9 turned mushrooms
heart-shaped croûtons
1 slice truffle (optional)
60 g (2 oz) butter (or margarine)
15 g (½ oz) meat glaze (Recipe 13)
chopped parsley

1 Truss and roast the pheasant, keeping it underdone; cut as for sauté chicken (Recipe 628) and chop the carcase in small pieces.
2 Skin the jointed pheasant and place in a buttered pan with the meat glaze and brandy; keep on the side of the stove to keep warm.
3 Pound the carcase and any trimmings and place them in a sauté-pan with the peppercorns, herbs, red wine, and shallots; and reduce the wine by half.
4 Add the jus lié; simmer until it reaches required consistency (coats a wooden spoon)' strain through a fine strainer; season and enrich with butter (optional).
5 Cook the mushrooms in butter.
6 Pour the sauce over the pheasant; dress it neatly on a silver serving-dish.
7 Garnish the dish with the mushrooms, truffle slices, and croûtons. (The carcase is not served.)

705 Salmis de caneton Montreuil – Salmis of duck

one 2 *kg (4 lb) duck*
45 *g (1½ oz) butter*
250 *ml (½ pt) jus lié (Recipe* 30) *or*
   well-reduced brown stock or
   demi-glace (Recipe 29)
62 *ml (⅛ pt) tomato sauce*
   (*Recipe* 34)
60 *g (2 oz) fine mirepoix*
   (*Recipe* 2)

125 *ml (¼ pt) sherry*
30 *g (1 oz) diced cooked ox-tongue*
2 *truffles (optional)*
9 *turned mushrooms*
4 *heart-shaped croûtons*
seasoning
chopped parsley
1 *bouquet garni*

1 Truss the ducks and partly roast.
2 Cut into joints and chop the carcase.
3 Butter a sauté-pan, cover the bottom with the vegetables and bouquet garni and place on top the pieces of duck and chopped carcase; season and place in the oven for 10 minutes.
4 Drain off the butter and pour in the sherry and add the two sauces; cook under cover until tender.
5 When cooked, place the duck in a large cocotte; remove all fat from the sauce; season and strain.
6 Cut the truffles (optional) and tongue into julienne; cook the mushrooms in butter and garnish the duck; pour over the sauce.
7 Garnish with the croûtons fried in butter with the ends dipped in parsley. (The carcase is not served.)

Salmis, General Note. All cooked game may be used in preparing salmis.

RABBIT AND HARE STEWS

706 Stewed rabbit

1 Rabbits should be drawn immediately they are dead.
2 Loosen the skin along the slit edges.

3 Pull the skin over the hind legs, cutting the tail away with the skin and first joint of each leg; the skin is then pulled right over the head.
4 The ears may be skinned or cut off the skin.
5 Take out the eyes; steep the rabbit in cold salt-water for 2 hours.

Note. This method of preparation applies to all rabbit stews. These are similar to poultry and meat stews. A basic example is given in the next recipe.

707 Ragoût de lapin à la jardinière – Stewed rabbit jardinière

1 *rabbit*	*bouquet garni*	*chopped parsley*
120 g (¼ lb) mirepoix	15 g (½ oz) tomato	jardinière of
(Recipe 2)	purée	vegetables
750 ml (1½ pt) brown	30 g (1 oz) dripping	(Recipe 750)
stock (Recipe 7)	seasoning	30 g (1 oz) flour

1 Joint the rabbit, fry in hot fat in a braising-pan. Add the mirepoix which has been previously fried; drain off all fat.
2 Dredge with flour and cook in the oven for 3 or 4 minutes.
3 Add the tomato purée and mix well; moisten with the brown stock.
4 Bring to boil, skim, add bouquet garni.
5 Cook under cover for approximately 1 hour.
6 When cooked, remove the rabbit and place in large entrée-dish.
7 Reduce the sauce to the correct consistency; remove all fat; season and strain over the rabbit.
8 Garnish with jardinière of vegetables and sprinkle with a little chopped parsley.

708 Hares

Present-day caterers are limited in their treatment of game such as hares, by hygiene considerations. For example, the old-style way to develop the game flavour was to retain the hares' insides for 3 to 4 days and hang the hares (always by their forelegs). Now it is unsafe (because of such risks as salmonella) to receive into a catering establishment any meat, poultry or game not previously eviscerated. EEC national and local regulations therefore make it difficult if not impossible to follow methods once practised, such as slitting the membrane at the end of the breast and removing the blood and offal (heart and liver) for subsequent use in the sauce or for hare soup.

709 Civet de lièvre à la bourguignonne – Jugged hare bourguignonne

1 *hare* 3 kg (6 lb)	45 g (1½ oz) flour	15 g (½ oz) parsley
500 g (1 lb) button	60 g (2 oz) dripping	stalk
onions	bouquet garni	120 g (¼ lb) sliced
240 g (½ lb) small	30 g (1 oz) tomato	carrots onions,
mushrooms	purée	celery
240 g (½ lb) lardons	Red-wine marinade:	1 clove crushed
16 heart-shaped	500 ml (1 pt) red wine	garlic
croûtons	62 ml (⅛ pt) oil	12 peppercorns
1 litre (2 pt) brown	1 sprig thyme	1.25 ml spoon [¼
stock (Recipe 7)		teaspoon] salt

1 Joint the hare (and in the traditional recipe retaining the blood and liver).
2 Place the hare in the marinade for at least 8 hours, frequently turning.
3 Remove the hare and vegetables from the marinade and fry in the dripping.
4 Dust with flour and brown in the oven for 5 or 6 minutes.
5 Mix in the tomato purée and the liquor from the marinade and stock; boil, skim, and add the bouquet garni; cover and cook in a moderate oven.
6 When cooked, remove hare and place in a clean pan; reboil sauce (and in the traditional recipe thicken with the hare's blood); season and strain over the hare.
7 Blanch the lardons and fry off; glaze the onions; fry the mushrooms and garnish the hare.
8 Fry the croûtons in butter or oil; dip the ends in parsley and decorate.

Traditional accompaniments:
(i) Chop the liver and mix with a little sausage-meat and redcurrant jelly; roll in balls, dip in egg and crumbs and deep-fry.
(ii) Serve also redcurrant jelly.

FURTHER DISHES OF MEAT, POULTRY, AND GAME

KEBABS AND MEAT PILAFFS

710 Kebab à l'orientale

2 *fillet mignon*	120 *g* (¼ *lb*) *lean pork*	7 *g* (¼ *oz*) *chopped*
4 *lamb's kidneys*	4 *large mushrooms*	*parsley*
8 *bay-leaves*	7 *g* (¼ *oz*) *powdered*	15 *g* (½ *oz*) *honey*
60 *g* (2 *oz*) *melted*	*thyme*	120 *g* (4 *oz*)
butter or margarine	*seasoning*	*breadcrumbs*

1 Skin the kidney and cut into roundels, 0.7 cm (⅓-inch) thick; sauté quickly in butter.
2 Cut the lamb and pork into 2 cm (1-inch) squares, 0.5 cm (¼ inch) thick.
3 Sauté the mushrooms cut into thick slices.
4 Alternate kidney, mushrooms, bay-leaf, pork, lamb, on a silver skewer and season.
5 Melt the honey and brush over the kebab.
6 Mix the breadcrumbs with the powdered thyme and parsley.
7 Brush over with melted butter and grill all over.
8 Serve with pilaff or risotto (Recipes 362 to 369) and leave on the skewers.

711 Pilaff d'agneau – Lamb pilaff

625 *g* (1¼ *lb*) *boned leg*	240 *g* (½ *lb*) *diced*	*bouquet garni*
of lamb	*onions*	30 *g* (1 *oz*) *flour*
750 *g* (1½ *lb*) *tomato*	*seasoning*	15 *g* (½ *oz*) *tomato*
concassé	750 *ml* (1½ *pt*) *brown*	*purée*
5 *ml spoon* [½ *dessert-*	*stock* (*Recipe* 7 *or* 8)	30 *g* (1 *oz*) *dripping*
spoon] *ground*		(*or oil*)
ginger		

1 Remove all fat from lamb and cut into 3 cm (1½ inch) squares.
2 Cook the onions in butter (or margarine).
3 Fry the meat to golden brown in a braising-pan; drain off all fat and add the ginger.
4 Sprinkle the meat with flour and cook for a few minutes in the oven.
5 Add the tomato purée and concassé and onions to the meat; mix well; boil, skim, and add bouquet garni.
6 Cover and simmer in moderate oven; when cooked, remove the meat and place in a clean pan.
7 Reduce cooking-liquor, check for seasoning and consistency and strain over meat.
8 Serve with rice pilaff (Recipe 366).

712 Pilaff de vilaille à la King

one 1½ kg (3 lb) chicken	*250 ml (½ pt) chicken velouté (Recipe 27)*	*60 g (2 oz) butter (or sunflower margarine)*
45 g (1½ oz) pimentos	*2 egg yolks* ⎫	
240 g (½ lb) white mushrooms	*62 ml (⅛ pt)* ⎬ *liaison*	*rice pilaff*
seasoning	*cream* ⎭	*(Recipe 366)*

1 Boil the chicken and carefully remove from the bone.
2 Cut the chicken into small pieces slantwise and toss in butter (or margarine).
3 Cook the mushrooms in a little butter and stock; dice and heat the pimentos in butter.
4 Add the garnish to the chicken and moisten with the chicken velouté and simmer for a few minutes.
5 Add the liaison and season; draw to the side of the stove.
6 Serve with a bordure of rice pilaff.

713 Émincé de volaille à la King

Prepare as Recipe 712 and serve within a bordure of pommes duchesse (Recipe 909).

HOT MOUSSES

714 Mousse de jambon – Hot mousse of ham

240g (½ lb) lean cooked ham	*15 g (½ oz) frangipane panada (Recipe 197)*	*pepper grated nutmeg*
1 egg white	*250 ml (½ pt) fresh*	
pinch of paprika	*double cream*	

1 Place the ham in a food processor and chop very finely to a paste.
2 Add the panada. Mix for 2 minutes.
3 Pass through a fine sieve if necessary.

4 Place in a basin over a bowl of crushed ice. Beat in the egg white vigorously. Season.
5 Gradually add the cream.
6 Grease a charlotte mould (or individual dariole moulds). Pipe the mixture into the moulds.
7 Poach in a bain-marie covered with greased, greaseproof paper:
  Charlotte mould approximately 20 minutes at 180°C (350°F).
  Dariole mould approximately 10 minutes at 190°C (375°F).
8 When cooked allow to cool slightly.
9 Serve in a suitable dish unmoulded, accompanied by sauce suprème (or a similar sauce) separately.

715 Basic recipe for hot mousse or mousseline de volaille

240 g (½ lb) chicken   1 egg white
salt, pepper   250 ml (½ pt) double cream

1 Remove all tendons and chop.
2 Season with salt, pepper and little grated nutmeg and chop in a food processor to a fine purée.
3 Add the egg whites and mix vigorously.
4 Rub through a fine sieve (if required) into a bowl; place bowl on ice.
5 Gradually add the cream with care to form an even mixture.
6 Butter a charlotte mould and gently poach in a bain-marie.
7 Present as for Ham Mousse (Recipe 714).

716 Quenelles de volaille (with panada)

one 1 kg (2 lb) chicken   Panada:
2 egg whites   30 g (1 oz) butter (or sunflower
seasoning   margarine)
125 ml (¼ pt) cream   60 g (2 oz) flour
                              125 ml (¼ pt) white stock (Recipe 6)

1 Melt the butter in a saucepan; stir in the flour; cook slightly; add the stock and work until it becomes a smooth paste and leaves the side of the pan clean, allow it to cool on a plate.
2 Remove the sinews from the chicken and chop to a fine purée in a food processor; mix with the panada and egg whites; season.
3 Rub the mixture through a sieve (if required; place in a bowl on ice and slowly work in the cream.
4 Mould with two spoons; gently poach.

Notes:
(i) Quenelles may be made from pheasant, veal, lean pork, using the same recipe and method.
(ii) Similar considerations apply in shaping and sizing for mousse, mousseline, and quenelles of chicken and other meats as for fish (see Recipes 459–61).

CHARCUTERIE DISHES – PORK-BUTCHER
AND SAUSAGE-MAKER DISHES

717 Boudin noir – Black pudding

4 *boudin*	120 g (¼ lb) white	8 slices bacon
French mustard	crumbs	

1 With a sharp knife, make little incisions on all sides of the boudin.
2 Brush with French mustard and roll in white crumbs; pour over melted butter and grill all sides gently.
3 Serve with grilled bacon.

718 Crépinettes de porc

500 g (1 lb) fine pork	250 ml (½ pt) sauce	seasoning
sausage-meat	Périgaux (Recipe 45)	1 egg yolk
30 g (1 oz) chopped	30 g (1 oz) melted	pig's caul
truffles (optional)	butter (or sunflower	
	margarine)	

1 Soak the caul in tepid water to make it pliable.
2 Mix the pork sausage-meat and truffle (optional) together and bind with egg yolks; season.
3 Divide into 60 g (2 oz) portions and shape into flat rectangles.
4 Wrap a piece of caul round each crépinette; brush with melted butter (or margarine) and grill or sauter both sides gently.
5 Arrange in a circle and serve creamed potatoes (Recipe 897) and the sauce separately.

719 Saucisses au vin blanc

500 g (1 lb) French or Cambridge	30 g (1 oz) finely chopped shallots
sausage (8 to the lb)	250 ml (½ pt) jus lié (Recipe 30) or
125 ml (¼ pt) white wine	well-reduced brown stock, or
8 oblong croûtons	demi-glace (Recipe 29)
45 g (1½ oz) butter (or sunflower	seasoning
margarine)	

1 Blanch and refresh sausages and sauté gently in butter (or margarine).
2 Remove sausages and cook shallots to golden colour.
3 Déglacer with wine and reduce.
4 Add the jus lié (or alternative) and reduce by half; enrich with butter, season.
5 Cook the croûtons in butter (or oil) and dress the sausage on top; coat each with sauce.
6 Garnish with a little chopped parsley.

720 Frankfurters Strasbourg

500 g (1 *lb*) *sauerkraut*
8 *frankfurter sausages*
120 g (¼ *lb*) *garlic sausage*
750 g (¾ *lb*) *boiled potatoes*
120 g (¼ *lb*) *bacon*
120 g (¼ *lb*) *bacon rind*

60 g (2 *oz*) *lard* (*or oil*)
¼ *bottle hock* (*or similar white wine*)
1 *onion clouté*
1 *whole carrot*

1 Line a thick pan with bacon rind.
2 Divide the sauerkraut in equal parts and place one half on top of the bacon rind.
3 Lay on the carrots, onions, lard and bacon, and cover with the remainder of the sauerkraut; place the garlic sausage on top and cover with the bacon rind, moisten with the hock.
4 Put a lid on top and seal with flour and water-paste; braise for 2 hours.
5 When cooked, remove vegetables and garnish with sliced garlic-sausage, bacon, boiled frankfurters and boiled potatoes.

Note. Frankfurters should be placed in cold water and brought to the boil.

COMPOSITE OR MADE-UP DISHES

The following made-up dishes are of cooked meat, poultry, and game and, in most instances, are regarded as a means of using left-overs.

721 Chicken and ham cutlets

240 g (½ *lb*) *finely diced cooked chicken*
120 g (¼ *lb*) *finely-diced cooked ham*
15 g (½ *oz*) *flour*
15 g (½ *oz*) *butter* (*or sunflower margarine*)

1 *egg yolk*
125 *ml* (¼ *pt*) *white stock* (*Recipe 6*)
seasoning
8 *cutlet-frills*
8 *pieces of raw macaroni* (*optional*)

1 Melt the butter (or margarine), add the flour and make a white roux.
2 Add the stock and mix to a smooth sauce.
3 Add the chicken and ham; mix well and cook for approximately 5 minutes at side of stove stirring frequently with the spatula.
4 Bind with the egg yolks; season, place on greased tray and leave to cool.
5 Shape into 8 cutlets; pass through flour, egg-wash and white breadcrumb. (Optionally place a small piece of macaroni in each end to resemble cutlet-bone.)
6 Fry in oil or clarified butter and garnish with fried parsley.
7 Place a cutlet-frill on each piece of macaroni (if used).

722 Cottage pie

500 g (1 *lb*) *finely chopped cooked beef*	500 g (1 *lb*) *duchesse potatoes* (*Recipe* 909)
125 ml (¼ pt) *jus lié* (*Recipe* 30), *or well-reduced brown stock or demi-glace* (*Recipe* 29)	120 g (¼ *lb*) *finely chopped onions* *seasoning* 15 g (½ *oz*) *butter* (*or margarine*)

1 Sweat the onions in butter and add the cooked beef.
2 Add the jus lié (or alternative) and simmer for approximately 15 minutes; season.
3 Place the meat in a pie-dish and pipe the duchesse potatoes on top.
4 Brush with egg-wash and brown in the oven.

Note. Shepherds pie is similarly made using cooked lamb or mutton.

Cromesquis (Alternative spellings – Cromeskis, Kromeskis): These are small rolls of savoury preparation composed of finely-chopped, cooked fowl, game, or other meat rolled into cork shapes, wrapped in bacon, dipped in frying batter, deep-fried in hot fat, and garnished with fried parsley. Tomato sauce is served separately.

723 Cromesquis à la russe

150 g (5 *oz*) *diced cooked chicken*	8 *slices bacon*
60 g (2 *oz*) *diced cooked tongue*	250 ml (½ *pt*) *frying batter*
7 g (¼ *oz*) *diced truffles* (*optional*)	*parsley sprigs*
1 *egg yolk*	125 ml (¼ *pt*) *white stock* (*Recipe* 6)
15 g (½ *oz*) *butter* (*or sunflower margarine*)	15 g (½ *oz*) *flour* *seasoning*
7 g (¼ *oz*) *diced cooked mushrooms*	

1 Melt the butter (or margarine), add the flour and make a white roux.
2 Add the stock and mix to a smooth paste.
3 Add the chicken, tongue, truffles (optional), and mushrooms; cook for 5 minutes at the side of the stove, stirring frequently with a wooden spatula.
4 Bind with the egg yolks, and season.
5 Pour on to a greased tray and allow to cool.
6 Roll into 8 equal-sized corks; wrap a thin slice of bacon round each, dip in batter and fry in deep fat; drain and garnish with fried parsley.

Croquettes is the name given to oval, round ball- or cork-shapes of minced meats, fish, poultry, or game. These shapes are floured, egged, and crumbed and are deep-fried or shallow-fried.

724 Croquettes de gibier aux truffes – Game and truffle croquettes

240 g (8 *oz*) *minced cooked game*	1 *egg yolk*	*seasoning*
15 g (½ *oz*) *finely chopped truffle*	15 g (½ *oz*) *flour* 15 g (½ *oz*) *butter* (*or margarine*)	125 ml (¼ *pt*) *game stock* (*Recipe* 12)

1 Melt the butter (or margarine), add the flour and make a blond roux.
2 Add the stock and mix to a smooth sauce.
3 Add the minced game and truffle; cook for a few minutes stirring frequently.
4 Bind with the egg yolks, and season.
5 Pour onto a greased tray and allow to cool.
6 Roll into 8 equal-sized corks; dip in flour, egg and crumb; fry in deep fat and garnish with fried parsley.

725 Croquettes de bœuf

360 g (12 oz) minced cooked beef	30 g (1 oz) finely chopped onions	1 egg yolk
120 g (¼ lb) dry mashed potatoes	7 g (¼ oz) chopped parsley	125 ml (¼ pt) sauce piquante (Recipe 46)
	seasoning	

1 Fry the onions to golden colour in butter.
2 Mix the meat, potatoes, parsley and onions together; bind with egg, and season.
3 Scale into approximately 90 g (3 oz) portions and shape into 5 cm (2½ inch) cylinders.
4 Dip in flour, eggwash and breadcrumbs and deepfry.
5 Garnish with a purée of fresh peas and serve sauce piquante separately.

726 Émincé de volaille

Though properly prepared from freshly-cooked chicken, émincés, such as émincé de volaille à la King, are sometimes adapted to make use of left-over cooked chicken.

727 Corned-beef hash

360 g (¾ lb) diced corned beef	stock (Recipe 7 or 8) as necessary
240 g (½ lb) finely diced cooked potatoes	chopped parsley
90 g (3 oz) butter (or sunflower margarine)	seasoning

1 Combine the cooked potatoes with the corned beef, season; use stock as necessary to form.
2 Shallow-fry in butter and when beginning to colour shape as a large omelette, continue to cook to golden colour; sprinkle with chopped parsley for service.

728 Mazagran

500 g (1 lb) duchesse potatoes (Recipe 909)	seasoning	125 ml (¼ pt) demi-glace (Recipe 29)
240 g (½ lb) cooked lean beef	500 g (1 lb) cooked lean ham	60 g (2 oz) finely chopped onions
	120 g (¼ lb) diced cooked mushrooms	

1 Fry the onions to golden colour in butter.
2 Dice the beef and ham small, and mix with the onions.
3 Moisten with the sauce and cook for a few minutes.
4 Place a layer of duchesse potatoes on the bottom of the serving dish then a layer of meat, and neatly pipe a layer of potatoes on top.
5 Brown under grill.

729 Moussaka

2 *large aubergines*	250 *ml (½ pt) béchamel sauce*
500 g (1 *lb*) *minced lamb* (*or beef*)	(*Recipe* 51)
60 g (2 *oz*) *finely chopped onion*	45 g (1½ *oz*) *raw, chopped*
120 g (¼ *lb*) *breadcrumbs*	*mushrooms*
30 g (1 *oz*) *grated cheese*	120 g (¼ *lb*) *tomato concassé*
½ *clove chopped garlic*	½ *tbsp. tomato purée*
oil, salt, pepper, bay-leaf	30 g (1 *oz*) *butter* (*or sunflower margarine*)

1 Peel and slice the aubergines, lightly sprinkle with salt and place between plates for an hour or so.
2 When moisture has drained away, wipe the slices dry.
3 Fry in hot oil until lightly browned, remove from pan and leave to drain.
4 Pouring off surplus, in the little remaining oil fry the onion and meat until browned.
5 Add tomato concassé and purée, parsley, bay-leaf, garlic, mushroom and seasoning and simmer for about half an hour; remove the bay-leaf then stir in the breadcrumbs. Adjust the seasoning.
6 Oil a large square or oblong pie dish (or deep baking tin) and line the bottom with aubergine, then a layer of meat mixture and another of aubergine.
7 Top with a layer of béchamel sauce (some chefs enrich this with one or two egg yolks) and a sprinkling of breadcrumbs, grated cheese and dots of butter (or margarine).
8 Bake in a moderate oven for half an hour until the top has a golden brown crust.

PUDDINGS AND PIES OF MEAT, POULTRY, AND GAME

The recipes in this section are mostly in the British tradition.

730 A Hot Chicken pie

one 2 *kg (4 lb) chicken*	240 g (½ *lb*) *button mushrooms*
240 g (½ *lb*) *button onions*	250 *ml (½ pt) white stock* (*Recipe* 6)
360 g (¾ *lb*) *parisienne potatoes*	*puff paste* (*Recipe* 994)
(*Recipe* 904)	4 g (⅛ *oz*) *parsley*

1 Joint the chicken (as for sauté (Recipe 628) and gently fry in butter and place in pie dish.

2 Add the onions, button mushrooms, parsley, potatoes, and season; add the stock.
3 Proceed to cover and decorate as for steak pie.
4 Approximate cooking-time, 1½ hours.

Note. There are several versions of chicken pie, including diced chicken in cream sauce etc. as fillings.

731 Cornish pasty

360 g (¾ lb) short pastry (Recipe 995)	62 ml (¼ pt) jus lié (Recipe 30) or demi-glace, cold (Recipe 29)
360 g (¾ lb) cooked meat	pinch mixed herbs
180 g (6 oz) cooked potatoes	pinch parsley
30 g (1 oz) diced cooked onions	salt, pepper

1 Cut the meat and potato into small dice; mix with the remainder of the ingredients, and season.
2 Roll out the pastry thinly and cut into rounds the size of a saucer.
3 Divide the meat mixture according to pastry.
4 Place a heap in the centre of each round and wet the edges.
5 Lift the edges of the pastry above the mixture and press the two together.
6 Flute the edges of the pastry with the fingers and prick each side to prevent bursting.
7 Brush over with milk and bake in a quick oven until browned, approximately 20 to 25 minutes.

732 Forfar Bridie

360 g (¾ lb) puff pastry (Recipe 994)	240 g (½ lb) minced steak
60 g (2 oz) cooked diced onions	7 g (¼ oz) chopped parsley
pinch mixed herbs	seasoning

1 Mix together the meat, onions, herbs and parsley; season and moisten with a little stock.
2 Roll out the paste thinly and cut into rounds the size of a saucer.
3 Place a heap of the meat mixture on one side of the round, wet the edges and turn over; make two small cuts on one side.
4 Egg-wash and bake in moderate oven for 20 to 25 minutes until browned.

733 Game pie (hot)

1 pheasant	500 ml (1 pt) brown stock (Recipes 7, 8)
1 partridge	
1 grouse	pinch mixed herbs
500 g (1 lb) rump steak	7 g (¼ oz) parsley
180 g (6 oz) diced onions	puff pastry (Recipe 994)
500 g (1 lb) diced mushrooms	

1 Joint the game and fry in butter until golden brown; cut the steak into small pieces.

2 Lay the game and other ingredients in alternate layers in the pie-dish and season.
3 Cover with the sauce.
4 Proceed to cover as for steak and kidney pie.
5 Cook for 1¾ hours, approximately.

734 Pigeon pie

2 pigeons	4 g (⅛ oz) chopped parsley
240 g (½ lb) rump steak	pinch mixed herbs
120 g (¼ lb) raw ham	salt, pepper
puff paste	250 ml (½ pt) brown stock
90 g (3 oz) chopped onions	(Recipe 7)

1 Joint the pigeons and cut the steak into small escalopes.
2 Place the pigeons and other ingredients in alternate layers in the pie-dish, season and cover with brown stock.
3 Cover with puff paste as for steak and kidney pie and cook for 1¾ hours approximately.

735 Pork pie (cold)

(Pie filling)

360 g (¾ lb) spare rib of pork	3 sheets gelatine	240 g (½ lb) hot-water paste
120 g (¼ lb) white breadcrumbs	125 ml (¼ pt) white stock (Recipe 6)	(Recipe 997)
	salt	pepper

1 Cut the lean and fat of the pork into 1 cm (½ inch) dice.
2 Add the breadcrumbs, stock, and seasoning.
3 Soak the gelatine in water.
4 Prepare hot-water paste and line the sides and bottom of a greased, oblong raised pie-mould, retaining sufficient paste to form a lid.
5 Place alternate layers of the meat-mixture and soaked, softened leaves of gelatine in the lined mould.
6 Moisten the edges of the mould, cover with paste, and decorate leaving a hole in the centre.
7 Cook for approximately 2 hours in a moderate oven.
8 When cold, fill with aspic jelly as necessary.

736 Rabbit pie

1 young rabbit	7 g (¼ oz) chopped parsley
120 g (¼ lb) raw ham	salt, pepper
90 g (3 oz) chopped onions	puff paste (Recipe 994)
250 ml (½ pt) brown stock	240 g (½ lb) mushrooms
(Recipe 7)	

1 Joint the rabbit (some chefs remove all bones) and soak in cold salted water for 2 hours; rinse well.
2 Dice the mushrooms and cut the ham into small pieces.

3 Place the rabbit and other ingredients in alternate layers in the pie-dish; season and cover with brown stock.

4 Cover as for steak and kidney pie and cook for 1½ hours.

737 Sausage rolls

500 g (1 lb) puff paste   360 g (¾ lb) sausage-meat
(Recipe 994)

1 Roll the puff paste into long strips 0.3 cm (⅛ inch) thick.
2 Roll the sausage-meat into long rolls using a little flour.
3 Place the sausage-meat along the centre of the paste.
4 Egg-wash the edges of the pastry and draw the bottom edge over the sausage, then turn over the egg-washed edge and seal carefully.
5 Cut through in slanting direction about 4 cm (2 inches) apart.
6 Make two slanting cuts on top of each and trim the ends.
7 Egg-wash, place on a damp tray, and bake in a hot oven for 20 to 30 minutes.

738 Steak, kidney, and oyster pie

500 g (1 lb) rump steak   250 ml (½ pt) brown stock
120 g (4 oz) ox-kidney   (Recipe 8) cold
60 g (2 oz) mushrooms   12 oysters
90 g (3 oz) diced onions   240 g (½ lb) puff paste (Recipe 994)
7 g (¼ oz) chopped parsley

1 Remove fat from meat and cut into escalopes about 2 cm (1 inch) in length.
2 Peel and slice mushrooms 0.5 cm (¼ inch) thick.
3 Beard the oysters.
4 Place meat, onions, parsley, and cold stock in a bowl and season; allow to stand for 1 hour.
5 Place a layer of meat, mushrooms, and oysters alternately in a 25 cm (10-inch) pie-dish.
6 Cover and decorate with puff paste, and egg-wash.
7 Bake in hot oven for approximately 1½ hours.

739 Steak and kidney pudding

500 g (1 lb) rump steak   Paste for pudding:
120 g (4 oz) ox-kidney   240 g (½ lb) sifted flour
7 g (¼ oz) chopped parsley   5 ml spoon [1 teaspoon] baking-
250 ml (½ pt) brown stock   powder
(Recipe 8)   120 g (4 oz) beef suet
salt, pepper   62 ml (⅛ pt) water (approx.)
90 g (3 oz) diced onions   pinch salt
                                 Worcestershire sauce

1 Cut the meat from fat, into small pieces; skin the kidney and cut to same size.

2 Place the meat in a bowl with the kidneys, chopped parsley, and onions; cover with cold stock, add a little Worcestershire sauce and season; allow to stand for 1 hour.
3 Prepare the paste by removing the skin from the suet and chopping finely with a little flour.
4 Sieve the flour, baking powder, and salt in a basin and mix it lightly with the suet and add water to form a soft paste.
5 Roll the paste to 0.5 cm (¼ inch) thickness and line a basin of suitable size, reserving sufficient paste for a lid.
6 Fill the meat into the lined basin; wet the edges and cover, pressing the edges down firmly.
7 Cover with a suitable cloth (or aluminium foil) and seal well, allowing room for the paste to expand.
8 Steam for 3½ hours.
9 Serve in the pudding-bowl or turn out.

Alternative method to reduce steaming time
By threequarters cooking the filling before placing in a basin with paste, steaming time is reduced to approximately 1 hour. In this case, cook the steak, kidney, onions, seasoning and parsley in brown stock with 2–3 drops of Worcestershire sauce on the stove top until threequarters cooked. Allow to cool before using.

740 Steak and oyster pudding

Prepare as Recipe 739 but allow 3 oysters (bearded) per person and place them in layers through the meat.

741 Steak pudding and mushrooms

Use the same method as for steak and kidney pudding (Recipe 739) but replace kidney by 250 g (½ lb) of sliced mushrooms.

742 Toad in the hole

| 8 *small sausages* | 240 *ml* (½ *pt*) *batter*
(*Recipe* 507) | 30 *g* (1 *oz*) *dripping*
(*or oil*) |

1 Skin the sausages and place in hot fat (or oil) and cook in a baking-tin.
2 Pour the batter over the sausages and cook in hot oven for 15 minutes.

Note. The batter should be a little thicker than when used for plain Yorkshire pudding.

743 Veal and ham pie (cold)

500 *g* (1 *lb*) *lean fillet of veal*	*grated rind of* ½ *lemon*
120 *g* (¼ *lb*) *raw ham*	240 *g* (½ *lb*) *puff paste* (*Recipe* 994)
1 *hard-boiled egg*	12 *slices streaky bacon*
125 *ml* (¼ *pt*) *aspic* (*Recipe* 122)	10 *ml spoon* [½ *tablespoon*]
250 *ml* (½ *pt*) *white stock*	*chopped parsley*
(*Recipe* 9)	30 *g* (1 *oz*) *chopped onion*

1 Free the veal from sinews and cut into small, thin slices and treat the ham in a similar fashion.
2 Arrange the veal, ham, and bacon in layers in a pie-dish.
3 Cover each layer with a few slices of hard-boiled egg; sprinkle each layer with onions, lemon rind, parsley, salt, and pepper.
4 Add 125 ml (¼ pt) stock); line the rim of the pie-dish and cover with puff paste; leaving a hole in the centre; decorate.
5 Egg-wash, bake in a moderate oven for approximately 1¾ hours; add a little stock from time to time if required.
6 When cold fill with cool, but not set, aspic.

744 Bouchées and vol-au-vents

Notes:
(i) The method of making the circular puff-pastry cases for vol-au-vents and bouchées (similar but smaller) is given in Chapter 8.
(ii) Vol-au-vents are used as hot entrées.
(iii) Bouchées are used also for appetizers (hot or cold).

Examples of fillings for vol-au-vents and bouchées.
Reine: quenelles, chicken, truffles, lié sauce suprême.
Montglas: tongue, quenelles, truffles, foie gras, sweetbread, chicken, lié sauce Madère.
Financière: quenelles, sweetbreads, tongue, olives, mushrooms, truffles, lié sauce Madère (cockscombs once listed are now never used).
Princesse: same as Reine, garnish asparagus tips, lié sauce suprême.
Diane: salpicon of game and truffles, blended with thickened salmis sauce.
Toulouse: chicken quenelles, mushrooms, sweetbreads, lié sauce suprême.

COLD DISHES OF POULTRY AND HAM

745 Poulet en belle vue – Chaud-froid of chicken

1 *large chicken*	2 *large truffles* (*or garnishing paste*)
500 *ml* (1 *pt*) *chicken stock*	2 *slices cooked tongue*
(*Recipe* 11)	*aspic jelly* (*Recipe* 122)
250 *ml* (½ *pt*) *white chaud-froid*	
(*Recipe* 134)	

1 Truss the birds with the legs entered.
2 Gently poach in chicken stock.
3 When cooked, cool and remove skins.
4 Reduce 250 ml (½ pt) of the cooking-liquor and stir into chaud-froid sauce.
5 Stir this mixture until nearly set and pour quickly over the birds to coat them completely.
6 Allow to set in the refrigerator.

7 Decorate with pieces of truffle (or garnishing paste) and tongue.
8 Mask with a coating of half-set aspic jelly.
9 Dress on a socle, neatly decorated, and garnish round the base with crescents of aspic jelly (or chopped aspic jelly. For chopped jelly add extra gelatine to the aspic).
10 To enhance appearance or for practicable serving and suitability on a cold buffet, small, appropriately decorated chicken collops or suprêmes may be added.

Note. Capon (Chapon), the castrated male bird which grows to large size, is now less commonly used for this dish (Chapon en belle-vue).

746 Mayonnaise de volaille

500 g (1 lb) cold boiled chicken   *125 ml (¼ pt) mayonnaise*
30 ml (¹⁄₁₆ pt) vinaigrette   *(Recipe 110)*
(Recipe 118)   *4 quarters lettuce hearts*
2 hard-boiled eggs   *4 anchovy fillets*
4 stoned olives   *12 capers*

1 Garnish the salad-bowl with shredded lettuce and season with salt and vinaigrette.
2 Skin the white meat of the chicken and cut into small collops.
3 Arrange the chicken, dome fashion, on top of the lettuce.
4 Cover chicken with mayonnaise sauce.
5 Decorate with olives, capers, and anchovy fillets.
6 Garnish with quarters of lettuce hearts and quarters of hard-boiled egg.

747 Salade de volaille – Chicken salad

Prepare as Recipe 746, with mayonnaise replaced by ordinary seasoning.

747a Pork pie

See Recipe 735.

748 Soufflé de jambon

120 g (¼ lb) cooked lean ham   *62 ml (⅛ pt) aspic jelly (Recipe 122)*
15 g (½ oz) butter (or sunflower   *62 ml (⅛ pt) double cream*
   margarine)   *4 g (⅛ oz) leaf gelatine*
7 g (¼ oz) finely chopped shallots   *salt, pepper*
1 egg white (optional)   *paprika*
125 ml (¼ pt) béchamel sauce
   (Recipe 51) or chicken velouté
   (Recipe 27)

1 Cut the ham into small dice and sweat in butter (or margarine) with the shallots.
2 Place the ham, shallots and sauce into a food processor, purée to a fine paste.

3 Rub through a sieve if required.
4 Season. Place into a basin. Add the aspic jelly, the soaked and melted leaf gelatine. Stir well.
5 Stir over a basin of ice.
6 On setting point, fold in the stiffly beaten egg white (optional) and half beaten cream.
7 Place into soufflé dish prepared with paper band attached. Chill in refrigerator for approximately 2 hours; remove paper band. Sprinkle with little paprika.

749 Veal and ham pie

See Recipe 743.

7 *Vegetables*

THE cooking of vegetables in a large professional kitchen operating on traditional *partie* lines was allotted to the chef entremettier (who also was responsible for the preparation and serving of eggs, pastas, and rice); but deep-fried items, particularly potatoes, were usually cooked under the supervision of the roast cook, and grilled vegetables such as tomatoes and mushrooms done by the grillardin. Vegetables for garnishes, when an integral part of the cooking, were normally done by the *partie* concerned, e.g. the saucier's preparation of the vegetables in bourgeoise. Otherwise, the chef entremettier not only prepared and cooked the vegetables for table d'hôte and à la carte service but also vegetable garnishes passed to other *parties*. Procedures and allocation of duties are nowadays adapted to meet an operation's particular requirements.

Pre-prepared and processed vegetables
Proven principles apply to the use of vegetables (and other commodities) prepared and processed in modern forms. Quick-frozen vegetables, for example, are widely used in the catering industry and the treatment outlined for fresh produce may be used for them provided that the preliminary steps in cooking are carried out in accordance with the processor's instructions given for the pack. In most cases quick-frozen vegetables are already blanched and basic treatment by the chef involves subsequent immersion in boiling water and continuous cooking as for blanched vegetables. (See further notes on page 263.)

Canned vegetables, such as rarer items like artichoke bottoms and okra, have long been in common use in professional kitchens. Dried pulses are similarly commonplace culinary items and kitchen craftsmen are also making use of dehydrated vegetables including the newer forms of accelerated freeze-dry. What is important is that once reconstitution and basic cooking have taken place, a good finish, as outlined in the recipes, must equally be given to processed forms.

Guide to vegetable portioning. In using the following approximate quantities as a guide, it should be noted that the portioning policy must be determined in the light of cost and selling price. The quality of produce also affects the amount required to gauge net portions.

Vegetables	*Gross Raw Portion*	*Net Raw Portion after Preparation*
Artichokes	1 per portion	120 g (4 oz)
Asparagus, fresh	8 or 9 sticks per portion	

Vegetables	Gross Raw Portion	Net Raw Portion after Preparation
Beetroot	90 g (3 oz)	60 g (2 oz)
Bamboo shoots	180 g (6 oz)	120 g (4 oz)
Bean sprouts	120 g (4 oz)	120 g (4 oz)
Broad Beans, fresh	180 g (6 oz)	120 g (4 oz)
Broad Beans, frozen	90 g (3 oz)	90 g (3 oz)
Broccoli, fresh	120 g (4 oz)	90 g (3 oz)
Broccoli, frozen	90 g (3 oz)	90 g (3 oz)
Brussels Sprouts, fresh	180 g (6 oz)	90 g (3 oz)
Brussels Sprouts, frozen	90 g (3 oz)	90 g (3 oz)
Button Onions	120 g (4 oz)	90 g (3 oz)
Cabbage, Chinese	180 g (6 oz)	120 g (4 oz)
Cabbage, red	240 g (8 oz)	90 g (3 oz)
Cabbage, winter	240 g (½ lb)	90 g (3 oz)
Cabbage, spring	180 g (6 oz)	120 g (4 oz)
Cardoons	120 g (4 oz)	90 g (3 oz)
Carrots, old	120 g (4 oz)	90 g (3 oz)
Carrots, new	90 g (3 oz)	60 g (2 oz)
Cauliflower, fresh	120 g (4 oz)	90 g (3 oz)
Cauliflower, frozen	90 g (3 oz)	90 g (3 oz)
Celeriac	120 g (4 oz)	90 g (3 oz)
Celery	1 head: 2 portions	
Chard, Swiss	180 g (6 oz)	120 g (4 oz)
Christophene (chayote)	180–240 g (6–8 oz)	160–220 g (5–7 oz)
Corn on cob	1 per person	
Corn salad	120 g (4 oz)	90 g (3 oz)
Courgettes (baby marrow, fresh)	180 g (6 oz)	120 g (4 oz)
Courgettes (frozen)	180 g (6 oz)	180 g (6 oz)
Cucumber	60 g (2 oz)	50 g (1¾ oz)
Egg-plant	90 g (3 oz)	90 g (3 oz)
Endive, Belgian	90 g (3 oz)	90 g (3 oz)
Fennel	120 g (4 oz)	90 g (3 oz)
Flageolets	180 g (6 oz)	120 g (4 oz)
French Beans, fresh	120 g (4 oz)	90 g (3 oz)

Vegetables	Gross Raw Portion	Net Raw Portion after Preparation
Jerusalem Artichokes	90 g (3 oz)	60 g (2 oz)
Kohl Rabis	180 g (6 oz)	90 g (3 oz)
Leeks	180 g (6 oz)	90 g (3 oz)
Lettuce, fresh (for serving as salad)	3 portions	
Lettuce (in cooking)	2 portions, depending on size	
Lettuce, cos	2 portions	
Lettuce, braised	1 portion	
Marrow	180 g (6 oz)	120 g (4 oz)
Marrow, baby (see Courgettes above)		
Mooli (white radish)	180 g (6 oz)	120 g (4 oz)
New Turnips	90 g (3 oz)	60 g (2 oz)
Onions	150 g (5 oz)	120 g (4 oz)
Palm hearts	normally canned	60 g (2 oz)
Parsnips	90 g (3 oz)	60 g (2 oz)
Peas, fresh, in pod	180 g (6 oz)	90 g (3 oz)
Peas, frozen	90 g (3 oz)	90 g (3 oz)
Pumpkin	180 g (6 oz)	120 g (4 oz)
Radish, white (see Mooli above)		
Salsify	120 g (4 oz)	90 g (3 oz)
Scotch Kale	180 g (6 oz)	120 g (4 oz)
Sea-kale	120 g (4 oz)	90 g (3 oz)
Spinach, fresh	180 g (6 oz)	120 g (4 oz)
Spinach, frozen	120 g (4 oz)	90 g (3 oz)
Squash	180 g (6 oz)	120 g (4 oz)
Swedes	180 g (6 oz)	75 g (2½ oz)
Sweet potato	180 g (6 oz)	120 g (4 oz)
Swiss chard	180 g (6 oz)	120 g (4 oz)
Tomatoes	90 g (3 oz)	90 g (3 oz)
Turnip tops	120 g (4 oz)	60 g (2 oz)
Yam (see Sweet potato above)		

EXAMPLES OF VEGETABLE GARNISHES
PREPARED BY THE ENTREMETTIER

750 Mixed vegetable garnishes

Guide to quantities for 4 covers

Bouquetière	Gross Raw Weight	Net Raw Weight
Turned carrots	120 g (4 oz)	75 g (2½ oz)
Artichoke bottoms	120 g (4 small)	120 g (4 small)
Turned turnip	120 g (4 oz)	75 g (2½ oz)
French beans	120 g (4 oz)	105 g (3½ oz)
Cauliflower	300 g (10 oz)	240 g (8 oz)

Served in small bouquets

Bourgeoise – Large turned vegetables

Carrots	240 g (½ lb)	180 g (6 oz)
Button onions	240 g (½ lb)	180 g (6 oz)
Completed garnish includes		
lardons of bacon	180 g (6 oz)	135 g (4½ oz)

Brunoise	Ingredients as for Julienne but all cut into fine dice
Duxelles	120 g (¼ lb) [cooked weight]

Guide to quantities for 4 covers

Jardinière	Gross Raw Weight	Net Raw Weight
Bâtons of carrots	90 g (3 oz)	60 g (2 oz)
Bâtons of turnips	90 g (3 oz)	60 g (2 oz)
Peas	60 g (2 oz)	60 g (2 oz)
Lozenge (diagonal cut) French beans	60 g (2 oz)	50 g (1¾ oz)

Julienne

Carrots	90 g (3 oz)	60 g (2 oz)
Celery	60 g (2 oz)	45 g (1½ oz)
Turnips	90 g (3 oz)	60 g (2 oz)
Leek	90 g (3 oz)	45 g (1½ oz)

Macédoine	As Jardinière but cut in dice
Primeurs	As Bouquetière using new or spring vegetables

Printanière

Small turned carrots	120 g (4 oz)	75 g (2½ oz)
Small turned new turnips	120 g (4 oz)	75 g (2½ oz)
Lozenge French beans	90 g (3 oz)	75 g (2½ oz)
Fresh shelled peas	90 g (3 oz)	90 g (3 oz)

Tomates farcies

4, 90 g (3 oz) tomatoes	360 g (¾ lb)	360 g (¾ lb)

751 Single vegetable and vegetable purée garnishes

Guide to quantities for 4 *covers*

In using this guide, note that weights depend on quality and on whether service is table d'hôte or à la carte, etc.

Garnish	Ingredients	Gross Weight	Approximate Cooked Weight
Argenteuil	Asparagus	750 g (1½ lb)	240 g (8 oz)
Bruxelloise	Brussels sprouts	500 g (1 lb)	300 g (10 oz)
Clamart	Fresh peas	300 g (10 oz)	180 g (6 oz)
Condé	Red beans	450 g (15 oz)	240 g (8 oz)
Conti	Lentils	240 g (8 oz)	180 g (6 oz)
Crécy	Carrots 150 g (5 oz) } Rice 60 g (2 oz) }	210 g (7 oz)	180 g (6 oz)
Du Barry	Cauliflower	360 g (12 oz)	240 g (8 oz)
Esaü	Lentils	240 g (8 oz)	180 g (6 oz)
Favorite	French beans	500 g (1 lb)	300 g (10 oz)
Florentine	Spinach	500 g (1 lb)	240 g (8 oz)
Freneuse	Turnip (with potatoes)	300 g (10 oz)	180 g (6 oz)
Maraîchère	Salsifis	360 g (12 oz)	240 g (8 oz)
Montagard	Chestnuts	660 g (22 oz)	180 g (6 oz)
Musard	Flageolets	300 g (10 oz)	240 g (8 oz)
Palestine	Jerusalem artichokes (with potatoes)	480 g (1 lb)	240 g (8 oz)
Parmentier	Potatoes	360 g (12 oz)	240 g (8 oz)
Piemontese	Cardoons 240 g (½ lb) and rice 60 g (2 oz)	300 g (10 oz)	180 g (6 oz)
Rachel	Artichoke bottoms	4 small	
Soubise	Onions } Rice }	120 g (4 oz) } 120 g (4 oz) }	250 g (8 oz)
St Germain	Peas	300 g (10 oz)	180 g (6 oz)
Vichy	Carrots, sliced	360 g (12 oz)	240 g (8 oz)

752 Boiling green vegetables

Green vegetables are cooked in boiling, salted water without lid or cover. Insufficient water is one reason why greens become yellow or brownish in colour; another cause of discolouration is over-long storing. To obtain good results, it is vital to use fresh vegetables and to cook and serve them promptly. When cooked, green vegetables should be drained of water, then returned to the pot, and put on the stove to dry-off any surplus moisture. Spinach is par-cooked and cooled under running water, and then gently squeezed in one hand to rid it of surplus water. Whether it is branch or purée spinach, it is stewed in butter to finish cooking. It is important that vegetables, to retain their full flavour, should not be over-cooked; preferably they should be firm. Finishing with butter (now optional) traditionally completed the cooking.

753 Cooking quick frozen vegetables

Most packers of frozen vegetables indicate on the packs the recommended cooking method. These are normally sound. After basic cooking has been effected, 'finishing' and dressing may be completed in accordance with the general methods outlined throughout this book's vegetable section.

Whilst packers' instructions should not lightly be disregarded the following points may be generally useful. As for fresh vegetables, cooking in the minimum amount of boiling water usually renders best results. Frozen vegetables should *not* be defrosted prior to cooking. If defrosted inadvertently use as soon as possible and *never* re-freeze.

The following points regarding specific vegetables merely indicate the approach and are not exhaustive.

Purée of Spinach:	Cook briskly without water in a buttered pan.
Frozen Broccoli:	Cook in minimum amount of boiling salted water until tender. Drain well.
Frozen Peas:	Cook in the minimum of boiling salted water. Drain, toss in butter with a little sugar. The peas may also be cooked gently under cover without water.
Frozen French Beans:	Cook under cover without water or cook in the minimum amount of salted, boiling water. Drain and season.
Frozen Leaf Spinach:	Blanch in minimum amount of boiling salted water. Refresh. Drain well. Squeeze into portions. Sauté in butter and season.

754 Glazing carrots and turnips

1 Glazing helps to ensure the retention of flavour and also enhances presentation for service: carrots and turnips are placed in a pan and just covered with water, butter, and sugar.
2 Allow 60 g (2 oz) butter and 30 g (1 oz) sugar per 500 ml (pint), bring to the boil and cook until the water evaporates; this leaves a syrup formed by the sugar and butter, which gives a gloss to the vegetables.

755 Glazing button onions (à blanc)

Onions are taken out of the blanc (Recipe 757) just before they are cooked; the liquor is reduced to a glaze and the onions rolled in this before service.

756 Button onions (à brun)

1 The method is different here, the butter (with a little oil) being melted in a sauté-pan first.
2 Put in the onions and lightly sprinkle with sugar.
3 Toss the onions until they acquire an even brown colour.
4 Cover with a lid and draw to the side of the stove.
5 Allow to cook slowly.

Alternative method
After step 3:
4 Add sufficient brown stock (Recipe 8) to cover.
5 Bring to boil, add sugar and simmer gently until the stock is reduced.
6 Toss the onions in the resultant glaze.

757 Blanc for vegetables

> 1 *litre* (1 *qt*) *cold water*   *juice of* 1 *lemon*   30 *g* (1 *oz*) *flour*
> salt

1 Whisk all ingredients in the pan.
2 Place on the stove and stir until boiling.
3 Place in the vegetables to be cooked.
4 When cooked, vegetables should be allowed to cool in blanc; leave until required.

Note. The blanc was thought to inhibit jostling in boiling and thus help to retain the white quality of the vegetable. During preparation and cleaning, the vegetable is put into acidulated water to prevent its blackening or becoming discoloured. It should be clearly understood that cooking in blanc or flour does not make the vegetable white.

758 Braising vegetables

1 For braising, wash well and trim the vegetables, then blanch and refresh; leeks, celery, and lettuces are squeezed gently by hand to express surplus water.
2 Line the bottom of a braising-pain with bacon or blanched pork-rind and then a bed of sliced carrots, onions, and bouquet garni (matignon); lay the vegetables on top, cover with a lid and place in the oven to sweat for 10 minutes. Cover with white stock, bring to the boil, and cook gently in the oven with the lid on.
3 When cool, express surplus juices by hand: celery and lettuce are cut in four or two, lengthwise, and folded.
4 Skim all fat from the cooking-liquor; reduce liquor to a glaze and add jus lié (or stock) to form a sauce (if desired); finish with lemon juice and butter.

VEGETABLE DISHES

ARTICHAUTS – ARTICHOKES

759 Artichokes (to boil whole)

4 *whole artichokes*	*sauce as required*	*lemon*

1 Cut top off artichoke approximately one-third of height.
2 Trim all round, string them and rub bottom with lemon.
3 Cook in salted, boiling water.
4 Drain well. Remove string and heart and chokes (inner fibrous section).
5 Serve on napkin.

Note. Melted butter, hollandaise (Recipe 70) or mousseline sauce (Recipe 75) may be served separately. If cold, serve vinaigrette sauce.

760 Fonds d'artichauts – Artichoke bottoms

1 Using a stainless knife, remove stalk, choke and all leaves to produce hollowed and rounded bottom-part.
2 Rub the artichoke bottoms with lemon juice to prevent discolouration and cook à blanc (Recipe 757).
3 Remove any remaining fibrous matter from the hollow of the fonds.

761 Artichauts à la barigoule

4 *fresh artichokes*	180 *g* (6 *oz*) *duxelles*	*prepared braising-*
4 *slices bacon*	(*Recipe* 102)	*pan*

1 Trim artichoke tops and outer leaves.
2 Parboil (as Recipe 759), remove heart and chokes (the inner fibre section).
3 Season inside, and stuff with duxelles.
4 Wrap in bacon-slice and tie up.
5 Place in pan and braise gently.
6 When cooked, remove string and bacon.
7 Dress and pour over reduced and prepared braising-liquor.

762 Fonds d'artichauts à la provençale

8 *small artichokes*	*seasoning*
250 *ml* (½ *pt*) *shelled peas* (*fresh*	*oil*
or frozen)	*lemon*
½ *lettuce*	

1 Trim artichokes to bottoms and rub with lemon.
2 Place in pan containing hot oil to cover bottom.
3 Cover and allow to cook slowly (10 minutes).
4 Add peas and lettuce, coarsely-shredded.
5 Cover and finish cooking; season.

763 Fonds d'artichauts farcis – Stuffed artichoke bottoms

4 *moderately large artichokes*   *blanc*
240 g (½ lb) *duxelle* (*Recipe* 102)   *melted butter* (*or margarine*)
½ *lemon*

1 Trim artichokes of leaves and chokes.
2 Trim bottoms and rub with lemon to prevent blackening.
3 Cook in a blanc, keep fairly firm.
4 Drain, remove any remaining fibrous matter and stuff with duxelle.
5 Place in buttered dish.
6 Sprinkle some breadcrumbs on top and a little melted butter.
7 Place in hot oven to form a gratin on top.

764 Fonds d'artichauts à la florentine

4 *medium-sized artichokes*   10 *ml spoon* [½ *tablespoon*]
120 g (¼ lb) *spinach purée*   *anchovy purée*
   (*Recipe* 833)   125 *ml* (¼ *pt*) *mornay sauce*
1 *clove crushed garlic*   (*Recipe* 58)
seasoning   *grated cheese*
15 *ml spoon* [1 *tablespoon*]
   velouté (*Recipe* 26) (*or yogurt*
   or double cream)

1 Prepare the bottom as for stuffing (Recipe 763).
2 Dry spinach in pan on stove.
3 Season, add garlic, velouté, and anchovy.
4 Cook gently for 2 to 3 minutes.
5 Stuff bottoms with the above mixture.
6 Coat with mornay sauce and sprinkle with cheese.
7 Place in buttered dish and glaze in hot oven.

765 Fonds d'artichauts aux pointes d'asperges

4 *medium-sized artichokes*   *grated cheese*
125 *ml* (¼ *pt*) *mornay sauce*   *seasoning*
   (*Recipe* 58)   12 *asparagus tips*
62 *ml* (⅛ *pt*) *cream* (*or fromage*   *butter* (*or sunflower margarine*)
   frais or yogurt)

1 Prepare artichokes as for bottoms.
2 Cook lightly in butter.
3 Bind asparagus tips with cream (or alternative).
4 Place tips in bottoms.
5 Coat with mornay sauce.
6 Sprinkle with cheese and glaze in hot oven.

766 Fonds d'artichauts sautés

4 *artichokes*   *butter* (*or sunflower*   *fines herbes*
                               margarine or oil)

1 Prepare in usual manner.
2 Slice artichokes raw.
3 Season with salt and pepper.
4 Toss in butter (margarine or oil), dish and sprinkle with herbs.

767 Fonds d'artichauts en purée – Purée of artichoke bottoms

4 *medium-sized artichokes*	*seasoning*
mashed potatoes (*Recipe* 896)	*butter* (*or sunflower margarine*)

1 Trim artichokes as for bottoms. (Some prefer to remove 'choke' *after* cooking.)
2 Half-cook in a blanc and drain.
3 Complete cooking in butter.
4 Remove fibrous matter. Pass through a a fine sieve.
5 Add mashed potatoes equal to half its bulk.
6 Mix well and serve with beurre noisette (optional).

ASPERGES – ASPARAGUS

Premier-quality asparagus, especially in early season, is the lauris. The smaller green Parisian type used for tips is also known as sprew. Asparagus from Argenteuil is highly esteemed, therefore 'Argenteuil' on menus describes asparagus dishes. English asparagus is good but inclined to be small. Asparagus should be used as fresh as possible.
To prepare asparagus. Lightly scrape from the bottom of the flower downwards, wash and then tie in small bundles. Level the heads then cut the bundles at the foot. Place in plenty of salted, boiling water and cook gently.

768 Asperges au beurre fondu – Asparagus with melted butter

4 *bunches asparagus* (8 *or* 9 *stalks per bunch*)	120 *g* (¼ *lb*) *butter*

1 Cook asparagus as above.
2 Drain and place in serving dish.
3 Melt butter and serve separately.

Notes
(i) Hollandaise (Recipe 70), or maltaise (Recipe 74), may be served.
(ii) If cold, serve vinaigrette dressing (Recipe 118) or mayonnaise (Recipe 110).

769 Asperges au gratin

4 *bunches asparagus*	250 *ml* (½ *pt*) *mornay sauce* (*Recipe* 58)	30 *g* (1 *oz*) *grated Parmesan cheese*

1 Dish asparagus in rows.
2 Coat with mornay sauce ⅓ down from heads.
3 Sprinkle with Parmesan cheese and glaze.

770 Asperges à la milanaise

4 *bunches asparagus*	120 *g* (¼ *lb*) *butter* (*or sunflower margarine*)	45 *g* (1½ *oz*) *grated Parmesan cheese*

1 Butter serving-dish well.
2 Arrange asparagus in layers, in successive rows.
3 Sprinkle heads with cheese.
4 Cover heads with noisette butter (or melted sunflower margarine) and glaze under salamander.

771 Asperges à la polonaise

2 *hard-boiled egg-yolks* (*sieved*) *chopped parsley*	4 *bunches asparagus* 120 *g* (¼ *lb*) *butter* (*or sunflower margarine or oil*)	*seasoning* 60 *g* (2 *oz*) *white breadcrumbs*

1 Dish asparagus (as Recipe 770).
2 Brown breadcrumbs in butter (or alternative) and season.
3 Add egg yolks and parsley.
4 Pour over asparagus and serve.

AUBERGINE – BRINJAL OR EGG-PLANT

772 Aubergines à l'égyptienne

10 *ml* (spoon [½ *tablespoon*] *chopped onion minced, cooked lean lamb or mutton*	2 *aubergines* 3 *tomatoes* *seasoning* *oil, butter*

1 Cut aubergines lengthwise into two.
2 Criss-cross centre with a knife.
3 Cook lightly in hot oil.
4 Drain and withdraw the pulp.
5 Cook onion in oil and add pulp chopped with an equal quantity of lamb or mutton.
6 Place shells in buttered dish.
7 Fill with prepared pulp.
8 Place in oven for 10 to 15 minutes.
9 A few slices of tomato cooked in oil are placed on top of each aubergine.
10 Sprinkle with chopped parsley.

773 Aubergines au gratin

dry duxelle (*Recipe* 102) *jus lié* (*Recipe* 30) *or demi-glace* (*Recipe* 29) (*or brown stock* (*Recipe* 8))	*breadcrumbs* 2 *aubergines*

1 Prepare as above.
2 Chop pulp and mix in equal quantity of dry duxelle.
3 Fill shells with preparation.
4 Sprinkle with crumbs and brown in oven.
5 Dish and serve a border of jus lié round the aubergines.

774 Aubergines frites

2 *aubergines*   *flour (seasoned)*

1 Skin aubergines and cut into rounds; season and flour.
2 Deep-fry in hot oil.
3 Drain and serve on napkin immediately.

775 Ratatouille – Provençale aubergine, courgette, pimento and tomato casserole

120 g (4 oz) aubergine	340 g (¾ lb) tomatoes
120 g (4 oz) courgette	3 tbsp. olive oil
120 g (4 oz) onion	2 cloves garlic crushed
120 g (4 oz) sliced peppers	salt, peppermill
(usually green)	

1 (i) Wash the aubergines (some prefer to peel this vegetable) and courgette and cut into 1 cm (½ inch) thick slices.
  (ii) Peel the onions and slice thinly.
  (iii) Skin and de-pip the tomatoes and slice.
2 In a sauteuse or casserole, sweat the onions. (The dish is casseroled or stewed, not fried.)
3 As the onions soften, add the pepper and aubergines.
4 After about 6 minutes add the tomatoes and garlic. Season with salt and pepper.
5 Cook for about half an hour, the first 20 minutes or so under cover, the remaining 10 minutes or so without lid to reduce the liquor; by this time the oil should be absorbed.

Notes
1 The traditional style is for the ingredients to be well-softened, but with modern taste for al dente vegetable times above are a little less than formerly given.
2 In Provence many assemble the vegetables in layers for final casseroling, so that, though softened, they retain their own shape and savour.
3 Some traditionalists think that pre-preparation and reheating the following day improve the dish's flavour.

BETTERAVE – BEETROOT

776 Beetroot (to boil)

1 Trim off the green leaves (these may be treated as turnip tops), wash the beets and boil until tender. Time varies according to age and size but will certainly be more than 1 hour and may be as much as 3 to 4 hours.
2 Remove the skin carefully with blunt edge of knife or by even rubbing with rough cloth.
3 Slice or dice according to mode of subsequent serving which may be, when hot, à la crème or braised with piquant, red-wine sauce as well as cold for salad use.

BLETTES – BLETT

777 Blettes – Blett or strawberry spinach

Cook the leaves as for spinach and the stalks as for salsifis (see Recipe 944).

BROCOLI – BROCCOLI

778 Brocoli – Broccoli

These are similar to cauliflower, though the purplish flowers are smaller and more scattered. Recipes for cauflower may be used.

CARDONS – CARDOONS

779 Cardons – Cardoons

1 Cut off the outer green-leaf stalks and discard them.
2 Cut the white stalks into lengths of 6–8 cm (3 or 4 inches).
3 Rub with lemon and place in acidulated water.
4 Take out the fibrous part of the heart and treat the heart like the white stalks.
5 Cook all à blanc (Recipe 757) for 1 to 1½ hours.

Note. Cardoons may be served with sauce bordelaise (Recipe 35), sauce hollandaise (Recipe 70), cream, Mornay sauce (Recipe 58), sauce italienne (Recipe 42); or treated and served as for celery.

780 Cardons au parmesan

30 g (1 oz) grated Parmesan cheese	*blanc (Recipe 757)*
125 ml (¼ pt) jus lié (Recipe 30) or demi-glace (Recipe 29) or concentrated brown stock (Recipe 8)	*750 g (1½ lb) cardons* *seasoning*

1 Remove the green stalks and cut white ones into 6 cm (3 inch) lengths; peel, and rub with lemon juice to keep white.
2 Remove the fibrous part from the heart and treat in the same manner.
3 Place the cardons in a boiling blanc.

4 Simmer for 1½ hours; drain and toss in butter (or margarine); build in layers and sprinkle Parmesan cheese on each one; season each layer.
5 Cover with jus lié (or alternative), sprinkle with Parmesan cheese and brown.

CAROTTES – CARROTS

781 Carottes glacées

750 g (1½ lb) peeled carrots
30 g (1 oz) butter (or sunflower margarine) per 500 ml (1 pt) of water

7 g (¼ oz) salt
15 g (½ oz) sugar

1 Cut carrots into 3 cm (1½-inch) lengths and quarter.
2 With a small knife trim them into barrel shapes (or jardinière).
3 Place in sauté pan and cover with cold water.
4 Add sugar, salt and butter, bring to boil.
5 Cook until water has evaporated, leaving a syrup glaze.

782 Carottes à la crème

1 As for carrottes glacées.
2 When cooked, lié with well-reduced cream.

783 Carottes Vichy

1 Slice carrots thinly on mandoline.
2 Finish as for carrottes glacées.

CELERIS – CELERY

784 Céleris braisés au jus

2 heads of celery
white stock (Recipe 6)

bouquet garni
60 g (2 oz) bacon rind

1 small carrot
1 small onion

1 Blanch and refresh celery and trim.
2 Cover bottom of pan with bacon rind.
3 Place sliced onions, carrots and bouquet garni on top.
4 Lay celery on top of vegetables.
5 Cover with lid and place in oven for 2 minutes.
6 Cover with stock, boil and cook in oven until tender.
7 Draw celery through hand to express surplus liquor.
8 Cut lengthwise in four, and fold.
9 Skim off fat from cooling-liquor.
10 Reduce and add some good jus lié (Recipe 30).
11 Coat celery with sauce.

785 Céleris au parmesan

1 Prepare as Recipe 784 then coat with jus lié (Recipe 30), concentrated stock (Recipe 8) or demi-glace (Recipe 29).
2 Sprinkle with Parmesan cheese and glaze.

786 Céleris Mornay

1 Prepare as Recipe 785, using Mornay sauce (Recipe 58) instead of jus lié.
2 Sprinkle with Parmesan cheese and glaze.

787 Céleris à la milanaise

Prepare as Recipe 785 but finish as for asparagus milanaise (Recipe 770).

788 Céleris à la moëlle

Prepare as Recipe 787, then place a slice of poached beef marrow on each piece of celery and coat with sauce bordelaise (Recipe 35).

789 Céleris with various sauces

1 Celery may be served with various sauces such as cream, hollandaise, italienne, mousseline or bordelaise.
2 Sauce may be served separately or coated over the vegetable.

CÉLERI-RAVE – CELERIAC

790 Céleri-rave à la crème

62 ml (⅛ pt) cream sauce	480 g (1 lb) celeriac
(Recipe 63)	1.25 ml spoon [¼ teaspoon] vinegar
juice of ½ lemon	62 ml (⅛ pt) cream
45 g (1½ oz) butter (or sunflower	salt, pepper
margarine)	

1 Peel celeriac thinly and place in water acidulated with lemon juice to retain colour.
2 Shape as for turned carrots; blanch in water with vinegar for about 5 minutes.
3 Sweat them in butter (or margarine) until tender, then mix with the sauce and cream, and season.

791 Céleri-rave aux fines herbes

500 g (1 lb) celeriac	1.25 ml spoon [¼ teaspoon] vinegar
4 g (⅛ oz) fines herbes (chopped	60 g (2 oz) butter (or sunflower
parsley, thyme)	margarine)
juice of ¼ lemon	salt and pepper

1 Cook as for à la crème (Recipe 790) and drain well.
2 Finish the cooking in butter (or margarine), add the fines herbes and season.

CHAMPIGNONS – MUSHROOMS AND OTHER FUNGI

Mushrooms (champignons), cèpes (flap mushrooms), morilles (morels), are all treated similarly. White, cultivated mushrooms need not be peeled but should be well washed to remove any sand which may adhere.

792 Cèpes à la bordelaise

15 ml spoon [1 tablespoon] finely-
  chopped onion
15 ml spoon [1 tablespoon] white
  breadcrumbs
¼ lemon

15 g (½ oz) chopped parsley
500 g (1 lb) cèpes
62 ml (⅛ pt) oil
salt, pepper

1 Cut cèpes in scollops and season.
2 Heat oil in pan, place in cèpes and sauté until well sizzled.
3 Add onions and cook for one or two minutes.
4 Finish with breadcrumbs.
5 When serving, squeeze lemon over and sprinkle with parsley.

793 Cèpes à la provençale

Prepare as bordelaise (Recipe 792) with the addition of garlic.

794 Champignons à la crème – Mushrooms in cream

50 g (1 lb) mushrooms
60 g (2 oz) butter (or sunflower
  margarine)

15 ml (spoon [1 tablespoon] finely
  chopped onion
250 ml (½ pt) cream
seasoning

1 Fry onions in butter without colouring.
2 Add mushrooms, cover and cook.
3 Drain and cover with cream.
4 Boil slowly until cream is well reduced.

795 Champignons farcis

large field mushrooms
  as required

duxelles stuffing
  (Recipe 102)

white breadcrumbs
butter

1 Peel, wash, and dry mushrooms.
2 Place on well-buttered tray.
3 Fill with duxelle stuffing.
4 Sprinkle with breadcrumbs.
5 Place in oven to cook.

796 Champignons grillés

500 g (1 lb) field mushrooms
salt
120 g (¼ lb) parsley butter
  (Recipe 89) (optional)

180 g (6 oz) butter (or sunflower
  margarine)
pepper

1 Peel, wash, and dry mushrooms.
2 Place in pan and season.
3 Coat with melted butter and grill gently.
4 When serving, place parsley butter in centre of each mushroom (optional).

797 Purée de champignons

500 g (1 lb) white mushrooms
250 ml (½ pt) Béchamel
    (Recipe 51)
nutmeg

62 ml (⅛ pt) cream (or fromage
    frais or yogurt)
45 g (1½ oz) butter (or sunflower
    margarine)
salt, pepper

1 Wash and dry mushrooms.
2 Rub through a fine sieve.
3 Reduce Béchamel by one-third.
4 Add mushroom purée and cream (or alternative).
5 Place on hot fire and reduce slightly.
6 Season and finish with butter (or margarine).

798 Champignons tournés – Turned mushrooms

white mushrooms as required

1 Cut stalks off flush with heads.
2 Groove head with point of small knife.
3 Wash well and cook quickly under cover in a little water acidulated with
  lemon juice together with a little butter.

799 Truffe – Truffle

To cook truffles:
1 Wash and brush, and soak in water for 3 hours.
2 Place in a cocotte, cover with sherry and add a few peppercorns.
3 Seal the lid with flour and water-paste and simmer in the oven for 30
  minutes.
4 Place in a jar and strain the liquid on top.

CHOU – CABBAGE

800 Chou à l'anglaise

one and a half 1 kg (2 lb) cabbages   salt

1 Trim the outer coarse leaves, and quarter cabbage.
2 Cut out coarse stalks.
3 Wash well and cook in plenty of boiling water (salted).
4 Drain and press between two plates.
5 Cut in portions and serve.

800a Scotch kale and Curly kale

Other varieties of spring 'greens' may be prepared as cabbage.

801 Petit chou au beurre – Small cabbage with butter

1 Separate outer green leaves keeping them whole.
2 Quarter rest of cabbage.
3 Blanch and refresh.
4 Place outer green leaves on clean board and place quarter on top.
5 Gather into a clean cloth and squeeze into a ball.
6 Place in well-buttered pan and dot each ball with a piece of butter.
7 Season and cover with buttered paper.
8 Cover pan and cook in oven until tender.

802 Chou étuvé

1 Shred cabbage after trimming.
2 Wash well in cold water.
3 Drain and place in pan with a good knob of butter (or sunflower margarine).
4 Add onion piqué, carrot and bacon rind.
5 Season with salt and pepper.
6 Cover with buttered paper and cover pan.
7 Cook in oven until tender.

803 Chou farci braisé – Braised stuffed cabbage

1 *medium-sized cabbage*	120 g (¼ lb) streaky bacon
60 g (2 oz) fresh white	1 egg yolk
breadcrumbs	120 g (¼ lb) sausagemeat
30 g (1 oz) finely chopped onion	120 g (¼ lb) bacon rind
120 g (¼ lb) matignon (Recipe 3)	seasoning
125 ml (¼ pt) jus lié or demi-glace	7 g (¼ oz) chopped parsley
(Recipe 29) or well-reduced	250 ml (½ pt) white stock (Recipe 6)
stock (Recipe 8)	

1 Cut the cabbage in quarters and remove the core.
2 Wash well; blanch for 10 minutes and refresh; remove stalky parts.
3 Mince the bacon and mix with sausage-meat, crumbs, onions, parsley, and seasoning; bind with egg yolks.
4 Roll the stuffing into 4 balls and wrap the cabbage leaves neatly around each ball.
5 Place the stuffed cabbage on the matignon and cover with the bacon rind.
6 Add the stock; season and cook under cover in the oven until tender.
7 Strain the cooking-liquid off; boil and remove all fat; reduce the liquid, add to the jus lié (or alternative).
8 Dress the cabbage on an oval dish and coat with the sauce.

Note. To keep the cabbage in shape, pack tightly in the braising-pan.

CHOU DE MER OR CHOU MARIN

804 Chou de mer à la crème – Sea-kale in cream

62 ml (⅛ pt) cream	500 g (1 lb) sea-kale	seasoning
sauce (Recipe 63)	15 ml (1 tbsp.) cream	

1 Wash and trim; tie in bundles.
2 Cook à blanc.
3 Drain well and pour a little cream sauce over the head before service.

805 Chou de mer à la hollandaise

500 g (1 lb) sea-kale   125 ml (¼ pt) sauce hollandaise
                                                                (Recipe 70)

1 Prepare as chou de mer à la crème (Recipe 804).
2 Serve plain on a serviette with sauce hollandaise separately.

CHOU-RAVE – KOHLRABI

806 Choux-raves à la crème

62 ml (⅛ pt) sauce   15 ml spoon [1   500 g (1 lb) kohlrabi
    allemande   tablespoon] cream   30 g (1 oz) butter
    (Recipe 54)   salt, pepper and grated   (or sunflower
125 ml (¼ pt) white   nutmeg   margarine)
    stock (Recipe 6)

1 Peel the kohlrabi thinly and shape as for turned carrots.
2 Blanch and refresh in salted water.
3 Stew them in butter (or margarine) till tender without colour.
4 Mix with the sauce and cream; adjust seasoning.

807 Choux-raves à la menagère

1 kg (1 lb) kohlrabi   30 g (1 oz) butter
250 ml (½ pt) jus lié (Recipe 30),   pepper
    demi-glace (Recipe 29) or well   salt
    reduced brown stock (Recipe 8)   nutmeg

1 Peel thin and neatly turn into olive shapes.
2 Blanch and refresh in salted water.
3 Stew in butter until tender, drain and add the jus lié (or alternative).

CHOUX ROUGES – RED CABBAGE

808 Choux rouges à la flamande

240 g (½ lb) bacon or pork rind   salt
120 g (¼ lb) diced apples (net wt)   bouquet garni
15 g (½ oz) caster sugar   120 g (¼ lb) (or sunflower
500 g (1 lb) red cabbage   margarine)
62 ml (⅛ pt) wine-vinegar   pepper

1 Cut the cabbage in quarters, remove stumps and stalks and faded leaves;
wash well in salted water.

2 Shred into rough julienne; season.
3 Place in a braising-pan with the butter and vinegar; cover with the bacon rind and cook under cover with the bouquet garni.
4 When 3-parts cooked, add the diced apples and sugar and finish off the cooking.
5 When cooked remove bouquet garni and bacon rind, adjust seasoning and serve in oval vegetable dish with a little of the cooking-liquor.

809 Choux rouges à la limousine

120 g (¼ lb) diced apples (net wt)	500 g (1 lb) red cabbage
125 ml (¼ pt) white stock	15 g (½ oz) caster sugar
(Recipe 6)	60 g (2 oz) butter (or sunflower
62 ml (⅛ pt) wine-vinegar	margarine)
120 g (¼ lb) diced raw chestnuts	bouquet garni
240 g (½ lb) bacon or pork rind	

1 Cut the cabbage in quarters, remove stump, stalks and faded leaves; wash well in salted water.
2 Shred into rough julienne and season.
3 Place the cabbage, chestnuts, stock and bouquet garni into a braising-pan; cover with bacon or pork rind, and cook under cover in the oven.
4 When 3-parts cooked remove the bacon rind; sprinkle the cabbage with vinegar; add the diced apples and the sugar; replace the rind and finish off the cooking.
5 When cooked, remove the rind and bouquet garni; adjust seasoning and serve with a little of the cooking-liquor.

810 Pickled red cabbage

red cabbage	1 clove garlic
pinch mixed herbs	salt
250 ml (½ pt) spiced vinegar	peppercorns
(Recipe 131)	

1 Trim off outer leaves and cut off stalk.
2 Cut into quarters then in fine julienne.
3 Place on tray and sprinkle liberally with salt.
4 Leave for two days.
5 Drain and place in jar with herbs, peppercorns and garlic.
6 Cover with spiced vinegar and leave to marinade.

CHOUX DE BRUXELLES – BRUSSELS SPROUTS

811 Choux de Bruxelles à l'anglaise

500 g (1 lb) Brussels sprouts	boiling water
	salt

1 Trim outer leaves of sprouts.
2 Cut a cross in the bottom of stem.
3 Wash well and drain.
4 Cook in plenty of boiling salted water.
5 Drain well and serve.

812 Choux de Bruxelles sautés

500 g (1 lb) Brussels sprouts   60 g (2 oz) butter (or sunflower margarine)

1 Prepare and cook as above, Recipe 811.
2 Drain well.
3 Heat some butter (or margarine) in pan and sauté sprouts until they are slightly browned.

813 Purée de choux de Bruxelles

500 g (1 lb) Brussels sprouts   butter (or sunflower margarine)
120 g (¼ lb) mashed potato   salt
(Recipe 896)

1 Trim sprouts and wash well.
2 Three-parts cook, drain and finish cooking in butter (or margarine).
3 Pass through sieve.
4 Add one-third of its bulk in mashed potato.
5 Mix well and add butter (or margarine) and salt.

814 Choux de Bruxelles limousine

1 Cook in salted water, strain well.
2 Toss in butter (or sunflower margarine) and garnish with pieces of cooked chestnuts.

815 Choux de Bruxelles polonaise

Finish as for chou-fleur polonaise (Recipe 821).

816 Choux de Bruxelles Mornay

1 Cook as for limousine (Recipe 814) but cover with Mornay sauce (Recipe 58).
2 Sprinkle with cheese and brown under grill.

CHOU-FLEUR – CAULIFLOWER

817 Cauliflower (to boil)

1 Remove outer leaves.
2 Hollow out stalk with a small knife.
3 Wash well in salt water.
4 Cook steadily in plenty of boiling salted water.

5 The stalk should be tender and care must be taken not to break the flowers; drain well and finish according to the appropriate recipe, such as those listed below.

818 Chou-fleur nature, sauce hollandaise

360 g (¾ lb) trimmed-weight cauliflower – approximately 1 *medium-sized cauliflower*

1 Cook as Recipe 817 – drain well.
2 Serve on a vegetable dish with flower uppermost.
3 Hollandaise sauce served separately (Recipe 70).

Note. Alternatives for hollandaise are beurre fondu (Recipe 80) or sauce divine (Recipe 72a).

819 Chou-fleur Mornay (or chou-fleur au gratin)

360 g (¾ lb) trimmed cauliflower	*190 ml (⅜ pt) Mornay sauce (Recipe 58)*	*30 g (1 oz) grated cheese*

1 Cook as for Recipe 817.
2 Drain well and place in buttered vegetable dish.
3 Coat with Mornay sauce (Recipe 58).
4 Sprinkle with grated cheese.
5 Brown in hot oven.

Note. May also be prepared in individual portions.

820 Chou-fleur à la milanaise

360 g (¾ lb) trimmed cauliflower	*45 g (1½ oz) grated cheese*	*60 g (2 oz) butter (or sunflower margarine)*

1 Cook as Recipe 817.
2 Place in buttered vegetable dish.
3 Sprinkle with grated cheese.
4 Glaze under grill.
5 Finish with beurre noisette (Recipe 82) (optional) (or brush with margarine).

821 Chou-fleur à la polonaise

360 g or ¾ trimmed cauliflower	*7 g (¼ oz) chopped parsley*
1 hard-boiled egg (sieved)	*120 g (¼ lb) butter (or sunflower*
60 g (2 oz) breadcrumbs	*margarine)*

1 Cook as Recipe 817.
2 Place in buttered vegetable dish.
3 Place butter in frying-pan and melt.
4 Add breadcrumbs and fry until golden brown and frothy.
5 Add most of the sieved eggs and chopped parsley; season.
6 Pour over the cauliflower evenly and sprinkle with remaining sieved egg and parsley.

822 Chou-fleur sauté au beurre

360 g (¾ lb) trimmed cauliflower   60 g (2 oz) butter (or sunflower
                                                                    margarine)

1 Cook as Recipe 817.
2 Cut into 4 equal portions.
3 Melt butter in frying-pan.
4 Add the cauliflower and colour evenly.
5 Season and serve in an oval vegetable dish.

823 Chou-fleur sauté aux fines herbes

To the above Recipe 822, when tossing in butter, add 15 g (½ oz) fines
herbes.

CONCOMBRE – CUCUMBER

824 Concombres à la crème – Cucumbers in cream

360 g (¾ lb) cucumber   62 ml (⅛ pt) fresh   30 g (1 oz) butter
salt and pepper   cream   (or sunflower
                                                                    margarine)

1 Peel, cut into 3 cm (1½-inch) sections and turn like olives.
2 Sweat in the butter without colouring.
3 Add the cream and simmer gently for 2 or 3 minutes; season and serve.

825 Concombres farcis – Stuffed cucumbers

360 g (¾ lb) cucumber   120 g (¼ lb) duxelles (Recipe 102)
15 g (½ oz) butter (or sunflower   15 g (½ oz) grated Parmesan cheese
margarine)   seasoning

1 Peel the cucumber and cut into 4 cm (2-inch) lengths and cut them
   lengthways.
2 Remove the centre seeds and blanch and refresh in salted water.
3 Heat the duxelles and place in savoy-bag and pipe the mixture neatly in the
   centre.
4 Brush the top with melted butter, sprinkle with the cheese and brown
   lightly under the grill.
5 Sprinkle a little chopped parsley on top before serving.

826 Concombres glacés

Prepare as for carottes glacées (Recipe 781).

827 Courgettes – Vegetable marrows

Prepare and cook as cucumbers.

CROSNES DU JAPON – JAPANESE ARTICHOKES OR STACHYS

828 Crosnes du Japon à la milanaise

500 g (1 lb) Japanese artichokes
blanc (Recipe 757)

30 g (1 oz) grated Parmesan cheese
45 g (1½ oz) butter

1 To clean: wash and peel (traditionally, place them in a sack with bay salt and shake well to remove skins).
2 Re-wash and cook à blanc.
3 Drain, toss in butter, season.
4 Sprinkle with cheese and brown under grill.

829 Crosnes du Japon à la polonaise

500 g (1 lb) Japanese artichokes
7 g (¼ oz) chopped parsley
1 sieved hard-boiled egg

120 g (¼ lb) breadcrumbs
60 g (2oz) butter (or sunflower
margarine)

1 Cook stachys as for milanaise (Recipe 828).
2 Fry the crumbs golden brown in butter (or margarine).
3 Add the eggs and parsley and coat over the stachys.
4 Sprinkle a little chopped parsley before service.

Note. May be used for fish garnish.

ENDIVE – CHICORY

830 Endive (to cook)

1 Wash, lay on buttered braising-pan, add salt and lemon juice.
2 Cover with tight-fitting lid (traditionally, sealed with flour and water paste).
3 Cook in moderate oven for 30 minutes.

Note. No water required as they contain sufficient in themselves.

831 Endive au jus

240 g (½ lb) endives

250 ml (½ pt) jus lié (Recipe 30)

1 Braise as Recipe 830.
2 When cooked, reduce cooking-liquor and add jus lié.
3 Coat over endives.

832 Endive Mornay

240 g (½ lb) endives

125 ml (¼ pt) mornay
sauce (Recipe 58)

15 g (½ oz) grated
Parmesan cheese

1 Braise as Recipe 830.
2 Drain; coat with Mornay sauce.
3 Sprinkle with cheese and brown.

ÉPINARDS – SPINACH

833 Épinards à la crème – Creamed spinach

125 *ml* (¼ *pt*) *cream sauce*   62 *ml* (⅛ *pt*) *fresh cream*
    (*Recipe* 63)   60 *g* (2 *oz*) *butter* (*or sunflower*
750 *g* (1½ *lb*) *leaf spinach*   *margarine*)

1 Prepare and cook as for en branches (Recipe 836).
2 Pass through a sieve.
3 Put in pan with butter (or margarine) and dry on stove.
4 Add one-quarter of its bulk in cream sauce and simmer gently for 10 minutes.
5 Dish and sprinkle some fresh cream over.

834 Épinards Viroflay

Soubise d'épinards (*as Recipe* 61)   500 *g* (1 *lb*) *blanched spinach leaves*
250 *ml* (½ *pt*) *Mornay sauce,*   *grated cheese*
    quarter quantities (*Recipe* 58)   *melted butter* (*or sunflower*
                              margarine)

1 Place leaves on table.
2 Place soubise on each leaf and fold.
3 Place on buttered dish.
4 Coat with Mornay sauce.
5 Sprinkle with cheese and melted butter.
6 Place in hot oven to glaze.

835 Épinards au gratin

750 *g* (1½ *lb*) *leaf spinach*   90 *g* (3 *oz*) *butter* (*or sunflower*
60 *g* (2 *oz*) *grated cheese*   *margarine*)

1 Cook spinach and pass through sieve.
2 Place in pan with butter and dry on stove.
3 Add 30 g (1 oz) grated cheese.
4 Place in buttered dish and sprinkle with remaining cheese and melted butter (or margarine).
5 Place in hot oven to glaze.

836 Épinards en branches – Spinach in leaf

750 *g* (1½ *lb*) *leaf spinach*   *boiling salt water*

1 Remove thick stalks from leaves.
2 Wash leaves well two or three times.
3 Half cook in plenty of boiling salted water.
4 Cool and squeeze in the hands to expel water.
5 Use as required.

837 Épinards en branches au beurre

750 g (1½ lb) leaf spinach
salt, pepper, grated nutmeg

pinch of caster sugar
60 g (2 oz) butter

1 Prepare and cook as Recipe 836.
2 Loosen leaves with a fork.
3 Melt butter in pan and finish cooking spinach in this.
4 Season with a pinch of sugar, salt, pepper and grated nutmeg.

838 Soufflé aux épinards

240 g (½ lb) spinach purée
125 ml (¼ pt) Béchamel sauce
  (Recipe 51)
30 g (1 oz) Parmesan cheese
12 anchovy fillets (optional)

60 g (2 oz) butter (or sunflower
  margarine)
3 eggs
seasoning

1 Heat spinach and Béchamel.
2 Add egg yolks and cheese; season.
3 Cool and add the beaten egg whites.
4 Place a layer of mixture in bottom of well-buttered soufflé dish.
5 Make a trellis of anchovy on top (optional).
6 Build up successive layers, finishing with anchovies.
7 Cook as for ordinary soufflé.

839 Subric d'épinards

125 ml (¼ pt) reduced Béchamel
  (Recipe 51)
750 g (1½ lb) spinach purée
60 g (2 oz) butter (or sunflower
  margarine)
1 egg

grated nutmeg
62 ml (⅛ pt) cream (or fromage
  frais or yogurt)
2 yolks
salt, pepper

1 Heat the spinach purée and add butter.
2 Dry in hot oven.
3 Add Béchamel, cream, eggs, seasoning and mix well.
4 Heat some butter in frying-pan.
5 Drop some spinach from a spoon into the pan.
6 Cook both sides like a pancake.
7 Dish and serve.

840 Fenouil – Fennel

Same weight and cooking procedure as cardons – cardoons.

FÈVES – BEANS

841 Broad Beans – Grosses Fèves (to boil)

500 g (1 *lb*) *shelled broad beans*   *salted water*
1 *small bunch savoury**   *seasoning*

1 Cook beans in salted water with savoury.
2 Drain and add savoury (chopped).

842 Fèves au beurre

Ingredients as for Recipe 841 with 60 g (2 oz) butter.
Cook beans as Recipe 841; drain and dry on fire and finish with butter.

843 Fèves à la crème

Ingredients as for Recipe 841 with 62 ml (⅛ pt) cream.
Prepare as Recipe 841 but lié with fresh cream.

844 Purée de fèves

Prepare as for purée of peas.

FLAGEOLETS

845 Flageolets – Small kidney beans (to boil)

500 g (1 *lb*) *flageolets*   *bouquet garni*
1 *small carrot*   *salted water*

1 Place all ingredients in pan and cover with cold water, salted.
2 Bring to boil and cook until tender.
3 Withdraw carrot, onion, and bouquet garni.
4 Drain beans and finish as required.

Note. Dried flageolets will require preliminary overnight soaking.

846 Flageolets au beurre

Prepare as Recipe 845 but finish with 60 g (2 oz) butter.

847 Flageolets en purée (or purée musard)

Prepare as for purée of peas (Recipe 885). Flageolet purée is also used for
thickening purée of French beans.

---

*This herb is also known as summer savoury.

HARICOTS

848 Haricots blancs – Haricot beans (to prepare)

240 g (½ lb) beans   1 small carrot
750 ml (1½ pt) cold water   1 small onion
bouquet garni   seasoning

1 Soak beans for 12 hours and wash.
2 Place all ingredients in pan and cover with water.
3 Bring to boil and allow to cook slowly until tender.
4 Withdraw aromatics and dry beans on top of stove.
5 Treat as required.

849 Haricots blancs à l'américaine

125 ml (¼ pt) tomato sauce   120 g (¼ lb) lean bacon
  (Recipe 34)   750 ml (1½ pt) water
1 small onion   250 ml (½ pt) beans
bouquet garni   1 small carrot

1 Prepare and cook as Recipe 848.
2 Cut bacon into dice and add to beans.
3 Bind beans with good tomato sauce.

850 Haricots blancs au beurre

1 Cook as for Américaine, Recipe 849, but without bacon.
2 Finish with 30 g (1 oz) butter.
3 Sprinkle with chopped parsley 4 g (⅛ oz).

851 Haricots blancs à la bretonne

Ingredients as for Recipe 849 with 120 g (¼ lb) tomato concassé, 30 g (1 oz)
butter, 1 clove garlic.

1 Prepare and cook as Recipe 848.
2 Drain and blend with the extra ingredients.

852 Haricots blancs en purée (or purée soissonnaise)

1 Prepare and cook in usual manner.
2 Drain and, while hot, pass through sieve.
3 Mix purée in pan with 45 g (1½ oz) butter and adjust consistency with hot
  milk.

853 Haricots rouges au vin – Red beans

240 g (½ lb) beans   120 g (¼ lb) bacon   125 ml (¼ pt) red
                                                   wine

1 Soak and prepare as Recipe 848.
2 Cook in a mixture of wine and water with the bacon.
3 Dice the bacon as a garnish.

854 Haricots verts au beurre – French beans

500 g (1 *lb*) *French*   60 g (2 *oz*) *butter*   *salted water*
    beans

1 If necessary, remove string from beans.
2 Place beans in boiling salted water.
3 When cooked, beans should be slightly firm.
4 Drain and dry on stove.
5 Finish with butter and seasoning.

855 Haricots verts en purée (or purée favorite)

360 g (¾ *lb*) *French beans*   125 *ml* (¼ *pt*) *purée of flageolets*
                                   (*Recipe* 847)

1 When cooked, drain and dry beans.
2 Place 45 g (1½ oz) butter in beans and stew slightly.
3 Pass beans through a sieve.
4 Mix flageolets purée 125 ml (¼ pt) with French beans purée 250 ml (½ pt).

JETS DE HOUBLON

856 Jets de houblon – Hop sprouts (or shoots)

1 *lb*) *for* 4 *covers*

1 Prepare as asparagus.
2 Serve with hollandaise sauce or melted butter.

LENTILLES

857 Lentilles – Lentils

Cook as for haricot beans.

LAITUE – LETTUCE

858 Laitues braisées – Braised lettuce

See Recipe 754 and dress as braised celery (Recipe 784).

859 Laitues farcies

Prepare as chou farci (Recipes 802 or 803) but riz pilaff (Recipe 366) may also be used as forcemeat.

MAIS – CORN

860 Mais nature – Corn on the cob

4 *corn on the cob*
10 *ml spoon* [½ *tablespoon*] *salt*
90 *g* (3 *oz*) *melted butter*

125 *ml* (¼ *pt*) *milk*
1 *litre* (1 *qt*) *water*

1 Boil the water with the milk and salt.
2 Wash the corn and cook whole with the leaves.
3 Cooking time, 20 minutes.
4 Drain, serve with leaves drawn back on a serviette.
5 Melted butter or sauce hollandaise served separately.

Note. For certain garnishes the grains are separated from the stalk and treated as required.

861 Maïs à la crème – Creamed corn

4 *corn on the cob*
10 *ml spoon* [½ *tablespoon*] *caster sugar*
62 *ml* (⅛ *pt*) *cream*

30 *g* (1 *oz*) *butter* (*or sunflower margarine*)
salt

1 Cook the corn and scrape off the ears.
2 Place the ears in a pan and sweat with butter (or margarine); add the cream, sugar and salt.

Note. Creamed corn or sweetcorn may be bought prepared in cans.

MARRONS – CHESTNUTS

862 Chestnuts (to shell)

1 Split open the shell with a small, sharp knife.
2 Place in a hot oven for 5 minutes and remove the shells when hot.

863 Marrons braisés – Braised chestnuts

500 *g* (1 *lb*) *marrons* (*gross weight*)
190 *ml* (⅜ *pt*) *brown stock* (*Recipe 10*)

15 *g* (½ *oz*) *butter* (*or sunflower margarine*)
pinch sugar
salt, pepper

1 Place in sauté-pan with butter and sweat for a few minutes.
2 Moisten with veal stock and simmer under cover until tender.
3 Strain and keep the chestnuts hot while reducing the liquor to a glaze.
4 Roll the chestnuts in the glaze; serve in a casserole, sprinkle with chopped parsley before service.

864 Marrons etuvés – Stewed chestnuts

1 With a pointed knife slit on side of the shell.
2 Place in frying-basket and plunge into hot fat.
3 Remove shell and skin.
4 Place in pan and cover with white stock (Recipe 6).
5 Stew gently until cooked.

865 Marrons glacés au jus – Glazed chestnuts

1 Prepare as Recipe 864.
2 Cook in strong stock.
3 When almost cooked, remove chestnuts.
4 Reduce stock to a glaze.
5 Roll chestnuts in the glaze.

NAVETS – TURNIPS

866 Navets de Suède en purée – Swede purée or
Navets en purée – Turnip purée

750 g (1½ lb) swedes or turnips   60 g (2 oz) butter (or sunflower
salt, pepper   margarine)

1 Wash, peel and cut into large dice.
2 Place in cold water with salt and simmer until tender.
3 Drain and dry well.
4 Rub through a sieve; beat until creamy and blend in butter (or margarine)
  and seasoning.
5 Place in hot vegetable dish and ridge with palette knife.

Lunch service usually.

867 Navets or navets de Suède glacés

As for carottes glacées (Recipe 781).

868 Turnip tops

Leaves of young turnip-tops may be treated and cooked as for choux verts à
l'anglaise or as spinach.

OIGNONS – ONIONS

869 Oignons braisés – Braised onions

Prepare as for other braised vegetables, e.g. Recipe 758.

870 Oignons farcis – Stuffed onions

duxelles stuffing (Recipe 102)   *prepared braising pan*
4 large Spanish onions

1 Peel and cut off top of onions.
2 Half-cook onions in water.
3 Drain and withdraw centre of onions.
4 Chop withdrawn section and mix with equal quantity of duxelles.
5 Stuff onions with this mixture.
6 Braise onions in usual manner.
7 Serve with sauce made by thickening (with fécule or roux), the cooking liquor.

871 Oignons frits à la française – French-fried onions

4 fairly large Spanish onions   *milk*
salt   *flour*

1 Slice onions into rings approximately 0.4 cm (⅕ inch) thick.
2 Separate rings and place in milk.
3 Drain and dredge in flour.
4 Shake well in a cane colander or sieve.
5 Fry in deep fat until crisp and golden brown; season.

872 Petits oignons glacés (bruns) – Brown-glazed button onions

Quantity. Allow 500 g–750 g (1 lb–1½ lb) for service as a principal vegetable accompaniment but only 240 g (½ lb) as garnish.

1 Carefully peel the onions.
2 Place butter (or margarine or oil) in the bottom of a sauté-pan; heat and place in the onions.
3 Sprinkle some sugar on top.
4 Allow to cook slowly; the sugar caramelizes to give glaze and colour.

Alternative method
After step 2:
3 Fry the onions quickly until browned.
4 Cover with brown stock (Recipe 8), sprinkle with sugar, bring to boil until cooked and the stock reduced.
5 Toss in the glaze.

873 Petits oignons glacés (à blanc) – White-glazed button onions

Quantity. As Recipe 872.

1 Cover the peeled onions with white stock, adding 30 g (1 oz) butter per 250 ml (½ pint) of stock.
2 Cook onions slowly.
3 Drain, reduce cooking-liquor to give a glaze.
4 Roll the onions in this glaze before serving.

OKRA – GUMBO OR LADIES FINGERS

874 Okra aux tomates

240 g (½ lb) tomato concassé   480 g (1 lb) fresh okra
15 g (½ oz) butter (or sunflower   salt, pepper
  margarine)   30 g (1 oz) sliced onions

1 Stew the onions in butter.
2 Add the tomatoes and sweat for a few minutes.
3 Add the cleaned, trimmed okra and stew for 10 minutes under cover; season.

875 Oseille – Sorrel

This astringent-tasting leaf is of the common dock family and may be prepared as spinach: it is used in soups and omelettes as garnish rather than as a separate vegetable.

Preparation of sorrel for garnish:
1 Shred the leaves finely and wash thoroughly two or three times in cold water.
2 Place in a well-buttered braising-pan, cover with buttered greaseproof paper and cover with lid.
3 Bring to the boil then transfer to the oven to complete cooking.
4 When cooked, fill small jars with the sorrel and allow to cool.
5 When cold, cover with melted butter (or margarine) and keep in refrigerator until required.

PANAIS – PARSNIPS

876 Panais à la crème – Parsnips with cream

62 ml (⅛ pt) cream sauce   750 g (1½ lb) parsnips
  (Recipe 63)   seasoning
30 g (1 oz) butter (or sunflower   62 ml (⅛ pt) cream
  margarine)   lemon juice

1 Wash, peel and cut the parsnips into sections and turn as for carrots.
2 Cook in salted, acidulated water until tender.
3 Drain well, toss in butter (or margarine), lié with the sauce and cream; season.

877 Panais au beurre

750 g (1½ lb) parsnips   60 g (2 oz) butter   seasoning

1 Prepare and cook as for à la crème (Recipe 876).
2 Drain and toss in butter; season.

878 Panais aux fines herbes

750 g (1½ lb) parsnips	*60 g (2 oz) butter (or*
	  sunflower
	  margarine)
		7g (¼ oz) fines
		  herbes

Prepare as for au beurre with addition of fines herbes.

PATATES (or *PATATES DOUCES*) – *SWEET POTATOES*

879 Patates en croquettes

500 g (1 lb) sweet
  potatoes
  egg-wash
	deep fat
	  1 egg yolk
	  flour
		120 g (¼ lb) white
		  crumbs
		  seasoning

1 Peel potatoes by hand, thinly.
2 Prepare as for duchesse (Recipe 909) and make into small croquettes.
3 Fry in deep fat.

Note. Sweet potatoes may be prepared as duchesse, au four, or sauté, or plainly boiled and rolled in caramelized sugar.

PETITS POIS – *PEAS*

880 Petits pois à l'anglaise

500 ml (1 pt) shelled
  peas
  salt
	30 g (1 oz) butter (or
	  sunflower
	  margarine)

1 Cook in plenty of salt water; drain and season.
2 Add a pinch of sugar and toss in butter (or margarine).

881 Petits pois à la bonne-femme

6 button onions
250 ml (½ pt) white stock
  (Recipe 6)
salt, sugar
60 g (2 oz) diced bacon
	500 ml (1 pt) shelled peas (fresh or
	  frozen)
	30 g (1 oz) butter
	15 g (½ oz) flour

1 Blanch and refresh bacon.
2 Put butter in pan and fry bacon lightly.
3 Add flour and cook slightly.
4 Moisten with stock and boil.
5 Add peas and onions and finish cooking.
6 Season with salt and sugar.

882 Petits pois à la française

500 ml (1 pt) peas *6 button onions* *½ lettuce*	*30 g (1 oz) butter* *salt, sugar* *pepper*	Beurre manié: *30 g (1 oz) butter* *30 g (1 oz) flour*

1 Shred lettuce.
2 Place in pan with rest of ingredients.
3 Half-cover with white stock or water.
4 Cover with lid and cook.
5 Lié with beurre manié.

883 Petits pois à la menthe

1 Same as for à l'anglaise (Recipe 880) but add a bunch of fresh mint.
2 Serve with blanched fresh mint leaves on top.

884 petits pois à la flamande

375 ml (¾ pt) peas   *120 g (¼ lb) carrots*

1 Prepare carrots as for glacé (Recipe 781) and par-cook.
2 Add peas. Complete the cooking. Adjust seasoning and serve.

885 Petits pois en purée – Purée of fresh peas

few parsley leaves	*½ lettuce*
boiling water to cover	*sugar, salt*
500 ml (1 pt) peas	*butter (or sunflower margarine)*

1 Cover peas with water.
2 Add lettuce and parsley (tied).
3 Season with teaspoonful each of salt and sugar, and cook.
4 Drain peas and reduce cooking-liquor.
5 Pass through a sieve.
6 Add 60 g (2 oz) butter (or margarine) per litre (quart) of purée and finish
  with liquor; reduce to a glaze.

886 Petits pois mange-tout

Mange tout, literally 'eat all', means that this type of pea is completely edible
including the pod. The unshelled, but stalked, peas are simmered then
dressed with butter.

PIMENTS DOUX – CAPSICUMS OR SWEET PEPPERS

The red and green sweet peppers are not really pimentos, though often so
called. True pimento yields the berry known as allspice. Although the seeds
must be removed from both red and green pappers, it is not necessary to skin
them though this is often done.

887 Piments doux farcis au riz – Peppers stuffed with rice

four 90 g (3 oz) pimentos	*190 ml (⅜ pt) brown stock*
120 g (¼ lb) rice pilaff (Recipe	*(Recipe 8)*
366)	*7 g (¼ oz) arrowroot*
	seasoning

1 If desired to remove the skins, brush with butter (or oil) and expose under
  grill momentarily.

2 Remove all seeds from inside.
3 Fill with rice pilaff.
4 Braise in stock until tender.
5 When cooked, remove and dress in oval dish – season.
6 Reduce cooking-liquor, thicken with diluted arrowroot (if desired), strain and serve separately.

888 Peppers for salads and hors-d'œuvre

Peppers, especially green ones, are widely used in salads; they may be shredded raw, mixed with onions and vinaigrette (Recipe 118) and served as hors d'œuvre.

POIREAUX – LEEKS

889 Poireaux au gratin

four 180 g (6 oz) *leeks*
15 g (½ oz) *grated Parmesan cheese*

190 ml (⅜ pt) *Mornay sauce* (*Recipe* 58)
seasoning

1 Wash and trim the leeks.
2 Tie in a bundle and cook until tender in boiling salted water.
3 Drain well: fold in two.
4 Coat with Mornay sauce, sprinkle with Parmesan cheese and brown under the grill.

890 Poireaux à la milanaise

22 g (¾ oz) *grated Parmesan cheese*

15 g (½ oz) *butter blanc* (*Recipe* 757)

four 180 g (6 oz) *leeks*

1 Prepare in bundles as Recipe 889.
2 Cook à blanc.
3 Place on a well-buttered dish.
4 Dress the leeks on top; sprinkle with cheese; brown under grill.

POMMES DE TERRE

Pommes de terre is the full French term for potatoes, and its literal translation is 'apples of the earth'. Usually, it is contracted to 'pommes'. As 'pommes' are apples, the context will indicate whether potatoes or apples are involved.

POMMES NOUVELLES – NEW POTATOES

891 Pommes nouvelles à l'anglaise

750 g (1½ lb) *new potatoes*

boiling salted water

1 Wash potatoes well, do not peel.
2 Place in pan and cover with boiling water, salted.
3 Bring to boil and cook slowly 20 to 25 minutes.
4 Drain and peel potatoes. Serve very hot.

892 Pommes nouvelles à la menthe – Minted new potatoes

750 g (1½ lb) new   boiling, salted water   2 or 3 sprigs mint
    potatoes

1 Cook as for à l'anglaise with mint added.
2 When peeled, dress potatoes with blanched mint leaf on top of each potato.

893 Pommes nouvelles persillées

750 g (1½ lb) new potatoes   boiling, salted water
45 g (1½ oz) butter (or sunflower   7 g (¼ oz) chopped parsley
    margarine)

1 Prepare and cook as for à l'anglaise (Recipe 891).
2 When peeled, toss in butter (or margarine).
3 Sprinkle with chopped parsley.

MAIN CROP OR 'OLD' POTATOES

894 Old potatoes (to boil)

1 Trim or turn to château (barrel) shape.
2 Cover with cold salted water.
3 Bring to boil and cook steadily (avoiding over-rapid, jostling boil which breaks up the structure).
4 May be dressed and served as above.

895 Pommes à la vapeur – Steamed potatoes

1 Trim to small château (large olive or barrel) shape.
2 Place on a tray preferably napkin-wrapped and cook in a steamer.
3 Serve with boiled fish, salmon, and turbot, etc.

896 Pommes en purée or pommes purées – Mashed potato

750 g (1½ lb) potatoes   62 ml (⅛ pt) boiled milk (whole,
30 g (1 oz) butter (or sunflower   semi-skimmed or skimmed)
    margarine)   grated nutmeg
cold, salted water   seasoning

1 Peel and quarter potatoes.
2 Cook as for à l'anglaise (Recipe 894).
3 Drain and dry potatoes.
4 Pass through sieve.
5 Place in pan and add milk and butter.
6 Season and beat until smooth and creamy over low heat.

897 Pommes en purée à la crème – Mashed potatoes with cream

750 g (1½ lb) peeled potatoes
62 ml (⅛ pt) boiled milk (whole,
   semi-skimmed or skimmed)
cold, salted water

30 g (1 oz) butter
grated nutmeg, pepper
30 ml (2 tbsp.) fresh cream

1 Prepare as for purée.
2 Dish potatoes on service dish.
3 Cover with cream which has been heated.

898 Pommes en purée au gratin

750 g (1½ lb) potatoes
62 ml (⅛ pt) (whole, semi-
   skimmed or skimmed)
cold, salted water

30 g (1 oz) butter
15 g (½ oz) grated cheese
grated nutmeg, pepper

1 Prepare as for purée (Recipe 896).
2 Dish on service dish.
3 Sprinkle with cheese.
4 Brown under the salamander.

899 Soufflé de pommes de terre – Potato soufflé

750 g (1½ lb) peeled potatoes
30 g (1 oz) butter
cold, salted water

62 ml (⅛ pt) boiled milk (whole,
   semi-skimmed or skimmed)
grated nutmeg, pepper
2 eggs

1 Prepare as for purée (Recipe 896).
2 Add the yolks of the eggs and beat well.
3 Whip the whites and fold into mixture.
4 Place in buttered soufflé-dish.
5 Cook as for ordinary soufflé.

Note. This method must not be confused with deep-fried pommes soufflées
(Recipe 931).

900 Pommes en robe de chambre – Steamed jacket-potatoes or belted
    potatoes

8 large, even-sized potatoes

1 Wash potatoes well and dry with a cloth.
2 Cut half-inch ribbon of skin full circumference of potato.
3 Place on tray and cook in steamer.
4 Dress on serviette with branch parsley.

ROAST, OVEN-BROWNED, AND DERIVATIVE METHODS

901 Pommes rôties – Roast potatoes

500 g (1 lb) even-sized potatoes   60 g (2 oz) fat (or oil)
      (peeled)   salt

1 Heat fat in roasting-tray.
2 Place in potatoes and roll until they are coated with fat or oil; sprinkle with salt.
3 Place in hot oven until cooked and golden brown; drain and serve.

902 Pommes château

750 g (1½ lb) potatoes turned to   30 g (1 oz) butter
      barrel-shape 4 cm (2 inches   60 g (2 oz) fat (or oil)
      long)   7 g (¼ oz) chopped parsley
salt

Cook as Recipe 901, but drain and toss in butter and sprinkle with chopped parsley.

Note. Par-boiling for pommes château (and also pommes rôties) is resorted to in some kitchens to reduce oven-times, but the result is less satisfactory.

903 Pommes noisettes

750g (1½ lb) potatoes   60 g (2 oz) butter (or sunflower
salt   margarine or oil)

Cut potatoes to hazel-nut size with the special spoon-shaped cutter and cook in butter (or alternative) until golden brown.

904 Pommes parisiennes

750 g (1½ lb) potatoes   60 g (2 oz) butter (or   meat glaze
salt   sunflower margarine   7 g (¼ oz) chopped
                                  or oil)   parsley

1 Cut with parisienne spoon (or scoop) in similar style to Recipe 903, but larger.
2 Cook in the same manner.
3 Before serving, roll in melted meat-glaze and sprinkle with chopped parsley.

905 Pommes Parmentier

750 g (1½ lb) potatoes in 1 cm   62 ml (⅛ pt) oil
      (½-inch) cubes   salt

1 Heat fat in roasting-tray.
2 Place in potatoes and toss until coated with oil.
3 Cook in hot oven until brown.
4 Drain and season.

906 Pommes pavées

750 g (1½ lb) potatoes in 2 cm   *62 ml (⅛ pt) oil*
(1-inch) cubes   *salt*

Prepare as for Parmentier, Recipe 905.

907 Pommes sablées

As for Parmentier but just before completion of cooking, sprinkle liberally
with 60 g (2 oz) white (or wholemeal) breadcrumbs; drain and serve.

908 Pommes olivettes

750 g (1½ lb) potatoes   *60 g (2 oz) butter (or sunflower*
salt   *margarine)*

Cut with special parisienne-type cutter in the shape of small olives and cook
as for noisette.

DUCHESSE POTATOES AND DERIVATIVES

909 Pommes duchesse

750 g (1½ lb) peeled	*30 g (1 oz) butter (or*	*salt*
potatoes	*sunflower*	*pepper*
2 egg yolks	*margarine)*	*grated nutmeg*

1 Boil potatoes until cooked.
2 Drain and dry well.
3 Mash potatoes and add butter (or margarine) and seasoning.
4 Beat in egg yolks.
4 Place potatoes in piping-bag with star-tube.
6 Pipe potatoes in rosette shape on to buttered tray.
7 Brush with egg-wash and brown in hot oven.
8 Finish by brushing with melted butter (or margarine).

910 Pommes marquise

750 g (1½ lb) pommes duchesse   *90 g (3 oz) tomato purée (or cooked*
(Recipe 909)   *tomato concassé, see note to*
     method below)

1 Beat purée of tomato into potatoes.
2 Pipe and finish as for pommes duchesse.

Note. Pommes marquise may be piped in the form of a duchesse nest with
tomato concassé filling. This style is now more popular.

911 Pommes St-Florentin

750 g (1½ lb) pommes duchesse   *90 g (3 oz) chopped lean ham*
(Recipe 909)   *60 g (2 oz) crushed vermicelli*

1 Mix duchesse with chopped ham, place on floured board and roll into cylinder.
2 Flatten into an oblong.
3 Slice into 60 g (2-oz) portions.
4 Dip in egg-wash and then in vermicelli. (Some chefs add also a little white breadcrumbs).
5 Fry in deep oil.

912 Pommes Berny

750 g (1½ lb) pommes   60 g (2 oz) chopped   flaked (or nib)
   duchesse (Recipe   truffles (optional)   almonds
   909)   egg-wash

1 Mix truffles through potatoes.
2 Form potatoes the size and shape of an apricot.
3 Dip in egg-wash and roll in almonds.
4 With the back of a small knife make a slight incision on top and insert a short piece of parsley stalk (optional).
5 Fry in hot deep oil.

913 Pommes croquettes

750 g (1½ lb) duchesse potato   egg-wash
   (Recipe 909)   flour and breadcrumbs

1 Place potatoes on floured board.
2 Roll into long cylinder.
3 Cut off in cork-sized lengths 60 g (2 oz each).
4 Dip in egg-wash then breadcrumbs.
5 Place in basket; fry in hot deep oil.

DUCHESSE WITH CHOUX-PASTE

914 Pommes Dauphine

750 g (1½ lb) pommes duchesse   250 g (½ lb) choux paste
   (Recipe 909)   (Recipe 999 but unsweetened)

1 Combine potatoes and choux paste.
2 Mould with tablespoons on greased paper and form into cylinders, 60 g (2 oz) each.
3 Fry in deep oil.

915 Pommes Lorette

750 g (1½ lb) pommes Dauphine   45 g (1½ oz) grated Parmesan
   (Recipe 914)   cheese

1 Mix cheese and potatoes.
2 Form into cigar shapes, 60 g (2 oz) each.
3 Fry in deep fat.

JACKET-BAKED AND DERIVATIVE

916 Pommes au four – Jacket-baked potatoes

8 *large potatoes*	45 g (1½ oz) butter (or sunflower
rock salt	margarine)

1 Wash potatoes and dry well with a clean cloth.
2 Cover bottom of tray with salt.
3 Place potatoes on top.
4 Bake in oven until tender.
5 Dress potatoes on serviette.
6 Make a cross-wise incision with pointed knife on potatoes.
7 Pull back potato-skin and place piece of butter in cavity.

917 Pommes Macaire

1 Prepare as for pommes au four (Recipe 916).
2 When cooked, scoop out pulp.
3 Season with salt and pepper.
4 Mash with fork and add 60 g (2 oz) butter (or sunflower margarine).
5 Shape like fish cakes.
6 Fry in pan with butter (or sunflower margarine and oil), browning both sides.

918 Pommes Byron

1 Prepare as for pommes Macaire (Recipe 917).
2 When fried, sprinkle with cream and grated cheese.
3 Glaze under salamander.

919 Pommes Robert

1 Prepare as for pommes Macaire (Recipe 917) with the addition of 3 egg yolks and a good pinch of chopped chives per 500 g (1 lb) of potato.
2 Finish as for Macaire.

920 Pommes de terre gratinées

1 Prepare as for pommes au four (Recipe 916) and when baked halve the potatoes lengthwise.
2 Withdraw the pulp and make as for pommes purée (Recipe 896).
3 With piping-bag refill the halves with the purée.
4 Sprinkle with grated cheese and brown in hot oven.
5 Serve on a serviette.

SAUTER OR SHALLOW-FRY

921 Pommes sautées

750 g (1½ lb) unpeeled potatoes

1 Wash potatoes well and cook in steamer.
2 Peel and cut in slices 0.5 cm (¼ inch) thick.
3 Sauté in oil in frying-pan until brown.
4 Drain well and season; sprinkle with chopped parsley.

922　Pommes sautées à la provençale

Prepare as sautées (Recipe 921) with the addition of chopped garlic.

923　Pommes sautées à la lyonnaise

1 Prepare as for pommes sautées (Recipe 921) with sauté onions mixed through.
2 Use one-third onions to potato.

DEEP FRIED

924　Pommes frites

> 1 *kg (2 lb) peeled potatoes*

1 Square off potatoes with knife.
2 Cut in 4 cm (2 inch) long bâtons 1 cm (½ inch) thick.
3 Wash well, drain, and fry in deep oil.
4 When cooked, drain and sprinkle with salt.

925　Pommes allumettes

Prepare as pommes frites (Recipe 924) but cut in 3 cm (1½ inch) long batons 0.5 cm (¼ inch) thick. (**Pommes mignonette** are similar but slightly thicker.)

926　Pommes bataille

Prepare as pommes frites (Recipe 924) but cut in cubes of 1.5 cm (¾ inch).

927　Pommes chips – Game chips (or crisps)

1 Cut in thin slices on mandolin.
2 Wash well: drain, and dry.
3 Cook in hot oil until golden and crisp.
4 Sprinkle with salt.

928　Pommes collerettes

1 Trim potatoes in cylinder-shape.
2 Groove sides with channel knife.
3 Slice thinly on mandolin.
4 Finish as for pommes chips.

929　Pommes pailles – Straw potatoes

1 Cut in julienne.
2 Wash well and cook in hot fat until golden and crisp.
3 Sprinkle with salt.

930 Pommes Pont-Neuf

Prepare as pommes frites (Recipe 924) but cut in 4 cm (2 inch) lengths 1.5 cm (¾ inch) thick.

931 Pommes soufflées

1 Trim the potatoes square.
2 Cut the slice 0.3 cm (⅛ inch) thick.
3 Dry well on clean cloth.
4 Put into moderately hot oil.
5 When cooked they rise to the surface.
6 Drain into frying-basket.
7 Plunge into hot oil.
8 Fry until golden brown and soufflée-d; salt.

STEWED AND CASSEROLE

932 Pommes à la dauphinoise (gratin dauphinois)

750 g (1½ lb) peeled potatoes
500 ml (1 pt) boiled milk (whole,
  semi-skimmed or skimmed)
1 egg
30 g (1 oz) butter (or sunflower
  margarine)

90 g (3 oz) grated Gruyère (or
  Cheddar) cheese
1 clove garlic
salt
pepper
grated nutmeg

1 Slice potatoes thinly.
2 Mix milk, egg and cheese, reserving 15 g (½ oz) cheese.
3 Mix potatoes with this mixture and season.
4 Rub an earthenware dish with garlic and butter (or margarine).
5 Fill with potato mixture.
6 Sprinkle with cheese and butter (or margarine).
7 Cook in moderate oven for 40 to 45 minutes.

933 Pommes à la savoyarde

750 g (1½ lb) peeled potatoes
500 ml (1 pt) white stock
  (Recipe 6)
45 g (1½ oz grated Gruyère (or
  Cheddar) cheese

salt
pepper
butter (or sunflower margarine)
grated nutmeg
garlic

Prepare as for pommes dauphinoise (Recipe 932).

934 Pommes Delmonico

750 g (1½ lb) potatoes cut in 1 cm
  (½-inch) cubes
white (or wholemeal)
  breadcrumbs

salt
375 ml (¾ pt) milk (whole, semi-
  skimmed or skimmed)

1 Almost cover potatoes with milk.
2 Season, bring to boil, and cook in oven.
3 Sprinkle liberally with breadcrumbs on top before they are cooked giving them time to brown.

935 Pommes maître-d'hôtel

750 g (1½ lb) medium-sized
   potatoes
375 ml (¾ pt) boiling milk (whole,
   semi-skimmed or skimmed)

cold salted water
7 g (¼ oz) chopped parsley
salt
pepper

1 Cook potatoes in salted water.
2 Peel while still hot.
3 Cut into round slices.
4 Cover with boiling milk
5 Season with salt and pepper.
6 Reduce the milk by half.
7 Place in service dish and sprinkle with chopped parsley.

936 Pommes maire

Prepare as for maître-d'hôtel (Recipe 935) using cream instead of milk and omitting parsley.

937 Pommes à la boulangère

750 g (1½ lb) peeled potatoes
240 g (½ lb) onions
chopped parsley (optional)
salt, pepper

white stock (Recipe 6)
60 g (2 oz) butter (or sunflower
   margarine)

1 Slice potatoes and onions finely.
2 Fry onions in butter (or margarine), slightly browning them.
3 Mix potatoes with onions and season.
4 Place in deep earthenware dish with bouquet garni.
5 Moisten with white stock and bring to boil.
6 Cook in oven until brown and stock has almost evaporated.
7 Withdraw bouquet garni; brush potatoes with melted butter (or margarine).

FONDANT STYLE

938 Pommes fondantes

750 g (1½ lb) potatoes turned to
   barrel shape [5 cm (2½ inches
   long)]
salt, pepper

45 g (1½ oz) butter (or sunflower
   margarine)
7 g (¼ oz) chopped parsley
white stock (Recipe 6)

1 Melt butter in tray.
2 Place in potatoes and toss.
3 Season, half cover with stock.
4 Bring to boil and place in oven.
5 Cook until golden brown and stock has almost evaporated.
6 Brush with melted butter (or margarine) and sprinkle with parsley.

939 Pommes à la berrichonne

750 g (1½ lb) château potatoes (Recipe 902)	120 g (¼ lb) diced onions 120 g (¼ lb) lardons	white stock (Recipe 6) 7 g (¼ oz) chopped parsley

As for pommes fondantes (Recipe 938).

ANNA AND DERIVATIVE STYLES

940 Pommes Anna

750 g (1½ lb) peeled potatoes   60 g (2 oz) melted butter (or
salt, pepper   sunflower margarine)

1 Trim potatoes in cylinder-shape.
2 Well oil (or butter) a pommes-Anna mould.
3 Slice potatoes thinly in circles.
4 Place potatoes in circles in bottom of mould overlapping each slice.
5 Butter and season each layer.
6 Build up layers until almost to the top of the mould.
7 Place in fairly hot oven and cook approximately for 30 to 40 minutes; turn out of mould.

941 Pommes Nana (for garnishes)

1 Prepare as for pommes Anna (Recipe 940) but cut into julienne.
2 Cook in well-buttered dariole moulds.

942 Pommes Voisin

1 Prepare as for pommes Anna (Recipe 940).
2 Sprinkle each layer of potato with grated cheese.
3 Cook as for pommes Anna.

POTIRON – PUMPKIN

943 Potiron à la provençale

750 g (1½ lb) pumpkin   500 g (1 lb) tomato concassé
120 g (¼ lb) sliced onions   4 g (⅛ oz) chopped parsley
62 ml (⅛ pt) oil   seasoning
1 clove crushed garlic

1 Skin the pumpkin and remove seeds.
2 Cut into small collops.
3 Sauté the onions to golden brown.
4 Remove onions and drain well.
5 Quickly sauté the scollops of pumpkin in the oil remaining from the onions; add the garlic and tomato concassé; season and add the cooked onions.
6 Serve with chopped parsley.

Note. Pumpkin may be plainly boiled and served with sauce hollandaise (Recipe 70), Mornay sauce (Recipe 58) or with cream. In such cases, cut into sizes of 6 cm by 4 cm (3 by 2 inches).

SALSIFIS – SALSIFY OR OYSTER PLANT

944 Salsifis à la crème – Salsify in cream

1 Wash and peel salsify and place in acidulated water.
2 Cook à blanc.
3 Drain and dry; cut into 4 cm (2-inch) lengths.
4 Bind with cream sauce.

945 Salsifis sautés

1 Cook in blanc (Recipe 757) and cut in 4 cm (2 inch) lengths.
2 Sauté in butter (or margarine) until well browned.
3 Season and serve.

946 Salsifis à la poulette

> 500 g (1 *lb*) *salsifis*   *seasoning*
> 125 *ml* (¼ *pt*) *sauce poulette*   30 g (1 *oz*) *butter* (*or sunflower*
>   (*Recipe* 59)   *margarine*)
> *blanc* (*Recipe* 757)   *lemon juice*

1 Wash well and scrape with peeler.
2 Place in lemon water as they are cleaned.
3 Cut into 4 cm (2 inch) lengths; cook à blanc.
4 Drain well; toss in butter, finish off in sauce poulette.

947 Salsifis aux fines herbes

> 500 g (1 *lb*) *salsifis*   60 g (2 *oz*) *butter* (*or sunflower*
> 7 g (¼ *oz*) *fines herbes*   *margarine*)

1 Cook as for salsifis poulette (Recipe 946).
2 Drain well, toss in butter with the fines herbes; season.

948 Salsifis frits

500 g (1 lb) salsifis	2.5 ml spoon	125 ml (¼ pt)
62 ml (⅛ pt) oil	[½ teaspoon]	coating batter
seasoning	chopped parsley	(Recipe 1001)
62 ml (⅛ pt) vinegar	½ lemon	

1 Wash and scrape with peeler.
2 Cut into 4 cm (2 inch) lengths.
3 Cook in salt water with lemon juice.
4 Drain and place in oil, vinegar, and parsley for 20 minutes.
5 Drain and dip in batter; fry in deep fat; drain.
6 Garnish with fried parsley.

TOMATOES

949 Tomates concassées – Chopped tomato

4 *large tomatoes*	30 g (1 oz) butter (or sunflower
1 *small finely chopped onion*	margarine)
seasoning	pinch sugar

1 Blanch and skin tomatoes.
2 Cut in half.
3 Scoop out seeds and express juice.
4 Cut tomato in dice.
5 Sweat onions in butter (or margarine) without colouring them.
6 Add diced tomatoes and seasoning.
7 Cook for 5 minutes and finish with a small pinch of sugar.

950 Tomates farcies au gratin

4 *tomatoes*	120 g (¼ lb) duxelles stuffing
30 g (1 oz) butter (or olive oil or	(Recipe 102)
margarine)	60 g (2 oz) white breadcrumbs

1 Blanch and peel tomatoes.
2 Cut off top of tomatoes and scoop out seeds.
3 Season inside with salt and pepper and fill with stuffing and brush with melted butter (or oil or margarine).
4 Sprinkle breadcrumbs on top; place on oiled tray and bake in oven.

951 Tomates farcies à l'italienne

250 ml (½ pt) rizotto à l'Italienne
   (Recipe 367)
4 *tomatoes*
15 g (½ oz) grated cheese

1 Prepare tomatoes as above but fill with rizotto italienne.
2 Sprinkle cheese on top and bake in oven.

952 Tomates farcies à la provençale

4 *tomatoes*	10 *ml spoon* [½ *tablespoon*]
1 *clove crushed garlic*	*chopped parsley*
60 g (2 oz) breadcrumbs	*salt, pepper*
	oil

1 Prepare as above but reserve seeds and pulp.
2 Place breadcrumbs in bowl and season adding the crushed garlic and parsley.
3 Strain tomato pulp over crumbs to moisten.
4 Fill tomatoes with breadcrumb mixture and cook in oil in oven.

953 Tomates grillées – Grilled tomatoes

4 *large tomatoes*	60 g (2 oz) butter (or oil or
seasoning	*margarine*)

1 Make an incision on the top in the form of a cross.
2 Brush liberally with butter (or oil or margarine), season.
3 Grill slowly under moderate heat.

954 Tomates sautées au beurre – Shallow-fried tomatoes

4 *large tomatoes*	15 g (½ oz) butter (or oil or
	margarine)

1 Cut in half and season.
2 Fry gently in butter flat-side down first, then turn over.

TOPINAMBOURS – JERUSALEM ARTICHOKES

955 Topinambours – Jerusalem artichokes (to boil)

1 Wash well and carefully peel thinly.
2 Place in acidulated water to retain whiteness.
3 Prepare à blanc (Recipe 757) and bring to the boil.
4 Add the artichokes and simmer until tender.
5 Drain well.

956 Topinambours à l'anglaise

750 g (1½ lb) topppinambours	240 ml (½ pt) Béchamel (Recipe 51)
seasoning	

1 Trim and shape as for olives.
2 Cook lightly in blanc as Recipe 955.
3 Bind with thin Béchamel and season.

957 Topinambours aux fines herbes

500 g (1 lb) topinambours	60 g (2 oz) butter (or sunflower
seasoning	*margarine*)
	7 g (¼ oz) fines herbes

1 Peel and trim the artichokes and toss in butter (or margarine).
2 Add the fines herbes and season.
3 Place in oval vegetable-dish and sprinkle with fresh parsley before service.

958 Topinambours frits

500 1 g (*lb*) *topinambours*
60 g (*2 oz*) *butter* (*or oil or margarine*)

Pâte à frire (*Recipe* 1001)
seasoning

1 Peel and slice topinambours.
2 Cook gently in butter.
3 When about to serve, dip in batter and fry in deep oil.

959 Topinambours en purée – Jerusalem artichoke purée

500 g (*1 lb*) *topinambours*
60 g (*2 oz*) *butter* (*or margarine*)

120 g (*¼ lb*) *mashed potatoes*
(*Recipe* 896)
seasoning

1 Peel and slice topinambours.
2 Cook in butter (or margarine).
3 Pass through sieve.
4 Season and add sufficient mashed potato to thicken mixture.

VEGETARIAN DISHES

Chefs, even in non-vegetarian restaurants, at times need to meet the increasing demand for vegetarian dishes. Many dishes featuring flesh foods or fish may be adapted to contain only vegetable products. The following small selection is intended merely to suggest the approach.

959a Bean goulash

240 g (*8 oz*) *red kidney* (*or haricot*) *beans*
60 ml (*⅛ pt*) *sunflower* (*or other vegetable*) *oil*
60 g (*2 oz*) *finely chopped onion*
1 *clove garlic* (*crushed*)
1 *yellow pepper*
1 *red pepper*
1 *green pepper*
} *halved, de-seeded and cut in 1 cm (½ inch) dice*

30 g (*1 oz*) *paprika*
4 *turned potatoes*
240 g (*8 oz*) *sliced button mushrooms*
60 g (*2 oz*) *tomato purée*
750 ml (*1½ pt*) *vegetable stock*
bouquet garni
seasoning

1 Soak beans for 24 hours in cold water.
2 Drain, place into a saucepan. Cover with cold water, bring to boil and simmer until tender.
3 Heat oil in a sauté pan, sweat onion and garlic without colouring for 2–3 minutes, add paprika, sweat for a further 2–3 minutes.

4 Add peppers and button mushrooms and sweat for a further 2 minutes.
5 Add tomato purée, vegetable stock and bouquet garni. Bring to boil and simmer until pepper and mushrooms are cooked.
6 Remove bouquet garni. Add drained cooked beans, correct seasoning and stir.
7 Garnish with potatoes and chopped parsley.
8 Serve wholegrain pilaff or wholemeal noodles separately.

959b Mexican beanpot

360 g (12 oz) dry red (or haricot)
  beans
120 g (4 oz) finely chopped onions
120 g (4 oz) sliced carrots
240 g (8 oz) tomato concassé
  (Recipe 949)
2 cloves crushed and chopped
  garlic
chopped chives
15 g (½ oz) paprika
4 g (⅛ oz) chopped marjoram
  (fresh or dried)
1 small chilli finely chopped
1 small red pepper finely chopped
7 g (¼ oz) yeast extract
seasoning

1 Soak the beans in cold water for 24 hours.
2 Drain the beans, place into a saucepan, cover with cold water, bring to the boil and simmer gently.
3 When three-quarters cooked, add all the other ingredients except the chopped chives.
4 Continue to simmer until all is completely cooked.
5 Serve sprinkled with chopped chives.

959c Vegetarian lasagne

10 lasagne sheets
125 ml (¼ pt) sunflower (or other
  vegetable) oil
12 g (4 oz) finely chopped onion
2 cloves crushed and chopped
  garlic
240 g (8 oz) sliced button
  mushrooms
2 medium sized courgettes cut in
  1 cm (½ inch) dice
250 ml (½ pt) single cream (or
  natural yogurt or fromage frais)
pinch of freshly chopped oregano
240 g (8 oz) tomato concassé
360 g (12 oz) broccoli florets
120 g (4 oz) carrots cut into ½ cm
  (¼ inch) dice
30 g (1 oz) pine kernels
250 ml (½ pt) Béchamel sauce
  (Recipe 51)
60 g (2 oz) grated parmesan,
  gruyère or cheddar cheese
120 g (4 oz) tomato purée

1 Cook the lasagne sheets in boiling salted water until al dente; refresh and drain.
2 Heat half the oil and sweat the onion and garlic.
3 Add the mushrooms and continue to cook without colour. Season.

4 Heat the remaining oil in a sauteuse, add the courgettes and lightly fry; sprinkle with the oregano. Cook until crisp, then add tomato concassé and tomato purée.
5 Add the broccoli florets and carrots previously blanched and refreshed. Mix together with the pine kernels.
6 Make a cheese sauce using the Béchamel and half the grated cheese; finish with cream (or alternative).
7 Well grease an ovenproof dish with oil, place a layer of lasagne in the bottom.
8 Cover with a layer of mushroom, then a layer of lasagne, followed by the broccoli and tomato mixture, lasagne, and cheese sauce. Continue this process, finishing with a top layer of cheese sauce.
9 Sprinkle with remaining grated parmesan cheese.
10 Bake in a pre-heated oven at 180°C (350°F) for 20–25 minutes.

959d Vegetarian Moussaka

60 g (2 oz) finely chopped onion
1 clove crushed and chopped garlic
60 ml (⅛ pt) sunflower (or other vegetable) oil
120 g (4 oz) textured vegetable protein soaked in cold water for 2–3 hours)
240 g (8 oz) tomato concassé (Recipe 949)
60 g (2 oz) tomato purée

pinch of oregano
seasoning
300 ml (1 pt) vegetable stock
7 g (¼ oz) yeast extract
15 g (½ oz) arrowroot
480 g (1 lb) potatoes
2 small aubergines
60 g (2 oz) grated parmesan, gruyère (or low fat cheddar) cheese

1 Cook the onion and garlic in the oil until lightly coloured.
2 Add the drained textured vegetable protein.
3 Add tomato concassé, tomato purée, oregano and seasoning.
4 Add vegetable stock to cover. Bring to boil, simmer for 5 minutes.
5 Add yeast extract, stir well.
6 Mix arrowroot with a little water and gradually stir into the textured vegetable protein.
7 Bring back to boil. Simmer for 2 minutes.
8 Cook the potatoes with the skins on by steaming or boiling. Peel and slice into ½ cm (¼ inch) slices.
9 Slice the aubergines in ½ cm (¼ inch) slices, pass through flour, and shallow fry in oil on both sides until golden brown. Drain on kitchen paper.
10 In an ovenproof dish arrange layers of tvp mixture and overlapping slices of potato and aubergines.
11 Pour the cheese sauce (see page 310) on top. Sprinkle with grated parmesan (or alternative) cheese.
12 Bake in a pre-heated oven at 190°C (375°F) for approximately 30 minutes.

Cheese sauce

30 g (1 oz) sunflower margarine
  (or butter)
30 g (1 oz) plain (or wholemeal)
  flour
250 ml (½ pt) milk (full cream,
  semi-skimmed or skimmed)

600 ml (⅛ pt) cream (or natural
  yogurt or fromage frais)
30 g (1 oz) parmesan (or low fat
  cheddar) cheese
1 egg yolk

1 With the flour, margarine and milk make a Béchamel sauce (Recipe 51).
2 Add the grated cheese, beat in the egg yolk and finish with the cream (or alternative).

959e Vegetarian Stroganoff

4 tbsp. sunflower (or other
  vegetable) oil
60 g (2 oz) finely chopped onions
190 g (12 oz) shredded Chinese
  leaves
120 g (4 oz) celery cut into
  paysanne
240 g (8 oz) mixed nuts (cashews,
  hazelnuts, Brazils)

190 g (12 oz) sliced button
  mushrooms
1 teasp. English mustard
1 teasp. paprika
125 ml (¼ pt) dry white wine
125 ml (¼ pt) single or double
  cream (or unsweetened vegetable
  creamer, smetana, natural yogurt
  or fromage frais)

1 Heat the oil and sweat the onions for 2–3 minutes.
2 Add the Chinese leaves, celery and mushrooms. Cook for 5 minutes.
3 Add the nuts whole. Stir in the paprika and diluted mustard.
4 Add white wine, bring to the boil and simmer for 5 minutes.
5 Season. Cool slightly; add the cream or smetana (or alternative).
6 Serve with plain boiled wholewheat noodles tossed in sunflower margarine or wholegrain pilaff rice.

959f Curried vegetables with wholegrain rice

720 g (1½ lb) mixed vegetables:
  cauliflower, broccoli, peppers,
  carrots, courgettes,
  mushrooms, aubergines
120 g (4 oz) sunflower margarine
  (or butter)
170 g (6 oz) finely chopped onion

30 g (1 oz) garam masala
30 g (1 oz) creamed coconut, or
  60 g (2 oz) desiccated coconut
500 ml (1 pt) curry sauce (Recipe
  32, but using vegetable stock,
  Recipe 12c, not brown meat
  stock)

1 Prepare vegetables: cut cauliflower and broccoli into small florets, blanch and refresh; cut peppers into half, remove seeds, cut into 1 cm (½ inch) dice; cut carrots into large dice; leave mushrooms whole; cut aubergines into 1 cm (½ inch) dice.
2 Heat the butter (or margarine) and sweat the onion.
3 Add garam masala, sweat together for approximately 5 minutes.

4 Add the curry sauce, bring to boil and gently simmer until all the vegetables are cooked but crunchy in texture.
5 Serve with a wholegrain rice pilaff garnished with flaked almonds and a curry tray including poppadoms and mango chutney.

959g Vegetarian terrine

480 g (1 lb) fresh washed spinach
30 g (1 oz) chopped chives
480 g (1 lb) carrots } washed and
480 g (1 lb) celeriac } peeled

375 ml (¾ pt) choux paste
  (Recipe 999)
190 ml (⅜ pt) double cream (or
  crème fraiche or fromage frais)
1 teasp. ground allspice
seasoning

1 Cook, refresh and drain spinach, purée in food processor and season with salt, pepper, allspice and chopped chives.
2 Cut carrots and celeriac into even pieces, cook and purée separately.
3 To each purée add 125 ml (¼ pt) of choux pastry and 60 ml (⅛ pt) of double cream (or crème fraîche or fromage frais).
4 Take a large well-greased loaf tin, preferably aluminium foil (disposable).
5 Layer carrot purée over the base. Next layer with celeriac and finish with the spinach.
6 Cover with foil. Cook in a bain-marie in the oven at 180°C (350°F) for approximately 1¼ hours.
7 Remove from oven, cool and serve cold and sliced, with a suitable sauce, e.g. green peppercorn and paprika (Recipe 78a).

8 Pastry and Sweets

THE pâtisserie department of a large hotel or restaurant is a highly specialized one. Cooks who wish to become chef pâtissier (chief pastry-cook) usually turn their attention exclusively to this partie early in their careers. Nevertheless, in many establishments, and in other fields of catering, a good chef will consider it essential to have a sound basic knowledge of pâtisserie work.

In providing recipes for this section, selection (and exclusion) presented problems but the aim has been to cover the basics or fonds to allow for a wide range of work. These even permit the making of many desserts and sweets that have not been listed. For example, using the basic paste-recipes, it is possible to prepare a variety of fruit pies, tarts, and flans even though a full range of pies and tarts is not given. If correctly exploited, baked- and steamed-pudding mixes can also yield a diverse numbers of sweets such as Eve's, and other fruit puddings.

Simple scones and griddle goods have been omitted. Though useful as exercises during apprentice-training, these are seldom prepared within catering establishments today, but, like ice-cream, are purchased as required.

The Gâteaux and similar pastries that are represented should be regarded as examples, as there are so many variants and alternatives. Nevertheless, from the recipes quoted within this section, a fair range of work for high-class service can be achieved.

BASIC PREPARATIONS IN THE PÂTISSERIE

SAUCES

960 Sauce à l'abricot – Apricot sauce

240 g (½ lb) apricot purée	500 g (1 lb) sugar	15 ml spoon (1 tbsp.) kirsch

Note. In place of apricot purée and sugar, apricot jam may be used.

1 Bring apricot purée and sugar (or sieved jam) to the boil, stirring occasionally to prevent burning.
2 When cool, add kirsch and reserve until required.

961 Sauce anglaise – Custard sauce

2 *egg yolks*   250 *ml* (½ *pt*) *milk* (*whole, semi-*
60 *g* (2 *oz*) *sugar*   *skimmed or skimmed*)
vanilla pod (*or vanilla essence*)

1 Bring milk and vanilla pod (or essence) to the boil; remove the pod, pour milk on to the egg yolks and sugar, stirring all the time.
2 Return to the stove and cook, but do not boil.
3 Continue cooking, without boiling, until the mixture coats the back of a spoon.

962 Sauce Arenberg or **Mousseline sauce**

2 *egg yolks* (*see note*   45 *g* (1½ *oz*) *sugar*   500 *ml* (1 *pt*)
    below)   62 *ml* (⅛ *pt*) *water*   *whipping cream*
vanilla essence

1 Whisk egg yolks, sugar, water and essence together over warm water until thick.
2 Whisk until cold, then add cream and continue whisking until it has the required light consistency.

Note. For safety, pasteurized egg yolk may be used.

963 Sauce au caramel

500 *g* (1 *lb*) *loaf* (*or granulated*)   125 *ml* (¼ *pt*) *water*
    sugar

1 Boil sugar to a light caramel.
2 Add carefully 125 ml (¼ pt) hot water; sauce is then ready for use.

964 Sauce au chocolat – Chocolate sauce

250 *ml* (½ *pt*) *water*   120 *g* (4 *oz*) *chocolate*
240 *g* (8 *oz*) *sugar*   62 *ml* (⅛ *pt*) *rum* (*optional*)
15 *g* (½ *oz*) *cocoa powder*

1 Boil the water and sugar together.
2 Whisk in the cocoa powder; add the chocolate, stirring until melted and smooth.
3 Strain through a fine strainer. Add the rum if desired. Use as required.

965 Sauce au citron – Lemon sauce

Juice and zest of 2 *lemons*   15 *g* (½ *oz*) *arrowroot*
250 *ml* (½ *pt*) *water*   *lemon colouring if desired*
60 *g* (2 *oz*) *sugar*

1 Dissolve arrowroot in a little of the water.
2 Bring remainder of ingredients to the boil and whisk in the dissolved arrowroot; sauce is then ready for use.

966 Custard sauce (with powder)

240 *ml* (*½ pt*) *milk*   30 *g* (1 *oz*) *sugar*
15 *g* (*½ oz*) *custard power*

1 Dissolve sugar and custard powder in a little of the milk.
2 Bring remainder of the milk to the boil and whisk in the dissolved powder.
3 Bring back to the boil and the sauce is then ready for use.

Note. This sauce is merely a substitute for Sauce Anglaise (Recipe 961).

967 Sauce à la framboise – Raspberry sauce

240 *g* (*½ lb*) *raspberry purée*   120 *g* (4 *oz*) *sugar*
colouring if necessary   125 *ml* (*¼ pt*) *water*

Bring all ingredients to the boil and the sauce is then ready for use.

968 Sauce à la fraise – Strawberry sauce

Prepare as for sauce framboisee (Recipe 967) substituting strawberry purée.

969 Jam sauce

150 *g* (5 *oz*) *jam*   5 *ml* (spoon [*½ dessertspoon*]
62 *ml* (*⅛ pt*) *water*   *arrowroot*

1 Boil jam and water together and thicken with diluted arrowroot.
2 Reboil, skim, and strain.

970 Melba sauce

120 *g* (*¼ lb*) *raspberry purée*   120 *g* (*¼ lb*) *strawberry purée*
cochineal (*if required*)   120 *g* (4 *oz*) *caster sugar*

Stir all ingredients together over heat to dissolve sugar; colour if necessary
and use when cold.

970a Sauce mousseline

See Recipe 962

971 Sauce Sabayon or Zabaglione

3 *egg yolks* (*advisedly*   *zest of ¼ lemon*
   pasteurized)   62 *ml* (*⅛ pt*) *white wine*
60 *g* (2 *oz*) *caster sugar*   125 *ml* (*¼ pt*) *marsala*

1 Whisk all the ingredients together over warm water until they rise to 3 or 4
  times their volume.
2 Continue whisking until the mixture thickens; do not boil.

Note. Sabayon or Zabaglione can be served in glasses as a dessert or in
sauceboats as an accompaniment to puddings such as soufflé.

972 Syrup sauce

> *60 g (2 oz) golden syrup*   *7 g (¼ oz) arrowroot*
> *125 ml (¼ pt) water*   *60 g (2 oz) sugar*
> *juice of ½ lemon*

1 Dissolve arrowroot in a little of the water.
2 Bring remainder of ingredients to the boil before whisking-in the dissolved arrowroot.
3 Re-boil to cook arrowroot.

972a Hard sweet sauces

Hard sauces for puddings such as Rum and Brandy Butters are, in effect, the sweet counterpart of the beurres composés, composed butters, referred to on page 30. Brandy butter, for example, may be made by creaming together 60 g (2 oz) butter and 60 g (2 oz) icing sugar and stirring in brandy [up to 62 ml (⅛ pt)] until blended. The sauce may be rolled and chilled for slicing or served creamy and non-chilled. Other types of liqueurs and essences may be used in similar proportions to provide variants.

GLAZES

973 Apricot glaze

> *240 g (½ lb) apricot*   *500 g (1 lb) sugar (loaf)*   *125 ml (¼ pt) water*
>   *purée*

1 Boil the sugar and water to 115°C (240°F).
2 Add the purée and re-boil until temperature reaches 110°C (230°F); strain.

Alternatively omit purée, sugar and water and substitute apricot jam. Boil and strain.

974 Syrup glaze

> *125 ml (¼ pt) water*   *apple peelings and cores*
> *30 g (1 oz) sugar*   *egg colouring*
> *7 g (¼ oz) arrowroot*

1 Dissolve arrowroot in a little water.
2 Boil remaining ingredients and strain.
3 Reboil and whisk in arrowroot.

Notes
(i) Pear or peach trimmings can be used to make syrup.
(ii) Proprietary pectin glazes are now used instead (follow manufacturers' instructions).

975 Syrup for glazing petits fours

240 g (½ lb) loaf (or   30 g (1 oz) glucose   30 g (1 oz) water
granulated) sugar   juice of ⅛ lemon

1 Boil sugar, glucose and water to 154°–157°C (310°–315°F).
2 Add lemon juice and shake in thoroughly.
3 Pass fruits or marzipans through syrup with the aid of a fork and place on a lightly-oiled marble slab to cool and set.

ICINGS AND COVERINGS

976 American icing

240 g (½ lb) loaf (or   30 g (1 oz) water   vanilla essence
granulated) sugar   1 egg white

1 Boil water and sugar to 120°C (245°F) and pour steadily on to the beaten egg white.
2 Add essence and continue beating until at the point of thickening.
3 Coat gâteaux or pastries.

977 Fondant

850 g (1¾ lb) cube (or granulated)   120 g (¼ lb) glucose
sugar   125 ml (¼ pt) water

1 Boil sugar and water to 110°C (230°F).
2 Add glucose and re-boil to 115°C (240°F).
3 Pour out on to a marble slab surrounded by fondant bars.
4 Allow to cool slightly and work into a white mass with the aid of a spatula.
5 Store in an earthenware jar or suitable container.

Note. Commercial fondant is frequently used.

978 Royal icing

240 g (½ lb) icing sugar   lemon juice or cream of   2 egg whites
tartar

1 Sieve icing sugar.
2 Add icing sugar gradually to whites of eggs, beating continuously with a wooden spatula.
2 Add lemon juice (or alternative acid). (For enhanced whiteness, some add 1 drop blue colouring.)

Note. If a softer setting icing is required, add a teaspoon glycerine.

979 Water icing

colouring and flavouring as   240 g (½ lb) icing sugar
desired   warm water

Add warm water to icing sugar; add colouring and flavouring if desired and beat to required consistency.

980 Sucre filé – Spun sugar

240 g (½ lb) loaf (or granulated)   15 g (½ oz) glucose
sugar   62 ml (⅛ pt) water
juice of ⅛ lemon (or pinch cream
of tartar)

1 Boil sugar, water and glucose to 155°C (312°F).
2 Add lemon juice (or cream of tartar).
3 Spin over an oiled wooden stick.

Note. Colouring may be added if desired.

981 Chocolate couverture

(a) Milk-chocolate couverture:
1 Grate the chocolate finely.
2 Place in a basin and warm to 45°C (112°F) over warm water stirring continuously with a spatula.
3 Cool to almost setting and re-warm to 31°C (88°F); the chocolate is then ready for moulding.

(b) Plain-chocolate couverture:
Prepare as above but warm to 46°C (115°F); cool to almost setting, and work at 32°–33°C (90°–92°F).

981a Almond mixture for shaping and baskets

480 g (1 lb) raw marzipan   120 g (4 oz) icing sugar
150 g (5 oz) egg white   60 g (2 oz) cornflour

1 Break down marzipan with half the egg white and mix.
2 Add the icing sugar, cornflour and then the remaining egg whites and mix well.
3 Bake at 190°C (380°F) on a greased baking sheet, noting the technique:
    (a) Par cook mixture until set lightly, i.e. just firm if touched with a finger.
    (b) Remove from oven and allow to cool.
    (c) Place back in oven to colour.
    (d) Remove from baking sheet immediately. Mould as required.

CREAMS FOR FILLINGS

982 Crème d'amandes – Almond cream

120 g (¼ lb) ground almonds   2 eggs
almond essence if necessary   120 g (¼ lb) butter (or margarine)
120 g (¼ lb) caster sugar   30 g (1 oz) soft flour

1 Cream butter (or margarine) and sugar together.
2 Beat in eggs, one at a time.
3 Fold through flour and ground almonds.

Note. This lighter preparation is often preferred to frangipane sponge (Recipe 1037) as a filling for items such as gâteaux, tartelettes, and petits fours.

983 Crème au beurre–I – Butter cream

6 *egg yolks*	60 g (2 oz) water
vanilla essence	240 g (½ lb) caster sugar
360 g (¾ lb) creamed butter unsalted	

1 Whisk yolks, water, sugar and essence over warm water until they rise to become 3 to 4 times their original volume.
2 Continue beating until the mixture thickens and beat until cold.
3 Add the creamed butter to the mixture, a little at a time, beating continually with a spatula until light and creamy.
4 It is advisable to use pasteurized yolks.

983a Crème au beurre–II – Butter cream (alternative recipe)

500 g (1 lb) butter	1 small egg
500 g (1 lb) icing sugar	vanilla essence

Beat butter and sugar together, before adding egg and essence.

Note. For chocolate butter-cream incorporate 90 to 120 g (3 to 4 oz) melted chocolate. Similarly, coffee butter-cream may be made by adding essence to taste.

984 Crème Chantilly

Crème Chantilly is whisked cream with the addition of a little sugar and flavouring (if desired), e.g. vanilla, kirsch, Grand Marnier, etc.

985 Ganache

500 g (1 lb) chocolate	15 ml spoon (1 tbsp.) rum may be
250 ml (½ pt) cream	added if desired

Bring the cream to the boil, pour on to melted chocolate and beat until cold and creamy.

Use as filling for gâteaux, etc.

986 Crème pâtissiere – Pastry cook's cream

120 g (4 oz) caster sugar	16 g (½ oz) custard powder
2 eggs	500 ml (1 pt) milk whole, semi-
60 g (2 oz) white soft flour	skimmed or skimmed
vanilla essence	

1 Whisk the egg and sugar in a bowl until almost white.
2 Mix in the flour and custard powder.

3 Boil the milk and then whisk it on to the eggs, sugar and flour. Mix well.
4 Return to saucepan, bring to boil and add vanilla essence.
5 Remove from the heat and pour into a basin.
6 Sprinkle the top with icing sugar to prevent a skin forming.

987 Crème St-Honoré

Crème pâtissiere (*Recipe* 986)   60 g (2 oz) caster sugar
3 egg whites   7 g (¼ oz) soaked gelatine

1 Beat the eggs to full peak. Fold in the caster sugar.
2 Add the soaked gelatine to the boiling pastry cream. Mix well.
3 Fold the beaten whites into the pastry cream.
4 Use as required while still warm and before setting point.

FURTHER FILLINGS AND FLAVOURINGS

988 Apricot marmalade

See Apricot Glaze (Recipe 973).

989 Caramel

250 g (½ lb) sugar   3 × 20 ml spoon (⅛ pt) water

1 Dissolve sugar and water; boil at approximately 170°C (340°F) until a light caramel is obtained.
2 Take care to brush down sides of sugar-boiler with cold water to prevent crystallization.
3 Carefully and slowly add 25 ml (2½ dessertspoons) hot water to the caramel to reduce the temperature to 115°C (240°F).
4 Pour into moulds and leave to set.

Used for caramel creams, lining dariole moulds, etc.

Note. When caramel is required for flavouring only, a slightly darker caramel may be used.

990 Marzipan

500 g (1 lb) caster sugar   125 ml (¼ pt) water
30 g (1 oz) glucose   375 g (¾ lb) ground almonds

1 Bring sugar, water and glucose to 115°C (240°F).
2 Add the almonds and beat thoroughly with a wooden spatula until quite stiff.
3 Cover with a damp cloth and allow to cool.
4 Work to a smooth paste with icing sugar.

991 Praline

120 g (¼ lb) hazel nuts   125 ml (¼ pt) water
120 g (¼ lb) almonds   500 g (1 lb) sugar, loaf or granulated

1 Toast nuts lightly in a cool oven.
2 Dissolve the sugar in the water and boil to a light caramel.
3 Add nuts and stir through with a spatula and turn on to an oiled marble-slab.
4 When cold, crush with a rolling-pin and store in a sealed container.

992 Stock syrup

500 g (1 lb) cube or granulated   250 ml (½ pt) water
    sugar

Bring sugar and water to boil and allow to cool.

Use for compotes, etc. See also Syrup for Savarins and Rum Babas (Recipe 1010).

BASIC PASTES

Substitutions
1 Butter, traditionally used for high quality pastry work, is often replaced by margarine with better creaming quality. Proprietary cooking fats have also been developed for specific usages, e.g. fats with high melting point for puff pastry. As previously indicated, polyunsaturated margarines are available for the health-conscious.
2 Except for specifically (and rarely) indicated dishes, white flour was invariably used in pastry making. In a more health-aware age, wholemeal flour is increasingly in demand. Complete substitution of wholemeal for white does not produce a comparable product; but more satisfactory results can be achieved by substitution as follows:
    Puff paste   70% white, 30% wholemeal.
    Short and other pastes: 50% white, 50% wholemeal.

993 Flaky and rough puff

240 g (½ lb) flour   125 ml (¼ pt) water (approx.)
120 to 180 g (4 to 6 oz) butter (or   pinch salt
    margarine)   ¼ lemon juice

Prepare as for pâte à feuilletage (Recipe 994) or with butter roughly distributed in lumps when forming dough followed by 6 turns (as in puff pastry-making).

Use for covering steak pies, puff pastries and gâteaux.

994 Pâte à feuilletage – Puff pastry

125 ml (¼ pt) (water (approx.))	240 g (½ lb) flour
juice of ¼ lemon (or pinch cream	240 g (½ lb) butter
of tartar)	pinch salt

1 Sieve flour on to a slab and form into a bay.
2 Add the water, salt, and lemon juice and mix to a smooth dough.
3 Allow to rest for 10 minutes.
4 Soften butter to similar consistency as dough.
5 Pin out the paste into a square, leaving it twice as thick in the centre.
6 Place the butter in the centre of the paste and envelop with the paste.
7 Pin out into an oblong, keeping the sides straight and the corners rectangular.
8 Give one half-turn; repeat this operation pinning to the open ends.
9 Allow the paste to rest for 15 to 20 minutes.
10 Repeat the above operation until the paste has had 6 half-turns.

Used for bouchées, vol-au-vents, covering steak pies, gâteaux, etc.

995 Pâte à foncer – Short pastry

120 g (¼ lb) flour	30 g (1 oz) lard	pinch salt
30 g (1 oz) butter	45 g (1½ oz) water	

1 Rub the butter and lard lightly through flour until a fine sandy texture is obtained.
2 Form into a bay, pour in the water, add the salt and mix into a smooth dough; do not over-work.

Used for savoury flans, tartelettes, croustades. Sufficient for lining one 12 cm (6-inch) flan-ring.

996 Pâte sucrée – Sweet short-pastry

120 g (¼ lb) flour	1 small egg
60 g (2 oz) butter (or margarine)	pinch salt
30 g (1 oz) sugar	

Mix egg and sugar for use as moistening, otherwise as for pâte à foncer (Recipe 995).

Used for flans, tartelettes. Sufficient for lining one 12 cm (6-inch) flan-ring.

997 Hot water paste

240 g (½ lb) flour	125 ml (¼ pt) water
75 g (2½ oz) butter or lard	2.5 ml spoon [½ teaspoon] salt

1 Add the salt to the flour and pass through a sieve.
2 Rub 30 g (1 oz) of fat in the flour.
3 Bring the water to the boil with the remainder of the fat.

4 Make a well in the centre of the flour; pour in the liquid partly cooled and mix quickly with a wooden spoon.
5 Knead lightly with the hands into a ball-shape making sure the paste is smooth and free from cracks.
6 Roll the pastry 0.5 cm (¼ inch) thick, reserving sufficient to form a lid; keep warm and cover with a damp cloth until required; (it is, however, desirable to use it while still warm).

Used for raised and pork pies, etc. (normally prepared in the garde manger or larder).

997a Suet paste

See Recipe 739 (Steak and Kidney pudding).

998 Pâte à brioche – Brioche paste

240 g (½ lb) strong flour	60 g (2 oz) butter	95 ml (⅕ pt) milk
15 g (½ oz) sugar	2 eggs	pinch salt
	15 g (½ oz) yeast	

1 Same method as for savarin (Recipe 1000), i.e. prepare a batter with the yeast, milk and a little of the flour and when showing signs of collapse dough up with the remainder of the ingredients.
2 Allow to prove, i.e. double its volume.
3 Knock back and it is ready for use.

Used for pastries, rusks, etc.

998a Pâte à ravioli – Raviole paste

See Recipe 353.

998b Pâte à nouilles – Noodle paste

See Recipe 353.

999 Pâte à choux – Choux paste

250 ml (½ pt) water	120 g (4 oz) butter (or margarine or
150 g (5 oz) strong flour	vegetable oil)
pinch salt	pinch sugar
4 eggs	

1 Bring water, salt, butter, and sugar to the boil.
2 Cast in the flour and beat with a non-metal spatula until the mixture leaves the sides of the pan.
3 Allow to cool slightly and beat in the eggs one by one.

Used for éclairs, carolines, cream buns, gâteaux Polka, and St-Honoré, etc.

1000 Pâte à savarin – Savarin paste

240 g (8 oz) flour	7 g (¼ oz) yeast
2 eggs	30 g (1 oz) milk at 90°F (36°C)
30 g (1 oz) butter (or margarine or	pinch salt
oil)	pinch sugar

1 Dissolve yeast in the warmed milk.
2 Warm the flour slightly and form into a bay on the table.
3 Place in eggs, salt, and sugar, and mix together, bringing in a little of the flour.
4 Add the dissolved yeast and remaining flour to form into a smooth dough.
5 Place in a basin; distribute the butter evenly over the dough and allow to prove; cover with a cloth to prevent skinning.

Used for Savarins and Babas.

1000a Filo pastry

960 g (2 lb) strong flour	2 teasp. salt
250–375 ml (½–¾ pt) water	4 tbsp. olive oil
1 tbsp. vinegar	

1 Sift the flour in a bowl.
2 Add water, vinegar and salt, and mix ingredients to a thick paste.
3 Add the oil very slowly while working the mixture.
4 Mix until the dough becomes smooth and elastic. Cover for 30 minutes.
5 First roll out with an ordinary rolling pin, then use a very thin rolling pin or pasta machine to make a wafer-thin paste.
6 The pastry is now ready.
7 Always cover filo pastry with a damp or oiled cloth or polythene when not being rolled out or before use, otherwise it dries quickly and is difficult to handle.

Note. Filo pastry may be (and usually is) purchased ready made.

BATTERS

1001 Pâte à frire – Fritter batter

120 g (¼ lb) flour	15 g (½ oz) sugar
125 ml (¼ pt) water at 90°F (36°C)	4 g (⅛ oz) yeast
7 g (¼ oz) oil	pinch salt

1 Dissolve the yeast in a little of the water.
2 Whisk the remaining ingredients together before adding the yeast.
3 Cover with a cloth and allow to prove for approximately 1 hour.

1002 Appareil à crêpes – Pancake batter

180 g (6 oz) soft flour	375 ml (¾ pt) milk	pinch salt
1 egg	45 g (1½ oz) oil	pinch sugar
2 egg yolks		

1 Whisk all ingredients together except half of the milk.
2 When smooth add remainder of milk.
3 Strain and set aside for use.

Used for crêpes au citron, crêpes Suzette, etc.

1003 Appareil à crêpes – Pancake batter (alternative)

250 *ml* (½ *pt*) *milk*	*pinch sugar*
120 *g* (¼ *lb*) *flour*	15 *g* (½ *oz*) *browned butter* (*beurre*
pinch salt	*noisette*) *oil oil*
1 *small egg*	

1 Whisk all ingredients together with half of the milk.
2 When smooth add the remaining milk.
3 Strain if necessary.

Note. A more economical batter may be made by substituting for the above ingredients:

120 *g* (4 *oz*) *soft flour*	45 *g* (1½ *oz*) *oil*
1 *egg*	*pinch salt*
250 *ml* (½ *pt*) *whole, semi-*	*pinch sugar*
skimmed or skimmed milk	

MERINGUES

1004 Ordinary or cold meringue (Made by machine)

4 *egg whites*	*pinch salt or lemon juice*
240 *g* (½ *lb*) *caster sugar*	

Note. When preparing by hand only half the amoung of sugar can be beaten in; the remainder is gently folded in.

1 Whisk whites, salt and one-third of the sugar to a stiff snow.
2 Whisk in half of the remaining sugar.
3 Fold in remaining sugar.
4 Pipe onto greaseproof paper and bake without colouring (dry out) in very cool oven.

Used for meringue shells as in Recipes 1004a and b.

1004a Meringue Chantilly

Sandwiched with crème Chantilly (Recipe 984).

1004b Meringue glacée

Filled with vanilla ice-cream in a sandwich style.

1005 Meringue italienne – Italian or boiled meringue

25 *ml spoon* (2 *dessertspoons*) water	240 *g* (8 *oz*) *cube* (*or granulated sugar*)
lemon juice (*or pinch cream of tartar*)	4 *egg whites*

1 Boil sugar and water to hard ball stage 121°C (400°F).
2 Pour steadily onto the stiffly-beaten egg-whites.
3 Continue beating until cold.
4 Cook as Recipe 1004 or as indicated when an ingredient of a dish.

Used for vacherin, mushrooms, swans, etc.

Note. For meringue mix for Soufflées en Surprise, see Recipe 1161.

1006 Heavy hot meringue

4 *egg whites*	*pinch salt*
240 *g* (½ *lb*) *caster sugar*	

1 Place sugar in oven to warm.
2 Add to the whites and salt.
3 Whisk until stiff.

Used for apple or lemon meringue pies, meringue rock cakes, topping Queen's pudding.

1006a Œufs à la neige

See Recipe 1083.

1007 Vacherin

Italienne meringue (Recipe 1005).

1 Prepare meringue onto greaseproof paper in three separate rounds.
2 Bake in a cool oven 104°C (220°F) for approximately 2 hours.
3 When cold, sandwich with cream and decorate.

SAVARINS AND BABAS

1008 Savarin Chantilly

savarin paste (*Recipe* 1000)	*syrup* (*Recipe* 1010) *whipped cream*	*apricot purée*

Soak savarin in syrup, brush with apricot purée and decorate with whipped cream.

1009 Savarin aux fruits

savarin paste (*Recipe* 1000)	*syrup* (*Recipe* 1010) *whipped cream*	*apricot purée* *fruit*

1 Bake the savarin mix in the customary ring-savarin mould.
2 Soak in syrup (rum is not necessary in this instance), and brush with a little apricot purée.
3 Place on a round silver flat and decorate the centre with fruit; finish décor with whipped cream and garnish with cherries, angelica, rose petals, and grapes, etc.

1010 Syrup for Savarins and Rum Babas

250 *ml* (½ *pt*) *water*	½ *sliced lemon*	15 *ml spoon* (1
240 g (½ *lb*) *sugar*	¼ *cinnamon stick*	*tbsp.*) *rum* (*when*
½ *sliced orange*	3 × 20 *ml spoon* (⅛ *pt*)	*for Rum Baba*)
	tea	

1 Bring all the ingredients except the rum to the boil.
2 Simmer for 10 minutes and strain; stir in rum.

Note. Rum is an essential ingredient when the syrup is for use with Rum Baba; for other savarins the rum may be omitted or another spirit or liqueur substituted.

1011 Baba au rhum

savarin paste (*Recipe* 1000)	*syrup* (*Recipe* 1010)
with the addition of:	*apricot glaze*
30 g (1 *oz*) *currants*	*whipped cream*
zest of ½ *lemon*	
30 g (1 *oz*) *sultanas*	

1 Prepare a savarin mixture with the addition of the fruit and zest of the lemon; pour into individual dariole moulds and bake in hot oven.
2 Soak in syrup and brush with apricot glaze.
3 When cold, split, and fill with cream.
4 Decorate with cherries, angelica, etc.

CHOUX PASTE

1012 Carolines

choux pastry (*Recipe* 999)   *pastry cream* (*Recipe* 986)

Prepare small éclairs, fill with pastry cream and dip in chocolate or fondant.

1013 Choux au chocolat

choux pastry	*chocolate*	*crème pâtissier*
(*Recipe* 999)		(*Recipe* 986)

1 Pipe choux paste into rounds onto a baking-tray through 1 cm (½ inch) plain tube.
2 Egg-wash and bake in a hot oven.
3 Fill with crème pâtissier and dip in chocolate.

1014 Éclairs

choux paste	*crème pâtissière*	*chocolate or*
(*Recipe* 999)	(*Recipe* 986)	*fondant*

1 Pipe in choux paste into rounds onto a baking-tray through 1 cm (½ inch) plain tube.
2 Egg-wash and mark with the back of a fork and bake in a hot oven.
3 When cold, fill with crème pâtissier; dip in chocolate or coffee-flavoured fondant.

1015 Salambos

Same as Recipe 1012 but round in shape; these small spheres are used for savouries (hot or cold) and for sweet petit fours.

1016 Profiteroles

Small spheres of choux paste; they may be piped with filling of crème Chantilly or pâtissière, heaped and masked with chocolate sauce (profiterau chocolat) or, when baked plainly as extremely tiny spheres used as a garnish for clear soup (Consommé aux profiteroles).

1017 Beignets soufflés

choux paste	*caster sugar*	*apricot sauce*
(*Recipe* 999)		(*Recipe* 960)

1 Prepare choux paste in small spheres on greased paper either (a) by moulding like quenelles between tablespoons or, (b) piping directly on to the greased paper.
2 Invert paper on surface of hot oil 121°C (about 250°F).
3 Remove paper and shake fritures in order that they may soufflé gradually, increasing temperature to 190°C (375°F) until they are a light-golden colour.
4 Drain well, roll in caster sugar.
5 Sauce apricot served separately.

1018 Beignets soufflés en surprise

Prepare as above but before rolling in sugar, fill with hot jam or pastry cream (Recipe 986).

PUFF-PASTRY GOODS

1019 Amandines

puff pastry (Recipe 994)	*almond cream (Recipe* 982)

1 Pin out puff pastry to 0.3 cm (⅛ inch) thick; place on baking sheet and spread 0.5 cm (¼ inch) thick with almond cream.
2 Decorate with strips of puff pastry and bake in a moderate oven.
3 Ice when cold with water icing.

1020 Dartois

puff pastry (*Recipe* 994)   *almond cream* (*Recipe* 982)

1 Pin out paste 0.3 cm (⅛ inch) thick, in long bands 14 cm (7 inches) wide.
2 Egg-wash one side and place almond cream in the centre; fold over other two sides to enclose the almond cream as in a turnover.
3 Egg-wash, mark with the point of a knife and bake in a moderate oven.
4 When almost ready, dust with icing sugar and glaze.

1021 Chaussons bruxellois – Vanilla turnovers

puff pastry (*Recipe* 994)   *pastry cream* (*Recipe* 986)

1 Pin out puff pastry 0.3 cm (⅛ inch) thick and cut into squares.
2 Egg-wash corners and place pastry cream in centre.
3 Taking opposite corners, stretch and close in the middle on the pastry cream; egg-wash and bake in a hot oven.
4 Glaze with icing sugar.

1022 Chaussons à la confiture – Jam turnovers

Use same ingredients and method as for apple turnovers (Recipe 1023) but substitute jam for apples.

1023 Chaussons aux pommes – Apple turnovers

puff pastry (*Recipe* 994)   *apples*
caster sugar   *cinnamon*

1 Pin out puff paste 0.3 cm (⅛ inch) thick and cut into rounds of the required size.
2 Egg-wash one side and place some finely-sliced apples, sugar, and cinnamon on it.
3 Fold over other side, and egg-wash; place on a baking-sheet and bake in a moderate oven.
4 When almost ready, dust with icing sugar and glaze.

1024 Fleurons – Small puff-pastry crescents

puff pastry (*Recipe* 994)

1 Pin out puff pastry to 0.45 cm (³⁄₁₆ inch) thick.
2 Lighly egg-wash and cut into small crescents.
3 Bake in a hot oven until golden brown.

Use as a garnish for poached fish dishes.

1025 Jalousies

puff pastry (*Recipe* 994)   *raspberry or strawberry jam*

Prepare in the same manner as for d'Artois (Recipe 1020) using jam instead of almond cream.

1026 Palmiers – Pigs' ears

> *puff paste trimmings (Recipe 994)*   *caster sugar*

1 Pin out trimmings to 0.5 cm (⅛ inch) thick and 24 cm (12 inches) wide.
2 Brush with cold water and sprinkle with caster sugar.
3 Fold the paste from either side in three; then fold in two; cut into 1 cm (½-inch) pieces.
4 Place on a baking-sheet and bake in a hot oven.
5 When almost ready, turn over with palette knife and finish baking to a golden colour.

1027 Vol-au-Vents

> *puff paste (Recipe 994)*

Two slightly-differing methods are given below. The first is often called the English and the second the French method:

Method I
1 Pin out the puff pastry to 1.5 cm (¾ inch) thick and cut into rounds with a 12 cm (6 inch) cutter.
2 Place on a baking-tray, lightly egg-washed.
3 Make a circular incision with a 10 cm (5 inch) cutter halfway through the paste.
4 Allow to rest before baking in a hot oven 204°C (400°F).
5 Remove top, and remove soft paste from centre while still hot.

Method II
1 Roll out puff pastry thinly 0.9 cm (¾ inch thick).
2 Use a 12 cm (6 inch) damp cutter and cut two rounds of pastry and turn over.
3 Place one round on a damp baking-tray and egg-wash the edges.
4 Using a small cutter approximately 2 cm (1 inch) less in diameter, make an incision on top of the second round of pastry and cut about halfway through.
5 Place the second round on top of the first and seal well together.
6 Egg-wash the top only and bake for 15 to 20 minutes in a hot oven.
7 When cooked, remove the lid with a sharp pointed knife and remove any soft paste inside.

1028 Bouchées

> Puff pastry (*Recipe* 994)

1 Pin out puff pastry from 0.7 cm to 1.0 cm (⅓ to ½ inch) thick and cut into rounds with a 6 cm (3 inch) cutter.
2 Continue as for vol-au-vents (Recipe 1027).

1029 Petites bouchées or Bonne bouches

> *Puff pastry (Recipe 994)*

1 Pin out puff pastry to 0.5 cm (¼ inch) thick and cut into rounds with a 3 cm (1½ inch) cutter.
2 Continue as for vol-au-vents (Recipe 1027).

FLANS, TARTS, AND GÂTEAUX WITH SWEET OR SHORT PASTE

1030 Bande aux fruits

pâte sucrée (*Recipe* 996)	*crème pâtissière* (*Recipe* 986)
apricot, pectin or syrup glaze	*fruit*
(*Recipe* 974)	

1 Pin out short pastry into a strip 24 × 10 × 0.5 cm (12 by 5 by ¼ inch thick) and decorate the edges with the aid of pastry pincers.
2 Egg-wash, stab the centre and bake in a moderate oven for 8 to 10 minutes.
3 When cold, spread pastry cream down the centre and decorate with appropriate fruit.
4 Mask with a glaze and decorate with whipped cream.

Note. Bandes aux fruits are also sometimes made with ribbon strips of puff paste to form the side edges on the short-pastry base.

1030a Black cherry cheesecake

105 g (3½ oz) caster sugar ⎫ for	6 egg yolks (pasteurized)
75 g (2½ oz) soft flour ⎬ sponge	zest of 1 orange
3 eggs ⎭	zest of 1 lemon
360 g (12 oz) caster sugar	480 g (1 lb) cream cheese
90 g (3 oz) caster sugar	30 g (1 oz) soaked gelatine
750 ml (1½ pt) whipped cream	3 egg whites (pasteurized)
240 g (8 oz) black cherries	vanilla essence or pod
1 × 20 cm (8 inch) disc sweet	
pastry (Recipe 996)	

1 Prepare the sponge (as Recipe 1043) and bake in a swiss roll tin.
2 Beat together the yolks, 360 g (12 oz) sugar and orange and lemon zest.
3 Mix the cream cheese until smooth.
4 Blend the egg mixture into the cheese.
5 Stir the gelatine (which has been soaked in cold water, and melted), and add while still warm.
6 Whisk the egg whites, adding 90 g (3 oz) caster sugar.
7 When the cheese mixture is on setting point, fold in the cream and egg whites and flavour with vanilla essence.
8 Line a 20 cm (8 inch) cake tin with a disc of cooked sweet pastry and line the sides with greaseproof paper.
9 Half-fill the mould with half the cheese mixture. Place on top a layer of well-drained black cherries.
10 Cover with a second layer of cheese mixture and finish with a layer of thinly sliced sponge.
11 Allow to set in the refrigerator for 3 hours.
12 Turn out of the tin and remove the greaseproof paper. Dust the sponge with icing sugar and mark trellis fashion with a hot poker.

Note. For varied cheesecakes, blackcurrants, strawberries, apricots, peaches and raspberries may also be used in place of black cherries.

1031 Flan aux fruits

pâte sucrée (Recipe 996)	*apricot, pectin or syrup glaze*
crème pâtissière	*(Recipe* 974)
	fruit

1 Line a flan ring with sweet short-paste and bake 'blind', i.e. with dried haricot beans as temporary filling to preserve shape.
2 When cold, half-fill with pastry cream.
3 Decorate the top with the appropriate fruit and glaze.

Use for pear flan – Flan aux poires, and soft fruit flans such as strawberry – Flan aux fraises, etc.

1032 Flan aux pommes – Apple flan

Apple purée:	Additional ingredients:
2 *apples*, 60 *g (2 oz) sugar*	1 *apple for decoration*
15 *g (½ oz) butter, cinnamon*	*pâte sucrée (Recipe* 996)
	apricot glaze (Recipe 973)

1 Line a flan ring with sweet short-paste.
2 Place in apple purée and decorate with sliced, quartered apples in a circular fashion.
3 Bake for 20 to 25 minutes in a moderate oven 175°C (350°F).
4 One minute before taking flan from the oven, remove flan ring and lightly egg-wash outside border.
5 Return to oven for a minute.
5 When cool, glaze with apricot glaze.

1033 Pomme en robe – Baked apple dumplings

pâte sucrée	2 *apples*	*puff or short paste*
(Recipe 996)		*trimmings*

1 Core, peel, and halve apples.
2 Pin out paste to 0.5 cm (¼ inch) thick and cut into 6 cm (3 inch) squares.
3 Place a half-apple in the centre of the square of paste and envelop.
4 Lightly egg-wash, then place a small round of puff-paste trimmings on top.
5 Bake for 15 to 20 minutes in a moderate oven.

1033a Tarte tatin

720 *g (1½ lb) cooking apples*	180 *g (6 oz) caster sugar*
(halved, peeled and cored)	*juice of ½ lemon*
120 *g (4 oz) butter*	270 *g (9 oz) puff pastry (Recipe* 994)

1 With the butter liberally grease a deep round oven-proof dish 26 cm (10 inch) in diameter and cover its base with sugar.
2 On this sugared base arrange the apples. Sprinkle with lemon juice.
3 Roll out the pastry 3 mm (⅛ inch) thick. Lay the pastry over the apples with an overlay of 2 cm (¾ inch) all round. Trim away excess (overhanging) paste.

4 Allow to relax for 20 minutes.
5 Place the oven-proof dish over fierce heat until the butter and sugar are bubbling.
6 Place in an oven at 200°C (400°F) until the pastry is cooked.
7 Immediately invert on to a round serving dish.
8 Serve immediately with a raspberry coulis (Recipe 1033b).

Note. Similar tartes may be made with pears or mangoes in place of apples and served with a passion fruit coulis.

1033b Rasberry coulis

*480 g (1 lb) raspberries (fresh or
     frozen)
60 g (2 oz) caster sugar*

*juice of ½ lemon
125 ml (¼ pt) white wine*

(i) Blend all ingredients together in a liquidizer.
(ii) Strain through a fine strainer, correct the consistency with a little water or fruit juice.

1034 Tartelettes et barquettes de fruits

*pâte sucrée (Recipe 996)
apricot or syrup glaze (Recipe
     974)*

*crème pâtissière (Recipe 986)
fruit*

Line tartelette or barquette moulds with sweet short paste and prepare as for fruit flan.

1035 Gâteau Alma

*boiled meringue (Recipe 1005)
frangipane (Recipe 1037)
fondant (Recipe 977)*

*pâte sucrée (Recipe 996)
raspberry jam
15 g (½ oz) angelica*

1 Prepare a Bakewell tart (Recipe 1036).
2 Prepare Italian meringue and build on Bakewell tart in a dome shape.
3 Dust with icing sugar and place in oven 177°C (350°F) for 10 minutes.
4 Allow to cool and mask with pink fondant.
5 Decorate with angelica.

1036 Bakewell tart

*pâte sucrée (Recipe 996)
frangipane (Recipe 1037)*

*raspberry jam
icing sugar*

1 Line one 12 cm (6 inch) flan-ring with sweet short-paste.
2 Spread the base of the flans with raspberry jam.
3 Two-thirds fill flans with frangipane sponge and decorate the tops with strips of sweet short-paste.
4 Bake in moderate oven 177°C (350°F) for 25 to 30 minutes.
5 Before taking from the oven, dust with icing sugar to give a glaze.
6 Serve on a d'oyley with custard sauce (Recipe 961 or 966) separately.

1036a Clafoutis aux pommes – Apple clafoutis

240 g (8 oz) short pastry	180 g (6 oz) caster sugar
(Recipe 995)	32 ml (1/16 pt) kirsch
480 g (1 lb) cooking apples	30 g (1 oz) granulated sugar
140 ml (1/4 pt) double cream	15 g (1/2 oz) flour
4 eggs	vanilla pod (or essence)
140 ml (1/4 pt) milk	

1 Line a well-greased 24 cm (9 inch) flan ring with short pastry.
2 Bake blind at 220°C (425°F) for 15–20 minutes.
3 Meanwhile peel, core and thinly slice the apples.
4 Boil the milk, cream and vanilla pod (or use vanilla essence). Cool to just under blood heat 32°C (90°F).
5 Whisk the eggs and caster sugar together until frothy. Add 15 g (1/2 oz) flour.
6 Remove the vanilla pod, pour the milk and cream onto the eggs and sugar. Add the kirsch.
7 Arrange the slices of apple neatly in the pastry case. Pour over the mixture while still warm.
8 Bake at 200°C (400°F) for 20–25 minutes.
9 When cooked sprinkle with granulated sugar.

1037 Frangipane sponge mixture

almond essence if desired	60 g (2 oz) caster sugar
45 g (1 1/2 oz) ground almonds	1 egg
60 g (2 oz) butter	30 g (1 oz) flour

Sugar-butter method:

1 Cream butter and sugar thoroughly.
2 Beat through eggs, one by one.
3 Fold through sieved flour and almonds.
4 Add essence if necessary.

Use for Bakewell tart. This mixture (and also crème d'amandes, Recipe 982) can be used for (a) Gâteau conversation (Recipe 1038); and (b) tartelette or gâteau Pithiviers (Recipe 1041).

1037a Pecan pie, maple-glazed

240 g (8 oz) sweet short-pastry	240 g (8 oz) caster sugar
(Recipe 996)	180 g (6 oz) melted butter
3 eggs	90 g (3 oz) soft flour
120 g (4 oz) maple syrup	240 g (8 oz) pecan halves
120 g (4 oz) corn syrup	vanilla essence
120 g (4 oz) chopped pecan nuts	
Glaze:	30 g (1 oz) melted butter
60 g (2 oz) maple syrup	

1 Line a 24 cm (9 inch) flan ring with short pastry and bake blind for approximately 15 minutes at 200°C (400°F).
2 Mix the caster sugar and eggs in a mixing bowl until light and frothy.
3 Add the maple and corn syrups, chopped pecans, butter and flour. Mix thoroughly.
4 Pour into the flan case. Arrange the pecan halves on top.
5 Return to the oven for approximately 10 minutes. Reduce the heat to 170°C (325°F) and continue to bake until the filling is set (approximately 20 minutes).
6 When cooked, brush with a glaze of melted butter and maple syrup.
7 Serve cold with whipped cream (which may be flavoured with brandy or Southern Comfort).

GÂTEAUX WITH CHOUX, PUFF OR SHORT PASTES

1038 Gâteau conversation

> *almond cream (Recipe 982)*   *puff paste (Recipe 994)*
> *royal icing (Recipe 978)*

1 Pin out puff paste 0.3 cm (⅛ inch) thick and cut into rounds 16 cm (8 inches) diameter.
2 Place 1 round on a baking tray, egg-wash and spread almond cream in the centre (Frangipane sponge, Recipe 1037 may be substituted).
3 Cover with other round of paste, carefully sealing the edges.
4 Coat puff paste evenly with royal icing and decorate with strips of puff paste.
5 Bake in moderate oven 165°–177°C (330°–350°F) for 30 to 35 minutes.

1039 Gâteau St-Honoré

> *sweet short-pastry (Recipe 996)*   *Crème St Honoré (Recipe 987)*
> *choux pastry (Recipe 999)*   *cherries*
> *boiled sugar (Recipe 975)*   *angelica*

1 Pin out short pastry 0.3 cm (⅛ inch) thick and cut into a round of 16 cm (8 inches) diameter.
2 Place on a baking sheet, slot with a fork, egg-wash and pipe a border of choux paste with 1 cm (½ inch) tube. Also pipe 16 small buns; egg-wash and bake in a moderate oven.
3 When cold, fill buns with crème St-Honoré and dip in boiled sugar.
4 Place in circular fashion on border of gâteau with crème St-Honoré.
5 Garnish buns with cherries and angelica.

1040 Gâteau mille feuilles

> *180 g (6 oz) puff-pastry trimmings*   *fondant (Recipe 977)*
> *(Recipe 994)*   *toasted almonds*
> *crème pâtissière (Recipe 986)*   *apricot jam*
> *raspberry jam*

1 Pin out pastry 0.2 cm (⅒ inch) thick, cut into 3 rounds of 16 cm (8 inches) diameter.
2 Thoroughly stab and bake until light brown and crisp.
3 Sandwich the three layers together with the pastry cream and jam, making sure that the underside of the last ring is on top.
4 Lightly press together and coat sides with crème pâtissière and mask with toasted almonds.
5 Coat top with fondant and pipe a spiral of raspberry jam, apricot jam, and chocolate fondant from the centre.
6 Pull a knife across the top while the fondant is still soft to form pattern.

1041 Gâteau Pithiviers

puff pastry (Recipe 994)   *icing sugar*
crème d'amandes (Recipe 982)

1 Pin out puff pastry 0.3 cm (⅛ inch) thick, cut into two rounds of 16 cm (8 inches) diameter.
2 Place one round on a baking tray, egg-wash and spread almond cream in the centre (frangipane sponge, Recipe 1037, may be substituted).
3 Cover with the other round and press the edges together with the back of a knife.
4 Egg-wash the top and mark the knife in arcs from centre to outside edge of gateau.
5 Bake in a moderate oven until almost ready and glaze with icing sugar.

1042 Gâteau Religieuse

choux pastry (Recipe 999)   *sweet short-pastry (Recipe 996)*
fondant icing (Recipe 977)   *whipped cream*
crème St-Honoré (Recipe 987)

1 Line a flan ring with sweet short paste and bake 'blind'.
2 Prepare 4 éclairs, one end slightly thicker than the other.
3 When baked, fill with crème St-Honoré and glaze with coffee and chocolate fondant.
4 Place remainder of crème St-Honoré in flan, cone-shaped, and arrange éclairs against the cream.
5 Decorate between each éclair with whipped cream and finish the top with a chocolate-iced cream bun.

1042a Schwarzwalder kirschtorte – Black Forest Gâteau

4 eggs	*25 ml (1 dessertspoon) kirsch*
120 g (4 oz) caster sugar	*250 ml (½ pt) stock syrup*
90 g (3 oz) flour	*1 × A2½ tin black cherries*
30 g (1 oz) cornflour	*30 g (1 oz) arrowroot*
60 g (2 oz) melted butter (or	*1 litre (1 qt) whipped cream (or*
margarine or vegetable oil)	*non-dairy equivalent)*
30 g (1 oz) cocoa powder	*240 g (8 oz) chocolate shavings*

1 Place the eggs and sugar into a mixing bowl and slightly warm.
2 Using a machine, whisk vigorously at full speed until ribbon stage (when the mixture stands on its own weight).
3 Sieve the flour, cocoa powder and cornflour together.
4 Carefully fold these into the egg mixture and then fold the melted butter (or margarine or vegetable oil) into the mixture.

Notes
(i) If using butter or margarine, this must only be at blood heat.
(ii) When folding in the flour and the fat, take special care not to overmix.

5 Pour into a well-greased and lightly floured 20 cm (8 inch) gâteau tin. (Alternatively line the tin with parchment paper.)
6 Bake at 150°C (300°F) for 30–40 minutes.
7 Turn out and allow to cool.
8 Split into three, making the bottom layer the top. Moisten all three layers with stock syrup and kirsch.
9 Boil the cherries and lightly thicken with arrowroot. Allow to cool.
10 Spread a layer of whipped cream on the bottom layer, with half the cherry mixture.
11 Cover with the next layer of sponge and repeat the procedure with cream and cherries.
12 Add the top layer of sponge and mask all over top and sides with whipped cream. Refrigerate for 15–20 minutes.
13 Remove from refrigerator and cover all over with chocolate shavings.
14 Decorate with rosettes of whipped cream and glacé or black cherries.

CAKES AND GÂTEAUX WITH CAKE MIXES

1043 Swiss roll sponge

butter cream (Recipe 983)   *90 g (3 oz) flour*
120 g (4 oz) caster sugar   *3 eggs*

1 Whisk eggs and sugar over hot water to ribbon stage.
2 Whisk until cold before folding through the sieved flour.
3 Spread on to a tray 28 × 40 cm (14 inches by 20 inches) lined with greaseproof paper.
4 Bake for 8 minutes – oven temperature 205°C (400°F).
5 Turn out on to a lightly-sugared cloth.
6 When cold, half spread with butter ceam and roll up tightly: to give 1 Swiss roll.

Note. Other examples of fatless sponge are Recipes 1048 and 1055.

1044 Génoise (Sponge-butter method)

30 g (1 oz) melted butter   60 g (2 oz) sugar
2 eggs   60 g (2 oz) flour

1 Whisk eggs and sugar over hot water to ribbon stage.
2 Continue beating until cold before folding through the flour and finally the melted butter.
3 Bake immediately in a moderate oven for 25 minutes.

Used for gâteaux, and petit fours.

1045 Chocolate génoise

2 eggs   60 g (2 oz) sugar   30 g (1 oz) melted
7 g (¼ oz) cocoa   50 g (1¾ oz) flour   butter

1 Sieve cocoa and flour together then follow method as for génoise (Recipe 1044).
2 Bake in a greased and floured gâteau-tin.

1046 Gâteau Mocha (or moka) – Coffee gâteau

génoise (Recipe 1044)   crème au beurre (Recipe 983)
roasted almond nibs   coffee essence

1 Bake génoise mixture ina greased and floured gâteau-tin.
2 When cold, split and sandwich with coffee-flavoured butter cream.
3 Mask sides with toasted almond nibs and decorate top with butter cream.
4 Generally the word moka (or mocha) is written across the top of the gâteau.

1047 Gâteau Suchard – Chocolate gâteau

chocolate génoise (Recipe 1045)   chocolate butter cream (Recipe 983)
chocolate vermicelli   120 g (¼ lb) melted chocolate

1 Bake génoise mixture in a greased and floured gâteau-tin and when cold, sandwich with chocolate butter cream.
2 Mask the sides with chocolate vermicelli.
3 Decorate the top with melted chocolate.

1048 Bûche de Nöel – Christmas log

vanilla butter cream   chocolate butter cream
marzipan holly-berries   120 g (4 oz) flour
20 ml spoon [4 teaspoons] water   150 g (5 oz) sugar
marzipan leaves   5 eggs

1 Use a biscuit à la cuillère mix (Recipe 1055) for Swiss roll.
2 When prepared bake in an oblong tray on greaseproof paper.
3 When cold, form into a roll with vanilla butter cream.
4 Decorate with chocolate butter cream, marzipan leaves and holly-berries.

1049 Fruit cake – (Slab-cake style)

240 g (½ lb) butter	5 eggs	180 g (6 oz)
240 g (½ lb) sugar	300 g (10 oz) flour	currants
60 g (2 oz) peel		180 g (6 oz) sultanas

1 Cream butter and sugar.
2 Add the eggs one by one beating them in thoroughly.
3 Fold through flour, fruit, and peel.
4 Pour into a cake-tin lined with greaseproof paper and bake in slow oven for 1½ to 2 hours.

1050 Christmas cake

240 g (½ lb) sugar	60 g (2 oz) minced peel
240 g (½ lb) butter	7 g (¼ oz) spice
300 g (10 oz) soft flour	15 ml spoon (1 tbsp.) rum
5 eggs	marzipan (Recipe 990)
240 g (½ lb) currants	royal icing (Recipe 978)
240 g (½ lb) sultanas	

1 Sugar-butter creaming method as for fruit cake (Recipe 1049).
2 When cold, mask with marzipan and decorate with royal icing.

1051 Wedding cake

600 g (1¼ lb) butter	240 g (½ lb) glace cherries
600 g (1¼ lb) sugar	30 g (1 oz) mixed spice
12 eggs	240 g (½ lb) ground almonds
750 g (1½ lb) sultanas	750 g (1 lb 9 oz) soft flour
1.6 kg (3¼ lb) currants	marzipan (Recipe 990)
480 g (1 lb) mixed peel	royal icing (Recipe 978)

As for Christmas cake (Recipe 1050).

BISCUITS AND PETITS FOURS

1052 Petits fours

There are two principal categories of petits fours:

Petits fours glacés: Glazed petits fours include fruits dipped in sugar, fondants and petit choux glazed.

Additionally, there are fondant petits fours, exemplified by small pieces of génoise masked with fondant icing and which are, in effect, miniature French cakes.

Petits fours secs: Dry petits fours are typically the various biscuits, macaroons and also meringue items and marzipan or almond paste dainties.

1053 Fruits glacés – Glazed fruits

Prunes:	Stone out and stuff with marzipan (Recipe 990).
Dates:	Stone out and stuff with marzipan (Recipe 990).
Cherries (glacés):	Stuff with marzipan (Recipe 990).
Cherries (fresh):	Keep in pairs, do not remove stalk.
Grapes:	Keep in pairs, do not remove stalk.
Oranges:	Peel and remove fillets without breaking the skin, dry out slightly overnight.
Strawberries:	Must be fresh and dry, hold by stalk of husk when glazing. Cochineal may be added to the syrup.

Note. To prepare syrup and for dipping see Recipe 975.

1054 Marzipan glacé

1 Condition marzipan (Recipe 990) by adding icing sugar, colour, and mould as desired.
2 Allow to dry out slightly before glazing (Recipe 975).

1055 Biscuits à la cuillère – Savoy biscuits

2 *eggs*	60 g (2 oz) *caster sugar*
15 *ml spoon* (1 *tbsp.*) *water*	60 g (2 oz) *flour*

1 Whisk egg yolks, sugar, and water over a bain-marie to ribbon stage.
2 Whisk egg whites to a stiff snow.
3 Begin folding the flour through the egg yolks; sugar and water before adding the beaten egg whites.
4 Pipe on to greaseproof or silicone paper, 6 cm (3 inches) long, turn on to caster sugar and bake immediately in a hot oven (204°C (400°F) for approximately 6 minutes).

Used for pastries; lining a charlotte russe; serving with ices, bombes, etc. The mix may also be used whenever a fatless sponge is required.

1055a Brandy snaps (yield approximately 10)

90 g (3 oz) *butter* (*or margarine*)	120 g (4 oz) *plain flour*
240 g (8 oz) *caster sugar*	6 g (¼ oz) *ground ginger*
240 g (8 oz) *golden syrup*	

1 Cream the butter (or margarine) and sugar until light and fluffy.
2 Add the golden syrup, and cream well.
3 Gradually fold in the sieved flour and ground ginger.
4 Place mixture into a piping bag with a ½ cm (¼ inch) plain tube.
5 Pipe on to a silicone-lined baking sheet into 1 cm (½ inch) diameter rounds.
6 Bake in a hot oven (approximately 220°C (425°F)) for approximately 5 minutes until golden brown on the edges.

7 Allow to cool until slightly firm. Roll round a wooden rod and allow to cool until crisp.
8 Remove from rod and use as required.

Note. Brandy snaps can be offered as petits fours and pastries. They can be shaped as required, e.g. tartlets, barquettes and used as containers for sweets, filled with, say, lemon syllabub, raspberries, whipped cream. etc.

1056 Langues de chat

60 g (2 oz) butter   90 g (3 oz) icing sugar   2 egg whites
60 g (2 oz) soft flour   vanilla essence

1 Cream butter and sugar lightly.
2 Add egg whites one by one taking care not to curdle.
3 Finally, fold through flour and essence.
4 Pipe on to a well-greased baking tray through 0.3 cm (⅛ inch) plain tube, 4 cm (2 inch) length; bake in a hot oven.

1057 Palets de dames

Ingredients as for Langues de chat (Recipe 1056).

1 As for Langues de chat but pipe into rounds of 1 cm (½ inch) diameter.
2 When cold decorate with chocolate.

1058 Macaroon tartelettes

sweet short-pastry (Recipe 996)   120 g (¼ lb) ground almonds
15 g (½ oz) ground rice or rice   240 g (½ lb) caster sugar
  flour   3 egg whites

1 Whisk whites lightly.
2 Add sugar, almonds, and ground rice, and beat thoroughly with a wooden spoon.
3 Line tartelette cases with sweet short-pastry.
4 Pipe in a little raspberry jam and cover with macaroon mixture.
5 Bake for 15 to 20 minutes at 165°C (330°F).

1059 Madeleines

60 g (2 oz) butter   90 g (3 oz) caster sugar   1 to 2 eggs
120 g (4 oz) soda flour   vanilla essence

1 Sugar-batter method; pipe into greased dariole-moulds; bake for 15 minutes at 165°–177°C (330°–350°F).
2 When cold, brush with raspberry purée and roll in coconut.
3 Pipe a dot of pink fondant on top.

Note. Dariole moulds produce 'Eiffel Tower' madeleines. Fluted coquille moulds are also accepted.

1060 Marquis biscuits

Langues de chat   *Praline (Recipe 991)*   *Ganache*
    (Recipe 1056)   *(Recipe 985)*

Sandwich biscuits together with ganache and praline and pipe the word 'Marquis' on top with chocolate.

1061 Ratafia biscuits

15 g (½ oz) ground rice or   *210 g (7 oz) caster sugar*
    semolina   *3 egg whites*
120 g (¼ lb) ground almonds

1 Lightly whisk egg whites and beat in remaining ingredients with a wooden spoon.
2 Pipe on to greaseproof or silicone paper to the size of a 2p piece.
3 Decorate with cherries, angelica, etc.; bake for 15 minutes at 160°C (320°F).

1062 Sables à la poche

120 g (4 oz) sugar   *1 egg yolk*   *240 g (½ lb) soft*
180 g (6 oz) butter   *1 egg*   *flour*
                                          vanilla essence

1 Cream butter and sugar until light in texture and colour.
2 Add yolk and egg one by one, beating thoroughly.
3 Fold through flour, ground almonds and essence lightly until smooth.
4 Pipe on to a greased and floured baking tray, using a star tube, into rosettes.
5 Decorate with cherry and angelica and bake in a moderate oven for 10 minutes approximately.

1062a Sables

Miniature version of Sables à la poche (Recipe 1062).

1063 Shortbread

210 g (7 oz) soft flour   *1 small egg yolk*
60 g (2 oz) sugar   *120 g (4 oz) butter*
30 g (1 oz) rice flour

1 Mix butter, sugar and egg yolk together.
2 Sieve flour and rice flour on to butter, sugar, etc., and knead.
3 Continue working on the table until smooth but do not oil.
4 Mould, stab and bake lightly (180–200°C for about 15 minutes); dust with caster sugar.

1063a Tuiles à l'orange – Orange tuiles

> 120 g (4 oz) nibbed almonds
> 120 g (4 oz) icing sugar
> 30 g (1 oz) flour
> 250 ml (½ pt) orange juice
> 90 g (3 oz) melted butter
> grated zest of ½ orange

1 Mix flour, nibbed almonds, icing sugar well. Stir in orange juice and zest.
2 Add the melted butter at blood heat.
3 Cover and refrigerate for 2 hours.
4 Well grease a baking sheet with compound fat.
5 Spoon the mix on to it according to size required – say 15 g (½ oz) mixture. Space tuiles well apart. Spread out with the back of a wetted spoon approximately 7 cm (2¾ inch) diameter.
6 Bake at 200°C (400°F) for approximately 5 minutes until golden brown at the edges.
7 Allow to cool for 1 minute before removing from the baking sheet.
8 With a large palette knife remove the tuiles carefully. Shape as required.
9 Use as petit fours or as accompaniment to ice creams, sorbets and other sweet dishes.

Note. Tuiles may also be baked on silicon paper.

SOUFFLÉS AND PUDDING SOUFFLÉS

1064 Soufflé à la vanille – Vanilla soufflé (basic baked soufflé mix)

For 6 portions

60 g (2 oz) butter	90 g (3 oz) sugar	250 ml (½ pt) milk
60 g (2 oz) flour	4 egg yolks	1 vanilla pod
6 egg whites		

1 Butter and sugar soufflé dish.
2 Melt butter and add flour.
3 Add milk, vanilla pod, sugar and bring to the boil, remove vanilla pod.
4 Cool slightly, beat through egg yolks.
5 Fold through stiffly beaten egg whites.
6 Pour into soufflé case and two-thirds fill only; bake for 20 minutes in moderate oven 177°–188°C (350°–370°F).
7 Serve immediately.

1065 Soufflé Arlequin

Half vanilla and half chocolate soufflé (Recipes 1064 and 1066).

1066 Soufflé au chocolat – Chocolate soufflé

1 Soufflé vanille with the addition of 90 g (3 oz) grated or powdered chocolate which should be added to the milk.

2 Add an extra egg white as the chocolate tends to stiffen the appareil.

1067 Soufflé Grand-Marnier

Soufflé vanille with the addition of 30 ml (2 tablespoons) Grand Marnier liqueur.

1068 Pouding soufflé à la vanille

vanilla pod or essence	*60 g (2 oz) butter*	*4 eggs*
60 g (2 oz) flour	*190 ml (⅜ pt) milk*	*60 g (2 oz) sugar*

1 Boil milk, sugar and essence and pour into creamed butter and flour.
2 Return to the stove and re-boil.
3 Cool slightly and beat through egg yolks.
4 Fold through stiffly beaten egg whites.
5 Two-thirds fill buttered and sugared dariole moulds.
6 Cook in a bain-marie 20 minutes in moderate oven 177°C (350°F).

1069 Pouding soufflé à l'orange

Prepare as for Recipe 1068 plus juice and zest of 1 orange and ½ lemon in lieu of 25 ml (1 oz) of milk.

1070 Pouding soufflé Rothschild

Prepare as Recipe 1068 plus 15 g (½ oz) candied fruit and 15 ml spoon (1 tablespoon) kirsch.

1071 Pouding soufflé à la saxone

Prepare as for Recipe 1068 plus juice and zest of 1 lemon.

Cold soufflés

See Recipe 1129.

STEAMED AND BAKED PUDDINGS

1072 Steamed sponge pudding (basic mix)

120 g (4 oz) flour	*60 g (2 oz) butter*	*60 g (2 oz) sugar*
1 egg	*25 ml spoon (1 fluid*	*7 g (¼ oz) baking*
vanilla essence	*oz) milk*	*powder*

1 Cream butter and sugar, beat in egg. Fold through sieved flour and baking powder. Add milk to adjust to piping consistency.
2 Pipe into buttered dariole moulds and steam for 45 minutes.

1073 Chocolate sponge pudding

100 g (3½ oz) flour
60 g (2 oz) sugar
7 g (¼ oz) baking powder
15 g (½ oz) cocoa

1 egg
60 g (2 oz) butter
30 g (1 oz) milk

As for Recipe 1072 with cocoa sieved with flour.

1074 Lemon sponge pudding

Prepare as Recipe 1072 without vanilla but plus juice and zest of ½ lemon.

1075 Pouding tunisien – Steamed date pudding

180 g (6 oz) breadcrumbs
90 g (3 oz) syrup or 180 g (6 oz)
  sugar
20 g (¾ oz) baking powder
180 g (6 oz) flour
360 g (¾ lb) dates

zest of 1 lemon
zest of 1 orange
180 g (6 oz) chopped suet
1 to 2 eggs
7 g (¼ oz) spice
310 ml (12½ fluid oz) milk

1 Mix all dry ingredients together.
2 Form into a bay; add milk, eggs and syrup and form into a soft mixture.
3 Half fill buttered dariole moulds and steam for 1½ hours.

1076 Christmas pudding

For 100 portions

2 kg (4 lb) sultanas
2 kg (4 lb) raisins
2 kg (4 lb) suet
2 kg (4 lb) currants
22 eggs
250 ml (½ pt) milk
zest of 2 oranges
2 kg (4 lb) peel

720 g (1½ lb) apples
1.6 kg (3¼ lb)
  breadcrumbs
1.6 kg (3¼ lb) brown
  sugar
30 g (1 oz) salt
250 ml (½ pt) spirit
zest of 2 lemons

1.6 kg (3¼ lb) flour
360 g (¾ lb) prunes
240 g (½ lb) ground
  almonds
120 g (4 oz) ginger
1.5 litre (3 pt) stout
45 g (1½ oz) spice

1 Soak fruit in spirit overnight and follow method for Recipe 1075.

Note. Steaming times depend on weight of puddings, but will be upward of 5 hours, i.e. 5 hours for 1 kg (2 lb) increasing to 6 hours for larger weights. it is customary to prepare and steam well in advance and to re-steam (approx. 3 hours according to size) on day of use.

1077 Baked sponge pudding

Prepare as Recipe 1072 but bake in a moderate oven 177°C (350°F) for 30 minutes.

MILK, CUSTARD AND KINDRED PUDDINGS

1078 Baked rice pudding

62 ml (⅛ pt) rice	500 ml (1 pt) milk	60 g (2 oz) caster
15 g (½ oz) butter	nutmeg	sugar
		vanilla essence

1 Butter a pie-dish and place in sugar and rice.
2 Pour in milk, add essence and grate a little nutmeg on top.
3 Bake for 1½ to 2 hours in a cool oven of 150°C (300°F).

1079 Semolina pudding

500 ml (1 pt) milk	62 ml (⅛ pt) semolina	60 g (2 oz) sugar
15 g (½ oz) butter	nutmeg	vanilla essence

1 Boil milk and essence, rain in semolina and cook gently at side of stove.
2 When cooked, add sugar, pour into buttered pie-dish; grate nutmet on top and brown under salamander or in oven, sitting in bain-marie.

1079a Sago and tapioca puddings

Proceed as for semolina pudding (Recipe 1079) using 3 × 20 ml spoon (⅛ pt) sago or tapioca instead of semolina.

1080 Bread and butter pudding (for 12 portions)

1 litre (1 qt) milk	30 g (1 oz) currants	60 g (2 oz) butter
120 g (4 oz) sugar	30 g (1 oz) sultanas	6 slices bread
5 to 6 eggs	vanilla esence	

1 Remove crusts and butter the bread, cut into triangles.
2 Butter a pie dish and sprinkle with half of the fruit.
3 Place in half of the buttered bread, the remainder of the fruit and top with the remaining bread.
4 Boil milk and essence, pour on to eggs and sugar; mix, strain and half fill pie-dish; allow to soak for 5 minutes before pouring in remainder of custard.
5 Cook in a bain-marie in a moderate oven at 175°C (350°F) for 45 minutes approximately.

1081 Cabinet pudding

500 ml (1 pt) milk	60 g (2 oz) diced	90 g (3 oz) sugar
vanilla pod	génoise	60 g (2 oz) ratafia
30 g (1 oz) cherries	(Recipe 1044)	biscuits
30 g (1 oz) sultanas	30 g (1 oz) angelica	(Recipe 1061)
4 eggs		30 g (1 oz) currants

1 Lightly butter a charlotte mould.
2 Dice génoise, ratafia, cherries, and angelica; add sultanas and currants, and half fill charlotte mould.

3 Whisk eggs and sugar together; add warm milk which has been infused with vanilla pod; strain.
4 Half fill charlotte mould with custard and let stand for 10 minutes.
5 Add remainder of custard; sit in a bain-marie of hot water and cook in a moderate oven for 30 to 40 minutes; do not allow water to boil.
6 Turn out and serve a jam or sabayon sauce (Recipes 970, 971).

1082 Pudding à la diplomate (cold)

270 g (9 oz) milk	60 g (2 oz) caster sugar	3 egg yolks
15 g (½ oz) gelatine	60 g (2 oz) water	270 g (9 oz) cream
(powdered)	30 g (1 oz) sultanas	30 g (1 oz) glacé
30 g (1 oz) currants	15 g (½ oz) angelica	cherries
2 × 15 ml spoon (⅛ pt)	8 savoy biscuits	125 ml (¼ pt) stock
kirsch	(Recipe 1055)	syrup
		(Recipe 992)

1 Lightly oil charlotte or dariole moulds and decorate with cherries and angelica.
2 Soak currants, sultanas and savoy biscuits in kirsch-flavoured syrup.
3 Prepare sauce anglaise as in Recipe 961.
4 Add dissolved gelatine to custard and strain.
5 When on point of setting, fold through stiffly beaten cream and place in mould in alternate layers with soaked savoy biscuits and fruit.
6 Allow to set in refrigerator.
7 When set, turn out and decorate with cream.

1083 Œufs à la neige

500 ml (1 pt) milk	120 g (4 oz) sugar	additional 180 g
4 eggs	vanilla essence	(6 oz) sugar for
		meringue

1 Prepare meringue with egg whites and 180 g (6 oz) sugar (Recipe 1004) and poach in warmed milk and essence; (mould meringues between two spoons).
2 Prepare a sauce anglaise (Recipe 961) with yolks of eggs and sugar and allow to set in a salad bowl.
3 Sprinkle meringue with flaked almonds; brown under grill and float on sauce anglaise.

1084 Pouding à la reine – Queen's pudding or Queen of puddings

250 ml (½ pt) milk	45 g (1½ oz) cake crumbs
60 g (2 oz) sugar	30 g (1 oz) apricot jam
15 g (½ oz) butter	60 g (2 oz) raspberry jam
2 eggs	icing sugar

1 Butter a pie-dish, spread with 30 g (1 oz) raspberry jam and sprinkle with cake crumbs (or bread crumbs).
2 Prepare an egg custard and half fill pie-dish allowing crumbs to soak.

3 Pour in remainder of custard, sit in bain-marie and bake for 45 minutes.
4 Prepare a meringue with whites of egg and sugar (Recipe 1006) and pipe on to custard; brown in oven before decorating the top by piping with alternate squares of jam (raspberry and apricot).

1085 Pouding soufflé à la samaritaine

190 ml (⅜ pt) milk
7 g (¼ oz) butter
90 g (3 oz) sugar for caramel
    (Recipe 989)
30 g (1 oz) semolina

zest of ½ lemon
3 egg whites
45 g (1½ oz) caster sugar
2 egg yolks

1 Boil milk, butter, lemon zest, and sugar; rain in semolina and allow to cook at the side of stove.
2 Prepare a caramel and line 4 dariole moulds with it.
3 Allow semolina and milk to cool slightly; beat through egg yolks.
4 Fold through stiffly-beaten egg whites and fill two-thirds of dariole moulds.
5 Sit in bain-marie and bake for 20 minutes.
6 Turn out on to entrée-dish and serve immediately.

Note. Additional caramel sauce (Recipe 963) can be served if desired.

SWEET OMELETTES

Although omelettes (including sweet ones) are made by the chef entremettier rather than by the chef pâtissier in a large professional kitchen, a few examples are listed here for convenience.

1086 Omelette à la confiture – Jam omelette

120 g (¼ lb) strawberry jam
    (warmed)
1 poker or heated iron bar

30 g (1 oz) (approx.) butter,
    clarified
120 g (¼ lb) caster sugar
8 eggs

1 Prepare omelette as Recipe 328.
2 Before folding, fill with warm jam.
3 When dished, sprinkle top copiously with sugar.
4 Burn sugar with hot poker, making any simple design as desired.

1087 Omelette au rhum – Rum omelette

8 eggs
120 g (¼ lb) caster sugar

30 g (1 oz) (approx.) butter,
    clarified
125 ml (¼ pt) rum

1 Make omelette (as Recipe 328), seasoning with a little sugar.
2 Sprinkle top with sugar.
3 Pour rum over sugar and set alight to serve.

1088 Omelette soufflée – Soufflé omelette

    8 eggs   *pinch of salt*
    60 g (2 oz) sugar   *30 g (1 oz) (approx.) butter*

1 Beat yolks separately from whites.
2 Beat whites and add sugar.
3 Fold whites into yolks.
4 Pour into hot buttered pan.
5 Place in oven or under grill to cook.

CRÊPES – PANCAKES

1089 To prepare pancakes (Pannequet – alternative name for Crêpe)

1 Heat oil or clarified butter in pan and pour away.
2 Heat sufficient batter (Recipes 1002 or 1003) to coat base of pan thinly and evenly.
3 Cook until lightly coloured, toss and cook other side likewise.
4 It is then ready for service, plain or otherwise as below.

1090 Crêpes au citron – Pancakes with lemon

Crêpes folded in four and accompanied by lemon quarters.

1091 Crêpes au confiture

Rolled with filling of warmed jam.

1092 Crêpes à la couvent

Filling of diced or purée of pears.

1093 Crêpes à la normande

With apple purée filling.

1094 Crêpes à la parisienne

Prepare with the addition of 30 g (1 oz) cream and 30 g (1 oz) crushed biscuits to crêpe batter (Recipe 1002 or 1003).

1095 Blinis – Unsweetened pancakes (for caviar)

    10 g (⅜ oz) yeast   *250 ml (½ pt) warm milk*
    125 ml (¼ pt) warm *for*   *2 egg yolks*
    2 egg whites (beaten *ferment*   *salt*
    stiff)
    180 g (6 oz) buckwheat flour

1 Sift the flour and make a bay.
2 Pour the 125 ml (¼ pt) warm milk and yeast in the bay, sprinkle with flour and allow to ferment.

3 Keep in a warm place for ¾ hour.
4 Make into a batter with the 250 ml (½ pt) of milk and egg yolks and allow to stand for 30 minutes.
5 Fold in the egg whites.
6 Make into small pancakes (as Recipe 1089 but about 7 to 8 cm (3½ to 4-inch diameter).
Note. When serving blinis with caviar, accompany with sour cream.

BEIGNETS – FRITTERS

Beignets soufflés
See Recipe 1017.

1096 Fruit for fritters (to prepare)

Apples: Core, peel and cut in rings. Flour before passing through batter (Recipe 1001).
Pears: Peel, halve and remove core. Cut into quarters depending on size. Flour before passing through batter.

Note. For soft fruit, pineapples, peaches, etc., flour before passing through batter.

1097 Fruit fritters (to cook)

1 Prepare fruit as necessary (e.g. stone, peel, and core), and if sliced, cut 0.5 cm (¼ inch) thick.
2 Flour, pass through batter (Recipe 1001) and remove excess batter before frying in hot fat.
3 Turn during cooking process.
4 Drain on cooling-wire and dust with caster sugar and glaze under salamander.
5 Serve apricot sauce or custard separately.

1098 Beignets de bananes – Banana fritters

Allow up to 2 bananas per portion depending on size:

1 Skin and lightly flour the bananas.
2 Pass through warm frangipane cream (Recipe 1099).
3 Allow to set before passing through batter (Recipe 1001).
4 Finish as for fruit fritters (Recipe 1097).

1099 Frangipane cream (for fritters)

250 ml (½ pt) milk	45 g (1½ oz) flour	3 egg yolks
1 egg	45 g (1½ oz) sugar	7 g (¼ oz) butter
1 vanilla pod or essence		

1 Boil milk, butter and vanilla pod.
2 Mix remainder of ingredients together to a smooth paste.
3 Add boiling milk to paste mixing smoothly.
4 Return to pan and bring to boil whisking continuously.
5 Pour in basin, cover with greased paper.

FRUIT COMPÔTES – STEWED OR POACHED FRUIT

1100 Syrup for compotes

500 g (1 lb) sugar   625 ml (1¼ pt) water

1 Bring sugar and water to boil.
2 Syrup should register 20° when tested by saccharometer.

1101 Compote de pommes – Stewed apples

660 g (22 oz) apples   250 ml (½ pt) syrup (Recipe 1100)

1 Quarter, core, and peel apples.
2 Place into boiling syrup.
3 Return to boil and immediately remove from stove.
4 Cover with a lid and allow to cool.

1102 Compote de pêches – Poached peaches

1 Blanch and skin peaches.
2 Cook in syrup until stone feels loose.
3 When cold, they are ready for service.

1103 Compote de poires – Poached pears

500 g (1 lb) pears   250 ml (½ pt) syrup (Recipe 1100)

Prepare as for apples (Recipe 1101).

1104 Compote de cerises – Stewed cherries

1 Place 360 g (¾ lb) cherries (with stalk removed) in boiling syrup.
2 Return to boil and allow to cool.

1105 Compote de prunes – Plum compote

Place 360 g (¾ lb) plums in boiling syrup and poach gently in the oven in a covered saucepan.

1106 Compote de reine-Claudes – Greengages

1106a Compote d'abricots – Apricots

1106b Compote de mirabelles – Mirabelle plums

1106c Compote de groseilles vertes – Gooseberries

May be prepared as for plums; allow 300–360 g (10–12 oz) fruit for 4 covers.

1107 Compote de framboises – Raspberry compote

1 Place 360 g (12 oz) raspberries in boiling syrup.
2 Return to boil and allow to cool.

1108 Compote de fraises – Strawberries

1108a Compote de groseilles rouges – Red currants

1108b Compote de cassis – Black currants

Prepare similar quantities in same manner as for raspberries (Recipe 1107).

1109 Compote de rhubarbe – Stewed rhubarb

1 Peel and cut 500 g (1 lb) rhubarb into equal lengths and place in a baking tin.
2 Sprinkle with sugar and a little water and red colouring if necessary.
3 Cover with wet greaseproof paper and poach until tender in a moderate oven.

1110 Compote de pruneaux – Stewed prunes

500 g (1 lb) prunes	*zest of ½ lemon*
120 g (¼ lb) sugar	*15 ml spoon [1 tablespoon] treacle*
¼ stick cinnamon	*250 ml (½ pt) water*

1 Soak prunes overnight.
2 Refresh, cover with cold water and add sugar, cinnamon, zest of lemon, and treacle.
3 Allow to simmer for ½ hour.
4 Ready to serve when cold.

1111 Compote de figues – Stewed figs

As for prunes, Recipe 1110, omitting treacle.

FRESH FRUIT SALAD

1112 Macédoine de fruit

Apples and *pears:*	Peel, core and slice evenly
Grapes:	Peel and stone
Oranges:	Remove cap of skin from top and bottom, and remove skin from sides in a circular manner. Cut out quarters which should not contain any skin.

Peaches:	Quarter and slice evenly
Pineapple:	Peel and cut rounds into eighths
Strawberries:	Remove husk and if large, cut into quarters
Bananas:	Skin and slice not too finely

Place in a silver timbale, add sugar, lemon juice and moisten with stock syrup (Recipe 992). See note on further fruits below.

FURTHER FRUITS

Since the first edition of this *Compendium*, many more tropical or exotic fruits have become commonplace in restaurants of the West. These may be served fresh in fruit baskets, as single items, in compôtes (as in preceding type of preparations), as additions to fresh fruit salad or in other dishes.

The following (indicative rather than exhaustive) suggest possibilities for some further fruits:

Cape gooseberries or Pok Pok
Small orange–yellow coloured fruits surrounded with white, feathery, open-ended outer covering. For sugar-dipping (and use as petit fours), this cover is drawn back and the amber-coloured fruit dipped in boiled sugar or white fondant. Also used in compôtes.

Custard apple – Corossal
This heart-shaped fruit is halved for removal of inedible seeds, and the flesh removed from the pine-comb textured skin. The custard-like flavour of the flesh (somewhat between that of pineapple and banana) may be used for service alone or with other fruit, or to flavour fools, mousses or other sweet dishes.

Guava – Goyave
Rounded (rather pear-shaped) fruit; colour varying from yellow to purple and flesh from greenish-white to pink. Washed, peeled and sliced for fruit salads, garnishes, fools and sauces.

Kiwi fruit (Chinese gooseberry)
Either wash the brown-skinned, oval fruit and halve for eating with a small spoon (teaspoon) or peel and slice into roundels for fruit salads or garnishes. Also usable in sauces and other items such as mousses.

Kumquat
A miniature fruit of orange style (some are round but they are usually oval). It is eaten whole, but its aromatic, edible skin and juice may be used like orange zest and juice for flavouring.

Lychee (Litchi) – Letchi (or litchi)
Plum-sized fruit with warty, purplish-red rind and interior stone. Peeled for eating fresh but often canned.

Mango – Mangue
As single fruit, usually halved, stone removed to spoon out flesh from the skin, or peeled and sliced for fruit salad, sauces, garnishes, mousses.

Papaya or Paw Paw – Papaye
Sliced for eating in melon style, with black seeds discarded, or cut for fruit salads, sauces, garnishes.

Passion fruit (grenadilla) – Barbardine
For eating fresh, halved and the seeds eaten with a small spoon (teaspoon) from the wrinkled skin (sometimes green but usually purplish). The seeds may also be added to fruit salads. Juice from the pulped seed makes a refreshing drink, sorbet or flavour for sauces, mousses.

Persimmon – Kaki (or figue caque)
Can be eaten halved to enable the flesh to be scooped out for service alone, or sliced in fruit salads or in flavouring mousses, jellies, sauces (for icecreams, etc.).

Pomegranate – Grenade
Chilled, top trimmed off to provide access to the fleshy seeds from the yellow tissue for service fresh and to be eaten with small spoon (teaspoon or sundae spoon). Juice expressed from the seeds only may be served as a chilled appetiser or made into grenadine syrup.

Sharon fruit – type of persimmon (see above)
Developed and improved in Israel. Eaten whole or sliced across (in kiwi-fruit style).

WARM FRUIT DISHES

1113 Charlotte aux pommes – Apple Charlotte

620 g (1¼ lb) apples		500 g (1 lb) bread
15 g (½ oz) margarine		120 g (¼ lb) butter
45 g (1½ oz) sugar	purée	250 ml (½ pt) apricot sauce
1 clove		(Recipe 960)
lemon zest		

1 Prepare a purée with the apples and other listed ingredients.
2 Line dariole moulds with buttered bread then fill with apple purée.
3 Bake in a moderate oven for 20 to 30 minutes.
4 Serve with apricot sauce (Recipe 960).

1114 Poire Bourdalouse

30 g (1 oz) crushed macaroons   120 g (¼ lb) frangipane cream
  (Recipe 1058) or   (Recipe 1099)
30 g (1 oz) flaked almonds   4 pears
                                       15 g (½ oz) butter

1 Poach pears in syrup and drain.
2 Halve pears and coat with frangipane cream.
3 Sprinkle with crushed macaroons or flaked almonds and melted butter.
4 Glaze under salamander and serve hot.

Note. Apricots, bananas, peaches, apples and nectarines may be prepared
similarly.

1115 Poires au vin rouge – Pears in red wine

4 pears   ¼ stick cinnamon   60 g (2 oz) sugar
125 ml (¼ pt) red wine   ½ lemon   125 ml (¼ pt) water

1 Prepare a syrup with water, wine, cinnamon, lemon, and sugar and allow
   pears to poach in it.
2 Pears should be served warm but not hot.
3 Serve with ratafia biscuits (Recipe 1061).

JELLIES, CREAMS, AND COLD RICE SWEETS

In the preparation of jellies and creams, it is possible to produce many
different kinds by changing the flavours. This can be achieved by including
different fruits, their pulp and juice, and liqueurs. Basic recipes for jelly,
bavarois (Bavarian cream), mousse of cold soufflé should, therefore, be fully
exploited.

1116 Basic jelly I – for warm-weather use

60 g (2 oz) gelatine   750 ml (1½ pt) water (or milk for
120 g (4 oz) sugar   milk jellies)

1116a Basic jelly II – for cold-weather use

870 ml (1¾ pt) water or milk   60 g (2 oz) gelatine
  (including cream, etc.)   150 g (5 oz) sugar

To both these jellies add fruit, flavouring, purée, and cream as required.

1117 Gelée au citron – Lemon jelly

750 ml (1½ pt) cold   60 g (2 oz) gelatine   1 bay-leaf
  water   3 egg whites   ¼ stick cinnamon
120 g (4 oz) sugar   zest of ½ lemon   coriander seeds
juice of 2 to 2½ lemons

1 Mix all ingredients together and bring slowly to the boil, stirring continuously.
2 Allow to simmer for ½ hour.
3 When straining, ladle from side of saucepan carefully.
4 Pass through a fine strainer (or jelly bag).

1118 Gelée à l'orange – Orange jelly

750 ml (1½ pt) water	coriander seeds
60 g (2 oz) gelatine	cochineal
3 egg whites	¼ stick cinnamon
juice and zest of 1 orange	1 bay-leaf
juice and zest of 1 lemon	120 g (4 oz) sugar

Prepare as for lemon jelly (Recipe 1117).

1119 Fruit jellies

Raspberry, strawberry, etc., are prepared in a similar manner to lemon and orange jellies (Recipes 1117 and 1118).

1120 Liqueur and wine jellies

Add kirsch, maraschino, white wine, etc., to lemon jelly (Recipe 1117) and colour accordingly.

BAVAROIS AND DERIVATIVE DISHES

1121 Bavarois à la vanille – Vanilla bavarois or basic Bavarian cream

500 ml (1 pt) milk	125 ml (¼ pt) cream
4 eggs	30 g (1 oz) gelatine (leaf)
120 g (4 oz) sugar	vanilla essence

1 Prepare a sauce anglaise (Recipe 961).
2 Add soaked gelatine and dissolve in the sauce anglaise.
3 Strain and place on ice, when on point of setting fold through beaten cream followed by stiffly-beaten egg whites.
4 Ladle into moulds before the preparation sets.

Note. Egg white need not be added; in which case the whipped cream may be proportionately increased (i.e. up to double the amount).

1122 Bavarois aux framboises I – Raspberry bavarois

1 Ingredients and method as for Recipe 1121 but replace 125 ml (¼ pt) of the milk with a 125 ml (¼ pt) of raspberry purée and the juice of ½ lemon and colouring, if necessary.
2 Purée is added before folding through the cream and egg whites.

1123 Bavarois aux framboises II

120 g (4 oz) raspberry purée	*125 ml (¼ pt) cream*
75 g (2½ oz) sugar	*red colouring*
7 g (¼ oz) gelatine	*juice of ¼ lemon*

1 Dissolve all ingredients together except the cream.
2 When dissolved, allow to cool and when almost setting, fold through the beaten cream.

1123a Bavarois, syrup-based (using a fruit purée)

500 ml (1 pt) fruit purée (see note below)	*15 g (½ oz) soaked leaf gelatine*
120 g (4 oz) caster sugar	*4 egg whites pasteurized (optional)*
250 ml (½ pt) whipping cream	*juice of ½ lemon*

1 Prepare the fruit purée, which should be the consistency of single cream.
2 Add the sugar, bring to the boil. Add the soaked gelatine.
3 Pass through a fine strainer.
4 Allow to cool. Add the lemon juice.
5 When on setting point, fold in the lightly whipped cream and stiffly beaten egg white (if egg whites omitted, a little extra whipped cream may be added up to a maximum 250 ml (½ pt).
6 Place into suitable moulds.
7 Allow to set in the refrigerator.
8 Turn out. Decorate and garnish as required.

Note. The purée may be made from raw, ripe, soft fruit or cooked hard fruits. Suitable fruits include strawberries, raspberries, mangoes, pears, apricots, peaches and nectarines.

1124 Bavarois au chocolat

Vanilla bavarois with the addition of 120 g (¼ lb) grated or powdered chocolate (Recipe 1121).

1125 Bavarois rubané – Ribboned (or tri-coloured) bavarois

Three layers of bavarois preparation, i.e.,

(i) Chocolate – Vanilla – Raspberry
or
(ii) Coffee – Raspberry – Chocolate

1126 Charlotte royale

Swiss roll	*125 ml (¼ pt) fruit jelly*	*Vanilla bavarois*
(Recipe 1043)	*(Recipe 1119)*	*(Recipe 1121)*

1 Set 1 cm (½ inch) of raspberry or strawberry jelly on bottom of charlotte mould.
2 Line the charlotte mould with slices of Swiss roll and fill with vanilla or strawberry bavarois.
3 Turn out when set.

1127 Charlotte russe

Savoy biscuits (Recipe 1055)   *Vanilla bavarois (Recipe* 1121)

1 Line a Charlotte mould with savoy biscuits and fill with vanilla or strawberry bavarois.
2 Turn out when set.

1128 Mousses I

Vanilla bavarois (Recipe 1121), omit 125 ml (¼ pt) milk and replace it with 125 ml (¼ pt) cream.

1128a Mousses II

¼ *lemon juice*	60 *g* (2 *oz*) *sugar*	125 *ml* (¼ *pt*) *fruit*
250 *ml* (½ *pt*) *cream*	*colouring if desired*	*purée*

1 Lightly whisk cream and sugar together and fold through the remaining ingredients.
2 Pipe into frosted goblets.
3 Serve with biscuits à la cuillère (Recipe 1055).

SOUFFLÉS FROID – COLD SOUFFLÉS

1129 Soufflé à la milanaise

125 *ml* (¼ *pt*) *cream*	120 *g* (¼ *lb*) *sugar*	2 *eggs*
1 *lemon*	*pistachio nuts*	*toasted almonds*
7 *g* (¼ *oz*) *gelatine*		

1 Surround a soufflé case with greaseproof paper.
2 Dissolve gelatine in the juice of ½ lemon.
3 Whisk egg yolks, sugar and lemon juice to ribbon stage over warm water.
4 Add dissolved gelatine and allow to cool.
5 When cold fold through whipped cream followed by beaten whites.
6 Pour into soufflé case and allow to set.
7 Remove paper, coat sides, with almond nibs, decorate with whipped cream and blanched pistachio n its.

CUSTARD CREAMS

1130 Crème au caramel – Caramel cream

60 *g* (2 *oz*) *sugar*	⎫ *Caramel*	*All ingredients as for Crème*
30 *g* (1 *oz*) *water*	⎭ *(Recipe* 989)	*Renversée (Recipe* 1131)

1 Prepare a caramel and cover the bottom of a charlotte mould.
2 When set, strain and continue in the same manner as for Crème renversée.
3 When cold, turn out on to a round silver flat.

1131 Crème renversée

250 *ml* (½ *pt*) *milk*	2 *eggs*
1 *vanilla pod* (*or essence*)	60 *g* (2 *oz*) *sugar*

1 Bring the milk and vanilla pod to the boil and pour over eggs and sugar.
2 Strain into a pie-dish or charlotte mould; place in a bain-marie and cook in the oven until set.
3 When cold, it is ready to serve.
4 Carefully turn out from mould and decorate with cream, if desired.

1132 Petits pots de crème au café

Crème renversée (Recipe 1131) with the addition of 45 g (1½ oz) coffee essence. As for petits pots de crème à la vanille (Recipe 1134).

1133 Petits pots de crème au chocolat

crème renversée (*Recipe* 1131)	45 *g* (1½ *oz*) *chocolate or*
	21 *g* (¾ *oz*) *cocoa powder*

As for petits pots de crème à la vanille (Recipe 1134).

1134 Petits pots de crème à la vanille

Crème renversée (*Recipe* 1131)

1 Prepare a Crème renversée and ladle into individual cocottes.
2 Bake in a bain-marie.

COLD SWEETS WITH MILK AND CREAM

1135 Junket

10 *ml spoon* [1 *dessertspoon*]	*grated nutmeg*
essence of rennet	250 *ml* (½ *pt*) *milk*
30 *g* (1 *oz*) *sugar*	

1 Warm milk and sugar to blood heat.
2 Pour over essence.
3 Place a little grated nutmeg on top.
4 Leave to set.

1136 Syllabub

250 *ml* (½ *pt*) *cream*	*zest and juice of* ½ *lemon*
125 *ml* (¼ *pt*) *white wine*	30–60 *g* (1 *to* 2 *oz*) *sugar*

1 Lightly whisk cream and add wine, zest, lemon juice, and sugar to taste.
2 Place on a sieve to remove excess moisture.
3 Place a little wine in frosted goblets and pour the syllabub on top.

Note. Red wine or brandy can be used.

1137 Fruit fools

250 ml (½ pt) fruit purée
60 g (2 oz) sugar

125 ml (¼ pt) cream
6 egg whites

1 Lightly whip the cream.
2 Whisk whites to a stiff snow.
3 Fold all ingredients together.
4 Add colouring if necessary.

TRIFLE

1138 Fruit trifle

sponge cake
raspberry jam
angelica, cherries
custard sauce

whipped cream
syrup { 240 g (½ lb) sugar
375 ml (¾ pt) water

1 Sandwich sponge with jam and place in a salad bowl.
2 Add the fruit and moisten with syrup.
3 Cover with custard sauce.
4 When cold, decorate with whipped cream, cherries, angelica, etc.

1139 Sherry trifle

120 g (¼ lb) sponge or
génoise
(Recipe 1044)
2 egg yolks
60 g (2 oz) sugar
62 ml (⅛ pt) stock
syrup (Recipe 992)

60 g (2 oz) ratafia
biscuits
(Recipe 1061) or
macaroons (or both
mixed)
30 g (1 oz) raspberry
jam

125 ml (¼ pt) cream
250 ml (½ pt) milk
1 vanilla pod
15 ml (1 tbsp.)
sherry
blanched almonds
cherries, angelica

1 Prepare a sauce anglaise with the milk, sugar, egg yolks, and vanilla pod
(Recipe 961).
2 Halve the génoise, spread with jam and cut into dice.
3 Place diced sponge and a few ratafia biscuits in a salad bowl and moisten
with sherry and stock syrup.
4 Napper with custard and leave to cool.
5 Decorate with stiffly beaten cream, split blanched almonds, cherries and
angelica, and remaining ratafia biscuits.

COLD RICE SWEETS

1140 Rice for Condé

625ml (1¼ pt) milk
60 g (2 oz) butter

120 g (¼ lb) sugar
250 ml (½ pt) cream

120 g (¼ lb) rice
vanilla essence

1 Boil milk and essence and rain in rice; bake in the oven for 1 hour approximately or simmer on stove until tender (20 to 30 minutes).
2 When soft, add sugar, butter and allow to cool.
3 When cold, fold through 250 ml (½ pt) of whipped cream.
4 Mould as required.

1141 Apricot Condé

1 Prepare as for Condé (Recipe 1140).
2 Place rice neatly in salad bowl and arrange appropriate poached fruit on top.
3 Glaze with kirsch-flavoured apricot sauce (Recipe 960).
4 Decorate with whipped cream, cherries, angelica, etc.

1142 Riz à l'impératrice

rice (Recipe 1140)   *vanilla bavarois (Recipe 1121)*
orange of strawberry jelly   *Melba sauce (Recipe 970)*

1 Set jelly, 0.5 cm (¼ inch) thick in dariole or charlotte moulds.
2 Pour in vanilla bavarois containing the cooked rice.
3 When set turn out on to silver, masked with jam sauce.

1143 Rice for créole

500 ml (1 pt) milk   *15 g (½ oz) gelatine*   *60 g (2 oz) sugar*
62 ml (⅛ pt) rice   *125 ml (¼ pt) cream*   *2 egg whites*
vanilla essence

1 Boil milk and essence, add rice and bake in oven or stove simmer until tender.
2 When cooked, add sugar and gelatine, place on ice to cool.
3 When on point of setting, fold through beaten cream and stiffly-beaten egg whites; mould as desired.

1144 Ananas à la créole – Pineapple creole

1 Prepare rice as Recipe 1143.
2 Mould rice in form of a pineapple, cut lengthwise.
3 Criss-cross to resemble pineapple skin.
4 Surround with half-rings of pineapple.
5 Glaze pineapple with apricot sauce (Recipe 960).
6 Decorate with angelica to resemble pineapple top.

ICES AND DESSERTS INCORPORATING ICE-CREAMS

1145 American ice-cream

250 ml (½ pt) milk   *½ can condensed milk*   *180 g (6 oz) sugar*
250 ml (½ pt) cream   *1 sheet gelatine*   *vanilla essence*

1 Dissolve gelatine and sugar in fresh milk.
2 Add essence – strain and cool.
3 Add remaining ingredients and freeze.

1146 Glace à la vanille – Vanilla ice-cream or Custard ice

500 ml (1 pt) milk	*4 egg yolks*	*90 to 120 g (4 to*
vanilla pod or essence		*5 oz) sugar*

1 Bring milk and vanilla pod to the boil.
2 Pour on to yolks and sugar; return to the stove and cook until custard coats the back of a spoon.
3 Strain, cool, and freeze.

Notes
(i) For *Glace au café* – Coffee ice, add coffee essence to the custard mix.
(ii) For *Glace au chocolat* – Chocolate ice, add 120 g (¼ lb) grated chocolate to milk before boiling to make custard.
(iii) Strawberry, raspberry and fruit-flavoured ices may similarly be made by flavouring with fruit pulp or purée and colouring if necessary.
(iv) Use pasteurized eggs where possible.

1147 Biscuit glacé

pâte à bombe	*6 egg whites*	*310 ml (⅜ pt) cream*
(Recipe 1149)		

1 Line the mould with greaseproof or silicone paper by cutting the paper to the size of lids and interior.
2 Place lid and paper on the bottom of one side and fill in the mixture evenly, taking care to prevent air bubbles.
3 Replace top lid with paper and place in deep-freeze cabinet to set.
4 For service, turn out on to a dish with wafers to form a base.
5 Tastefully decorate the top with crème Chantilly and appropriate fruit such as Tutti Fruitti, Ananas, Framboise, Fraises.

Note. Biscuits glacés are normally cut by the waiter at the service table.

1148 Bombes

Ice bombes are usually made in a shaped mould, shell-shaped rather than the older-fashioned bomb-like sphere originally used. They may contain various layers of flavoured ice-cream or biscuit ices and when served are usually decorated with cream, crystallized fruits, violets, rose petals, etc.

1149 Pâte à bombe – Ice-bombe mix

3 eggs	*flavouring*
190 ml (⅜ pt) cream	*3 × 20 ml spoon (4 tbsp.) water*
90 g (3 oz) sugar	*(⅛ pt)*

1 Whisk yolks, sugar, and water together over a bain-marie until stiff.
2 Remove from heat and whisk until cold.
3 Add flavouring and fold through beaten cream.
4 Mould as desired.

1150 Bombe andalouse – Apricot ice-cream

vanilla biscuit ice-cream   *juice of ½ lemon*
(Recipe 1147)   *whipped cream*
custard ice (Recipe 1146)   *half apricots*
250 *ml* (*½ pt*) *apricot purée*

1 Prepare a custard ice (Recipe 1146) and when partly frozen add 250 ml (½ pt) apricot purée plus the juice of ¼ lemon.
2 Fill bombe mould, freeze.
3 When frozen, hollow centre and fill with vanilla biscuit ice.
4 Freeze.
5 To turn out: plunge into tepid water and set on to a silver lined with wafers.
6 Decorate with cream and apricots.

1152 Bombe Nesselrode

vanilla ice-cream   120 *g* (*¼ lb*) *glacé*   190 *ml* (*⅜ pt*) *cream*
(Recipe 1146)   *chestnuts* (*puréed*)

1 Prepare a custard ice and clothe the bombe mould.
2 Fill with lightly beaten cream and purée of chestnuts.
3 Freeze – turn out and decorate with half-chestnuts and whipped cream.

1152 Parfaits

Parfait nowadays describes a single-flavoured unclothed ice made from biscuit glacé preparation. *Parfait au Rhum* for example, is made as for biscuit glacé (Recipe 1147) with the addition of 50 ml (¹⁄₁₀ pt) rum and moulded in a bombe mould. Alternatives may be prepared with cognac or other liqueurs, and also *parfait aux Café* (strong essence of coffee to flavour).

1152a Parfait praliné

This is a biscuit glacé with praliné (Recipe 991).

SORBETS

1152b Sorbet au citron – Lemon water ice

240 *g* (*8 oz*) *granulated sugar*   2 *lemons*
½ *litre* (1 *pt*) *water*   1 *egg white*

1 Grate the zest and squeeze the juice from the lemon.
2 Bring sugar, water ,zest and lemon juice to the boil.
3 Remove from the heat and allow to cool. The saccharometer reading for the syrup should be at 20° beaume.
4 Mix in the egg white thoroughly.
5 Pass through a strainer and freeze in a sorbet machine.

1152c Sorbet à l'orange – Orange water ice

As for Recipe 1152b, substituting oranges for lemons.

1152d Sorbet aux fraises – Strawberry water ice

240 g (8 oz) granulated sugar   1 lemon
375 ml (¾ pt) water   1 egg white
125 ml (¼ pt) strawberry purée

Prepare and freeze as for lemon water ice (Recipe 1152b).

COUPES

Coupes are in fact the cups or silver goblets in which garnished ices are presented. The following are but a few examples:

1153 Coupe Alexandra

fruit salad   kirsch   strawberry ice-
                                                        cream

1 Place fruit salad, flavoured with kirsch into a coupe.
2 Place a rocher (scooped portion) of strawberry ice-cream on top of fruit and decorate with cream and cherry or strawberry.

1154 Coupe andalouse

orange fillets   maraschino   lemon ice-cream

1 Place orange fillets soaked in maraschino in coupes.
2 Place a rocher (scoop portion) of lemon ice-cream on top; decorate accordingly.

1155 Coupe Edna-May

cherries   vanilla ice-cream
Melba sauce (Recipe 970)   whipped cream

Coat ice-cream and cherries with Melba sauce and decorate with cream.

1156 Coupe Jacques

fruit salad   maraschino   lemon ice-cream
  (Recipe 1112)   strawberry   whipped cream
sugar

1 Soak fruit in maraschino and sugar and place into coupes.
2 Place ice-cream on top of fruit and decorate with whipped cream.

1157 Coupe Jamaïque

rum-flavoured apricot	*coffee ice-cream*	*sliced pineapple*
(Recipe 960)	*whipped cream*	*crystallized violet*

1 Soak pineapple in rum-flavoured apricot sauce.
2 Rocher of coffee ice.
3 Decorate with cream and crystallized violet.

1158 Poire Belle-Hélène

Poached pear with vanilla ice-cream and with hot Sauce chocolat (Recipe 964) served separately.

1159 Pêche Melba

1 Blanched, skinned, and poached whole peaches.
2 Vanilla ice-cream and peaches coated with sauce Melba (Recipe 970).

1160 Pêche ou Poire Dame-Blanche – Peach or Pear

4 rochers vanilla ice-cream	*2 peaches or 2 pears*
mousseline (or Arenberg) sauce	*crushed violet*
(Recipe 962)	*whipped cream*

1 Place 4 rochers of vanilla ice-cream in a timbale.
2 Place, between the ice-cream, 4 halves or 4 whole peaches, or pears, and coat with mousseline sauce.
3 Decorate with cream and crushed violet.

Note. Mousseline sauce is almond-flavoured.

OMELETTE SOUFFLÉE OR SOUFFLÉE EN SURPRISE

1161 Meringues for omelettes soufflées en surprise

8 egg whites (one egg	*pinch salt or cream of*	*180 g (6 oz) caster*
yolk if desired)	*tartar*	*sugar*

Whisk all ingredients together into a stiff snow before adding the yolk.

Note. Some chefs add a little pâte à bombe to the prepared meringue.

1162 Omelette soufflée or Soufflée en surprise

génoise	*angelica*
cherries	*meringue (Recipe 1161)*
ice-cream	*15 g (½ oz) caster sugar*

1 Hollow out a piece of génoise and moisten with fruit syrup and kirsch.
2 Place on ice-cream: half vanilla, half strawberry.
3 Mask with meringue, decorate with cherries, angelica, and sprinkle with caster sugar.
4 Brown off in a hot oven or under the salamander.

1163 Omelette soufflée Alaska

Recipe 1162, using only vanilla ice-cream on génoise but topped with méringue.

1163a Omelette soufflée Paquita

As for soufflé Alaska, with the addition of macédoine of fruit (Recipe 1112).

1163b Omelette or soufflée My Lord

Same as Paquita using pears.

1163c Omelette or soufflée My Lady

As for My Lord using peaches.

BREADS, ROLLS, AND DANISH PASTRY

1164 Pâte à croissants – Crescent paste or dough

240 g (½ lb) strong flour	Plus 60 g (2 oz) butter or 90 g (3 oz)
2 eggs	puff paste (Recipe 994)
15 g (½ oz) sugar	62 ml (2½ fl oz) milk
15 g (½ oz) yeast	15 g (½ oz) salt
60 g (2 oz) butter	

1 Same method as for pâte à savarin (Recipe 1000).
2 When proved, beat through butter and pin out into an oblong.
3 Place on butter or puff paste to cover two-thirds of the paste.
4 Give four half-turns as for puff paste; dough is then ready for use.

1165 Vienna rolls and bread

120 g (¼ lb) soft flour	7 g (¼ oz) lard	4 g (⅛ oz) sugar
120 g (¼ lb) strong flour	7 g (¼ oz) milk powder	100 ml (⅕ pt) water
7 g (¼ oz) yeast	4 g (⅛ oz) salt	(approx.)

1 Dissolve the yeast in a little of the water.
2 Place the flour on to the table and form into a bay.
3 Cream the lard, sugar and salt in the centre of the bay before adding the remainder of the ingredients.
4 Work into a smooth dough.
5 Cover with a cloth and allow to prove, for 2 hours approximately; scale as required.

1166 Bridge roll dough

45 g (1½ oz) strong	15 g (½ oz) yeast	2 egg yolks
flour	15 g (½ oz) sugar	60 g (2 oz) butter
200 g (6½ oz) soft flour	7 g (¼ oz) salt	90 ml (c. ⅕ pt) milk

1 Prepare a batter with 45 g (1½ oz) strong flour, the yeast and a little milk; leave aside to prove for ½ hour approximately.
2 Work the remainder of the ingredients in to a smooth dough until it does not adhere to the hands or basin.
3 Add fermented sponge or batter to the dough and set aside in a warm place to prove (double its volume) for ½ hour approximately.

1167 Tea-bread dough

45 g (1½ oz) strong	15 g (½ oz) yeast	2 eggs
flour	15 g (½ oz) sugar	7 g (¼ oz) salt
200 g (6½ oz) soft flour	60 g (2 oz) butter	90 ml (c. ⅕ pt) milk

Prepare sponge and dough as for Bridge rolls (Recipe 1166).

1168 Doughnuts

240 g (½ lb) strong flour	1 egg
10 g (⅜ oz) yeast (fresh, live)	60 g (2 oz) butter (or margarine)
125 ml (¼ pt) milk and water	30 g (1 oz) caster sugar

1 Sieve the flour into a bowl and warm.
2 Dissolve the yeast in a basin with a little of the liquid.
3 Make a well in the centre of the flour.
4 Add the dispersed yeast, sprinkle with a little water, cover with a cloth, leave in a warm place until the yeast ferments (bubbles).
5 Add the beaten egg, butter (or margarine), sugar and remainder of liquid. Knead well to form a soft, slack, smooth dough, free from stickiness.
6 Keep covered and allow to prove in a warm place.
7 Pin out to 0.5 cm (¼ inch) thick and cut into rings using two cutters (6 cm (3 inch) and 3 cm (1½ inch)).
8 Deep fry to gold brown and toss in sugar.
9 Serve either hot or cold.

1169 Danish pastry

625 g (1¼ lb) flour	60 g (2 oz) sugar	2 eggs
250 ml (½ pt) milk	60 g (2 oz) yeast	420 g (14 oz) butter
7 g (¼ oz) mixed spice		

1 Dissolve the sugar in cold milk and add the crumbled yeast.
2 Stir in the egg until it is well mixed.
3 Sieve the flour and spice together into the liquid and mix to a dough.
4 Place in the refrigerator for ½ hour.
5 Roll the dough into a rectangular shape.
6 Spread the butter in walnut-size pieces over two-thirds of the surface of dough.

7 Fold over the remaining dough and then over again so that 3 layers of dough enclose 2 layers of fat.

8 Roll out the pastry keeping the shape rectangular, brush off surplus flour and fold in three.

9 Half-turn the pastry, roll again and fold into three.

10 Cover paste with damp cloth and place in refrigerator for 1 hour.

11 Repeat the rolling and folding process again, so that the paste has been rolled and folded 4 times.

Note. Keep the paste very cold during manipulation.

1170 Danish pockets

Ingredients as for Recipe 1169.

1 Roll out basic paste into a sheet 0.5 cm (¼ inch) thick and cut into squares 7 × 8 cm (3½ by 4 inches).

2 Place almond paste, with sultanas worked in it, in the centre of the squares; fold the corners and press each tip well down in the middle of the almond paste.

3 Egg-wash and prove slowly; bake at 215°C (420°F).

1171 Danish butterflies

Ingredients as Recipe 1169.

1 Roll out basic paste 0.3 cm (⅛ inch) thick and 24 cm (12 inches) wide.

2 Wash surface with melted butter.

3 Sprinkle with caster sugar and roasted almond-nibs and roll the paste cylindrically.

4 Cut into pieces 1.5 cm (¾ inch) wide.

5 Open out the folds to right and left by pressing with the back of a knife down the centre.

6 Arrange on trays, egg-wash, prove slowly, and bake at 205°C (400°F).

7 Brush with apricot glaze.

9 Savouries and Supplementary Breakfast Dishes

SAVOURIES

SAVOURIES as a final course to complete a meal have long been in demand in Britain. French chefs, though they helped to develop many of them, tend to be contemptuous of savouries and do not include them among items prepared in the continental tradition. Just as cheese is nowadays often served before the pudding or dessert so there has been a tendency also to serve a savoury in that menu position. However, its original purpose was to leave the diner with a savoury tang after eating. For that reason the canapé, croûte or other items need not be large. Neatness and daintiness are essential features.

1172 Anges à cheval – Angels on horseback

4 oblongs toast (6 × 4 cm)   15 g (½ oz) butter (or margarine)
(3 × 2 inches)   12 oysters
12 bacon rashers

1 Butter the toast.
2 Flatten the bacon and wrap a slice round each oyster.
3 Skewer and grill.
4 Garnish with a few straw potatoes and watercress.

1173 Beignets soufflés au parmesan

60 g (2 oz) flour   2 eggs   125 ml (¼ pt) water
15 g (½ oz) grated   pinch salt   oil (or fat) for deep
  Parmesan cheese   30 g (1 oz) butter (or   frying
                             margarine)

1 Boil water and butter.
2 Sift flour and salt and mix into the water and butter.
3 Cook until mixture leaves the side of the pan.
4 Add the eggs one by one beating well; add the cheese.
5 Pipe on to greased paper.
6 Fry in deep oil (or fat); drain well.

1174 Buck rarebit

Method and ingredients as Welsh rarebit (Recipe 1194) but each portion topped with a well-rounded, soft-poached egg.

1175 Canapé Chang Wang

4 *slices tomato*	*Welsh rarebit mix*	4 *bacon rashers,*
15 g (½ oz) chutney	(Recipe 1194)	*rolled*
		4 *rounds of toast*

1 Prepare as for Welsh rarebit and place a slice of tomato on top of each before glazing; add a little chutney to each portion and place a bacon roll on top.
2 Glaze slowly; garnish with parsley.

1176 Canapé des gourmets

4 *small rounds of toast*	15 g (½ oz) butter
30 g (1 oz) mustard butter	10 ml spoon [½ tablespoon] cream
240 g (½ lb) finely chopped ham	paprika

1 Butter toast, which has been cut with a round 6 cm (3 inch) cutter.
2 Heat the ham with the mustard butter (Recipe 91) and cream and flavour with a little paprika.
3 Heap evenly on the buttered toast; brush with butter and pass under the grill.
4 Garnish with sprigs of parsley.

1177 Canapé Diane

4 *oblongs toast* 6 × 4 *cm*	12 *bacon rashers*
(3 × 2 *inches*)	15 g (½ oz) butter (or margarine)
240 g (½ lb) chicken-liver	

1 Butter the toast.
2 Flatten the bacon and wrap a slice round each piece of liver.
3 Skewer and grill.
4 Remove skewer and place 3 on each piece of toast.
5 Garnish with a few straw potatoes and watercress.

1178 Canapé écossais – Scotch woodcock

8 *eggs*	4 *rounds of toast*
30 g (1 oz) butter (or margarine)	15 ml spoon (1 tbsp.) cream
8 *fillet anchovies*	16 *capers*

1 Butter toast, which has been cut with a round 6 cm (3 inch) cutter.
2 Prepare scrambled egg (Recipe 300) add cream.
3 Heap the mixture evenly on toast.
4 Garnish with criss-cross of anchovy.
5 Place a caper in each section.
6 Garnish with parsley.

1179 Canapé Ivanhoë

240 g (½ lb) findon (finnan or
   smoked) haddock
3 × 20 ml spoon (⅛ pt) Béchamel
   (Recipe 51)
4 small grilled mushrooms
15 g (½ oz) butter (or margarine)

10 ml spoon [½ tablespoon] cream
cayenne pepper
seasoning
250 ml (½ pt) milk
4 rounds of toast

1 Cook haddock in milk (Recipe 1206).
2 Skin and chop very fine.
3 Sweat in butter, bind with Béchamel, add cream and season.
4 Heap evenly on buttered toast, cut with a round 6 cm (3 inch) cutter.
5 Place a grilled mushroom on top of each.
6 Pass under salamander.
7 Garnish with parsley.

1180 Canapé Quo-Vadis

4 oblongs toast 6 × 4 cm
   (3 × 2 inches)
4 grilled mushrooms
120 g (¼ lb) flour

125 ml (¼ pt) milk
seasoning
30 g (1 oz) butter (or margarine)
240 g (½ lb) herring roes

Prepare as for Laitances sur croûte (Recipe 1187) but with a garnish of grilled mushrooms.

1181 Canapé à la yorkaise

Prepare as for Croûte Derby (Recipe 1184) with grilled mushroom on top.

1182 Croûte aux anchois – Anchovy toast

4 oblongs toast 6 × 4 cm
   (3 × 2 inches)
60 g (2 oz) fillet anchovies
15 g (½ oz) butter (or margarine)

½ lemon
parsley
paprika

1 Butter the toast.
2 Lay the anchovies lengthwise on the toast.
3 Brush with butter and heat under the salamander.
4 Dust with paprika, garnish with small pieces of lemon and picked parsley.

1183 Croûte baron

4 small rounds of toast
8 slices beef-bone marrow
7 g (¼ oz) white (or wholemeal)
   breadcrumbs

8 large, grilled mushrooms
4 rashers streaky bacon
15 g (½ oz) butter (or margarine)
parsley

1 Butter toast, which has been cut with a round 6 cm (3 inch) cutter.
2 Place grilled mushrooms on toast.
3 Grill bacon and place on mushrooms.
4 Heat the marrow in a little stock; drain and place on the bacon.
5 Sprinkle lightly with breadcrumbs and pass under the salamander.
6 Garnish with sprig parsley.

1184 Croûte Derby

4 *small rounds of toast*   2 *pickled walnuts*
240 *g* (½ *lb*) *finely chopped ham*   15 *g* (½ *oz*) *butter* (*or margarine*)
15 *ml spoon* [1 *tablespoon*] *cream*

1 Butter toast, which has been cut with a round 6 cm (3 inch) cutter.
2 Heat the ham in butter, add the cream and season with paprika.
3 Heap the mixture on the toast and garnish each one with half a walnut.
4 Pass under the salamander.
5 Garnish with parsley.

1185 Croûte Windsor

This is the alternative name for canapé yorkaise (Recipe 1181).

1186 Diables noirs or Diables à cheval – Black devils or devils on horseback

4 *oblongs toast* 6 × 4 *cm*   12 *cooked prunes*
(3 × 2 *inches*)   15 *g* (½ *oz*) *chutney*
12 *slices streaky bacon*   15 *g* (½ *oz*) *butter* (*or margarine*)

1 Stone prunes and fill with chutney.
2 Flatten bacon and wrap a slice round each stuffed prune.
3 Skewer and grill.
4 Remove skewer and place 3 on each piece of toast.
5 Garnish with parsley.

1187 Laitances sur croûtes – Soft roes on toast

4 *oblongs toast* 6 × 4 *cm*   *paprika*
(3 × 2 *inches*)   *salt*
240 *g* (½ *lb*) *herring roes* (*soft*)   30 *g* (1 *oz*) *butter* (*or margarine*)
pepper   125 *ml* (¼ *pt*) *milk*
120 *g* (¼ *lb*) *flour*

1 Soak the roes in milk, drain and dust with flour.
2 Place evenly on buttered tray and brush butter (or margarine) on each one and season.
3 Grill for 5 minutes.
4 Dress lengthwise on buttered toast.
5 Dust with paprika and garnish with parsley.

1188 Paillettes d'or – Cheese straws

60 g (2 oz) flour
30 g (1 oz) Parmesan cheese
cayenne pepper
little water

30 g (1 oz) butter (or margarine)
1 small egg yolk
salt

1 Sift flour, salt and pepper.
2 Rub in the butter.
3 Blend in the cheese.
4 Add the egg yolk and water to make a firm dough.
5 Roll out 0.3 cm (⅛ inch) thick.
6 Cut 6 cm (3 inch) long and 0.5 cm (¼ inch) wide.
7 Twist the straws.
8 Lay on greased baking sheet.
9 Bake in moderate oven for 7 minutes.
10 Sprinkle with salt.

Note. Cheese straws are also frequently made with puff paste.

1189 Quiche lorraine

Paste:
120 g (¼ lb) flour
30 g (1 oz) butter
30 g (1 oz) lard
1 egg yolk
pinch salt
2 or 3 × 10 ml spoon
  [2–3 dessertspoons] water

Filling:
30 g (1 oz) diced bacon
½ clove chopped garlic
1 egg
125 ml (¼ pt) milk
seasoning
21 g (¾ oz) grated Gruyère cheese

Paste:
1 Sift flour and salt.
2 Rub in the fat.
3 Make a bay, add egg yolks and water; work to a paste.
4 Line a 14 cm (7-inch) flan-ring and allow to stand.

Filling:
1 Heat the milk with the garlic.
2 Beat the eggs and seasoning.
3 Add the milk and mix well.
4 Fry the diced bacon and garnish the bottom of the flan.
5 Strain liquid over the top.
6 Sprinkle with cheese.
7 Cook in moderate oven until firm, serve hot.

1190 Ramequins au gruyère

4 *croustades* (*tartlet cases of*   125 *ml* (¼ *pt*) *milk*
    pastry)   1 *egg*
21 *g* (¾ *oz*) *Gruyère cheese*   *seasoning*
    (*grated*)

1 Boil the milk.
2 Beat the eggs and seasoning, and combine with cheese.
3 Add the milk, mix well.
4 Strain into the cooked croustades.
5 Cook in moderate oven until set.

1191 Ramequins suisses

Ingredients as Recipe 1190 with the addition of 30 *g* (1 *oz*) *diced, cooked mushrooms*, 1 *sherry-glass white wine*.

1 Add the sherry-glass of white wine to the above recipe (1190).
2 Garnish bottom of croustades with diced, cooked mushrooms.

Note. Ramequin-style savoury-tartlets may be prepared in barquettes or other shaped pastry-cases.

1192 Sardines sur croûte – Sardines on toast

1 *small can sardines*   4 *oblongs toast*   ½ *lemon*
15 *g* (½ *oz*) *butter*   6 × 4 *cm*   *paprika*
                          (3 × 2 *inches*)

1 Skin both sides of sardines.
2 Lay 2 sardines on each piece of toast; brush with butter and heat under salamander.
3 Garnish with small pieces of lemon and parsley.

1193 Soufflé au parmesan – Cheese soufflé

190 *ml* (⅜ *pt*) *stiff Béchamel*   21 *g* (¾ *oz*) *grated Parmesan cheese*
    (*Recipe* 51)   2 *egg yolks*
3 *egg whites*   1 *small soufflé case*
15 *g* (½ *oz*) *butter*

1 Heat Béchamel.
2 Beat in the egg yolks and cheese; season.
3 Allow to cool slightly.
4 Beat the egg white stiffly.
5 Fold into the mixture gently.
6 Grease the soufflé case and dust with Parmesan cheese.
7 Pour in the mixture.
8 Bake in hot oven for 20 minutes.

Note. Variant savouries may be made by cooking this mixture in barquettes or croustades.

1194 Welsh Rarebit (or Welsh Rabbit)

120 ml (¼ pt) stiff Béchamel	1 egg yolk
(Recipe 51)	seasoning
5 ml spoon [½ dessertspoon]	4 rounds toast cut with 6 cm (3 inch)
Worcester sauce	round cutter
120 ml (¼ pt) beer	240 g (½ lb) grated Cheddar or
1.25 ml spoon [¼ teaspoon]	Cheshire cheese
mustard	

1 Make a reduction of the beer and mustard.
2 Add the Béchamel and melt the cheese into a smooth paste; add the Worcester sauce.
3 Bind the mixture with the egg yolk, and season.
4 Allow to cool.
5 Butter the toast and cover like a pyramid with the Welsh rarebit.
6 Set to glaze slowly at the bottom of the grill.

Note. Béchamel is added to stabilize and ensure creamy texture; traditionalists may prefer to prepare Welsh rarebit without this aid.

1195 Hot club sandwiches

In addition to the foregoing croûtes and canapés listed amongst savouries, there is a certain demand on hotels and restaurants for the hot sandwich or club sandwich as a light snack or savoury. This type of sandwich is made from sandwich-loaf bread, with crust removed, and toasted and buttered. Club sandwiches may be made in one or two layers, garnished with slices of ham, chicken, mushrooms, bacon, minute steaks, and sausages.

1196 Open hot sandwiches

In addition to the named canapés there are more substantial open sandwiches made from one slice of toast and topped with various types of cheese, canned fish, shell-fish, liver and meat pâté, eggs, salpicon, and so on.

BREAKFAST COOKERY

Simple breakfast dishes are tasks customarily left to a semi-skilled cook rather than to one fully-trained. Many dishes in the preceding chapters are suitable for breakfast service. This is especially so of: preliminary breakfast items such as half-grapefruit, tomato and fruit juices, and similar appetizers mentioned in the section on hors-d'œuvre; Macédoine of fruit and fruit compotes listed among the recipes in Chapter 8; simple fish dishes from Chapter 5.

Moreover, vegetables may accompany many fried and grilled items from Chapter 6 including offal, such as kidney, liver, and sausages. Plainer methods from the vegetable recipes of Chapter 7 may be used. Potatoes, tomatoes and mushrooms, particularly in shallow-fried and grilled modes are suitable.

Breakfast cookery is little used in continental systems but in Great Britain, the Commonwealth and America there is still demand for cooked courses. For breakfast in the American manner, the customary grills and fried dishes of bacon, sausage, and meats, and the usual fish dishes are also augmented by specialities such as corned-beef hash (see Recipe 727), by pancakes and by American-style biscuits.

While chefs in charge of kitchens interest themselves in beverages accompanying meals, making items such as tea, coffee, and chocolate is normally carried out in the still-room under the supervision of the maître d'hôtel or restaurant manager. Other than toasts which may be prepared for canapés and hot open sandwiches, toast is normally prepared in the still-room and not by the chef. Toast split and re-toasted is known as toast Melba, but extremely thin slices of toasted bread are now more often substituted.

EGGS

(See Chapter 4 for range of egg dishes)

1197 Œufs à la coque – Eggs (to boil)

Though precise cooking-times depend on the size of the egg, large, high-grade eggs are cooked by plunging into boiling water as follows:

1 Hard-boiled: 8–10 minutes.
2 Soft-boiled: 5 minutes.
3 Lightly soft-boiled: 3½–4 minutes.

1198 Coddled eggs

There is a small demand for eggs lightly boiled. This is done by immersion of the egg in boiling water for 1 minute, withdrawing the pan from the heat, retaining tight covering on the vessel, and allowing the cooking to be completed by standing for a further 5 minutes.

FISH

(See Chapter 5 for further range of fish dishes)

1199 Harengs grillés – Grilled herrings

4 *herrings*	120 g (¼ lb) *seasoned flour*
60 g (2 oz) *melted butter* (*or*	*seasoning*
margarine)	

1 Clean the herrings by gutting, scaling, trimming tails and fins and removing head.

2 Ciseler both sides of herring.
3 Pass through seasoned flour.
4 Brush with melted butter on both sides; season.
5 Grill both sides under moderate heat for approximately 5 minutes.
6 Served with mustard sauce or mustard butter (Recipes, 65, 91).

1200 Herring meunière

Prepare as for mackerel meunière (Recipe 1202).

1201 Oatmeal herrings

4 *boned herrings*	*chopped parsley*
240 g (½ *lb*) *fine oatmeal*	*seasoning*
120 g (¼ *lb*) *butter* (*or margarine*)	

1 Dip herrings in melted butter (or margarine) and then into the seasoned fine oatmeal.
2 Shallow-fry in butter (or margarine) and sprinkle with a little chopped parsley before serving.

1202 Mackerel meunière – Maquereau meunière

4 *mackerel*	120 g (¼ *lb*) *seasoned flour*
120 g (¼ *lb*) *butter*	1 *lemon*
chopped parsley	125 ml (¼ *pt*) *oil.*

1 Prepare as for grilling herrings (Recipe 1199).
2 Pass through seasoned flour.
3 Shallow-fry in hot oil.
4 Garnish with lemon slices.
5 Cover with a beurre noisette (Recipe 82) (optional, or brush with melted margarine).
6 Add a dash of lemon juice.
7 Sprinkle with chopped parsley.

1202a Grilled mackerel

Prepare as grilled herrings (Recipe 1199).

1203 Fish kedgeree

4 *hard-boiled eggs*	180 g (6 *oz*) *plain boiled rice*
240 g (½ *lb*) *white cooked fish or*	(*Recipe* 362)
cooked Finnan haddock	250 ml (½ *pt*) *curry sauce*
	(*Recipe* 32)

1 Place the rice in silver dish and make a hollow in the centre.
2 Mix the cooked fish with the curry sauce and add the sliced, hard-boiled eggs and place in the centre of the rice.

1204 Fishcakes

240 g (½ lb) cooked white fish
15 g (½ oz) melted butter (or
  margarine)
60 g (2 oz) seasoned flour
240 g (½ lb) dry mashed potato

2.5 ml spoon [½ teaspoon] anchovy
  essence
120 g (¼ lb) white breadcrumbs
seasoning
1 egg (beaten)

1 Break fish into small pieces removing all skin and bone.
2 Mix with the dry mashed potatoes and bind with the beaten egg, season.
3 Cut into even-sized pieces and form into neat cakes.
4 Pass through seasoned flour, egg-wash, and crumbs.
5 Fry in deep oil (or fat) or shallow-fry.

1205 Salmon fishcakes

Ingredients and method as Recipe 1204 substituting cooked or canned salmon for white fish.

Note. Croquettes or cutlets of fish or salmon may be made from the two preceding recipes.

1206 Finnan haddock in milk

4 small findons   60 g (2 oz) butter (or   375 ml (¾ pt) milk
  (smoked haddocks)   margarine)   pepper

1 Trim off the lugs and tail.
2 Butter a dish large enough to hold the fish flat.
3 Lay the fish skin-side down.
4 Cover with milk and sprinkle with butter.
5 Cover with greased kitchen paper.
6 Cook in moderate oven for 10 minutes.
7 When cooked, remove vertebrae.
8 Reduce cooking-liquor slightly.
9 Pour over the Finnan before serving.

1207 Haddock Monte Carlo

Prepare as Recipe 1206 with the addition of a poached egg on top of each portion.

1208 Arbroath smokies in milk

For these smoked haddock – a speciality of Arbroath – ingredients and method are the same as for Finnan haddock in milk (Recipe 1206).

1209 Grilled Arbroath smokies

4 smokies   90 g (3 oz) butter (or margarine)

1 Brush with melted butter.
2 Grill for 3 minutes on each side.

1210 Smoked cod fillet

500 g [1 lb] fish (120 g or 4 oz per   120 g (4 oz) butter (or margarine)
    person)]   750 ml (1½ pt) milk
pepper

Treat as Finnan in Milk (Recipe 1206).

1211 Grilled kipper

8 kippers   90 g (3 oz) butter (or margarine)

1 Remove head and tail and brush with butter.
2 Grill slowly for approximately 4 minutes.
3 Remove bone before serving and again brush with butter (or margarine).

1212 Bloaters

8 bloaters   90 g (3 oz) butter

Trim as for grilled herring then treat as kippers or alternatively place in a pan with little water and butter, cooking quickly under cover.

1213 Grilled turbot steak

four 180 g (6 oz) steaks   62 ml (⅛ pt) oil   60 g (2 oz) seasoned
½ lemon   parsley   flour
                                                    seasoning

1 Pass the steaks through the seasoned flour.
2 Brush with oil.
3 Grill both sides.
4 Remove centre bone and black skin before service.
5 Brush with melted butter (or margarine).
6 Garnish with lemon slices and sprigs of parsley.

1214 Grilled, fried, and meunière fish

Most white fish as well as those listed above are suitable, when cooked in a simple style, for breakfast services, especially whiting, cod, plaice, fresh haddock, and halibut; trout is also an acceptable fish.

1215 Potatoes for breakfast

Sauté potatoes (Recipe 921) and croquettes (Recipe 913) are examples of potatoes suitable to accompany breakfast items such as grilled bacon and eggs. Even composite forms of hashed potatoes such as Bubble and Squeak (with cooked cabbage) can also be used.

Glossary

SHORTENED LIST OF CULINARY TERMS

THIS brief list defines terms used in the compendium, together with others encountered in the professional kitchen. Many words whose meaning is made apparent in the text have not been included.

Abats.	Offal.
Ail.	Garlic.
Ailerons de volaille.	Chicken winglets used, for example, as a garnish for clear soup (e.g. petit marmite) or rizotto. For consommé: singe and trim tips, then cook in white stock. When cooked, bones may be removed.
Anglaise, à l'.	Plainly cooked in English style: usually boiled, steamed, or plain roasts or frieds.
Animelles.	Lamb's fry.
Appareil.	The food items or mixture for preparing a dish: hence, appareil à crèpes – pancake batter.
Aromates.	Aromatics: sweet-smelling herbs and spices.
Au bleu.	Method of boiling live fish (especially trout) in plain court-bouillon.
Au four.	In the oven: thus, pommes au four – jacket potatoes.
Au gras.	Richly-cooked or dressed.
Au naturel.	Plainly-cooked and served.
Bain-marie.	Double saucepan or bath of hot water for slow cooking or keeping hot.
Ballotine.	Boned and stuffed form of poultry or game birds.
Bande.	Band or strip, hence bande aux fruits, strip-type flan.
Bard, to.	To cover with slices of fat (e.g. in roasting game birds).
Barquette.	Boat-shaped pastry tartlet.
Bâtarde.	Rudimentary white sauce of water (or stock) thickened with white roux or flour and used as 'extender' to increase the volume of a sauce.
Bâton.	Stick-shaped garnish or stick-like French bread.
Blanch.	Foods are blanched by being covered with cold water, brought to the boil, drained and refreshed by being plunged again into cold water. The term is, however, also used loosely to indicate processes like plunging

	tomatoes in boiling water and peeling and the preliminary par-frying of pommes frites.
Bombay duck.	Dried Indian fish served as accompaniment to curry.
Bouquet garni.	Bundle of herbs, usually thyme, bay-leaf, and parsley tied within strips of celery or leek.
Broche, à la.	On the spit (roasted).
Brochette.	Skewer: thus, à la brochette – cooked on a skewer.
Brûlé.	Burnt.
Brunoise.	Mixed vegetable garnish cut into tiny dice.
Casserole, en.	Cooked in casserole (or vessel for oven use).
Chapelure.	Browned breadcrumbs.
Chaud-froider.	To coat with chaud-froid sauce.
Chemiser.	To line a mould with jelly (including aspic).
Chiffonnade.	Fine ribbon-cut of lettuce or sorrel for soup or sauce garnish.
Chinois.	Conical strainer not unlike Chinese coolie hat in shape.
Ciseler.	To cut gashes on: e.g., incising herring for grilling, or to slice finely.
Clouter.	To pierce and stick with, for example, cloves or truffle fragments.
Cocotte, en.	In small oven-proof dish.
Concasser.	To chop; especially used of peeled and pipped tomatoes.
Contiser.	To incise (meat, fish, poultry); to insert truffle slice, clove of garlic, etc.
Coquille.	Shell.
Cordon.	Ribbon; refers also to ribbon or thread of sauce circling a dish.
Créole, à la.	In Creole style: tradition of cookery from the southern states of the U.S.A. usually implies with rice.
Croustadine.	Flat puff-paste bouchées of various shapes.
Cru.	Raw.
Cuit.	Cooked.
Darioles.	Small baba-shaped moulds.
Daube, or Daubiére.	En daube is oven-stewed or -braised; hence daubiére – the oven cooking pot or casserole.
Demidoff knife.	Grooving cutter used to channel decorative strips of vegetable subsequently cut into serrated roundels for Demidoff garnish.
Dépouiller.	To remove scum and fat by skimming during slow bringing-to-boil, and during cooking.
Dorure.	Egg-wash for gilding pastry.
Doux, douce.	Sweet.

Ébarber.	To beard; to remove inedible fringe from shellfish, e.g. oysters and mussels.
Émincer.	To cut into small pieces.
Escalope.	Collop or slice.
Espagnole, à l'.	In Spanish style often with onion: a Spanish-style omelette is flat.
Faire revenir.	To fry quickly; to give colour without cooking through.
Faire suer.	To sweat (q.v.).
Fécule.	Starch flour (fécule de riz – rice flour; fécule de pommes de terre – potato flour).
Feuille.	Leaf; hence, mille feuilles (literally, thousand leaves) describes a puff-pastry gâteau.
Feuilletage.	Puff pastry.
Fines herbes.	Finely-chopped mixed herbs such as parsley, chives, tarragon, and chervil.
Flamande, à la.	Flemish style, with Flamande garnish.
Flamber.	To flame (flambé, flamed).
Fouetté.	Whipped; hence, crème fouettée – whipped cream.
Française, à la.	Cooked in the French style; for example, vegetables in butter.
Frappé.	Iced.
Friandises.	Small dainties (particularly, nowadays, sweet items). Alternative name for petits fours.
Friture.	Deep-frying vessel or bath (also food which has been deep-fried).
Garam-masala.	A blend of freshly ground spices (usually including caraway, cardomom and coriander seeds, black peppercorns, cloves and cinnamon) widely used in the preparation of Indian and Pakistani dishes.
Gaufrette.	Wafer: wafer biscuit serve with ice.
Girofle.	Clove; hence, clou de girofle (literally, stud of clove) when piercing onion for onion clouté.
Glacé.	Iced, frozen or glazed with glossy sauce, jelly, etc.
Grecque, à la.	In Greek style, usually with rice garnish.
Gros sel.	Coarse salt, freezing salt.
Hâtelet.	Small skewer, usually decorative and of silver.
Hongroise, à la.	Hungarian style; usually signifies use of paprika.
Huile.	Oil (hence à l'huile, cooked or dressed with oil).
Indienne, à l'.	Indian style, usually indicates garnish of curry sauce and rice.
Irlandaise, à l'.	Irish style, probably with potatoes as garnish.
Italienne, à l'.	In Italian style, usually signifies garnish of pasta with tomato sauce.

Julienne.	Cut into match-size strips.
Lard (Fr.).	Bacon or salt fat pork.
Lardons.	Dice of bacon.
Lyonnaise, à la.	In Lyon style, usually with onions.
Macédoine.	Mixed fruit or vegetables cut in dice [about 0.5 cm (¼ inch) cubes].
Macérer.	To macerate; e.g. to steep fruit in sugar and flavouring liquors.
Madère.	Madeira; fortified wine of Madeira is extensively used in cooking.
Mandoline.	Implement incorporating a blade within a frame to make fine slicing possible.
Manié.	Literally, handled, manipulated; hence beurre manié (butter worked into flour).
Marmite.	Soup pot or stock pot (petite marmite: small earthenware soup pot).
Mask, to.	Cover with sauce or aspic.
Médaillons.	Medallions: round, flat pieces of meat or fish, or preparations of meat or fish.
Mélange.	Mixture.
Mexicaine à la.	Mexican style, possibly with pimento.
Mijoter.	To simmer slowly.
Mille-feuille.	Literally, a thousand leaves: a puff-pastry gâteau.
Miroton.	A dish of cooked meat, sliced and re-heated in sauce.
Moëlle.	Beef-bone marrow.
Monter au beurre.	To enrich a sauce by tossing while adding small pieces of butter.
Moulin.	Mill (pepper mill).
Napper.	To coat or mask with sauce or aspic.
Noques.	French version of Gnocchi.
Normande, à la.	In Normandy style, usually with apple or cider or calvados.
Panaché.	Mixed.
Pané.	Breadcrumbed.
Panure.	As chapelure: browned breadcrumbs.
Passer.	To pass, to sieve, or strain.
Pastillage.	Sugar-and-gum paste used by pâtissier for sugar boxes, and cake decoration, etc.
Paysanne, à la.	In peasant (or simple) style: vegetables (or other items) sliced in small pieces for garnish.
Pluches.	Leaves or shreds (e.g. of chervil).
Poivrade.	Peppery dish.
Poivre.	Pepper, hence au poivre with pepper as predominant flavouring.

Polonaise, à la.	In Polish style, possibly with beetroot, sour cream and red cabbage accompanying.
Portugaise, à la.	Portuguese style, usually cooked in oil with tomato and onion.
Potage.	Soup.
Provençale, à la.	In southern French style, usually cooked in oil with garlic and tomato flavouring.
Rascasse.	Mediterranean fish, 'hog-fish'.
Ravier.	Small dish for hors-d'œuvre items.
Réchauffer.	To re-heat.
Recherché.	Unusually fine.
Reduce.	By rapid open boiling to evaporate a sauce or liquor; to concentrate and make richer.
Reduction.	The result of reducing.
Rissole.	Minced meat in deep-fried paste cases. Commonly (but less correctly) used to describe medallions of left-over minced meat.
Rissoler.	To toss rapidly in hot fat to colour.
Rocher.	Literally rock, used to denote portion of ice-cream in coupes and similar dishes.
Royale.	An unsweetened custard; cut into dice as garnish for soup (usually clear soup).
Sable.	Literally, sand; used to describe a type of shortbread.
Saccharometer.	Measuring instrument to test sugar content.
Saindoux.	Lard (pork dripping).
Salamandre.	A top fired grill for glazing or to make gratins; originally a portable metal utensil made hot and passed above a dish.
Sec, sèche.	Dry.
Sel.	Salt.
Spatule.	Spatula: a flat, spoonlike implement of wood or metal for stirring and mixing.
Suer.	To sweat (q.v.).
Suprême.	Alternative name for fillet, fine cut of game, poultry, meat or fish.
Sweat, sweat on.	To cook in fat without colouring.
Tamis.	Sieve or strainer; a tammy.
Tapénade.	A Provençal sauce of pounded capers and anchovies emulsified with olive oil and flavoured with lemon juice and mignonette pepper for service with cold meats, fish or eggs.
Tasse.	Cup: therefore, en tasse – served in cup.
Terrine.	Earthenware dish used for pâtés of meat, liver, and game, etc. Therefore, used as an alternative name for pâtés.

Timbale.	A deep circular dish.
Tomaté.	Tomatoed, i.e. flavoured with tomato or tomato purée.
Tomber.	To reduce (q.v.), therefore, tomber à glace; to reduce to a glaze.
Tourner.	See *turn*.
Truffle essence.	Liquor in which truffles are canned or cooked.
Turn.	To turn (vegetables, mushrooms etc). is to trim with small knife to regular shape.
Vert-pré.	Green stuff: watercress.
Vin.	Wine.
Vinaigre.	Literally, sour wine. True wine vinegar is to be preferred for all culinary and table purposes.
Voiler.	To veil or cover with spun sugar.
Xérès, vin de.	Sherry wine.
Zeste.	Rind of orange or lemon.

Index

References are to recipe numbers, not page